A·N·N·U·A·L E·D·I·T·I·O·N·S

World History Volume II
1500 to the Present

Seventh Edition

EDITOR

David McComb
Colorado State University

David McComb received his Ph.D. from the University of Texas at Austin and is currently a professor of history at Colorado State University. Dr. McComb has written eight books, numerous articles and book reviews, and he teaches courses in the history of the United States, sports, and the world. He has traveled twice around the world as a Semester at Sea faculty member of the University of Pittsburgh, and he has spent additional time in India and Mexico.

McGraw-Hill/Dushkin
530 Old Whitfield Street, Guilford, Connecticut 06437

http://www.dushkin.com

Credits

1. The World and the West, 1500–1900
Unit photo—Illustration from the Virginia State Library.

2. The Ferment of the West, 1500–1900
Unit photo—Reproduced from the collections of the Library of Congress.

3. The Industrial and Scientific Revolutions
Unit photo—Courtesy of the National Archives.

4. The Twentieth Century to 1950
Unit photo—Courtesy of the National Archives.

5. The Era of the Cold War, 1950–1990
Unit photo—United Nations photo by Yutaka Nagata.

6. Global Problems, Global Interdependence
Unit photo—© 2001 PhotoDisc, Inc.

Cataloging in Publication Data
Main entry under title: Annual Editions: World History, vol. II: 1500 to the present. 7/E.
    1. World history—Periodicals. 2. Civilization, Modern—Periodicals. 3. Social problems—Periodicals. I. McComb,
David, comp. II. Title: World history, vol. II: 1500 to the present.
ISBN 0–07–250309–2   905   90–656260   ISSN 1054–2779

Seventh Edition

Cover image © 2002 PhotoDisc, Inc.

Printed in the United States of America   1234567890BAHBAH5432   Printed on Recycled Paper

Copyright

Members of the Advisory Board are instrumental in the final selection of articles for each edition of ANNUAL EDITIONS. Their review of articles for content, level, currentness, and appropriateness provides critical direction to the editor and staff. We think that you will find their careful consideration well reflected in this volume.

Editors/Advisory Board

Staff

iii

To the Reader

In publishing ANNUAL EDITIONS we recognize the enormous role played by the magazines, newspapers, and journals of the public press in providing current, first-rate educational information in a broad spectrum of interest areas. Many of these articles are appropriate for students, researchers, and professionals seeking accurate, current material to help bridge the gap between principles and theories and the real world. These articles, however, become more useful for study when those of lasting value are carefully collected, organized, indexed, and reproduced in a low-cost format, which provides easy and permanent access when the material is needed. That is the role played by ANNUAL EDITIONS.

After 1500, world affairs were increasingly influenced by the power and problems of Western civilization—more so than by any other civilization. Europe and its offspring in North America experienced a unique transformation during the industrial and scientific revolutions, with the result that Western guns and ships were able to establish dominance over global trade and culture. Moreover, Western ideas about capitalism, commerce, private property, socialism, Christianity, democracy, education, nationalism, law, and human rights traveled on the caravels, steamships, railroads, and airplanes. It was a European who dispelled the myth of the "sea of pithy darkness" on the western coast of Africa where sea dragons supposedly destroyed ships and ate sailors. It was also an intrepid European who uncovered a New World, another who rounded Cape Horn to find a water route to the distant Far East, and yet another who first circumnavigated the globe. It was not a Chinese mariner who sailed up the Hudson River or an African who forced open the Japanese ports at gunpoint. It was not an American Indian in a canoe who transferred potatoes to Ireland or corn to France or manioc to Africa. With all of their faults and virtues, it was Europeans and, later, Americans who ventured around the earth and on to the surface of the moon.

The history of the modern world, the period after 1500, therefore, intimately concerns the circumstances of the West and the ambitions of its people. As Westerners reached into the world they established trading posts, colonies, and empires carved out of foreign lands. Early conquerors in the Americas and the Pacific, motivated by religion and a lust for wealth, used swords, horses, dogs, disease, and gunpowder. Later invaders in Africa, China, and India used railroads, telegraphs, quinine, steamboats, and machine guns. European scientists cataloged flora and fauna, explored extinct civilizations, and transported useful plants to distant locations. The nineteenth century was a time when the English were so widely dispersed that the sun was always shining somewhere on the British Empire. Then, after the disasters of two world wars, an economic depression, and a cold war in the twentieth century, the West drew back while other civilizations asserted themselves. The West left behind, however, a residue of ideas, religion, technology, and language.

No person, no remote tribe, no plant or animal was left untouched by this global penetration of Western civilization. Radio, television, movies, computers, tin cans, mass-produced clothes, bicycles, and automobiles are everywhere. Wealthy tourists travel to the Antarctic, the Caribbean, or the Seychelles for vacations. People everywhere wear digital wristwatches, listen to transistor radios, and talk on cell phones. The World Wide Web of information is truly worldwide. Young people across the globe wear blue jeans, listen to rock music, play basketball or soccer, and endure vaccinations to prevent childhood diseases. There is now a mixing of cultures and an interdependence of economies. Indigenous peoples have had to react in one way or another to the Western influence—adopt, adapt, rebel, or avoid. The human species has become culturally richer for all of the global interaction and, at the same time, increasingly imperiled by diseases, pollution, exploitation, warfare, and overpopulation.

The purpose of *Annual Editions: World History, Volume II* is to provide a sense of the modern world and how it developed through a selection of timely, fresh, and interesting articles from popular sources. The units are organized into large chronological periods with special segments about the scientific and industrial revolutions, the intellectual ferment of the West, and current global problems. The progress of science and technology is ongoing and still has a pervasive influence upon the history of the world. The subject, moreover, is fundamental in the history of Western civilization. There are other subjects contained in the units—war, politics, women's history, geography, for example—that cut through the time periods. The *topic guide* and *index* can provide direction for these subjects. There are also *World Wide Web* sites, which are cross-referenced by number to the topic guide to allow further exploration for students. These sites can also be hot-linked through the *Annual Editions* home page at http://www.dushkin.com/annualeditions.

The world is not perfect and *Annual Editions: World History, Volume II* is not a perfect anthology. By its nature, an anthology must be selective, and not everything can be covered. Some important historical subjects, moreover, are lightly discussed in recent popular literature. In such cases an older article is used to maintain balance. Please feel free to recommend articles that might improve the next edition. You can use the *postage-paid rating form* at the back of this volume. We would like to have your suggestions and comments.

David McComb

Editor

Contents

UNIT 1

The World and the West, 1500–1900

Ten articles show how
the West extended and dominated
much of the world. Topics include
the age of discovery, the emergence
of Western colonial powers, the
European impact on the Far East,
and the relationship between the
British and the Zulus after the
Boer War in Africa.

UNIT 2

The Ferment of the West, 1500–1900

Six articles examine the cultural and economic development of the West, including such topics as women in eighteenth-century society and the controversy between mercantilism and free trade.

The concepts in bold italics are developed in the article. For further expansion please refer to the Topic Guide and the Index.

UNIT 3

The Industrial and Scientific Revolutions

Eight selections discuss the revolution in the industrial and scientific world. Topics include the scientific method, the industrial revolution in Great Britain, the development of the computer, and the development of space exploration.

The concepts in bold italics are developed in the article. For further expansion please refer to the Topic Guide and the Index.

vii

UNIT 4

The Twentieth Century to 1950

Eight articles examine the effect of war and economic depression on modern world history. Topics include the dynamics of Japan, World War II, and the war crimes trial at Nuremberg.

The concepts in bold italics are developed in the article. For further expansion please refer to the Topic Guide and the Index.

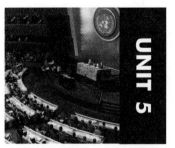

UNIT 5

The Era of the Cold War, 1950–1990

Seven articles discuss the evolution of a new world order. Topics include the Korean and Vietnam conflicts, the nuclear accident at Chornobyl, and the end of the cold war.

The concepts in bold italics are developed in the article. For further expansion please refer to the Topic Guide and the Index.

UNIT 6

Global Problems, Global Inter-dependence

Six selections examine the effects of
interdependence on some world
problems, including overpopulation,
the spread of nuclear technology, the
AIDS crisis, and the conflict between
Uganda and Rwanda.

Topic Guide

This topic guide suggests how the selections in this book relate to the subjects covered in your course.

The Web icon (⊙) under the topic articles easily identifies the relevant Web sites, which are numbered and annotated on the next two pages. By linking the articles and the Web sites by topic, this ANNUAL EDITIONS reader becomes a powerful learning and research tool.

TOPIC AREA	TREATED IN	TOPIC AREA	TREATED IN
Africa	2. Potato Connection 10. Zulus and the Boer War 43. Congo's Hidden War 44. 10 Million Orphans ⊙ *1, 2, 7, 11, 34, 35, 38*	**Culture**	1. That Fateful Moment 4. Dutch in Japan 6. Macartney Embassy to China 8. After Centuries of Japanese Isolation 9. Chinese Burns 11. First Feminist 16. Strange Case of the Surgeon 35. Tibet Through Chinese Eyes 45. American Century ⊙ *4, 7, 9, 12, 13, 19, 33*
Americas	1. That Fateful Moment 2. Potato Connection 12. George Mason 13. Founding Rivalries 22. Transatlantic Telegraph Cable 23. Father of the Computer Age 24. Greetings From Mars 33. Plan and the Man 45. American Century ⊙ *1, 2, 11, 38*		
		Economics	2. Potato Connection 5. 400 Years of the East India Company 7. Coffee, Tea, or Opium? 8. After Centuries of Japanese Isolation 14. From Mercantilism 15. As Good As Gold? 19. Workshop of a New Society 20. X Factor 33. Plan and the Man 45. American Century ⊙ *7, 10, 18*
Asia	3. Making Memories 4. Dutch in Japan 5. 400 Years of the East India Company 6. Macartney Embassy to China 7. Coffee, Tea, or Opium? 8. After Centuries of Japanese Isolation 9. Chinese Burns 20. X Factor 25. On the Turn—Japan, 1900 29. Exposing the Rape of Nanking 34. Korea: Echoes of a War 35. Tibet Through Chinese Eyes 37. Vietnam's Forgotten Lessons ⊙ *1, 2, 7, 11, 24*		
		Environment	2. Potato Connection 32. Short-Lived Miracle of DDT 38. Ten Years of the Chornobyl Era 40. Like Herrings in a Barrel 41. Weather Turns Wild ⊙ *1, 2, 3, 6, 10, 34, 35, 38*
		Europe	1. That Fateful Moment 3. Making Memories 4. Dutch in Japan 5. 400 Years of the East India Company 6. Macartney Embassy to China 9. Chinese Burns 10. Zulus and the Boer War 11. First Feminist 14. From Mercantilism 19. Workshop of a New Society 26. Home at Last 27. Maginot Line 28. Women in the Third Reich 30. His Finest Hour 31. Judgment at Nuremberg 33. Plan and the Man 38. Ten Years of the Chornobyl Era ⊙ *4, 12, 19, 22, 25, 26, 27, 30*
Business	3. Making Memories 4. Dutch in Japan 5. 400 Years of the East India Company 6. Macartney Embassy to China 7. Coffee, Tea, or Opium? 8. After Centuries of Japanese Isolation 15. As Good As Gold? 19. Workshop of a New Society ⊙ *7, 10, 17, 18*		
China	3. Making Memories 5. 400 Years of the East India Company 6. Macartney Embassy to China 7. Coffee, Tea, or Opium? 9. Chinese Burns 20. X Factor 29. Exposing the Rape of Nanking 34. Korea: Echoes of a War 35. Tibet Through Chinese Eyes ⊙ *7, 10, 14, 24, 36*	**France**	14. From Mercantilism 27. Maginot Line ⊙ *8, 26, 27*
		Geography	2. Potato Connection 24. Greetings From Mars 41. Weather Turns Wild ⊙ *11, 12, 21*
Cold War	33. Plan and the Man 34. Korea: Echoes of a War 36. Day We Shot Down the U-2 37. Vietnam's Forgotten Lessons 39. End of the Cold War ⊙ *3, 8, 11, 28, 29, 30, 33*	**Germany**	27. Maginot Line 28. Women in the Third Reich 31. Judgment at Nuremberg ⊙ *8, 9, 25, 27*

3

● AE: World History, Volume II

The following World Wide Web sites have been carefully researched and selected to support the articles found in this reader. The sites are cross-referenced by number and the Web icon (●) in the topic guide. In addition, it is possible to link directly to these Web sites through our DUSHKIN ONLINE support site at *http://www.dushkin.com/online/*.

The following sites were available at the time of publication. Visit our Web site—we update DUSHKIN ONLINE regularly to reflect any changes.

General World History Sites

1. CNN On Line Page
http://www.cnn.com
This is a U.S. 24-hour video news channel. News, updated every few hours, includes text, pictures, and film. It has good external links.

2. C-SPAN Online
http://www.c-span.org
See especially C-SPAN International on the Web for International Programming Highlights and archived C-SPAN programs.

3. Historical Text Archive
http://historicaltextarchive.com
This award-winning site contains links to world history, regional or national, and topical history and resources. For speed, use the text version.

4. History Index
http://www.ukans.edu/history/VL/
Here you will find an immense collection of links to sites devoted to different aspects and periods of history, some with graphics and sound.

5. History of Science, Technology, and Medicine
http://www.asap.unimelb.edu.au/hstm/
This database of information on science, technology, and medicine, with an alphabetical listing of resources, has search features and multiple links.

6. HyperHistory Online
http://www.hyperhistory.com
At this Web site, click on "hyperhistory" and navigate through 3,000 years of world history. There are links to important historical persons, events, and maps.

7. International Network Information Systems at University of Texas
http://inic.utexas.edu
This gateway has pointers to international study sites for Africa, India, China, Japan, and many other countries.

8. Military History
http://www.cfcsc.dnd.ca/links/milhist/
Here is a good place to start exploring military history. The site includes a timeline of major wars and links to military history by period.

9. National Humanities Institute Home Page
http://www.nhumanities.org
This Web site includes philosophical, cultural, and historical worldwide links, including archives, history sites, and an electronic library of full texts and documents, which is useful for research in history and the humanities.

10. United Nations System
http://www.unsystem.org
Everything is listed alphabetically at this official Web site for the United Nations system of organizations. Examples: UNICC; Food and Agriculture Organization.

11. U.S. Department of State Home Page
http://www.state.gov/index.html
Organized by categories: Hot Topics (i.e., Country Reports on Human Rights Practices), International Policy, Business Services, and more.

12. World Lecture Hall/History
http://www.utexas.edu/world/lecture/his/
At this Web site you can locate professors' lectures on many history topics by clicking on subjects, such as Europe in the Twentieth Century, History of Western Civilization, and Renaissance Creativity, among many others.

13. WWW Virtual Library—Humanities
http://www.hum.gu.se/w3vl/VL.html
This main subject index leads to many humanities-related research subjects, many of which relate to historical studies.

The World and the West, 1500—1900

14. The Boxer Rebellion of 1900
http://www.geocities.com/CollegePark/Pool/6208/title_page.htm
Visit this site to explore details and quotations concerning the Boxer Rebellion.

15. Commodore Matthew Perry
http://members.tripod.com/MickMc/perry.html
Here you will find information about Matthew Perry and his expedition to Japan. There is also a brief history of Japan and its isolation from trading and the West before Perry arrived.

16. The East India Company
http://www.theeastindiacompany.com/contents.html
The East India Company has had a long history. Explore their history and products on its official Web site.

The Ferment of the West, 1500—1900

17. The Adam Smith Institute
http://www.adamsmith.org.uk
This company and its Web site are dedicated to the economic principles and theories of Adam Smith. Visit here to explore those theories and Smith's original texts.

18. Britannica.com: Mercantilism
http://www.britannica.com/eb/article/eu=53378
This entry from the online Encyclopedia Britannica explains the economic theory and practice of mercantilism. It also provides links to information and popular sites on mercantilism.

19. Victorian Web
http://www.stg.brown.edu/projects/hypertext/landow/victorian/victov.html
At this Web site, open up links to Victorian Times, which includes social context, visual arts, politics, and Victorianism. This is an expansive collection of links.

The Industrial and Scientific Revolutions

20. A Trip to the Past
http://members.aol.com/mhirotsu/kevin/trip2.html
This site contains art, pictures, and text concerning the Industrial Revolution. Follow the links to an essay, innovative inventions, advances in art, and modifications in medicine.

21. Center for Mars Exploration
http://cmex-www.arc.nasa.gov
A starting place for an exploration of the history of Mars, with links to the Whole Mars Catalog and Live from Mars information about Pathfinder and Global Surveyor.

22. Sir Isaac Newton
http://www.newton.org.uk
Newton.org is a virtual museum about Isaac Newton and the history of science.

The Twentieth Century to 1950

23. Czar Nicholas II Assassinated
http://www.hiltonheadhigh.com/coolwork/newspapers/ nicholas/nicholas.htm
This is an online replication of the *Moscow Times* July 18, 1918, front page, which reports that Czar Nicholas II and his family were killed by Bolshevik guards. There are also other relevant historical stories from that issue on this site.

24. The Nanking Atrocity
http://web.missouri.edu/~jschool/nanking/
This is a Master's Project created by Masato Kajimoto for the University of Missouri–Columbia. It contains information and links to information about the atrocities at Nanking.

25. U.S. Holocaust Memorial Museum
http://www.ushmm.org
From this site you can access the official trial records, with photographs, of the Nuremberg trials, along with complete information about the Holocaust.

26. World War (1914–1918)
http://www.cfcsc.dnd.ca/links/milhist/wwi.html
This page is dedicated to World War I and features links to many subjects, including trench warfare, the Versailles Treaty, individual countries' participation, and lost poets of the war.

27. World War II on the Web
http://www.geocities.com/Athens/Oracle/2691/ welcome.htm
From this page you can explore 445 links to World War II material, including Pacific War Chronology, Women at War, Rescuers During the Holocaust, and the Rise of Adolf Hitler.

The Era of the Cold War, 1950–1990

28. The Chornobyl Nuclear Accident
http://www.infoukes.com/history/chornobyl
This site contains Dr. Zuzak's Chornobyl Files, Chornobyl maps and photo gallery, and a Chornobyl bibliography. There are also essays and projects about the disaster and its ramifications.

29. David Price's Homepage to Cold War Hot Links
http://www.stmartin.edu/~dprice/cold.war.htm
Here you will find material about the cold war, used by an anthropologist, which will also be of interest to a historian. There are many images and formerly classified documents, information on Joseph McCarthy, and period speeches, as well as clips from Soviet archives.

30. The Marshall Plan
http://www.nara.gov/exhall/featured-document/ marshall/marshall.html
Here is a brief overview and a set of links concerning the Marshall Plan.

31. Russia on the Web
http://www.valley.net/~transnat/
Among other links at this very complete site, click on History for a virtual tour of the palace where Nicholas II and Alexandra lived, Mikhail Gorbachev's home page, or Russian Studies on the Internet, a listing of sites related to Russian history and culture.

32. Tibetan Government in Exile
http://www.tibet.com
This is the official Web site of the Exiled Tibetan Government. Visit here to gather information about the history, exile, and status of Tibet.

33. WWW Virtual Library: Russian and East European Studies
http://www.ucis.pitt.edu/reesweb/
Through the NewsWeb at the University of Pittsburgh, there is a massive collection of links to both historic and contemporary information about Russia and Eastern Europe. At this Web site, there is everything from maps of the former Soviet Union to Bucharest's home page.

Global Problems, Global Interdependence

34. Africa News Web Site: Crisis in the Great Lakes Region
http://www.africanews.org/greatlakes.html
The African News Web Site on the Great Lakes (i.e., Rwanda, Burundi), Zaire (now Democratic Republic of the Congo), Kenya, Tanzania, and Uganda is found here, with frequent updates plus good links to other sites.

35. Africa Notes
http://www.csis.org/html/2africa.html
CSIS Africa Notes is published monthly. Check into this Web site for what's new in efforts to help sub-Saharan countries.

36. Amnesty International
http://www.amnesty.org
Information about the current state of human rights throughout the world is available at this Web site.

37. Population Awareness
http://www.overpopulation.org/nav.html
This page contains fact sheets and statistics about population as well as answers to the questions: Why does population matter and what are the impacts of overpopulation?

38. Reliefweb
http://wwwnotes.reliefweb.int
This is the UN's Department of Humanitarian Affairs clearinghouse for international humanitarian emergencies. It has daily updates, including Reuters, VOA, and PANA.

We highly recommend that you review our Web site for expanded information and our other product lines. We are continually updating and adding links to our Web site in order to offer you the most usable and useful information that will support and expand the value of your Annual Editions. You can reach us at: *http://www.dushkin. com/annualeditions/*.

www.dushkin.com/online/

Unit Selections

Key Points to Consider

❖ What was the importance of technology in the expansion of the West?

❖ What was the motivation of Westerners in their global explorations?

❖ What was the "Columbian Exchange"? What items were involved? What were the long-term consequences of the exchange?

❖ Compare the influence of the Portuguese, Dutch, British, and Americans on the Far East.

❖ Explain the role of the East India Company in the British government.

❖ In your opinion, did "might make right" in regard to Cortés, the Opium War, the United States in Japan, the Macartney embassy, the Zulus, and the Boxers?

❖ How did Japan escape the fate of China in its encounter with the West?

 **Links** **www.dushkin.com/online/**

These sites are annotated on pages 4 and 5.

Searching for trade opportunities, the small, seafaring nation of Portugal began the great European explorations of the fifteenth century. They followed the western coast of Africa, eventually rounded the Cape of Good Hope, and sailed on to India and the spice islands of the Far East. They were the first Europeans to reach Japan, and they introduced the Japanese to both guns and Christianity. They established the port of Macau on the southeastern coast of China in 1557, which, consequently, they returned to China in 1999. Macau became known for its Jesuit background and its tolerance of sin and diverse peoples. The Portuguese were never as aggressive as the British who later occupied Hong Kong, but, nonetheless, they were pushed out of Japan in favor of the Dutch. "Making Memories" tells the story of this last European port in China while the article, "The Dutch in Japan," relates the restricted, but long, association of the Dutch merchants with the people of Japan.

The small Dutch port of Deshima Island, located on an isolated, man-made island, provided the Japanese with their only window to the West. The Japanese were not much interested in the rest of the world and had actually suppressed gunmaking in favor of the honored Samurai swords. It was a shock, therefore, when Matthew Perry of the United States arrived with his small flotilla and forced Japan to open its ports under the threat of naval gun power. James Fallows in his article, "After Centuries of Japanese Isolation, a Fateful Meeting of East and West," provides an account of this event. Following the forced opening of its ports, Japan undertook a large-scale industrialization that brought it power in the Far East and allowed it to avoid the humiliation visited upon China by Western nations.

Western countries, particularly Great Britain, followed the Portuguese and the Dutch to the Far East. At the end of the eighteenth century, an English delegation led by Lord George Macartney tried to arrange a trade agreement with China. The Chinese arrogantly rejected the overture and, at the same time, exposed their own weaknesses.

Meanwhile, the East India Company consolidated British power in India with Robert Clive's victory over an Indian and French force at the Battle of Plassey during the Seven Years' War. The article, "400 Years of the East India Company" explains this remarkable imperialism carried out by a commercial organization.

The East India Company established trade in China and paid for the tea it bought with opium grown in India. The Chinese effort to halt this debilitating drug trade failed when the British government authorized the use of its warships to legalize the transactions. Worse, as explained in the article, "Coffee, Tea, or Opium?" five ports and Hong Kong fell under British influence. Other European nations moved in to exploit the weakness of China. In 1900 China's hatred of outsiders boiled over in the Boxer Rebellion. "Chinese Burns: Britain in China 1842–1900," by Robert Bickers describes this event and explains why it was so readily suppressed by Western troops. China was left on the verge of dissolution.

The Chinese suffered under the heavy hand of Western imperialism; so did the Zulus of South Africa. The British acquired the Cape Colony during the Napoleonic Wars and the Dutch who had settled it moved to the north. At the end of the nineteenth century the British and Dutch settlers clashed in the Boer War. To aid in their battle, the British recruited and armed Zulu warriors. After winning the war, the British, who were concerned with reconciliation with the Boers, disarmed the natives, broke promises, and left them worse off than before the conflict. Jabulani Maphalala explains this story in "The Zulus and the Boer War."

Perhaps, the most important legacy of this long history of Western imperialism, however, was the quiet exchange of food products that Alfred Crosby writes about in "The Potato Connection." This part of the "Columbian Exchange," which involves especially white potatoes, manioc, and corn, has had a continuing global impact by improving nutrition for the world's people.

That fateful moment when two civilizations came face to face

Cortés and his men were out for gold and glory; Montezuma's Aztec empire was shaky; the cruel result was a tragedy of history

Charles L. Mee Jr.

Even before anyone came, there were amazing events: a comet appeared and split into three; the waters of the lake boiled up in a rage; a sign like a tongue of fire burned up into the sky, up to the heavens.

These and other remarkable things began to happen ten years before the Spaniards landed: omens that foretold their coming, said the old men who drew pictographs of them some 30 years afterward for the Franciscan missionary Fray Bernardino de Sahagún.

According to Sahagún's aged native informants, a messenger brought word of "towers or small mountains floating on the waves of the sea." The ships came in the spring of 1519, off the northern shore of the Yucatan peninsula. There were 11 all told (or, according to other sources, 10 or 12 ships), carrying 10 large bronze cannon, 4 falconets, or light cannon, stores of powder and shot, 16 horses, some large dogs, 550 soldiers (including 32 crossbowmen and 13 musketeers), 100 sailors along with 200 Cuban natives, several black people and a few Indian women.

The Spaniards, with their white skin, their suits of armor, their cannon and their horses, were an arresting sight. "They were very white," the old men told Sahagún. Their faces were like chalk. Indian amazement, in any case, has been the theme of most historians for the past four centuries and more, who have written of the Spanish ships of supernatural size and appearance. The newcomers were observed riding on the backs of extraordinary deerlike beasts, which snorted and bellowed, and whose running made tremors "as if stones were raining on the earth." Perhaps these creatures who rode such beasts were gods, white gods.

Yet the natives of the Yucatán and of Mexico could hardly have been quite as astonished as all that. In truth, just a year before, in 1518, the Indians had seen Spaniards cruise precisely this same coastline, in an expedition led by the adventurer Juan de Grijalva. The Indians had met the Spaniards and traded native gold ornaments and jewels for green glass beads, some scissors, pins and other trinkets. And the year before Grijalva, Francisco Hernandez de Córdoba had sailed into the Gulf of Mexico looking for gold and silver and slaves.

The new lot of Spaniards was led by Hernán Cortés, a soldier of fortune whose parents had destined him for the law until he had quit school at the age of 16. According to an account written years later by Cortés' private secretary and chaplain, Francisco López de Gómara, this "vexed his parents exceedingly.... He was a source of trouble to his parents as well as to himself, for he was restless, haughty, mischievous, and given to quarreling, for which reason he decided to seek his fortune." Cortés arrived in the New World in 1504, and eventually was chosen by Diego Velázquez, governor of Cuba, to command an expedition to Mexico—for exploration and trade but, officially at least, *not* to conquer or colonize.

Even so, many of those who sailed with him were experienced soldiers of fortune, men who had signed up in the hope of getting fame and riches, as well as conquering lands for Spain. Tough as they were, they were also committed, in a way we can hardly understand today, to the mission of converting the Indians to Christianity. Along the route of their journey, searching for members of an earlier journey, they picked up Jerónimo de Aguilar, a Spaniard who had been shipwrecked eight years before, then enslaved by the Maya, learning their language. The Spaniards also picked up a woman sold to the Maya by allies of the Aztecs. They called her Doña Marina. She spoke Nahuatl, the language of the Aztecs, as well as Maya. As the Spaniards moved into Aztec territory, she was helpful, translating from Nahuatl into

From *That Fateful Moment When Two Civilizations Came Face to Face,* by Charles L. Mee, Jr., October 1992. Published by *Smithsonian,* pp. 57-69. Used by permission of the Wallace Literary Agency, Inc.

Maya, while Aguilar translated from Maya into Spanish.

On Holy Thursday, 1519, the fleet found safe harbor on the island of San Juan de Ulúa, as the Spaniards called it, off Mexico's eastern shore. As Bernal Díaz, one of Cortés' foot soldiers who chronicled these events years later, tells the story, they no sooner had dropped anchor than two large canoes came out filled with Aztec ambassadors. The Indians brought with them some gifts, and they were taken aboard the flagship and given food and wine and some blue beads.

"They said that their lord," relates Bernal Díaz, "a servant of the great Montezuma [as the Spanish spelled it], had sent them to find out what kind of men we were and what we were seeking." According to Gómara, the Indians also asked the Spaniards, with exemplary diplomatic tact, "whether they intended to stop or continue on beyond." Cortés replied that the Spaniards had come to speak to the lord of the Aztecs. (According to Sahagún's native informants the Spaniards were not as polite as all that. They put the Indians in irons and fired off a cannon to scare them.)

By Easter Sunday, a local Aztec governor had arrived. His name was Tentlil, and he was accompanied, says Gómara, by more than 4,000 men, all unarmed, handsomely dressed and loaded with presents. Tentlil had brought along some artists, who made portraits in the style of Aztec picture-writing, of Cortés, his captains and soldiers, his ships and horses and guns—a detailed report to send back to Montezuma. When Cortés asked to see Montezuma himself, saying that the Spaniards came as ambassadors from the greatest king on earth, Tentlil graciously replied that word would be sent to Montezuma. Some sources say that Tentlil at first inquired testily, "How is it that you have been here only two days, and demand to see the emperor?" Cortés asked whether Montezuma had any gold, and Tentlil replied that he did. It was then, apparently, that Cortés said, in a phrase that has rung down through

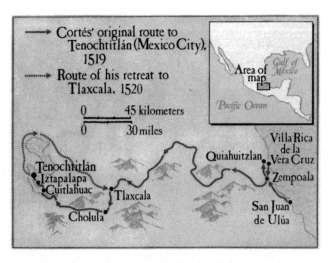

The route of the Spanish conquest of Mexico includes Cortés' retreat to Tlaxcala in the summer of 1520.

the ages, "Send me some of it, because I and my companions suffer from a disease of the heart which can be cured only with gold."

From his capital city of Tenochtitlán, the present site of Mexico City, the emperor Montezuma II ruled over a vast imperial domain in central Mexico stretching from the Gulf Coast to the Pacific Ocean, and as far south as present-day Guatemala. He was chosen by a group of about a hundred of the richest and most powerful members of the ruling class, and he had to maintain his rule with subtle and skillful maneuvering. Central Mexico at the time probably had a population of perhaps 25 million, with 2 million or so in the region about Tenochtitlán. Of these, perhaps a total of 500,000 could be mustered as soldiers, though the offensive force here comprised, on average, probably about 50,000 men.

Montezuma's reply to Cortés came back to the coast accompanied by more extremely lavish gifts, and word that Montezuma "rejoiced to learn about" Cortés' great king, and that Cortés should determine what he needed for himself and "the cure of his sickness," as well as whatever supplies he needed for his men and his ships. But, as for Montezuma and the Spanish leader meeting, that would be "impossible."

Undismayed, Cortés gathered a sample of Spanish wealth to send to the emperor, inquiring again about a meeting

and the possibility of trade. While he waited he had some surprise visitors, five Indians from the city of Zempoala—a city, they said, that had recently been brought under Montezuma's yoke by force of arms.

This piece of news electrified Cortés. As Díaz puts it, he learned "that Montezuma had opponents and enemies, which greatly delighted him." Very quickly, Cortés would come to learn how extraordinarily fragile this great empire of Montezuma's was. Mexico was a loose organization of villages and city-states linked together in an uneasy alliance. Their inhabitants spoke more than 20 different languages and hundreds of different dialects. Their local loyalties made them resentful of central government. The empire, in short, was based upon the conquest and subjugation of many embittered peoples. Cortés instantly saw the possibility of revolt in Mexico, with himself as the leader.

Eager to be rid of Cortés, Montezuma apparently reiterated in his next communication that the Spaniards might have whatever they needed but then must take their fleet and leave. Now surer of his ground, Cortés refused. It was impossible, he insisted, for the Spaniards to leave without seeing the emperor. Montezuma had provided men to wait on the Spaniards, but about this time Cortés saw that these people had disappeared. He called his captains together and told them to prepare for war.

The route the Spaniards eventually took to Montezuma's capital city was circuitous. First they headed north, to Zempoala, finding the people ready to join in an uprising against Montezuma. From there, gathering allies, they moved on to Quiahuitzlan, where they came across some of Montezuma's tax collectors—and had them arrested. (Later Cortés quietly set them free for diplomatic purposes.) As soon as the chiefs of the neighboring towns heard that the Spaniards had arrested Montezuma's tax collectors, they joined forces with Cortés against Montezuma, and even took an oath of allegiance. Almost overnight his tiny force was increased by thousands of fighting men.

STONES CAME LIKE HAIL FROM INDIAN SLINGS

After establishing a base at Villa Rica de la Vera Cruz, the Spaniards and their new allies ventured into the territory of the Tlaxcalans, where their mettle was tested in battles with several thousand warriors. The Indians fought with clubs, spears, slings, arrows and darts; the Spaniards with lances, artillery, muskets, crossbows and swords. Some days of nearly continuous hand-to-hand fighting occurred. Stones came like hail from the Indians' slings, Díaz says, and "their barbed and fire-hardened darts fell like corn on the threshing-floor."

The Spaniards "wondered what would happen," Díaz adds, "when we had to fight Montezuma if we were reduced to such straits by the Tlaxcalans, whom our Cempoalan allies described as a peaceful people." But in the end they had the victory, the first of many.

How, in fact, was it possible for this little band of Spaniards to march into unknown territory, defeat the vast armies brought against them, and lose only two score or so Spanish lives in such encounters?

First of all, not too much faith should be placed in the numbers used to describe the size of the enemy. Though the various Spanish estimates range from 30,000 to 100,000 warriors, it is clear that if such numbers were accurate, only a miracle could explain a Spanish victory. That miracle would seem less necessary if, say a decimal point were moved, giving the Tlaxcalans 10,000 warriors at most. Even so, the Spaniards were greatly outnumbered.

Not too much credit can be given to the Spanish crossbows. Although they outclassed Indian bows, they were difficult to use. Nor can too much credit be given to the purely material effects of gunpowder. Spanish powder was often wet, and the rate of fire of cannon and muskets was appallingly slow.

The psychological effect of gunpowder and horses and glistening armor, though, must have been phenomenal. The Span-

iards must have impressed the Indians in the way that street demonstrators are impressed—and suddenly made to feel vulnerable—when heavily armed, modern riot police wade into the midst of a crowd. Besides, some Indian tactics helped the Spaniards. They tended not to kill their enemies, hoping to wound and capture them mainly for use as sacrifices to the gods. They also stopped fighting periodically to remove their dead and wounded from the battlefield. At close range, the Indians used wooden clubs tipped and ridged with razor-sharp obsidian—a vicious weapon against other Indians, but one which probably shattered against Spanish helmets.

The Spaniards brought their swords into this close combat, and they were dreadfully effective. Pointed and double-bladed, they could stab, and slash left and right, quickly killing or maiming. Driving directly at warriors clustered around their leaders, the Spaniards would often capture or kill a local chief. Once their chief was taken, his men usually fell back.

After two weeks the Tlaxcalans surrendered, agreeing to join Cortés against the Aztecs. As the Spaniards penetrated farther and farther into Mexico, they recruited allies until, when they reached Tenochtitlán at last, their force included about 5,000 Indians.

As the Spaniards advanced, they laid waste to the town of Cholula. It was there that Cortés killed 3,000 Indians, because, he said, they had plotted with Montezuma to attack him. Other sources describe it as an unprovoked massacre. In any case, as they approached Tenochtitlán the Spaniards' reputation for savagery and invincibility grew greater and greater.

By the time they had reached the city of Cuitlahuac, just southeast of Tenochtitlán, they had entered the lake country in the Valley of Mexico, where the towns were sometimes built entirely in the water, connected to the land by broad causeways. The towns and stone buildings, says Díaz, "seemed like an enchanted vision. . . . Indeed, some of our soldiers asked whether it was not all a dream."

As they approached the Aztec capital the Spaniards set foot on a causeway—wide enough for ten horsemen to ride

abreast. And partway along it, Gómara says, they were met by 4,000 "gentlemen of the court" of Tenochtitlán "richly dressed after their fashion," who, each in turn, bowed to the Spaniards as a sign of peace. Then, just across a little bridge, the Spaniards saw Montezuma. "He walked," Gómara adds, "under a pallium of gold and green feathers, strung about with silver hangings, and carried by four gentlemen." He was supported on the arms of two royal princes.

Courtiers walked ahead of Montezuma, sweeping the ground and laying down thin mantles so that his feet would never touch the earth. Then came 200 lords, all barefoot, but wearing rich cloaks. Cortés stepped forward to embrace Montezuma; but the two princes put out their hands at once to prevent it. The two leaders exchanged brief greetings. Only then was Cortés permitted to step forward and take a splendid necklace of pearls and cut glass and put it around the neck of Montezuma.

The emperor ordered that Cortés and many of his Indian allies be shown to a beautiful palace. There, Montezuma himself took Cortés by the hand, bidding him, Cortés says, to "sit on a very rich throne . . . and then left saying that I should wait for him." In the heart of Montezuma's empire, the Spaniards and their allies were surrounded. The Aztecs, in turn, were surrounded by more of Cortés' allies outside the city. Frozen in this balance of forces, they commenced a curious diplomatic dance, one whose end was entirely unpredictable.

Montezuma, Díaz reports, was about 40 years old, "of good height, well proportioned, spare and slight." He bathed every afternoon, according to Díaz—twice a day, according to Gómara. The Spaniards, who sometimes slept in their armor without even removing their shoes, were impressed by the frequency of Montezuma's bathing.

For a time the Spaniards were left alone. The city in which they found themselves would have impressed anyone. Tenochtitlán lay at the center of a vast bowl dominated by high mountains. At the bottom was a large plain and many shallow lakes, including Lake Texcoco, a large body of salt water. The Aztec capital had been built up atop mudbanks and islands until, like Venice, it was a wonder of human artifice, laced with canals and bridges. Three long and wide causeways connected it to the mainland. An aqueduct brought fresh water from a hillside spring into the middle of the city.

Cortés describes a marketplace "twice as big as that of Salamanca, with arcades all around, where more than sixty thousand people come each day to buy and sell." The array of goods on sale reflected the far-flung trade that the Aztecs had developed: all manner of birds—chickens, partridge, quail, turtledoves, falcons—used for food, for feathers, for hunting; gold or featherwork in the form of butterflies, trees, flowers; a silver monkey that moved its feet and head; carved turquoise and emeralds; stuff made of conchs and periwinkles; toys for children; ointments, syrups and culinary delicacies, such as little barkless dogs that had been castrated and fattened. There were even cakes made from a sort of scum skimmed from the ooze on the lake's surface and dried, to be eaten like cheese. "Delicious," says Gómara.

All around the city, according to Cortés, were many temples, "beautiful buildings," but among them all, there was one "whose great size and magnificence no human tongue could describe." The main temple occupied a site about 70 by 80 yards at its base, with two staircases leading up nearly 200 feet to a terrace and twin shrines. There the stones were splattered black with the blood of human sacrifices.

Most often, the victim would be led or dragged to the top of the temple steps and stretched out over a block of stone by five priests. A priest would cut him open, reach in and pluck out his still-beating heart. The heart was offered up in a sacred vessel, often to placate the Sun. The body was thrown down the temple steps and then flayed and cut up. Its skull went to a great skull rack (where, according to Gómara, there were 136,000 skulls, arranged in rows, teeth outward), and the remainder was sometimes ceremoniously eaten, usually by the warriors who had captured the victim.

In the days to come, as Cortés and Montezuma met, Cortés broached his wish to convert Montezuma to Christi-anity and spoke of the evils of the Aztec gods—a topic of conversation that must have struck Montezuma as outrageously rude, and irrelevant to the business of conducting trade or to negotiations between an emperor and a visiting captain general.

A COMMANDER "BESET WITH MISGIVINGS"

For their part, the Spaniards evidently became increasingly uneasy about the absurdity and perilousness of their position. Even Cortés himself came to feel "beset with misgivings," sharing a dreadful sense of being caught in a web from which he and his men could never escape. It had begun to dawn on them that there was no reason for Montezuma to let them leave Tenochtitlán alive. Eventually, they devised a most astounding way out of their dilemma. They decided to seize Montezuma and hold him hostage in his own city.

And so, says Gómara, Cortés took some of his soldiers with him to pay a call on the emperor. Cortés greeted Montezuma "as usual, and then began to jest and banter with him, as he had done before." But soon enough Cortés got to the point, and told the emperor that he would need to come and stay with the Spaniards. Montezuma was "profoundly shaken," says Gómara, and replied, "My person is not such as can be taken prisoner, and even if I should consent to it, my people would not suffer it."

According to Díaz, Cortés and Montezuma spent more than half an hour discussing the question. Cortés' soldiers grew jittery. "What is the use of all these words?" one of them burst out. "Either we take him or we knife him. If we do not look after ourselves now we shall be dead men." In the end Montezuma went peacefully with the Spaniards.

How was it that the Aztec emperor could have allowed himself to be placed in such a position? Sahagún's informants gave an explanation of the mystery that has endured ever since: Montezuma and the Aztecs thought that Cortés was none other than the ancient god-king Quetzalcóatl, the Feathered Serpent, who, according to religious myth, had been driven from his kingdom vowing one day to return and reassert his rule. Therefore some historians believe that Montezuma was a prisoner of his own mythology. The myth is a wonderful explanation but, as British archaeologist Nigel Davis points out, it "has been rather overplayed in popular accounts." Besides, purely diplomatic protocol provides a reasonable explanation—Montezuma waited for Cortés to arrive at Tenochtitlán simply because it was the Aztec custom that an ambassador was immune from harm.

Or it may be that, as word came of Spanish military and diplomatic victories, Montezuma came to comprehend that these strangers needed to be handled with great care. This, in any case, appears to have been Cortés' view. As Gómara explains, Montezuma "did not wish to stir up trouble for himself (and this was the truest reason)" by offering open resistance to Cortés and thus perhaps encouraging more of his discontented subjects to join the Spaniards in an attempt to unseat his power. He would pursue the strategy of the spider and the fly; he would bring Cortés into Tenochtitlán and informally hold him hostage, in the same way that he customarily held numerous rival chiefs as permanent hostages.

While the Spaniards kept Montezuma in captivity—sometimes, indeed, in manacles—the myth of Montezuma's rule had to be maintained. Each day the Spaniards would ask him what his orders and his wants were, and these were carried out. Sometimes Cortés and Montezuma would sit together and play to *totoloque,* a game that involved tossing small pellets of gold for higher stakes, usually more gold or jewelry.

Eventually, perhaps trying to quench the Spanish thirst for gold, Montezuma agreed not only to open up his personal treasure but to call in gifts from his whole empire and give them to Cortés. The list of what he gave is breathtaking: gold and silver and pearls, golden nose crescents and necklaces, blowguns inlaid with silver, silver plates and cups, pitchers and saucers. There was so much gold treasure from Montezuma's gifts alone, says Díaz, that it took the Spaniards three days just to examine it all.

Soon afterward it appeared that some of the Aztec leaders, tired of seeing their emperor truckling to the Spaniards, told Montezuma that either the Spaniards should leave or the Aztecs should kill them. Aware of the danger, Cortés ordered that the horses be kept saddled and bridled day and night; Spanish soldiers slept in their armor, their weapons beside them.

But just at the critical point—it was May 1520—Montezuma's messengers brought news that another Spanish fleet, captained by Pánfilo de Narváez, had been spotted back at San Juan de Ulúa where Cortés had originally landed. A picture painted on cloth was brought to Montezuma. There were 18 ships, 80 horses and 900 soldiers.

Cortés greeted the news with an appearance of relief, even joy. However, out of Montezuma's presence he grew "very thoughtful," Díaz says. He guessed that Diego Velázquez had sent the fleet to put a stop to his enterprise, and he sensed the presence of rivals for the Aztec riches as well as a possible split among the Spaniards that the Aztecs might exploit. Cortés left for the coast, taking about 120 soldiers with him and leaving fewer than 100 at Tenochtitlán, under the command of Pedro de Alvarado, a man with the reputation of being brave but cruel.

At Zempoala, Cortés took Narváez's army by surprise at night. Narváez himself got a pike thrust that cost him an eye and was put into irons. Most of his men joined Cortés, augmenting his force with a large and fresh lot of soldiers, including, as Gómara reports, "a Negro sick with the smallpox"—who would, as we now know, turn out to be a very significant figure in the final tragedy.

Back in Tenochtitlán, however, the whole city had exploded in violence. The Indians had been celebrating the annual festival of Toxcatl in the courtyard of the great temple square with "drums, conch trumpets, bone fifes" and other instruments. They were covered with necklaces and jewels, feathers and pearls, and danced in circles, accompanied by sacred singing. In the midst of the dancing the Spanish soldiers abruptly closed off all the exits and, with swords drawn, waded into the midst of the dancers.

"They attacked the man who was drumming," according to Sahagún's native informants, "and cut off his arms. Then they cut off his head, and it rolled across the floor. They attacked all the celebrants, stabbing them, spearing them. . . . Others they beheaded . . . or split their heads to pieces. . . . Some - at tempted to run away, but . . . they seemed to tangle their feet in their own entrails."

The next day the Aztecs who had not been trapped in the courtyard counterattacked. Full-scale fighting swept through the city, bringing about all of the horrors that Montezuma apparently had feared and labored for so long to avoid. The emperor watched, powerless, as the city, which had thus far been saved from bloodshed, was threatened with disaster. The Aztecs closed off the causeways, destroyed some of the bridges over which the Spaniards might escape and threw up barricades around the palace, hoping to starve the Spaniards out.

TRAPPED INSIDE THE AZTEC CITY

Hearing the news, Cortés at once rushed back toward Tenochtitlán. As he passed through the countryside, he discovered "all the land was in revolt and almost uninhabited." In late June, when he reentered Montezuma's city, he found the streets almost deserted. There was an ominous quiet, as the Aztecs let the Spaniards back into the trap. By next morning, the roads around Tenochtitlán were filled with angry warriors, all of them enemies of the Spaniards. The thousands of Cortés' native allies now seemed to melt away, except for the few thousand Tlaxcalans trapped with the Spaniards inside the city.

"Such a multitude" of Aztecs now swarmed in to surround the Spaniards' quarters, says Cortés, "that neither the streets nor the roofs of the houses could be seen for them." And soon, so many stones began to be "hurled at us from their slings into the fortress that it seemed they were raining from the sky. . . ."

Wave after wave of Aztecs repeatedly attacked, often running headlong into Spanish guns, cannon and swords. Some tried to scale the walls of the palace. Finally, they shot burning arrows into the fortress, hoping to smoke the enemy out. One whole section of the palace fell, but the attackers never got in.

At last Cortés sent for Montezuma and asked him to go up to the roof of the palace and tell his people to stop the fighting and let the Spaniards leave in peace. According to Díaz, Montezuma mounted to the roof, and a great silence fell over the thousands who swarmed over the streets and nearby rooftops. The emperor begged his people to put down their arms and let the Spaniards go. But, Díaz says, the chiefs replied to Montezuma—"in tears"—that they no longer recognized him as their leader, and they would not stop now until all the Spaniards were dead, "and they begged for his forgiveness."

And then, a shower of darts and stones was thrown at Montezuma. The Spanish soldiers rushed the emperor back inside the palace. But soon thereafter, because he refused to eat or have his wounds tended, Montezuma died.

While most sources agree with this account, some, mostly native sources, say that Montezuma was murdered by the Spaniards back in their palace quarters.

It was now imperative for the Spaniards to get out of the city. In the middle of the night of June 30, 1520, they brought the gold and jewels and silver out into the middle of a hall in the palace. Those who wanted some, took it and stuffed it into their packs and clothes. Shortly before midnight, Cortés and his men made a run for it across one of the causeways.

The horsemen went out first, presumably to charge and scatter any Aztecs who might block the way. They were followed by soldiers carrying a makeshift wooden bridge to be used in place of the bridges the Aztecs had destroyed. The retreating Spanish managed to slam the bridge down across the first break they came to. They had caught the Aztecs by surprise, and so a good many Spaniards slipped past the main mass of Indians. But then an alarm sounded—trumpets, cries and whistles—and their retreat became a headlong dash down the causeway. Crowds of Aztec warriors threw stones and spears at them, and, as Díaz says, they had to leave the bridge behind at the first gap.

Trying to get over the next gap without the bridge was a disaster. As horses slipped and fell into the water, cannon and bundles and boxes followed. The Spaniards rushed on from gap to gap, fleeing ahead of the Aztec warriors, braving the improvised gauntlet of warrior-filled canoes on either side of the causeway. Those who had been most greedy about stuffing gold into their clothes were among the first to sink with the weight of it as they crossed. "So those who died," Gómara notes dryly, "died rich."

According to Díaz, there had been 1,300 Spanish soldiers in Tenochtitlán in those last days (much of Cortés' original army, plus Narváez's reinforcements) as well as 2,000 native warriors, mostly Tlaxcalans. Estimates of those killed in the siege and flight from the city range from 450 to 860 Spaniards and 1,000 to 4,000 Tlaxcalans.

The survivors continued to flee, all the way to the city of Tlaxcala, where their strongest allies took them in. For Cortés and the Tlaxcalans, there was no quitting the struggle with the Aztecs.

Realizing that to take back the Aztec capital he would have to attack and seize the city from both the causeways and the surrounding water, Cortés had boats built so they could be carried piecemeal over land and then assembled to operate in the shallow lake waters. In late December of 1520, Cortés reentered the Valley of Mexico, secured the shores of the lake, and destroyed the aqueduct that brought the main supply of fresh water into the city.

In late April 1521 the siege began, Cortés sending his boats across the water, and his foot soldiers down the causeways. The Aztecs had prepared their defenses by planting sharpened stakes just under the water at the gaps in the causeway. As fighting continued, the Spanish kept filling in the gaps with stones and rubble, but at night the Aztecs reopened them. Once, when the Aztecs took prisoners, they cut off the heads of some and bowled them at the approaching army.

Day and night, the fighting went on. The Spaniards would secure a street, only to find it taken back the next day. At last Cortés instructed his men to advance, slowly and deliberately, removing every Aztec barricade, destroying every Aztec tower and house as they went. The slow, grinding reduction of Tenochtitlán went on for three months, and toward the end the stench of unburied bodies piled high in the streets and rotting in the water was appalling. In the last offensive, so "piteous" was the wailing of women and children, says Gómara, that Cortés urged his men to spare the populace, but they kept on. As the city began at last to collapse, a gush of old men, women and children came flooding out toward the causeways with such force "that they pushed each other into the water, where many drowned."

The end came on August 13, 1521. The few Aztec warriors still alive gathered on the rooftops of the houses that still stood, and "stared at the ruins of their city in a dazed silence." As the Spaniards walked at last down the inner streets of the conquered city, they tied handkerchiefs over their noses to guard against the stench. They went through town, seeing the stagnant and briny water that had served as drinking water in these last days of Tenochtitlán and the remnants of what the Aztecs had had for food: lizards and salt grasses from the lake, twigs, roots and tree bark.

Among the piles of bodies were people who had died not so much of wounds as of starvation and of various diseases, especially smallpox—the virus that had been brought ashore by the man in Narváez's crew, a virus that had made its way across Mexico with Cortés' army. The populations of the Americas had no resistance to it.

In some regions of Mexico, the mortality rate was so great that the living could not bring themselves to bury the dead. It was said that the Indians, overwhelmed by the task, sometimes pulled down the houses on top of the dead to bury them.

Cortés' story did not end here. Like many other New World adventurers, he went on to great wealth and power. But in the end, accused of murder and mismanagement, he died broken-hearted in Spain. The pestilence that his invasion brought did not end with the death of Tenochtitlán, either. Smallpox and other epidemics spread throughout the countryside, subsided and recurred, subsided and recurred, until, eventually, of a total population of perhaps 25 million, as many as 22 million died.

And with the death of so many, a civilization died—not simply a city or a government or an empire, but most of the accumulated knowledge of life and art and skill, so that, in time, practically all that remained of it were its artifacts and its story of the inevitability, in life and in history, of tragedy, and surprise.

The Potato Connection

How the New World Fed the Old

Alfred W. Crosby

In the 16th century, Francisco López de Gómara, biographer of Hernán Cortés and historian of Spain's new empire, declared that the European discovery of the New World was one of the two most important events since Creation—the other being the incarnation of God. To Gómara's fellow Europeans, the Americas did indeed provide golden opportunities for conquest and evangelization. But they had no idea that their most influential acquisitions would be the food crops they took home, chiefly maize and the white potato.

For those of us who live in the Western Hemisphere, the importance of Christopher Columbus's landfall in 1492 is self-apparent. But what difference did it make for the peoples on the other side of the Atlantic Ocean?

For some, the impact of contact was undoubtedly negative. The forced migration of millions of Africans to America's plantations, for example, was to Europe's advantage, but certainly not to Africa's. Most Asians, until the mid-19th century, were indifferent to the discovery of the Americas.

But in Europe the fallout from Columbus's find was immense. Europeans extracted enormous sums—in Spanish dollars, French livres and British pounds—from the New World's mines, soils and waters, capital that may have spurred the industrial revolution in Europe. And what would European history, plagued by riot and war, have been like without America to receive 50 million or so people? How would modern science have developed if the unknown plants, animals and peoples of America

had not exploded old concepts? The authorities of antiquity had known nothing of America's existence. They had envisioned one-legged men, phoenixes and griffins, which could not be found anywhere; but they had not written of animals with pockets (opossums), birds that fly backwards (hummingbirds) or snakes that rattle, all of which awaited discovery in the New World. Never had they dreamed of the variety of peoples native to America, whose very diversity inspired the invention of anthropology, a scientific outlook many Europeans could not yet embrace, reverting instead to the ancient concept of the subhuman heathen or creating new fictions like Jean Jacques Rousseau's "noble savage." Both concepts still stalk our scholarship and popular culture today.

While such examples of America's shaping influence on Old World *thought* are impressive, they do not reflect direct influence in the way that the transfer of plants and animals does.

Biologically, America was indeed a new world to Europeans, Africans and Asians. It had been separate from the Old World for an immense stretch of time, except for connections in the frigid north, and free from even that frosty link for the past 10,000 years. It had been independent for long enough to have raccoons, skunks, chipmunks, hummingbirds and rattlesnakes, and for Americans to have developed their own distinct civilizations. Politically, America may have become a satellite of the Old World—specifically of Europe—after 1492, but biologically the Old and New Worlds were near equals. The Old World

proffered its distinctive flora and fauna—smallpox virus, malaria plasmodia, horses, cattle, sheep, house cats, starlings, wheat, rice, barley, turnips, peas and so on. The New World's most influential contributions were food crops.

A few other life forms—largely valueless exports—made their way over. Turkeys crossed the Atlantic early but never replaced any of the Old World's domesticated fowl; North American gray squirrels have largely displaced the indigenous red squirrels in Great Britain; and American muskrats have spread from central Europe beyond the Urals. But the impact of such transplants has been minimal. The exception may be the spirochete of syphilis, which many scientists and historians claim is as American as the rattlesnake. Europeans first recognized the disease in the mid-1490s, shortly after Columbus's return from America. Voltaire vested his pie-in-the-sky Pangloss with the infection. Pangloss caught it from Paquette, who caught it from a monk and so on back to an early Jesuit, who had caught it from one of Columbus's companions. Did the real Columbus, as many have insisted for the last half millennium, transport the disease across the Atlantic?

THE SCIENTIFIC RECORD IS FRUStratingly unclear. Syphilis is one of a close-knit family of diseases, or perhaps one manifestation of an ancient and widely distributed infection. Proving that a given lesion on an ancient bone was caused by syphilis and not by a similar infection is a shaky

 From *Civilization,* January/February 1995, pp. 53–57.

proposition. In fact, the disease has provoked far more literature than more important illnesses—tuberculosis or malaria, for instance. (Sin is catnip for scientists and scholars alike.) Certainly it has had a decisive influence on the lives of particular individuals—including Gustave Flaubert and Lord Randolph Churchill, Winston's father. But syphilis has not deflected the course of human history. American crops have.

A mention of the important American food crops immediately reveals their significance for Old World agriculture and diet. Who can imagine Italian cooking without the tomato, Indian curries without the chili pepper, or an Irish stew without potatoes to mop up the gravy? Protein-rich American beans (kidney, navy, string, lima, butter, pole, French, haricot, snap, frijol, but not the soybean) have served as "poor man's meat" in Europe, Africa and Asia. These, along with the peanut and fruits like the guava, papaya, squashes, avocado and pineapple, have fed Old World peoples for centuries, but their effects on the course of history are negligible compared with those of America's four abundant sources of carbohydrates: manioc, maize and the two potatoes.

Potatoes, white and sweet, are related not botanically, but only by an accident of comprehension. The Taino Indians of the Greater Antilles and Bahamas used the word "batata" for sweet potato; in the 16th century, the Spanish mistakenly transferred the word to the Andean tuber, and their names have been confused ever since. (The fact that Old World yams are also often called sweet potatoes does not help.)

Manioc, maize, sweet potatoes and white potatoes are extraordinarily hardy and more productive than the staples of Old World agriculture, except for rice. Their cultivation requires human labor, of which the Old World had a surplus, plus a stick, some sort of spade and perhaps a knife. American Indians, who had few beasts of burden and no metal farming equipment, had bred crops that required neither. Their needs adapted these crops for the peasants and poor of the Old World.

Most inhabitants of the temperate zones know manioc only as tapioca, the

bulk element of certain desserts. Since its transfer (probably by Portuguese slaves) from Brazil, it has become one of Africa's most basic staples and is often considered a native plant. More than three times as much manioc root is now produced there as in South America. Often known as cassava, it is one of the developing world's great staples. Tropical peoples eat its tender shoots and leaves but value it chiefly for its starchy roots, which can weigh as much as 11 pounds. It is an amazingly hardy plant, resistant to pests and infections, thriving from sea level to 7,000 feet in poor soils, both in flood and drought. In Indonesia, it flourishes where thirsty rice cannot, in the hills and mountains.

The sweet potato probably arrived in the 17th century in New Guinea (brought over by Chinese and Malay traders), where its generous productivity in the highlands may have triggered a population explosion—just as the white potato did in Ireland during the same period. In warm lands the sweet potato (which, like manioc, was first seen by Europeans in the West Indies) also does well on marginal ground. It is important as a staple and particularly as a backup crop or famine food in Africa, China and regions of Indonesia where rice won't grow. Unlike manioc, it thrives in frostless temperate zones; it carried thousands of Japanese through the famines of 1832, 1844, 1872 and 1896 when other crops failed.

BUT MORE IMPORTANT THAN MANioc and sweet potatoes for feeding the masses of the Old World were maize and the white potato. Their distributions overlap, with more of the grain in warm lands, more of the tuber in cooler. The one spurred population growth in Africa, the other in northern Europe.

The scientific name, *Zea mays,* and the common maize were both derived from the Taino word for the crop, whose fields of it were the first ever seen by Europeans. But somehow English speakers of North America tagged the American cereal "corn," the generic term used in Britain for all cereals (which is incidentally what the word refers to in the King James version of the

Bible—Abraham, Joshua, David, Solomon, Jesus and St. Paul never saw an ear of the American grain).

The Maya and a number of other American Indian peoples had maize gods—and no wonder. It provides for more of humanity's needs than any other crop. It is one of the most versatile, thriving in climates as diverse as torrid Nigeria and the cool plains of northern China. In times of need, it can be eaten green. In times of war, it can be left on the stalk after it ripens, protected at least for a while from weather, birds and rodents by its husk. Once harvested and dried, it can be stored for years without spoiling. Its grain makes as good feed for livestock as for humans, and its leaves, unlike those of the other grains, make good fodder. Huts and sheds can be built of its stalks, and smoking pipes fashioned from its cobs.

In 1498, according to Columbus, maize was already growing in Castile, but Europeans hesitated before adopting it. Northern Europe was too cool, and in much of the south the crop required irrigation during dry Mediterranean summers. Iberian Jews and Muslims, fleeing Christian persecution, may have brought it to the eastern Mediterranean, where population pressure was greater than in western Europe in the 16th century, and maize was recorded in the 1570s growing "six, seven or eight cubits high" in fields along the Euphrates and around Jerusalem and Aleppo.

The slave trade, which placed a premium on cheap food that would survive the heat and damp of equatorial passage, was what brought maize to Africa (although linguistic evidence suggests that the grain also came down the coast from the Middle East). West Africans were cultivating maize at least as early as the last half of the 16th century, and shipwrecked Portuguese saw fields of it on the coast of South Africa's Indian Ocean as early as 1630. By the latter half of the 19th century, maize was one of the most widely cultivated of all foods in Africa.

Indonesian chroniclers paid little attention to the arrival of maize (food tends to receive much less attention than kings and battles), but, like manioc, the crop grew in countryside unsuitable for paddy rice, such as the lofty interior of Java. It proved a boon to China, where in the 16th century almost all the level, wet land for rice was already under cultivation, and the Chinese had few crops that would do well in hilly, drier and colder lands. Today China is second only to the United States as a producer of this American grain, and in China, unlike the United States, it is used almost entirely to feed humans.

The potato is to the temperate zone what rice is to the tropics. Given plenty of water, this Andean plant will produce more calories per unit of land in a cool climate than any alternative. Its tuber (a fleshy part of the underground stem) is a rich source of starch and provides some protein and even vitamin C, which was often in chronic shortage in northern winter diets. One can almost live on a diet of potatoes alone, which the Irish proved: A man with no more than a spade, even a wooden one, and an acre and a half of land in potatoes could, with a few supplements such as buttermilk, keep a family of five healthy. Adam Smith, the Scottish economist, recognized the potato's increasing value in this backhanded compliment to it and the Irish:

> *The chairmen, porters, and coal-heavers in London, and those unfortunate women who live by prostitution, the strongest men and the most beautiful women perhaps in the British dominions, are said to be, the greater part of them, from the lowest rank of people in Ireland, who are generally fed with this root [sic]. No food can afford a more decisive proof of its nourishing quality, or of its being peculiarly suitable to the health of the human constitution.*

The potato's disadvantage is that it does not keep well, and before modern refrigeration those who relied on it were always dependent on the success of the next harvest.

The Old World was slow to take to the potato. European farmers already had the earthy turnip and parsnip, and the fact that the leaves of the potato plant are toxic did not encourage its wholesale cultivation or consumption. But the potato had another appeal: Europeans considered it (like the tomato) an aphrodisiac. That's why when Shakespeare's Falstaff sees the object of his affection approaching in *The Merry Wives of Windsor,* he lustily shouts, "Let the sky rain potatoes."

The plant arrived in Europe—as an ornamental—in the 16th century. In the 17th century the Irish, pushed off the most fertile land by the English after siding with the Stuart kings against Parliament, adopted the American tuber for its caloric productivity—more than twice that of any alternative in Ireland's climate. In the next century the French and Prussians, driven by war, did likewise. (Not only does the potato fill soldierly bellies cheaply, but when soldiers requisition food, they may leave potatoes in the ground while they trample crops in the field and cart off grain in the barn.)

Eighteenth-century Russians paid little attention to Catherine the Great's suggestion that her subjects plant potatoes, but the failures of the traditional crops in the 19th century convinced them. In the last 40 years of the century, potato production went up 40 percent in the dominions of the czar. Today, the former Soviet Union is the biggest producer of potatoes in the world.

Maize and potatoes were undoubtedly the New World's most precious gifts to the Old World, more valuable than all the silver from Potosí or gold from the Sacramento Valley, but gifts, like swords, can be double edged. The wide spread of maize cultivation in southern Europe, Hungary and the Balkan provinces of the Ottoman Empire made it *the* cash crop for growing cities. But lacking the vitamin-B complex constituents, especially niacin, a diet exclusively of maize causes pellagra, the disease of the three *D's*: dermatitis, dementia and death. In 1755, a medical journal described just such an illness common in Spain's province of Asturias. Soon northern Italian physicians recognized the same symptoms, and by 1856 more than 37,000 cases were reported in Lombardy. Today, with the benefit of vitamin supplements, only in the Third World and in South Africa do maize farmers suffer from the disease.

Too great a dependence on maize eased people into the grave. Too great a dependence on white potatoes killed them swiftly. Many northern Europeans, notably the Irish, bet their lives on the unvarying productivity of the potato. But as the 19th century progressed and steamship technology reduced the number of days' voyage between America and Europe, American parasites caught up with the plant.

Between 1750 and 1841 the potato-loving population of Ireland had grown from 3 million to more than 8 million, making it one of the most densely populated countries in Europe. In the 1840s ("the hungry '40s") an American parasite, *Phytophthora infestans,* arrived, reducing the tuber to black slime. Between 1841 and the next census, a generation later, Ireland's population dropped by half because of famine, disease and emigration. Ireland became, for its size, the chief exporter of humans on earth; the northeast coast of the United States took on a Celtic cast; and Patrick and Bridget Kennedy, great-grandparents of the first Catholic president of the United States, set sail across the Atlantic (and so did two of my great-grandparents).

THE MOST IMPORTANT CHANGE OF the last few centuries, more important than the propagation and shriveling of Marxism, or the industrial revolution, is the population explosion. Between the mid-18th century and the present, the total number of humans on this planet rose from fewer than 800 million to 5.5 billion. Among the various causes of that increase is the nourishment associated with the cultivation of American crops overseas. In some places the connection is undeniable. In China, for example, where the population has grown from 330 million to more than a billion, people depend on a supply of food of which about 37 percent is American in origin.

With little prospect of worldwide population control, we need every productive variety of food plant whose requirements of climate, soil or space differ from our staples. We need strains of maize and potatoes resistant to the insects, worms, rusts and blights that threaten our popular strains. We need plants that will prosper in seasons when we leave the land fallow. We need to squeeze two and three harvests into a single year. We must use the odd corners of land too steep, too dry, too wet, too acidic or too alkaline for our current crops. We need species that will preserve the land's fertility rather than diminish it.

In short, we need another descent of the sort of vegetable manna that Columbus inadvertently introduced to the Old World. Fortunately, we have only begun to exploit the pre-Columbian larder. When Europeans first arrived, the agriculturists of Mesoamerica were cultivating some 67 species of plants (for food and other purposes), those of the Inca region about 70. And this does not include plants first domesticated by the farmers of the Amazon and Orinoco basins. Native American crops account for about one-fifth of the world's crops.

Most of us, except botanists and anthropologists, are ignorant of all but a few of these plants and will remain so, because they do not fit our immediate needs. Other plants will soon be familiar, because they are productive despite saline soils and can survive overabundance or shortage of water, and so on. They make good insurance policies for our uncertain futures. For instance, which of our staple crops is especially tolerant of ozone? None, I suspect; but what about the Andean cereal quinoa, which produces great quantities of starch and protein at 13,000 feet, an altitude at which it is subject to high levels of ozone?

Another neglected crop, amaranth, was cultivated by American Indians all the way from the desert borderlands of the southwestern United States to the southern Andes. It was one of the most ancient of Mexico's crops: The Aztecs collected half as much of this cereal in tribute as they did of their staff of life, maize. But cultivation fell off sharply soon after the European arrival, probably because the Spaniards saw that it was intricately involved in the old religious practices: Images of the gods were made

Future Crops

Some traditional Andean crops that have been preserved by native peoples may play an important role in food production around the world:

Achira Starch from the huge rhizome of this lilylike plant is easily digested, making it an ideal foodstuff for invalids, infants and the elderly. Part of a traditional feast (along with roast guinea pig) in the Andes, achira is already commercially cultivated in Australia and elsewhere.

Kaniwa Andean farmers regard this grain as a welcome "weed" because it thrives on poor, rocky soil and is resistant to salt, drought, frost and pests. Such resilience along with its richness in protein and amino acids may one day make kaniwa popular in other tropical highlands.

Lucuma A single tree of this bronze-yellow starchy fruit is said to be able to feed a family year round. Pulped lucuma tastes rather like maple syrup, and is a popular addition to drinks, puddings, pies and cookies. In Switzerland it is used today to flavor ice cream.

Maca Found at high altitudes—where it endures intense sunlight, violent winds and chilling cold—this relative of the radish has a sweet, tangy root that can be dried and stored for years. It is also said to enhance fertility.

Oca Brilliant color and pleasant flavor give this potatolike tuber immediate consumer appeal. It is also easy to propagate and can be prepared in so many ways that New Zealanders now serve it with their national dish—roast lamb.

Pepino A "decadent fruit for the '90s," the versatile but exotic yellow-streaked-with-purple pepino tastes like sweet melon and has now entered international commerce in California, New Zealand and Japan.

Tarwi This spectacular legume produces protein-packed seeds that contain as much vegetable oil as soybeans. It is being experimentally grown in Europe, South Africa and Australia.

Source: LOST CROPS OF THE INCAS, **National Academy Press 1989**

from its dough, which was even called the "bones of god." (Amaranth is available today in Mexican markets as blocks of candy—seeds bound together with honey or molasses—called *alegría,* joy.)

Yet the crop is a nutritional marvel. Its stems and leaves are as edible as spinach and richer in iron; its prolific seeds are a source of a good grade of starch and are 16 to 18 percent protein of a quality comparable to that of cow's milk. Amaranth flour mixed with wheat or maize flour is about as protein-rich as eggs.

The plant does well at various altitudes in different soils, even tolerating salinity (the curse of irrigated land) better than many cereals. It weathers droughts and cold, though not frosts,

and is now being grown in China, Nepal, India and Kenya.

Few Europeans, Africans and Asians know about amaranth—or quinoa, achira, ahipa, oca, maca, kaniwa, lucuma, pepino or tarwi, among scores of other native American crops—but how many Americans knew about China's soybean 75 years ago? Very few indeed. Yet it is now a major crop, nutritionally and economically, in the United States and Brazil, both of which produce far more soybeans than China. And if Europeans, Africans and Asians continue to be as smart about importing crops as American farmers have recently been about soybeans, New World crops will continue to make history in the Old World.

Making memories

Catholic Macau's relationship with China was quite different from Protestant Hong Kong's. Portugal's handover of Macau on December 20th will be quite different too from Hong Kong's in 1997

MACAU

LAST year Lisbon reclaimed acres of industrial wasteland beside the River Tagus to hold a huge celebration of the world and Portugal's place in it. One part millennium fever and one part nostalgic throwback to 19th-century world fairs, it brought to mind far-off celebrations of European empire and progress. By far the most popular feature of Lisbon's "Expo 98" was the Macau pavilion. It received 4m visitors, ten times the population of the Chinese enclave itself. But the Portuguese colony of Macau, which reverts fully to China on December 20th, has long had a special place in foreigners' imaginations.

It no longer looks as it did to the 18th century artist who highlighted the romance of the port in the charming promotional scene above. Grimly plain tower blocks now smother the old city and its outlying islands. Yet much of Macau's spirit remains, including the

omnipresence of the past, a tolerance of diversity and an outsider's sense of mischief. In a tiny studio high in one of those tower blocks an unusual painting is taking form that marks the coming handover. The young artist, Konstantin Bessmertny, is Russian, but the work is somehow typical of the place. A keen student of the old masters, he depicts members of the Portuguese government and the local administration handing back the keys of the city to Chinese dignitaries in front of the Praia Grande bay. The picture is a bow to "The Surrender of Breda" by Velazquez, though without the sense of chivalry between the Spaniards and the defeated Dutch. Egos are stripped of their masks, and those all-too human frailties—the gambling and whoring for which outwardly respectable Macau is well known—are on naked display.

Not all the Portuguese dignitaries shown in Mr Bessmertny's work will

like his sense of humour. A few may wish they could pay him to paint them out (just as Hong Kong worthies are supposed to have paid to be included in a grotesque but earnest glorification of Hong Kong's return to China two years ago, a piece of Communist triumphalism that is said to have fetched the highest price ever for a Chinese oil painting). Others will probably make a wry, self-deprecating smile. What they will all share with the Russian artist is a feel for the peculiar place that Macau holds in the history of Europe's involvement with the East.

You can trace the reasons for the Portuguese lodging on Chinese shores almost as far back as you like. Macau was officially founded in 1557. But Portuguese ships had plied the China seas for decades before that. Their presence was part of a tussle between Spain and Portugal, Europe's expansionary powers, over how the mid-Atlantic lines of de-

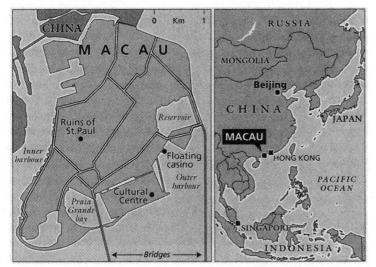

marcation (drawn up under the aegis of the pope in the Treaty of Tordesillas of 1494) should be applied to the Pacific. More than anything, the Portuguese had got as far as Macau (via their base at Goa on the west coast of India) because they were the first to solve the problems of navigating the open Atlantic. Thus the seminal feat was the rounding by a Portuguese ship of Cape Bojador, on the tip of West Africa, in 1434. The later voyages of Vasco da Gama, who gave the Cape of Good Hope its name, and the great Magellan built on that accomplishment. Meanwhile, the Spanish vaulted into the Pacific by way of their new world empire, establishing their base at Manila in the Philippines.

China's tolerance of the Portuguese in Macau (in stark contrast to its views of the rapine British in Hong Kong up to 1997) dates back to that early occupation. Disputes over Macau's sovereignty did routinely erupt, usually over whether the ground-rent the Portuguese paid for Macau constituted an admission of Chinese sovereignty. But, as an earlier historian of Macau pointed out, money acted more as a salve than a sore. The "endless contentions" between the Celestial Empire and these forbidding "long-bearded and large-eyed men", were usually resolved with a "good round sum of money for adjusting matters".

NOT EVEN A PIMPLE

Portugal never really projected power in Asia and Macau's position remained precarious. Centuries later, a British of-

ficial described Hong Kong as "a pimple on China's backside". Macau was not even that. Pimples colonise backsides, as the British did when, from their Hong Kong base, they opened China to trade in the 19th century, and even briefly occupied Peking to make a point. Macau was always a frontier, but it never had a hinterland.

Only occasionally did Macau prosper but when it did, it boomed. Portuguese ships arriving from Goa and Malacca on the south-west monsoon may have contained their share of conquistadors ready to plunder Asia's wealth (particularly its spices), or of expansionists who dreamt of a long-range economic exchange between East and West. But it was the singular skill of the Portuguese to realise that more money was to be made in the interstices of a rich, regional trade. After all, Asians, if anything, seemed wealthier than Europeans, though it was not clear quite what rich Asians might want from Europe. The Chinese, wrote one visitor, "sell everything and buy nothing."

At the same time, though, there were political impediments to regional trade. In the late 16th century China exercised a policy of seclusion, mainly because of a fear of pirates. A Japanese passion for Chinese silks therefore went unmet. The Portuguese, for a brief period between 1560 and their final expulsion from Japan in 1639, met the passion in a way that so enriched Macau that the city was able to survive through centuries of later vicissitudes.

From Macau, the Portuguese would each summer load the *naus do trato,* the

India-built carracks that the Japanese called the "black ships", with Chinese silks, porcelain and gold. The convoy would then waft up to Nagasaki in Japan on the south-west monsoon, praying to avoid the typhoons. Later the same year, the convoy would tear back on the north-east monsoon, full of Japanese silver. It was the only thing for which China seemed to have an insatiable demand: silver there fetched almost the same price as gold, weight-for-weight. For the Portuguese, it was an extremely profitable arbitrage.

Nearly half of the New World's silver is reckoned to have found its way to China. Where the trade went, the Jesuits followed, and not purely in search for spiritual conversions. It was the perceptive Jesuits, as a historian, David Howe, says, "who noted that sophisticated Japanese, completely sceptical over the existence of a world to come, were eager to create a paradise of consumption and pleasure in the present." The Jesuits helped them realise their earthly Utopia, and even financed their own ships to Japan.

Even so, the Jesuits' success at Japanese conversion—150,000 Japanese Christians by 1582—was astounding, so much so that it aroused the envy of the Franciscans in Manila. An unseemly and very public fight for Japanese souls was one of the reasons for Japanese Catholics' eventual persecution by the authorities, and for the expulsion of the missionaries and many of their converts. That may have helped destroy Macau's Japan trade, but at least it filled the city's marital beds with Christian virgins.

Converting China was the greatest dream. In 1552 Ignatius Loyola's most fervent disciple, Francis Xavier, died off Macau, never having realised his hopes of entering China: no missionary had. Converting the Chinese, lamented a colleague, was going to be like trying to "whiten an Ethiopian". Those Jesuits who eventually penetrated the Middle Kingdom did so by being more Chinese than the Chinese. The first missionary, Michele Ruggieri, studied Chinese in Macau with a Chinese classical painter. His successor in 1600, Matteo Ricci (probably the most famous westerner ever in China before the 20th century), not only learnt to read and write Chinese, but studied Chinese philosophy and wore Chinese dress. Ricci also argued to his superiors that the Chinese at the Ming court would be most impressed if the Jesuits were to share modern western knowledge with them. So there followed mathematicians, astronomers and builders of scientific instruments in what, even now, was the most enlightened period of cultural exchange between China and the West.

Macau, which was known as the city of the Name of God, and whose diocese extended from Malacca to Timor, China, Korea and Japan, was the fount of this enlightenment. Today, the backless facade of the church of St Paul in Macau, one of the most striking Christian monuments in Asia, bears witness to an extraordinary period of cultural dissemination.

Macau long refracted western views of China, which shimmer to this day. The Jesuits believed that the Chinese empire was more perfect than any in the West. Though this missed the essential point of China's economic and cultural stagnation—invisible before European mercantilism and the industrial revolution laid it bare—it was certainly a more enlightened view than the Chinese one of the West. Chinese officialdom thought that, if need be, the constipated western powers could be made to submit simply by withholding from them supplies of their treasured rhubarb.

It was also through Macau that the Utopian view of China later swung to a dystopian one, though this time the arrogant British were the agents of change. It was Commodore George Anson who, in 1743, was the first to practise gunboat diplomacy on the Chinese. Contrary to an age-old Chinese ban, he insisted on being allowed up the Pearl River from Macau, thus dealing a fullfrontal insult to the Celestial Empire. Anson's disparaging views of the Chinese—he had met prevarication and corruption in spades—greatly outraged Voltaire, who was shocked that "the oldest and most polished nation of the world" should be judged by the shenanigans of "the populace in a corner of a province". Anson's views of China were indeed shocking, even for the time:

"Thus much may undoubtedly be asserted, that in artifice, falsehood, and an attachment to all kinds of lucre, many of the Chinese are difficult to be paralleled by any other people."

BRITAIN STEPS IN

It was but a small step for Lord George Macartney to conclude, after his famously futile mission to Peking in 1793, that the China of the Qing dynasty was like "an old crazy first-rate man-of-war", of more harm to herself than to others. It was but a small step further for Britain and other powers to realise how easily China was open to plunder.

The role that the British forced Macau to play in this plunder was only reluctantly acknowledged by the Portuguese, who had rarely resorted to force against the Chinese. Gunboat diplomacy was finally to spell Macau's ruin, when the British founded the free port of Hong Kong in 1843. The enclave lost its special role as western go-between with the Chinese, and it sunk into a torpor enlivened only by the infamous coolie trade in the 1850s, half-hearted opium dealing (legal until 1947), gambling (first legalised a century-and-a-half ago) and its sister pleasure, prostitution. In the 1930s W.H. Auden was to write that Macau was just "a weed from Catholic Europe" where " . . .the childish vices/Will safeguard the low virtues of the child,/And nothing serious can happen here."

THE TOLERANCE OF MACAU

This essential difference between Catholic and Protestant experiences of China colours the view the Portuguese now have of Macau's handover later this year. They will not, they say, leave with the hypocritical sentimentality of the British departure from Hong Kong (as if the forceful British occupation was much more warranted, say, than the Chinese occupation of the Isle of Wight). Rather, says Macau's under-secretary for culture and tourism, Antonio Salavessa da Costa, the handover is "not a sad moment, but a proud one. It's a moment fulfilled."

Many of the visitors in Lisbon might echo similar sentiments. After all, every Portuguese schoolchild learns of the supposed stay in Macau of their national poet, Luis de Camoes, and many will know the 1902 history of Macau by C. A. Montaldo de Jesus, which lauds the "ever memorable landmark whence the light of the West first irradiated upon China, and where in the noblest of epics Camoes sang the dawn of European intercourse with the Far East." Imagine Shakespeare in Hong Kong. Imagine the British taking such intercourse to the literal extent of the Portuguese in Macau. Even this century, the British imported white prostitutes to Hong Kong for their sole pleasure, and as recently as two decades ago the young "officers" of the Hongkong and Shanghai Bank were forbidden from marrying local Chinese girls without their superiors' permission. The faces in Macau speak of centuries of mixing amongst Portuguese, Chinese, Japanese, Brazilians, Malays and Armenians.

One long-time Portuguese in Macau tells a small anecdote about Macau's famed tolerance, which was nurtured by racial mixing, by the existence of the Macau legislative assembly whose age some claim gives Macau the title of the first republic of Asia, and by Macau's reputation as a haven from Japanese atrocities in China and Hong Kong during the second world war. Earlier this year, he says, the Chinese new year celebrations happened to fall on a big Catholic feast day. Firecrackers were let off in droves, and there was much commotion on the street. Then a Catholic procession swung into sight. The crowds fell silent, out of respect, and only resumed the orgy of noise when the procession had passed.

Yet other Macau residents suggest that Macau's tolerance may have been too easy, allowing a full-scale takeover of Macau by Chinese Communist influences—political correctness, corruption, hot money and cultural atrophy—long before the official handover. Once formal Portuguese rule is over, they say, little will distinguish Macau from any mainland Chinese boom-and-bust town. Since Portugal's democratic revolution in 1974, which overthrew the Salazar dictatorship, sovereignty has for practical purposes been ceded to China, with the Portuguese acting as mere administrators. This pliancy has long roots: in 1926 an edition of Montaldo de Jesus's history was publicly burnt in supposedly tolerant Macau, for suggesting that the city's precarious position be formally protected by the League of Nations.

Today, some of the more rueful Macanese regret that their city's cultural heritage at least was not protected under the United Nations. That might have helped limit the worst effects of the construction and landfill that have disfigured the once graceful enclave. The Praia Grande, a perfect *mezzoluna* lined with pink, cream and yellow villas, was perhaps the most painted vista in all of Asia. Five years ago, the waterfront's sweep was still apparent. Today, it is just another ugly landfill.

The Portuguese have built an imposing cultural centre on some of it. Macau will be left with music and art festivals, its own airport and all the other trappings of a world-class city, they say.

Others are less impressed: "that is a mere veneer of cosmopolitan refinement, mainly for touristic show," says Oscar Ho, the director of the Hong Kong Arts Centre and a lover of Macau. The local arts scene, Mr Ho argues, is suffocating. A group of young artists in Macau agrees.

One, Frank Leih, disputes the claim, often made by Portuguese officials, that Macau is not really even a colony, but three colonies at once. It is certainly a Portuguese one (all the senior administrators are Portuguese, and few Portuguese, he points out, have bothered to learn the lingua franca, Cantonese). It is a Chinese one, since a wave of immigration in the past decade now puts mainland-born Chinese in the majority. And it is a Hong Kong one, for from that territory come most of the gamblers, loan-sharks, pimps and clients. Macau, agrees one of Hong Kong's best-known artists, Yank Wong, is "just a theme park for Hong Kong people. They have no sense of the history or the culture." Mr Leih and his film-making and

theatre friends say they have a political agenda, which is to reinforce a sense of identity amongst Macau's residents before it is too late.

TURNING A BLIND EYE

Meanwhile, mainstream Macau pretends not much has changed, or is about to change. The more respectable denizens of the city have a wondrous ability to feign ignorance of the source of the enclave's wealth (more than half of the government's revenues come from the gambling monopoly). Mr Bessmertny laughs when he recounts how long it took him and his piano-teaching Russian wife to become accepted by the establishment: being Russian, she was automatically taken for a prostitute. He does not mind, he says: he knows who uses the viewing rooms behind the two-way mirrors at the Crazy Horse show, and they are not the visiting Hong Kongers. It is all grist to his tableau.

The Dutch in Japan

Paul Doolan *describes the unique 400-year-long trading, intellectual and artistic contacts between the Dutch and the Japanese.*

MANY OF US have read James Clavell's *Shogun* (1975), the fictional account of the adventures of the crew of the Dutch ship *De Liefde,* or have seen the television series starring Richard Chamberlain. April 2000 marks the 400th anniversary of the *Liefde*'s arrival in Japan in 1600, an event which began four centuries of Japanese-Dutch relations.

The Portuguese had been the first Europeans to settle in Japan in the mid-sixteenth century, seeking both riches and souls. In the 1570s Nagasaki was opened as the main port for foreign trade by the local *daimyo* (lord), and became the centre for the Jesuit Francis Xavier's mission to convert Japan to Christianity. The Portuguese also brought firearms with them. Japan at this time was wracked by power struggles, and the last *shogun* (military ruler) of the Ashihara clan was deposed in 1573. Over the next thirty years Toyotomi Hideyoshi built up his position as the most powerful man in Japan, though he never claimed the title of shogun. One of his former rivals, Tokugawa Ieyasu, went over to his side and on Hideyoshi's death in 1598 Ieyasu continued to battle the regional *daimyo* for control over the whole of Japan.

Then, in 1598, a fleet of four ships left Rotterdam intending to circumnavigate the world. After a disastrous voyage, the one surviving vessel, the *Liefde* (Charity), reached southern Japan in April 1600. Of the original 110 crew members only twenty-four survived, six of whom died shortly after arriving. By this time Tokugawa Ieyasu had grown suspicious of the Portuguese and was

pleased to learn that the Dutch were their enemies. He also wished to break the influence of the Portuguese mission, and the Dutch assured him that they had no interest in converting his subjects to Christianity. In October 1600 Tokugawa Ieyasu decisively defeated his main rivals at the Battle of Sekigahara in central Honshu. For the battle he was able to call on the help of Dutch gunners and eighteen cannons from the *Liefde,* and his favourable impression of these new Europeans was confirmed. He appointed two of the crew, the Englishman Will Adams and Jan Joosten van Lodensteijn, as senior advisors to his government. Both remained in the service of Japan for the rest of their lives.

In 1603 Ieyasu established himself as shogun, setting up the Tokugawa Shogunate that ruled Japan until 1868. Then in 1609 two ships of the recently formed Dutch East India Company (VOC) sailed into the port of Hirado in southwestern Japan. They carried a letter from the Dutch leader Maurice of Orange, in which he invited the Shogun to commence official relations between the two countries. The Shogun was so flattered by the tone of the letter that he presented the Dutch with a permit giving them access to all Japanese ports. The VOC opened its first trading post in Hirado. The Portuguese trade monopoly was finally broken.

Ieyasu continued to distrust the Christian missionaries, fearing the new faith would provide a focus for opposition to his rule, and in 1612 and 1614 he prohibited Christianity, initiating a period of ever-worsening persecution. During the 1630s, the Portuguese were

also increasingly penalised by the Japanese with trade restrictions, while the English abandoned as hopeless their attempt to break into the Japanese market. In 1641 the Portuguese were expelled altogether and the Dutch were ordered to move their trading post from Hirado to the tiny artificial island of Deshima in Nagasaki Bay. In order to ensure its own survival Japan now closed itself off from the rest of the world almost completely.

From 1641 until the arrival of the Americans in 1853, the strictly-controlled Dutch post on Deshima was Japan's sole window on the Western world. This created a bilateral relationship unique in history. Crucial Western developments during these centuries—from Newton's work on gravity to the development of the technique of smallpox vaccination—entered Japan via the VOC's seemingly insignificant little outpost. Dutch became the imperative language for Japanese scholars interested in the outside world.

Throughout the seventeenth century the VOC went from strength to strength, becoming the largest business organisation in the world. During the 200 years of its existence nearly a million Europeans left Holland on one of the VOC's ships. Its overseas bases employed about 25,000 workers. Deshima was only a tiny base on the periphery of the VOC's world. In 1687–88 the company's Ceylon and Batavia offices had over 2,500 employees each; on Deshima there were only twenty-seven. On the other hand, the Dutch enjoyed an envied monopoly with an extremely important partner. Until 1688, when the shogun banned the export of silver, Japan was the source of a plentiful and inexpensive supply of this precious metal. During the seventeenth century the profit on the annual trade with Japan was over 50 per cent, making Deshima the VOC's richest trading post. The Dutch supplied the Japanese with Chinese silk, textiles from Europe, spices from the Dutch-controlled East Indies, hides from Thailand and Taiwan and ivory from Africa and South East Asia. The VOC's exports from Japan included silver, gold, copper, camphor, porcelain, lacquerware and grains.

In the eighteenth century, though, the VOC's profits in Japan began to dwindle. In Europe the Dutch Republic was losing its preeminent place as a trading power to England and France. London replaced Amsterdam as the world's financial centre. In the early part of the century a series of disastrous shipwrecks in East Asia proved costly for the company. These difficulties were compounded by increasing Japanese trade restrictions. In 1728 there was talk within the VOC of closing the Japanese office. In 1743 the Deshima trade post made a loss for the first time.

Ironically, as trade decreased Dutch influence on Japanese culture was growing. By the late fifteenth century, Portuguese had become the language of commerce. By the eighteenth century it had been all but forgotten, however, replaced by Dutch. In the second half of that century the term *Rangaku*—Dutch studies or 'Hollandology'—appeared. Specialists in the study of Europe became known as *Rangakusha* or 'Hollandologists'. These Japanese scholars threw themselves into the study of Western medicine, astronomy, maths, botany, physics, chemistry, pharmacy, geography and the military arts—all studied in Dutch of course. Early *Rangakusha* contributed to the development of a new spirit of enquiry in Japan. Those who studied Dutch medical techniques were impressed by the accuracy of Western science. This led to a Japanese questioning of some of their beliefs and, ultimately, contributed to an attitude of scepticism towards the entire feudal system. By the mid-nineteenth century civil servants and young men from all over Japan were attending the Tekijuku, a

school in Osaka to study Dutch language and Western sciences, founded by the physician and teacher Ogata Koan. The Dutch-inspired premise of free enquiry propagated at this school was revolutionary for Japan. One graduate of the school, Fukuzawa Yukichi, became the founder of Keio University, arguably the most prestigious and influential private university in Japan today. Remembering his years in Osaka, he wrote:

We students were conscious of the fact we were the sole possessors of the key to knowledge of the great European civilisation ... The resources of our minds were beyond the reach of any prince or nobleman of the whole nation.

We can only imagine the astonishment and disappointment that many Japanese must have felt when the country opened its doors to the outside world in the 1850s, only to discover that Dutch

---

By the late 18th century the Dutch settlement had become a tourist attraction for visitors to Nagasaki.

---

was far from being an international language. *Rangaku* scholars had worked hard to conquer the language of the Netherlands but now it turned out to be incomprehensible to all but a few foreigners. But the Dutch influence on the Japanese language can still be found today. Plenty of Japanese words in current usage derived from Dutch. For example, '*birru*', from the Dutch '*bier*', meaning beer; '*garasu*', from the Dutch '*glas*', meaning glass and '*kohii*' from the Dutch '*koffie*' meaning coffee. All these words entered the Japanese vocabulary in the eighteenth century. Clearly, the Japanese saw the Western world through a Dutch lens—and the Japanese word '*renzu*' comes from the Dutch world '*lens*'.

By the late eighteenth century the Dutch settlement on Deshima had be-

come something of a tourist attraction for visitors to Nagasaki, who would try to catch a glimpse of a 'red-headed' on the little island. As a result, woodblock prints depicting the foreigners or their mighty ships began to be sold as souvenirs. These prints had become a speciality of Nagasaki publishers by the nineteenth century.

Elsewhere, the annual journey undertaken by the Dutch from Nagasaki to pay their respects at the shogun's residence at Edo might afford a glimpse of the red-headed ones. Not surprisingly, misconceptions regarding the foreigners were common. It was widely believed that the Dutch never reached fifty years of age; that they had the eyes of a dog; their feet had no heels (which explained why they wore shoes with wooden heels), and that they raised a leg, in the manner of a dog, when urinating. As is often the case with stereotypes, the Dutch were considered to have ferocious sexual appetites. The large number of ladies of pleasure that were employed in Nagasaki might have contributed to this impression, as well as babies born in Nagasaki with European facial features and, it was said, no heels. Of course, some *rangakusha* attempted to correct popular misconceptions. When the artist and pioneer of Westernisation Shiba Kokan (1747?–1810) was asked to explain how the Dutch, who belonged to the animal world, exceeded the Japanese in some areas of science and technology, he replied dryly: 'apparently human beings are not as clever as animals'.

For Europeans, Japan remained an enigma. Members of the VOC were the sole contact between Japan and Europe and a few of these officials threw themselves into the role of interpreter of this strange civilisation. The German VOC surgeon Englebert Kaempfer compiled his *History of Japan* in the late seventeenth century, a work that remained the standard European description of the country for nearly 150 years. In the eighteenth century Hendrik Doeff and Isaac Titsingh immersed themselves in Japanese culture, while the Swede Carl Peter Thunberg, a student of Linnaeus, used his time as surgeon for the VOC on Deshima to collect hundreds of plants. His botanical drawings were

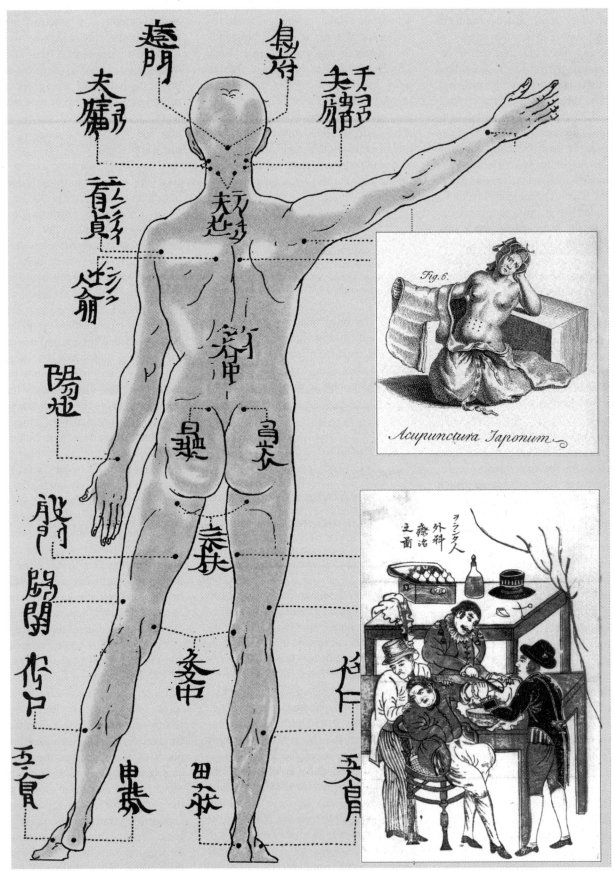

Non-invasive techniques: Japanese acupuncture was studied by the Dutch; the figure of a man shows the points on which moxa (smouldering herbs) should be applied for various illness, while the sketch of the woman shows acupuncture points, though somewhat less convincingly. From Kaempfer's *History*. The Japanese were equally fascinated with Western surgery: the print of an amputation (insert) was made in about 1810.

published as *Flora Japonica* in 1784. The giant among these VOC scientists was the naturalised Dutchman Philipp Franz von Siebold. Von Siebold, who lived in Japan from 1823 to 1829, was allowed a great deal of freedom of movement by the Japanese government. He lectured on Western medicine in Nagasaki and his daughter by a Japanese woman became the first female doctor in Japan. His collection of Japanese ethnographic objects became the basis for the present day National Museum of Ethnology in Leiden and his book *Nippon* (1832–58) is a monumental study of Japanese culture.

In the nineteenth century it became obvious to the Dutch that it was only a matter of time before one of the Western powers would force its way into Japan. In the early morning of July 8th, 1853, four American warships appeared off the Japanese coast. They carried a message from the US president that Japan was to open its doors to trade or suffer the consequences. American gunboat diplomacy proved successful and Japan's isolation came to an abrupt end. So, too, did the unique relationship that had existed between the Netherlands and Japan for over two centuries.

Dutch influence did not disappear overnight. During the turbulent mid-nineteenth century, Dutch scientists and technical experts helped to shape modern Japan. Koenrad Gratama, a chemist, was instrumental in founding the medical faculty of the University of Osaka, for example, while engineer Cornelius van Doorn introduced the modern principles of water management. At first the Dutch were much needed as secretaries and interpreters, too, for Dutch remained the *lingua franca* in Japan for a few years more. Inevitably, however, the Dutch gradually lost their special place in the Japanese view of things and the Netherlands became a minor player on the world stage.

Yet the Dutch may have bequeathed to the Japanese nation one legacy of great symbolic value. In 1855 William III of the Netherlands decided to donate a paddle steamship, the *Soenbing,* to Japan. During the transfer ceremony, one Admiral Fabius lowered the Dutch flag only to discover that the Japanese

Ramanas Rosa, from von Siebold and Zuccarini's *Flora Japonica* of 1835.

authorities had no national flag available to hoist in its place. The quick-thinking Dutch admiral grabbed the nearest available flag to hand. No one knows exactly what flag it was he raised. Perhaps it was the standard of the Satsuma clan, who were then challenging the shogunate for power. But eye-witness reports describe the flag which flew over the *Soenbing* as a red ball on a white field. Was this the accidental origin of the *hinomaru,* the flag that has symbolised the Land of the Rising Sun ever since?

The friendly relations that had existed between Holland and Japan turned to deep suspicion in the twentieth century when the Japanese empire began to expand. Japanese imperialism clashed head on with Dutch imperialism in the Dutch East Indies, present-day Indonesia. The Japanese invasion of Indonesia

commenced on January 10th, 1942. Victory was swift, and nearly 150,000 Dutch citizens found themselves prisoners of the Japanese. The Japanese occupation only lasted three-and-a-half-years but it all but brought to an end Dutch rule in this area.

The trauma of war gradually faded and relations between the Netherlands and Japan were normalised during the 1950s. Since then commercial, cultural and scientific contacts have grown. One sign that the Netherlands still holds a special place in the imagination of many Japanese is the success of the theme park Huis ten Bosch. This piece of Holland nestles among the volcanic mountains of southern Japan, not far from Nagasaki. It boasts a replica of the Soenbing, canals, cobble-stoned streets, a cosy brown café typical of Amsterdam,

Friendly relations between Holland and Japan turned to deep suspicion in the 20th century.

as well as lifesize replica landmarks such as the Dom of Utrecht, the city hall of Gouda and, of course, the royal residence, Huis ten Bosch. All the buildings are lifesize and one could almost be in Holland but for the absence of graffiti, and the fact that this Holland attracts far more Japanese visitors than the real one.

One issue concerning the two countries' shared past remains sensitive: when an exhibition—organised by the Dutch National Institute of War Documentation and partly subsidised by a Japanese grant—on the relationship between the Dutch, Indonesians and Japanese during the Second World War, opened in the Rijksmuseum, Amsterdam, last summer, the Japanese ambassador to the Netherlands turned down his invitation. The exhibition was due to open in Tokyo in December 1999, but it has still not reached Japan. Indeed a proposed venue for the exhibition in Tokyo was picketed in February while a leading newspaper carried an article expressing outrage at the exhibition. At the time of going to press, discussions regarding the 'modification' of the exhibition for the Japanese public were still taking place. Any indiscreet reference to 'The Great East Asian War' is likely to ignite the fury of nationalists, including Tokyo's elected mayor, Ishihara Shintaro.

Nevertheless, there is much to be celebrated in both countries. In August 1999 the Vincent Van Gogh Museum in Amsterdam opened a new wing designed by a Japanese architect and paid for by a Japanese donation—a gift from one country to another for 400 years of almost continual friendship. In the Amsterdam suburb of Amstelveen, home to more than half of the five thousand Japanese residents of the Netherlands, a street will be renamed 'Deshima Avenue'. This month [April 2000] Dutch television will broadcast an extended series on the 400-year relationship. Dutch orchestras will visit Japan throughout the year. Paintings by the Japanese artist Shiba Kokan will be exhibited in Amsterdam, while works of Rembrandt and Vermeer and other Dutch masters will be taken to Japan. The football club Feyenoord of Rotterdam will also tour Japan.

As for the *Liefde,* it has long since disappeared. But in 1926 a statue was discovered among the Buddhas in a temple north of Tokyo. No one knows how it got there or how long it had been there. It clearly was not an image of Buddha as the facial features were Caucasian. In fact it was a statue of Erasmus and it had once decorated the stern of the *Liefde,* which had previously been known as the *Erasmus.* It is all that remains of that fateful ship. Today the statue can be found in the Tokyo National Museum, a solid reminder of the arrival of Will Adams and his Dutch shipmates 400 years ago.

FOR FURTHER READING

C. R. Boxer, *Jan Compagnie in Japan, 1600–1850* (The Hague, 1950); C. R. Boxer, *The Dutch Seaborne Empire: 1600–1800* (London, 1965); Grant Kohn Goodman, *The Dutch Impact on Japan* (Leiden, 1967); Willem van Gulik, *Nederlanders in Nagasaki —Japanese prenten uit de 19de eeuw/ The Dutch in Nagasaki—19th Century Japanese Prints* (Amsterdam 1998); K. Vos, *Assignment Japan. Von Siebold: Pioneer and Collector* (The Hague, 1989).

Paul Doolan is Head of History at the International School of the Sacred Heart in Tokyo.

400 Years
of the East India Company

__Huw V. Bowen__ asks whether the East India Company was one of the 'most powerful engines' of state and empire in British history.

THE YEAR 2000 MARKS THE 400th anniversary of the founding of the English East India Company, the trading organisation that acted as the vehicle for British commercial and imperial expansion in Asia. For over two hundred years, the Company stood like a colossus over trade, commerce and empire, and contemporaries could only marvel at its influence, resources, strength and wealth. Writing at the beginning of the nineteenth century, the political economist David Macpherson was unequivocal in his assessment that the Company was 'the most illustrious and most flourishing commercial association that ever existed in any age or country.'

Today even the most powerful firm pales by comparison in terms of longevity and wide-ranging economic, political and cultural influence. In an era before fast travel and instant communication, the East India Company established a far-flung empire and then set about governing, controlling and exploiting it from a great distance in London. It managed to do this until it was finally rendered obsolete by the tumultuous events surrounding the Indian Mutiny in 1857.

The Company was granted its first charter by Elizabeth I on the last day of 1600, and it had to survive an uncertain first century or so as it sought access to Asian markets and commodities. At home, it was restructured several times, notably between 1698 and 1708 when an 'old' and 'new' East India Company

The frontispiece of Isaac Pike's *Journal of the Stringer* (1713) showed the Company robustly defending its trading position.

co-existed before merging to form the United Company of Merchants Trading to the East Indies. In the East, the Company came under such pressure from its Dutch rivals during the mid-seventeenth century that it was obliged to shift the main focus of its activities from the Malay archipelago and the Spice Islands to South Asia. Over time, it managed to establish a commercial presence in India centred upon three 'presidencies' established at Madras, Bombay and Calcutta.

These tenuous footholds were fortified and defended by the Company as it sought to consolidate its position in an often hostile commercial and political world. This in turn gave rise to the growth of a small private army that was eventually to rival the regular British army in terms of size and manpower. The Company's role in India was thus defined by both commercial activity and a military presence: it was considered legitimate to use force in support of trade, and the overseas personnel were organised and deployed accordingly. In the words of one contemporary, it was a 'fighting company'.

By the mid-eighteenth century, the Company had begun to assert itself over rival European companies and Indian powers alike, and this placed it in a position from which it could begin to carve out an extended territorial and commercial empire for itself. The actions of men such as Robert Clive (1725–74), Warren Hastings (1732–1818) and Charles Cornwallis (1738–1805) helped to transform the Company from trader to sovereign, so that during the second half of the eighteenth century millions of Indians were brought under British rule. As William Playfair put it in 1799:

> From a limited body of merchants, the India Company have become the Arbiters of the East.

The Company created the British Raj, and as such it has left a deep and

Today's casual observer finds few signs of the leading role the Company once played in the life of the nation.

permanent imprint on the history and historiography of India. The story, once almost universally described as the 'rise of British India', not so long ago formed part of the staple reading diet of British schoolchildren and students. In the post-colonial era, when imperial history has ceased to be fashionable, the legacies of British India are still hotly debated and contested. It is within this context that the history of the East India Company remains to the fore.

Rather less obvious, perhaps, is the part played by the East India Company in the domestic development of Britain. Indeed, today's casual observer finds few signs of the leading role it once played in the nation's business, commercial, cultural and political life. In terms of architecture, for example, there is lit-

The Old East India House in Leadenhall Street, as it was between 1648 and 1726, with ostentatious paintings and wooden statues expressing the Company's ambition.

tle surviving evidence in London of the Company's once-extensive property empire. The London docklands, home to the East India dock complex, has been reshaped. Although Commercial Road and East India Dock Road—the purpose-built link with the City—survive, the docks themselves have been filled in and redeveloped, leaving only a few poignant reminders of the Company's once formidable presence in the area. To the West, the great fortress-like warehouses built by the Company at Cutler Street were partially demolished and refurbished in controversial circumstances during the late 1970s. There is no trace remaining whatsoever of the Company's headquarters in Leadenhall Street. Charles Dickens once described the 'rich' East India House 'teeming with suggestions' of eastern delights, but it was unceremoniously pulled down in the 1860s, and in its place today stands the new Lloyd's Building, also a monument to commercial capitalism, but displaying rather different architectural qualities. In recent years, the only obvious local clue to the Indian connection was provided by the East India Arms, a tavern in nearby Lime Street, but that too has now fallen victim to the modern re-naming and re-branding process. As a result, the East India Company is now out of sight and out of mind.

It was not always like this. During the late eighteenth century, the Company played a key role in London's economy, employing several thousand labourers, warehousemen and clerks. Returning fleets of East Indiamen moored in Blackwall Reach, before their Indian and Chinese cargoes were transferred via hoys and carts to enormous warehouses where they awaited distribution and sale in Britain's burgeoning consumer markets. The profile of the Company in London was always high and the eyes of many were on Leadenhall Street. Political infighting at East India House regularly captured the attention of the metropolitan chattering classes. The Company itself was repeatedly subjected to inquiry by a Parliament uneasy about the turn being taken by events in the East.

The Company's domestic tentacles extended well beyond London, however,

and its influences were widely felt across the south of England. Provincial outposts were established in the form of the agencies in ports such as Deal, Falmouth, Plymouth and Portsmouth. Over the years the Company maintained camps for its military recruits at Newport in the Isle of White, Warley in Essex and at Chatham in Kent. Educational establishments were set up for the purpose of preparing those destined for service overseas. During the first half of the nineteenth century, the East India College at Haileybury in Hertfordshire educated boys for the civil service, while Addiscombe Military Seminary near Croydon trained military cadets.

More generally, the Company touched many sectors of British society and the economy, as some contemporaries acknowledged. In 1813, for example, a friend to the Company, Thomas William Plummer, set about identifying what 'proportion of the community' had a connection with the Company. Without mentioning several million purchasers of tea, spices, silks, muslins and other Asian commodities, he listed investors, Company employees of many types, tradesmen, manufacturers, shipbuilders, dealers, private merchants, military personnel and ship crews, before concluding that:

> Scarcely any part of the British community is distinct from some personal or collateral interest in the welfare of the East India Company.

There was more than a grain of truth in what Plummer wrote, and by the beginning of the nineteenth century many interests across the country had been tied closely to the Company. This was particularly the case with the several thousand or so well-to-do individuals who chose to invest in Company stocks and bonds. For much of the eighteenth century East India stock was the most attractive investment available in the nascent stock market, not least because it always paid out an annual dividend of more than 5 per cent. The India bonds that provided the Company with its short-term working capital were also highly prized, with one early stock market analyst describing them as 'the most

Charles James Fox, as an oriental potentate, rides on an elephant with Lord North's face and led by Edmund Burke towards India House: cartoon of 1784 opposing Fox's India Bill, by Sayers.

convenient and profitable security a person can be possessed of'.

The fortunes of Company and nation had become so tightly intertwined that they had begun to move in tandem with one another as those who took a broad view of political and economic matters were able to see. When the Company flourished, the nation flourished. Equally, as Edmund Burke put it, 'to say the Company was in a state of distress was neither more nor less than to say the country was in a state of distress'. Such logic dictated that the effects of any crisis or catastrophe experienced by the Company in India would be deeply felt in Britain and the wider British Empire, and this was well understood by close observers of the imperial scene. One pamphleteer wrote in 1773 that the loss of India would occasion a 'national bankruptcy' while the imperial theorist Thomas Pownall suggested that such an event would cause 'the ruin of the whole edifice of the British Empire'. These concerns lay behind the increased levels of government anxiety about Company adventurism, misrule, and mismanagement in India that became evident after 1760.

Late eighteenth-century concerns about events in the East reflected the fact that the East India Company was no longer an ordinary trading company.

It had evolved into an immensely powerful hybrid commercial and imperial agency, and after the conquest of Bengal it fundamentally reshaped its traditional commercial policy based upon the exchange of exported British goods and bullion for Asian commodities. Instead, the Company concentrated its efforts on the collection of territorial and customs revenues in northeast India. The right to collect these revenues had been granted by the Mughal Emperor Shah Alam II in 1765, an event which both confirmed British military supremacy in the region and served to elevate the Company to the position of *de facto* sovereign in Bengal and the neighbouring provinces of Bihar and Orissa. Thereafter, trade was used to facilitate the transfer of 'tribute' from Asia to London as surplus revenue was ploughed into the purchase of Indian and Chinese commodities for export to Britain. As Edmund Burke later remarked, this marked a 'revolution' in the Company's commercial affairs.

By the 1770s the Company was akin to a semi-privatised imperial wing of the Hanoverian state.

The Company's empire had now become self-financing to the point that further military expansion could be sustained, but it was also believed that generous payments could be made to domestic stockholders and the British government alike. This proved to be a vain hope, but the transfer of tribute helped to define the essential characteristics of the late-eighteenth-century state-Company relationship. Successive ministers declared the state's 'right' to a share of the Bengal revenues, but in return for the promise of annual payments into the public treasury they allowed the Company to continue in its role as the administrator, defender and revenue collector of Bengal. This brought the British government the benefits of empire

without any expensive administrative or military responsibilities. It was a welcome and convenient arrangement at a time when the national debt was spiralling ever-upwards and parts of the Empire, most notably North America, were proving increasingly difficult to control and subdue.

By the 1770s the Company thus found itself as something akin to a semi-privatised imperial wing of the Hanoverian state, with its operations being defined by the dual pursuit of both private and public interest. It was charged with the protection, cultivation, and exploitation of one of Britain's most important national assets, and contemporary observers described its new role accordingly. In 1773 the prime minister, Lord North, declared that the Company was acting as '[tax] farmers to the publick', while a late-century pamphleteer suggested that the Company had become 'stewards to the state'. In this scheme of things, there was a greater need for the Company to become more accountable, efficient, and reliable, and this desire lay behind the reforms embodied in North's Regulating Act of 1773 and Pitt's India Act of 1784.

The Company's importance to the British state was not, however, simply to be assessed in terms of its role as the licensed agent through which metropolitan administrative, fiscal and military influences were brought to bear upon the Indian empire. The Company had been present at the birth of the eighteenth-century state during the troubled period following the 'Glorious Revolution' of 1688–89. As a hard-pressed nation struggled to cope with the demands of the Nine Years' War, ministers had drawn heavily on the financial resources of the 'new' East India Company that had received its charter in 1698. This meant that when the United Company was established in 1709 it was already deeply embedded in both the public finances and the City of London where, together with the Bank of England, it formed part of the 'monied interest'.

The financial relationship between state and Company took several different forms, all of which were a variation on a theme that saw the Company's monopoly privileges periodically confirmed

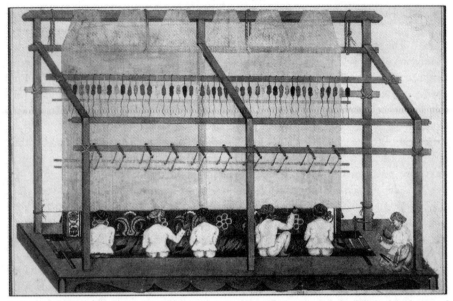

Indian weavers at work on a handloom in the early 19th century; their skill had endangered the livelihood of European producers in the previous century.

or extended by the Crown in return for loans or payments made to the public purse. Indeed, by the 1720s the entire paid-up share capital of the Company, almost £3.2 million, was on longterm loan to the state at 5 per cent interest. This sizeable advance was extended to £4.2 million before prime minister and chancellor Henry Pelham's restructuring of the national debt in 1749–50 saw the reduction of interest payments to 3 per cent and the creation of the East India annuities. This extensive underwriting of the post-settlement regime was such that a Chairman of the Company, Jacob Bosanquet, was later to borrow a phrase from Adam Smith and declare that the Company, together with the Bank of England, had become one of the 'most powerful engines of the state'. As Chairman of a company under great pressure from critics by 1799, Bosanquet was hardly likely to say anything else, but his comments were not altogether inaccurate. His organisation had established itself as a cornerstone of the City of London, and as such it had played a key role in supporting the state and public credit.

By the end of the eighteenth century, apologists were thus arguing that the Company formed part of the very foundations of Britain's state and empire, yet within sixty years it had ceased to exist at all. What happened to make the great 'engine' run out of steam so rapidly?

There are a great many answers to this question but the most basic one is undoubtedly the most important. Quite simply, in economic terms the Company failed to deliver what it had promised since the 1760s. As the military and administrative costs of empire multiplied, the Company proved itself unable to generate a revenue surplus for transfer to Britain. A great many attempts were made to remodel the Company's fiscal and commercial operations but successes in one area were always off-set by failures and setbacks elsewhere. Only the striking growth of the China tea trade offered the Company any prospect of success, but that in itself was not enough to satisfy the demands of profit-hungry stockholders and ministers. Indeed, the annual flow of 'tribute' to the state Treasury promised by the Company in 1767 had dried up almost at once. By 1772 the Company was teetering on the edge of bankruptcy, having failed to master the complexities of its new role in India, and a degree of desperation forced it into the measures that ultimately led to the Boston Tea Party the following year. Thereafter, the Company staggered from crisis to crisis, requiring government loans to enable it to continue functioning. In effect, this meant that roles had been reversed, and the Company had become dependent upon the state for financial support.

A dose of economic reality, coupled with widespread metropolitan unease about 'despotic' Company government in India, caused many commentators rapidly to reassess their views of Britain's eastern empire. Nowhere was this more evident than with Edmund Burke who became one of the Company's harshest critics and campaigned long and hard for reform and the punishment of British misdemeanours in India. Initially, though, Burke had been as captivated as any observer by the prospect of Britain gaining very real material advantage from the Company's successes in Bengal. He had outlined the economic potential of India to the House of Commons in 1769 before concluding that 'The Orient sun never laid more glorious expectations before us.' This type of view was commonplace during the 1760s, but it was replaced by much gloomier assessments of the situation in the decades that followed. Commentators soon tired of hearing about the promise of Indian wealth being used to the advantage of the metropolis, and began instead to expose the flaws that were evident in the Company's calculations and methods. The figures did not seem to add up, leaving one MP, George Tierney, to complain that 'Our Indian prosperity is always in the future tense'.

Criticism such as this only strengthened the case of those in Britain who were campaigning vigorously for the East India trade to be opened up to free competition. Just as the utility of the Company to the nation began to be discussed, old mercantilist assumptions about the organisation of trade were being called into question. Taking a lead from Adam Smith, who had condemned chartered companies as being 'nuisances in every respect', critics exposed the Company to searching analyses of its methods and practices.

Under such attack, the Company proved unable, indeed almost unwilling, to answer the charges levelled against it. Although it began to emphasise the contribution it made to intellectual and scientific life in Britain, it failed to argue convincingly that it alone offered the best way forward for the further development of the Anglo-Asian connection. Part of the reason for this was that the

The company failed to argue convincingly that it offered the best way forward for the Anglo-Asian connection.

Company believed it had already taken the organisation of its commercial and financial affairs to the highest possible level. It proved to be remarkably complacent and, together with a deep-rooted institutional conservatism, this meant that any change was regarded with the deepest suspicion. As one director of the Company put it, 'Innovations in an established system are at all times dangerous'. Few friends of the Company could see any need to alter an organisation that was thought to be beyond improvement, and this case was restated time and again. Most would have agreed with Thomas Mortimer who argued during the 1760s that the Company had 'brought the commerce and mercantile credit of Great Britain to such a degree of perfection, as no age or country can equal.' To alter anything would be to invite trouble. Sustained failure and. disappointing performance, however, flew in the face of such opinion, and this ensured that pressure for change continued to grow from outside the Company.

In the end, the Company's failure was essentially two-fold as far as many of those in the metropolis were concerned. It failed to deliver to Britain the great financial windfall that had been anticipated after the conquest of Bengal; and because of this it was unable to sustain much beyond 1760 its position as one of the major institutional and financial props of the Hanoverian state. When charges related to misrule, despotism, unfair monopoly practices and a host of other complaints were added to the scales, they served eventually to tip the balance of political opinion.

The immediate and outright abolition of the Company, however, was never an option because the state did not possess the resources, skills or will necessary to govern a large empire in India. Instead, successive breaches were made in the Company's commercial position. Trade with the East was opened up to a limited degree in 1793; the Indian monopoly was ended in 1813; and the exclusive trade with China was abolished in 1833. The Company survived for another twenty-five years as Britain's administrative and military representative in India, but by then it was a trading company in name only. The Company had achieved the full transition from trader to sovereign, amply fulfilling Adam Smith's prediction that trade and government were incompatible within a 'company of merchants'.

The Company ended its days in the aftermath of the Indian Mutiny when no case at all could be advanced for its survival in any form. Its powerful legacy endured in India for many more years in the form of the Indian army and civil service, but sight was soon lost of the importance of its contribution to the development of the metropolitan state and to imperial Britain itself. Today the Company has been almost entirely removed from the geographical and historical landscape and it has been more or less erased from our national consciousness. As the 400th anniversary of the founding of the Company approaches, this make it all the more necessary for us to reflect on the deep, but now hidden, impression left on British history by this quite extraordinary institution.

FOR FURTHER READING

H.V. Bowen, 'Investment and Empire in the Later Eighteenth Century: East India Stockholding, 1756–1791', *Economic History Review* (1989); K.N. Chaudhuri, *The English East India Company: The Study of an Early Joint-Stock Company* (Cass, 1965); John Keay, *The Honourable Company: The History of the English East India Company* (Harper Collins, 1991); Philip Lawson, *The East India Company: A History* (Macmillan, 1993); Martin Moir, *A General Guide to the India Office Records* (British Library, 1996); Jean Sutton, *Lords of the East: The East India Company and its Ships* (Conway Maritime Press, 1981). Information about the records of the East India Company can be found on the British Library's website http://www.bl.uk/ (follow the links to the Oriental and India Office collections).

Huw Bowen is Senior Lecturer in Economic and Social History at the University of Leicester and the author of *War and British Society 1688–1815* (Cambridge UP, 1998).

The Macartney Embassy to China, 1792–94

Two hundred years ago, a motley collection of Wedgwood china, clocks, a planetarium and a hot-air balloon accompanied an expedition to Peking, designed to open up the Imperial Kingdom to British commerce and diplomacy. How and why it failed, according to **Paul Gillingham,** *offers valuable lessons, even today, on the perils of cultural misunderstanding.*

Paul Gillingham

Paul Gillingham is a freelance writer and presenter and author of At The Peak: A History of Hong Kong Between the Wars *(Macmillan, 1983).*

Lining the boardroom of Coutts Bank in London's Strand is a striking and unusual wallpaper. Made of mulberry paper, a cross between rice-paper and silk, it depicts scenes of everyday life in Imperial China in the sort of detail that makes it a wallpaper equivalent of a documentary film.

Shopkeepers keep accounts with their abacuses, labourers collect birds' nests for making soup, women adorn a tea house-cum-brothel, barefooted servants wait on their masters, and horses, dogs and children hang about courtyards. Tea is picked, dried, packed and sold and the stages of silk production are shown, from collecting cocoons off mulberry trees, to spinning and weaving.

Such is the wallpaper's importance to the bank that it has survived being moved twice since it was first hung nearly two hundred years ago. In 1978 it was found to be so firmly glued on that the walls were dismantled and rebuilt as part of the modern bank—just to save the wallpaper.

The wallpaper was a present to the bank's director, Thomas Coutts, from one of his customers, Lord Macartney of Lissamore, who had recently returned to England, in 1794, after a two-year expedition to China. He had seen the paper on the walls of a palace where he and his entourage had stayed in Peking, the home of a Collector of Customs who was in jail awaiting execution for misappropriating the profits of European trade!

It was because of people like the Collector of Customs that the Embassy set off for China in the first place. Trade between Britain and China had been expanding fast throughout the eighteenth century, but not fast enough to satisfy all the merchants involved in it. There was an insatiable desire for things Chinese in Britain, especially China tea, porcelain and silk.

As the directors of the East India Company, which held a monopoly on trade with India and China, grew prosperous on the huge profits to be made, there were nevertheless frustrations at the rigid controls imposed on the one port into China which was open to overseas trade, Canton. Foreigners were allowed to stay there only during a five-month trading season, and then only in 'factories'—which served as warehouse, office and home—in a foreign ghetto outside the main Chinese city. Women, both local and European, were forbidden, as were Chinese servants and sedan-chair bearers, and any Chinese caught teaching the language to a European could face the death penalty.

Moreover, profits were hit by the graft and corruption built into a system dominated by a guild of Chinese merchants known as the Hong or Cohong and the Collector of Customs himself, the all-powerful Hoppo, once of whom owned the palace that provided the Coutts Bank wallpaper.

Thus it was with a view to liberalising the system and opening up trade with China that George III despatched an embassy to the Imperial Court in Peking in 1792 under one of his most experienced ambassadors, Lord George Macartney. The fifty-five year old Irishman had earlier made a name for himself by charming Catherine the Great and performing sterling work as secretary for Ireland, governor-general of British West Indies and governor of Madras.

Lord Macartney's was not the first European embassy to China, but it was certainly the largest. The three ships to set sail from Spithead on September 26th, 1792, carried 700 men including diplomats, scholars, botanists, scientists, painters, musicians, technicians, soldiers, servants and sailors. Also on board were two Chinese interpreters, priests from the Collegium Sinicum in Naples, who spoke no English, but passable Latin.

The emperor's new toys: Gillray's 1793 cartoon 'Tribute from the Red Barbarians' shows a disdainful emperor receiving the British and plays up the mutually xenophobic under-currents of the meeting.

Because none of the adult members of the embassy spoke Chinese, communication was to prove a major problem during the expedition. English was first translated into Latin and then into Chinese, and vice versa, a cumbersome process which left much room for misunderstanding.

Only one Briton of the 700 who set sail could read and write Chinese, and that was a boy of twelve, Macartney's page and the son of his second-in-command, Sir George Staunton. Young Thomas Staunton, who was to play a key part in Sino-British relations for the next fifty years, was a precocious child who could recite a page of *The Times* after one reading and spoke Latin, Greek, French and German. He learnt his Chinese from the two priests during the ten-month voyage and was later to prove useful in trans-

lating some of the key documents Macartney sent to the emperor, including his views on the *kowtow*.

Aboard the inevitably slow boats to China—the voyage took ten months and went via Rio de Janeiro, Tristan da Cunha, Java and Vietnam—Macartney and his entourage had ample opportunity to reflect on what they might see and experience when they got there. Chinoiserie and 'things Chinese' had been all the rage in Europe for much of the eighteenth century and there was a tendency to idealise China, largely as a result of the writings of European Jesuits who had access to the Peking court. English country estates were landscaped with Chinese gardens, complete with marble pagodas; wall tapestries bore Chinese motifs, and even the Queen of England wore Chinese-style clothes.

Philosophers were impressed by the idea of Confucianism, which seemed to hold the key to ideal government and a harmonious social order based on respect for age and authority.

But by the end of the century the love affair with the idea of China was beginning to pall. Louis-Sebastien Mercier wrote: 'What wretched luxuries these Chinese porcelains are! With a touch of its paw, a cat can do more damage than the plunder of twenty acres of land'. Montesquieu was much more devastating in his critique of Chinese government: 'China is a despotic state whose principle is fear', he wrote. 'The stick governs China'.

Apart from the diplomatic and commercial aims of the embassy, there was a powerful need to explore the real China, to separate myth from reality.

This was, after all, the age of scientific enquiry when everything under the sun was being weighed, measured and assessed. Sir Joseph Banks who accompanied Captain Cook to the South Seas and was establishing the Royal Botanical Gardens at Kew, gave full instructions to Macartney on what specimens to collect. Both he and Staunton were happy to oblige, being enthusiastic amateur botanists themselves.

On July 20th, 1793, the embassy eventually reached Dengzhou, a city of first rank in the province of Shandung. From there they were to transfer to junks for the journey up-river, stopping briefly at Tientsin, and then marching overland to Peking.

After such a long voyage, first reactions to China were ecstatic. 'O brave new world', Macartney wrote, quoting Shakespeare in his journal. Then, more matter-of-factly, 'great numbers of houses . . . built of mud and thatched, a good deal resembling the cottages near Christchurch in Hampshire'.

Shortly after arriving, he received a letter form the emperor extending a warm welcome to him and the 'others of England, country of the red hairs' with a promise to replenish their much-depleted stores. Within days, a consignment of 20 bullocks, 120 sheep, 120 hogs, 100 chickens, 100 ducks, 10 chests of tea, 160 bags of flour, 14 boxes of tartar bread and 2,000 melons was lined up on the quayside ready to be loaded on board.

But apart from the significance of having travelled from the other end of the world, the Chinese regarded the embassy as little different from the regular tribute-bearing missions they received from vassal states bordering China, like Burma, Vietnam, Korea and Tibet. As the Chinese script on the yellow pennants fluttering above the junks declared: 'The English Ambassador bringing tribute to the Emperor of China'.

Macartney, however, had no intention of accepting the status of tribute-bearer on the same level as Burma. His aim was to become accredited as an ambassador on equal terms with China, in the European diplomatic tradition of mutual recognition between sovereign states. True, his ships bore gifts for the Chinese emperor and his entourage, but they were intended as presents and not as 'tribute' in the Chinese sense.

Although a basic principle of Chinese good manners is to understate the value of a gift in order not to humiliate the recipient, Macartney did the opposite. It would not, he wrote in the catalogue listing the presents:

> . . . be becoming to offer trifles of momentary curiosity, but little use. His Britannic Majesty has been, therefore, careful to select only such articles as might denote the progress of science, and of the arts in Europe.

Macartney was hoping to impress the emperor with British ingenuity and doubtless win orders for British goods.

The *pièce de résistance* among the presents was a planetarium which, with the aid of complicated gears, showed the movement of the heavens. Also crated up were telescopes, clocks, guns, cannon, Wedgwood china, two carriages, a diving bell used to repair Ramsgate harbour and a newly-invented hot-air balloon.

There were also paintings of people and places, including portraits of George III and Queen Caroline, which later caused a stir among mandarins who thought of portraiture only in terms of 'ancestral portraits' of the dead. A Reynolds portrait of the Duke of Bedford, painted when he was a child was also seen as rather odd. How, the mandarins asked could a mere boy be a member of the House of Lords when they had to study for years and pass tough exams to achieve a similar rank?

The cultural differences between East and West were especially marked when it came to the *kowtow*. To the Chinese, the act of self-abasement in the form of kneeling three times and 'knocking' the head on the floor nine times was a vital element in court ritual. Its significance went far deeper than merely showing respect, as a deep bow or curtsey might indicate in the West. The kowtow was an acknowledgement of the rights and obligations owed to a higher by a lower power. In Chinese eyes the emperor was the intermediary between heaven and earth, a lynchpin in the preservation of universal order against the forces of chaos, both human and divine. He was, after all, the 'Son of Heaven' and brooked no human equal.

But for Macartney, dropping down on both knees was reserved for begging for mercy, praying to God and proposing marriage. To kowtow to the Emperor of China was an act of abject humiliation which he, as the emissary of an equally proud nation, was simply not prepared to do.

The emperor's mandarins did all they could to persuade the English to change their minds. Zhengrui, Wang and Qiao, who escorted the embassy to Peking, offered to give lessons in kowtowing. They advised the English to replace their tight court breeches, knee buckles and garters in favour of the loose Chinese-style garments that made kowtowing so much easier.

But Macartney remained adamant. How could he make an obeisance before the emperor which he would never perform before his own king? The only terms under which he might agree were if the emperor's emissaries agreed to kowtow before the portrait of King George, which, for the Chinese, was impossible. The furthest he would go was to drop on one knee and kiss the emperor's hand, which was how he greeted his own sovereign. Eventually, the Chinese agreed that Macartney could do as he would at home, though they drew the line at hand-kissing. The concession was granted on the grounds that these were, after all, distant barbarians who could not be expected to understand the real significance of the kowtow anyway.

On August 21st, the embassy eventually reached Peking. Macartney, the Stauntons and the Chinese interpreter entered the city at the Western Gate, carried aloft in palanquins ahead of a procession of 90 wagons, 40 handcarts, 200 horses and nearly 3,000 men. By now, the members of the embassy—unwashed, dishevelled and suffering from lack of sleep and mosquito bites—were hardly a prepossessing sight. According to Macartney's valet, Aeneas Anderson, the Chinese crowds burst into laughter when they saw them. The embassy bore 'greater resemblance to the sight provided by the removal of paupers to their parishes in England than the expected dignity of the representative of a great and powerful monarch', he lamented.

They were given accommodation in the only building in Peking large enough to accommodate the whole embassy, the Palace of Eleven Courtyards with the wallpaper which now graces the board-room of Coutts Bank. This was to be a short stay, as the imperial audience was to take place not in Peking's Forbidden City, but in the emperor's summer residence 120 miles to the north, at Jehol in Manchuria.

On September 2nd, 1793, the party set out along the Imperial Way. In Peking they had left behind a team to set up the display of the 'presents' and make arrangements for transforming the Palace of Eleven Courtyards into the British embassy. This was an especially bitter blow to the artist William Alexander—and to posterity—because he knew he was losing the opportunity of painting the most dramatic events of the whole expedition.

The Imperial Way was a superbly made road of compacted sand and clay, and travelling along with the young Staunton in his own carriage, 'the first piece of Long Acre machinery that ever rattled up the road to Jehol', Macartney could imagine he was back in England.

But he was soon left in no doubt that this was China, not Surrey, by the Great Wall which loomed ahead of them. 'The most stupendous work of human hands', wrote Macartney, who ordered his men to measure every possible dimension, except of course its 4,000 mile length. As they prepared to leave, some were seen pocketing fragments of the Wall, no doubt to sell to antiquity dealers' back home.

Beyond the Great Wall they were in the land of Tartary—or Manchuria—a barren landscape of mountains and remote valleys. Rising above the plains into cooler air, they approached the emperor's summer retreat at Jehol.

The Emperor Qianlong had been watching the embassy's arrival, unseen, from a hilltop pergola. A remarkably clear-eyed man of benign countenance, he wore his eighty-three years well. Staunton later described him as 'so hale and vigorous that he scarcely appeared to have existed as many years, fifty-seven, as in fact he had governed the

empire'. That empire had grown substantially during Quianlong's reign, the population having doubled, along with the area over which it held sway. His energy was prodigious, not least in being able to handle an extensive harem and the whims of the notorious 'perfumed muslim' Xiangfei, his consort. As a young man Qianlong had fallen passionately in love with his father's concubine, Machia, and in his sixties the passion was transferred to a male lover, Heshen, Machia's supposed reincarnation. As a result Heshen enjoyed rapid promotion, becoming the emperor's 'Grand Colao' or chief minister. But he was no friend of the embassy and did much to engineer its failure.

In contemplating the audience he was about to give to the English, Qianlong was highly ambivalent. On the one hand he was flattered by their visit. But, as imperial archives show, he had become increasingly annoyed by what he saw as English bad manners, especially over the kowtow. 'The more magnanimous we are towards them, the more conceited they become,' he wrote. He was especially angered by a letter from the king suggesting China would benefit from English progress and that Qianlong should consider George III his 'friend and brother'. As far as Qianlong was concerned, to imply that China needed anything or that a barbarian could be the equal of the Son of Heaven was clearly preposterous.

On Saturday, September 14th, the big day arrived. After setting off at 3am and getting caught up in roaming bands of pigs, cattle and dogs in the darkness, they eventually reached the Garden of Ten Thousand Trees, where Qianlong was to receive them. Approaching a large compound of ceremonial Mongolian tents—or yurts—they could see by the light of paper lanterns that they were in the presence of the entire imperial court. All the Tartar princes were there, plus viceroys, district and city governors and 5–600 mandarins of varying ranks, together with their servants. In addition, there were ambassadors from tributary states, soldiers, balladeers and musicians, all expectantly awaiting the arrival of the Khan of Khans, his arrival perfectly stage-managed to coincide with the rising of the sun.

They waited three hours. Then, at 7am, as the sun flooded the great park, the emperor arrived, carried in an open chair by sixteen men dressed in gold, followed by his ministers and chief mandarins. As he passed the lines of courtiers, everyone present fell to their knees, sweeping their heads to the ground in the kowtow, except for the British, who dropped to one knee, heads bowed.

The emperor entered the largest, most elaborate yurt, followed by the vassals and four members of the British embassy: Macartney, Staunton senior, young Staunton and the Chinese translator. Once inside, they saw that Qianlong was now seated on a raised dais. The nine prostrations were performed again by all present, except the British.

Macartney, followed by Staunton senior, stepped up on the dais. He handed a pair of enamelled watches to Qianlong, together with a letter from George III in a gilt box. Staunton gave the emperor two airguns. In return, Qianlong presented the two men with a ceremonial jade sceptre each and one in white agate for the king.

Wearying of the long-winded translation provided by Li, the emperor asked if any of the British could speak Chinese. The young Staunton was ushered forward, man and boy conversed briefly and Qianlong presented the twelve-year-old with a yellow silk purse for areca nuts, which had been hanging by his side.

Although the meeting at Jehol had been the high point of the embassy's visit to China, Macartney had no more idea than when he started out whether the British requests would be granted. The answer, in the form of two edicts from Qianlong to George III, came as a shock. There was to be no British ambassador to China and China had no need of British goods. 'As your ambassador can see for himself', Qianlong wrote, 'we possess all things. I set no value on objects strange or ingenious, and have no use for your country's manufactures'.

In the second edict, Qianlong rejected Britain's six proposals for opening up China to British trade. 'Do not say that you were not warned in due time', he concluded. 'Tremblingly obey and show no negligence!' Imperial records show that Qianlong had decided on rejection well before the embassy set foot in China.

Three months later, after a journey across China by land, river and canal, Macartney and his entourage finally rejoined their ships at Canton and set sail for home on January 8th, 1794.

The embassy had been a diplomatic failure, but the long-term effects were profound. Within five years of Macartney's return, six books were published by members of the expedition, all of them best-sellers. Combined with the gossip circulating in England's stately homes and London's salons, they dispelled any romantic notions the West had of China. The celestial empire was now revealed, warts and all.

Macartney chose not to publish his own detailed journal, doubtless for diplomatic reasons. He had concluded that the Chinese were 'barbarians' and the government a 'tyranny of a handful of Tartars over more than three hundred millions of Chinese'. China was like 'an old, crazy, first rate man-of-war' which over-awed its neighbours by its bulk and size but would flounder under the command of a weak leader.

Staunton and John Barrow wrote the semi-official accounts, but it was the populist books by Macartney's valet, Aeneas Anderson, and the soldier, Samuel Holmes, that caught the public imagination. Tales of Chinese peasants eating the fleas they picked off their clothes and defecating in public were far removed from the earlier, idealised, Jesuit versions of China. 'There is not a water-closet, nor a decent place of retirement in all China', despaired Anderson. His phrase—'We entered Peking like paupers; we remained in it like prisoners; and we quitted it like vagrants'—stood out as a reminder of the humiliation the embassy had suffered, which, by implication, would one day need to be avenged.

Neither Macartney himself nor any of the books on the embassy advocated using force against China. Yet within fifty years Lord Palmerston had launched the first Opium War against her, extracting by gunboat diplomacy what Macartney had failed to achieve by more peaceful means. Ironically, the leading politician

to advocate war against China in the Commons in 1840 was the fifty-nine-year old Sir George Thomas Staunton, that same youth who had conversed with the Emperor Qianlong years before at Jehol.

It is sometimes argued that China missed a golden opportunity and that the history of the country might have been radically different if Qianlong, like Japan's Meiji emperor later, had adopted European techniques of production. But the China of the 1790s was very different from the Japan of the 1860s and China was neither able nor willing to adapt to Western industrialism. Besides, one might ask, what was the relevance of the planetarium—Macartney's great showpiece 'present'—to modern industrialism?

How significant was Macartney's failure to kowtow? Did it cause the failure of the embassy as some, especially the Jesuits in China at the time, believed? The Chinese records of the period significantly make no mention of the kowtow at all. Possibly the embassy might have stayed longer in China and received more courtesies had Macartney agreed to kowtow, but maybe not. Either way, willingness to kowtow did not guarantee success, as a Dutch envoy later discovered. He was treated with disdain after losing face in public when he kowtowed before the emperor so low that his wig fell off!

The Collision of Two Civilisations, by the French historian and former Gaullist diplomat, Alain Peyrefitte, describes the encounter of 1792–94 as 'a collision of two planets . . . one celestial and lunar; the other with its feet firmly on the ground—mercantile, scientific and industrial.' For him it is a striking instance of the clash between a dynamic, advanced society and a traditional and unchanging one. Although the book is superbly researched and written, the underlying thesis surely represents a nineteenth century Eurocentric view, which minimises the dynamic, changing aspects of China and the conservatism of much of Britain.

Does the Macartney embassy have a relevance now, 200 years on? On the face of it, yes. China is today an ideological state ruled with an iron hand by an octagenarian. The forces of tradition-

alism remain strong, Westerners are confined to 'special economic zones' and the capitalist world is knocking hard to enter. Tea, the drink which gave the impetus to eighteenth-century attempts to open up Chinese markets has its modern day equivalent in Coca-Cola. Interestingly, some of the language used recently in connection with Hong Kong Governor Chris Patten's face-off with Beijing over democratic reforms in the colony, echoes 1793. One Hong Kong official praised Britain for standing firm against China over the reforms and refusing to 'tremble and obey', and Britain and Hong Kong are urged by the popular press not to 'kowtow' to Beijing, which must be treated 'like any other country'.

Perhaps it is true that history can repeat itself, but 1793 is not 1993. Qianlong is no more Deng Xiao Ping than George III is John Major or Macartney Chris Patten. What the Macartney embassy offers us is, in the words of Professor Peter Marshall of London University, 'the beam of a searchlight', a fascinating glimpse at the preconceptions two great civilisations had of each other at a particular time in a certain place. No more nor less than that. But it is a thumping good story!

FOR FURTHER READING:

Sir George Leonard Staunton, *An Authentic Account of an Embassy from the King of Great Britain to the Emperor of China* (J. Nicol, 1797); William Alexander, *Picturesque Representations of the Dress and Manners of the Chinese* (John Murray, 1805); Aeneas Anderson, *A Narrative of the British Embassy in China* (J. Debrett, 1795); N. Cameron, 'Kowtow: Imperial China and the West in Confrontation' *Orientations,* Hong Kong, January 1971; J.L. Cranmer-Byng, *An Embassy to China 1793–94* (Longman Green & Co, 1962); Alain Peyrefitte, *The Collision of Two Civilisations: the British Expedition to China in 1792–94,* (Harvill, 1993); Helen Robbins, *Our first Ambassador to China* (John Murray, 1908); Aubrey Singer, *The Lion and the Dragon* (Barrie & Jenkins, 1992).

Coffee, Tea, or Opium?

In 1838, a Chinese drug czar confronted the Age of Addiction

Samuel M. Wilson

Samuel M. Wilson teaches anthropology at the University of Texas at Austin.

In 1839, China's commissioner for foreign trade, Lin Zexu (Lin Tse-hsü), was running out of diplomatic options. Traders from the East India Company and other European enterprises were pressing him ever more forcefully to turn a blind eye to the illegal importation of opium into his country. They were implicitly backed by Britain's heavily armored warships—such as the *Blenheim* and *Wellesley,* carrying seventy-four cannons each—which could crush China's navy and lay waste to her ports. But the opium trade was damaging public health and bleeding China of her wealth. In 1838, the Manchu emperor had given Lin extensive power and ordered him to control the demand of China's people for opium and force the barbarian merchants to cut off the supply.

After his appointment, Lin began to study European culture, looking for clues to barbarian behavior. He obtained a partial translation of Emer de Vattel's 1758 *Le Droit des Gens* ("The Law of Nations"), and he bought and studied the British ship *Cambridge.* Although it was not the largest of the "East India-men"—big defended freighters—and although it had been stripped of its guns and its intricate rigging was a mystery to Lin's sailors, the ship was ample evidence that these British were clever at naval warfare.

Lin also visited Macao, the Portuguese trading entrepôt near Canton, and carried out some anthropological fieldwork:

> As soon as I entered the wall of Macao, a hundred barbarian soldiers dressed in barbarian military uniform, led by the barbarian headman, greeted me. They marched in front of my sedan playing barbarian music and led me into the city. . . . On this day, everyone, man and woman, came out on the street or leaned from the window to take a look. Unfortunately the barbarian costume was too absurd. The men, their bodies wrapped tightly in short coats and long "legs," resembled in shape foxes and rabbits as impersonated in the plays. . . . Their beards, with abundant whiskers, were half shaved off and only a piece was kept. Looking at them all of a sudden was frightening. That the Cantonese referred to them as "devils" was indeed not vicious disparagement. [Chang Hsin-pao, *Commissioner Lin and the Opium War* (Cambridge: Harvard University Press, 1964)]

Although the Chinese forbade opium importation, willing trading partners were easily found among the Chinese merchants. And if trade became too difficult for the foreigners in the principal port of Canton, there were a thousand miles of coastline, and thousands of miles more of inland borders, through which opium could be transported. Lin saw that the opium trade was ruining China. Informed by his reading of de Vattel and by his extensive dealings with the British representatives, in early 1839 he appealed to Queen Victoria, attempting to conceal the sense of superiority that the Chinese rulers felt toward Westerners:

> We have heard that in your honorable nation, too, the people are not permitted to smoke [opium], and that offenders in this particular expose themselves to sure punishment. . . . Though not making use of it one's self, to venture nevertheless to manufacture and sell it, and with it to seduce the simple folk of this land, is to seek one's own livelihood by exposing others to death, to see one's own advantage by other men's injury. Such acts are bitterly abhorrent to the nature of man and are utterly opposed to the ways of heaven. . . . We now wish to find, in cooperation with your honorable sovereignty, some means of bringing to a perpetual end this opium, so hurtful to mankind: we in this land forbidding the use of it, and you, in the nations of your dominion, forbidding its manufacture. [Chang Hsin-pao, *Commissioner Lin and the Opium War*]

The British were the biggest traders in China, but merchants from the United States were present too. Lin considered petitioning this other, possibly significant state, but understood that twenty-four chiefs governed the American people, and thought that communicating with them all would be too difficult.

In his letter to Queen Victoria, Lin sought to explain the situation logically. Earlier communications from the Chinese government had not been so diplomatic. The commander of Canton had sent an edict to the Western traders demanding, "Could your various countries stand one day without trading with China?" This threat came in part from the Chinese leaders' delusion that the British would die if deprived of tea, China's largest export (a delusion the British may have shared). The same edict took note that, according to the Western press,

> your motives are to deplete the Middle Kingdom's wealth and destroy the lives of the Chinese people. There is no need to dwell on the topic that the wealth of the Celestial Empire, where all five metals are produced and precious deposits abound, could not be exhausted by such a mere trifle, but for what enmity do you want to kill the Chinese people?

China had withstood barbarian traders without difficulty for two thousand years. But now it was feeling the aftershock of the Western encounter with the Americas and with the closely related expansion of European influence across the globe. The importation of opium reached staggering proportions in the early nineteenth century after the British-run East India Company took control of the drug's production in India. During the trading season of 1816–17, about forty-six hundred 150-pound chests of opium entered China. This number rose to 22,000 by 1831–32 and 35,000 by 1837–38. That was more than 5.25 million pounds of opium, the carefully collected and dried sap extruded from 4.8 trillion opium poppies.

The period from the seventeenth century to the present could be termed the Age of Addiction, for the international economy and the fortunes of nations depended on trade in addictive or semiaddictive agricultural products. The young United States exported tobacco, the habit for which spread rapidly across Europe, Africa, and Asia. The Spaniards carried the New World practice of tobacco smoking to Europe and the East Indies, and as its popularity spread, the plant came to be widely cultivated throughout the Old World. In their Indonesian colonies the Dutch tried filling their pipes with a combination of opium and tobacco. The Chinese continued to smoke the opium, but left out the tobacco.

The British became addicted to the carefully processed leaves of *Camellia sinensis,* or Chinese tea (originally, China was the only exporter). Caffeine-rich coffee was another drug for which Europeans and others developed a craving. A native plant of Ethiopia, coffee's range of cultivation expanded hand in hand with European colonialism. Perfect growing conditions were found in both the New World and Southeast Asia, giving rise to the exotic names for coffee familiar today: Jamaica Blue Mountain, Mocha Java, Guatemalan, Sumatran, and Colombian. These and other nonessential but deeply desired plant products—cocaine, chocolate, and marijuana—have captured huge markets.

Addictive substances are wonderful exports for the countries that produce and ship them. They are highly valuable and compact agricultural products that can be exchanged for hard currency, and the demand of addicts is—for physiological reasons—what economists would call highly inelastic. Farmers get much more from their land and effort than they would by growing things for a local market, and middlemen on both sides of the border get rich. The losers in the transaction—apart from the users themselves—are the importing countries, which run up uncontrollable trade deficits.

From the opening of the Silk Road in the Middle Ages, Western countries were eager to obtain Chinese spices, fabrics, and tea, viewing them as superior to European products. The problem for England and other nations was that they had very little that China wanted, so they had to pay in the most respected and accepted international currency, Spanish silver dollars. With good reason, the Chinese thought the British could not live without tea. About all China would take in trade was British woolen and cotton cloth. American merchants, lacking England's textile manufacturing infrastructure, struggled still more to find anything the Chinese would take in trade. They too paid mainly with Spanish silver, but they also brought natural products—sealskins and other furs from the Northwest Coast, aromatic wood, cotton, wild American ginseng—with which to trade (*see* "Yankee Doodle Went to Canton," *Natural History,* February 1984).

By capitalizing upon a massive addiction to smoked opium in China—and in substantial measure helping to create it—England and the other Western nations shifted the balance of trade in their favor. As social historian Fernand Braudel put it, "China was now literally being paid in smoke (and what smoke!)." Most of the rest of what England traded was woven cotton, also grown and spun in India. In return, at the time of Commissioner Lin's appeal to Queen Victoria, the Chinese were trading about 60 percent tea, 12 percent silks, and most of the rest, about 25 percent, silver and gold.

The opium trade was not the only alarming foreign influence in Lin's day. The barbarians seemed to have designs on Chinese territory. The port of Canton lay thirty miles upriver from the great Gulf of Canton, twenty miles wide and fifty miles long. At the western approach to the bay was the Portuguese trading colony of Macao, which the Chinese had allowed to exist since 1557. On the other side of the gulf lay the island of Hong Kong, which the British sought to turn into a secure headquarters for their trading operations. Even if the Europeans had lacked naval superiority, they could have defended both places from invasion by land or sea. China had always insisted that barbarians of any stripe carry out their trade and then leave, but instead of acting as temporary visitors, the Western traders were staying longer and longer, becoming in effect permanent residents.

Another major grievance was that the foreigners would not submit to Chinese laws when in China. Some European sailors murdered Chinese citizens, but their leaders would not turn over the culprits to the Chinese magistrates. Lin's research revealed that foreigners in England were required to obey British law, but when he confronted the British commanders with this double standard, they merely conceded that he had a case and again refused to turn over British subjects to almost certain execution. Other European and American traders acted similarly.

Despite the barbarian offenses, Lin preferred negotiation and reasoned discussion to fighting a battle that he felt would be difficult to win. In a final, carefully worded letter to Queen Victoria, he wrote:

> Let us suppose that foreigners came from another country, and brought opium into England, and seduced the people of your country to smoke it. Would not you, the sovereign of the said country, look upon such a procedure with anger, and in your just indignation endeavor to get rid of it? Now we have always heard that Your Highness possesses a most kind and benevolent heart. Surely then you are incapable of doing or causing to be done unto another that which you should not wish another to do unto you. [Chang Hsin-pao, *Commissioner Lin and the Opium War*]

Moral persuasion has not, historically, proved very effective in dealing with drug smuggling or rulers who sanction it. Unofficially, the contents of the letter were probably widely known but, as with his previous attempts, Lin received no official response. Britain was determined that the opium trade would continue, by force if necessary, and because China had been unwilling to open formal diplomatic channels, the British government would not accept a letter to the queen from a commissioner.

Lin's efforts to rein in the barbarians and subdue the Chinese appetite for opium were ultimately unsuccessful, and the emperor harshly accused him of failing:

> Externally you wanted to stop the trade, but it has not been stopped. Internally you wanted to wipe out the outlaws, but they are not cleared away. . ... You are just making excuses with empty words. Nothing has been accomplished but many troubles have been created. Thinking of these things I cannot contain my rage. What do you have to say now?

Lin replied that the Chinese should address the threat and fight the British, falling back to the interior and fighting a guerrilla war if necessary. He warned the emperor not to attempt to placate the British: "The more they get the more they demand, and if we do not overcome them by force of arms there will be no end to our troubles. Moreover there is every probability that if the English are not dealt with, other foreigners will soon begin to copy and even outdo them."

In June of 1839, Lin had 20,000 chests of opium destroyed in Canton, and the foreign merchants fell back to Macao. The British sent a fleet of their most powerful warships on a punitive expedition, and they overwhelmed the Chinese fleet whenever they faced it. Among their warships were the "ships-of-the-line," massively armed vessels that demonstrated the advantage of superior technology over superior numbers in modern warfare. In the summer of 1842, China was forced to sign the humiliating Treaty of Nanking, which required $21 million in reparations, opened five ports to British trade (including Canton and Shanghai), and ceded Hong Kong, surrounding islands, and part of the mainland to Queen Victoria. China also agreed that future Chinese–British relations would be on terms of "complete equality." This condition seems ironic, because the terms

of the treaty were certainly in the Western merchants' favor. This wording was insisted upon by the British, however, because previously China had dealt with Westerners as barbarian traders, never recognizing them as official representatives of foreign governments. Nowhere did the treaty mention opium, but everyone knew that the drug had been at the heart of the war.

One hundred fifty years later, China still feels the sting of this defeat. The recently negotiated treaty for the return of Hong Kong in 1997 is viewed as just a fraction of the restitution owed. In 1990, writing in the *Beijing Review,* historian Hu Sheng, president of the Chinese Academy of Social Sciences, lamented the cost of the war in terms of Chinese health, hard currency, and national honor. He also observed that for the next hundred years China was under continuous attack by the West and Japan, but because the emperors were willing to tolerate their presence, the people were unable to rise up and throw out the foreigners. In his view, and in that of many Chinese, "Only the Chinese Communist Party could do this."

For his failure to curb the barbarians, Lin Zexu was demoted and disgraced, and spent the last few years before his death supervising irrigation projects and the repair of dikes. In retrospect, he is regarded as a hero. "The Chinese army, commanded by Lin," writes Hu, "resisted the invaders together with the local people. However, the corrupt Qing court was unable to continue the resistance and succumbed to the invaders."

Commissioner Lin would no doubt feel vindicated, and perhaps even take some pleasure in the way many Western nations are now on the receiving end of the drug policies they helped invent.

After Centuries of Japanese Isolation, a Fateful Meeting of East and West

When Japan's rulers finally let in Yankee trade and technology, they changed the history of their country and of the world

James Fallows

James Fallows, Washington editor of the Atlantic Monthly, *has published* Looking at the Sun, *a Study of Japanese and East Asian economic systems.*

From the deck of the USS *Susquehanna* the sailors watched the sea around them fill with little boats. The *Susquehanna* and its sister ships—the *Mississippi,* the *Saratoga,* the *Powhatan*—had been traveling for more than half a year. From Norfolk, Virginia, they had sailed in the late fall of 1852 across the Atlantic, then down around Capetown, and across the Indian Ocean to the South China Sea. Through the spring of 1853 they labored northward past Macao, Hong Kong, Okinawa and the Bonin island chain—Iwo Jima and Chichi Jima—toward the main islands of Japan.

On the evening of July 8, 1853, they rounded a promontory and came to the entrance of the Uraga Channel, itself the entrance to Edo Wan, now known as Tokyo Bay. At the head of the bay, less than a day's sail away, lay Edo itself, Japan's largest city, insulated from foreign contact for nearly 250 years.

The Japanese guard boats that teemed around the American flotilla in the Uraga Channel were made of wood, with sharply angled prows. Sweating oarsmen propelled the boats through the ocean chop. Above the rowers' heads flapped the geometric- or floral-patterned standards of the Tokugawa shoguns who ruled Japan. The American sailors could not understand the shouts that came to them in Japanese. Yet every crew member knew that in the past, uninvited visitors to Japan had often been jailed, tortured or decapitated.

As the lead guard boat approached the *Susquehanna,* the Americans peering down from the deck found, with relief, that they could make out a few familiar characters from the Roman alphabet, rather than the gracefully swirling *hiragana* of Japanese phonetic writing or the intricate *kanji* ideograms the Japanese had adapted from written Chinese. As the guard boat drew closer still, sharp-eyed crewmen sounded out the first word: *"Départez!"* The entire message was in French, not English. It said, "Depart immediately and dare not anchor!" The two nations that would become the main Pacific powers made their first significant contact in a language neither really understood.

THE LENGTHENED SHADOWS OF TWO MEN

Japan's rulers had not in any way invited the encounter; indeed, the more imminent it had become, the more it filled them with dread. America forced the encounter on Japan for a confused tangle of reasons, many of which the American instigators did not honestly discuss among themselves. Yet the aftereffects of this moment prepared Japan for the most impressive feat in its history, and one of the most surprising in the history of any nation. At the same time American interests were more shrewdly advanced by the man who sat hidden in his cabin on the *Susquehanna* than by other American leaders almost any time in U.S. history. Ninety years afterward, Japan and America would be at war, but that was not the fault of the two men who guided this encounter on a hot summer day in 1853; Masahiro Abe, in the shogun's council at Edo, and Matthew

Calbraith Perry, in command of the vessels known today in Japan as *kurofune*, "black ships."

Matthew Perry, bearing the title not of Commodore but of "Commander in Chief, United States Naval Forces Stationed in the East India, China, and Japan Seas," was 59 years old when his fleet reached Uraga. For the era, that was old—especially for a man undertaking a prolonged voyage to an essentially unknown destination. Perry suffered from arthritis and other maladies that confined him to his cabin during much of the long trip. Even at age 25 he had been remarked on for his gravitas; as he grew older he took on the air of a mandarin. This demeanor proved a great asset. Like Douglas MacArthur, another American too regal to fit easily into his home culture, Matthew Perry was well prepared by training and temperament for negotiations in Japan. An aw-shucks, unassuming manner might be an asset on the American frontier, but not surrounded by little boats in Tokyo Bay.

Perry's career, indeed his whole life, was devoted to the expansion of the U.S. Navy. His older brother, Oliver Hazard Perry, had become a hero at the Battle of Lake Erie before Matthew was out of his teens. Matthew, by contrast, spent his early career in a peacetime navy "where members of a small clique of senior officers scrambled for the limited command opportunities, where feuding, backbiting, and even dueling were a way of life," as Peter Booth Wiley puts it in *Yankees in the Land of the Gods.* "During the navy's first fifty years, thirty-three officers were killed in duels." Perry's first important mission, in 1819, was to transport freed slaves to Africa during the founding of Liberia. He did not see combat until he was in his 50s, at the Battle of Veracruz in the Mexican War, as the nation kept expanding westward toward a second sea frontier on the Pacific.

One great struggle over America's maritime future turned on the relative future roles of clipper ships versus steam-powered vessels. By the 1850s the fast and graceful clippers had given America the lead in the shipping trade. But the British were outbuilding America in steamships, and by the 1840s, Britain's steam-powered Cunard line was winning the battle for passengers and valuable freight on the transatlantic route.

Steam power required coal, and at the time no ship was large enough to carry all the coal it needed to cross the vast Pacific. Clipper ships had to choose routes to China on the basis of favorable winds, but steamers could be more deliberate, following a "great circle" route up toward Alaska and then down the Japanese archipelago. With coaling stations along the way, the great circle route would be possible, and in 1851 Americans learned that Japan had deposits of coal. "The moment is near when the last link in the chain of oceanic steam navigation is to be formed," said Senator Daniel Webster of New Hampshire, not stinting on rhetoric, as he endorsed an American expedition to Japan. The point of this link would not be to buy from the Japanese their own handicrafts and manufactures but to obtain a "gift of Providence, deposited, by the Creator of all things, in the depths of the Japanese islands for the benefit of the human family"—that is, Japan's coal.

The desire to expand a coal-using, steam-powered navy was not the only reason for the expedition to Japan. Beyond lay China, where Americans hoped to find markets to develop and souls to convert. For a century before the age of steamships, American whalers had worked the waters of the North Pacific surrounding Japan. Frequently the ships did not come home. American sailors stranded by typhoon or shipwreck had washed ashore in Japan since the late 1700s. Often they were executed; usually they were jailed; a few were forced to perform ritual disrespect to Christian symbols, for instance by walking on a portrait of the Virgin Mary.

GETTING THE JUMP ON DUTCH, FRENCH AND ENGLISH

These icons of the Blessed Virgin were leftovers from Portuguese Jesuits, who had proselytized in Japan for nearly a century before being driven out in the early 1600s. The shipwrecked Americans, mainly Protestants, found this ordeal less excruciating than the Japanese expected, yet news of such episodes, especially one involving the whaler *Lagoda,* filtered back to America, where at a minimum they stirred a passion for better protection for whalers, and among some people a desire to make the "pagans" atone. "If that double-bolted land, Japan, is ever to become hospitable, it is the whale-ship alone to whom the credit will be due," Herman Melville wrote in *Moby-Dick* in 1851.

The British had won their Opium Wars against China. From the north came Russian vessels. Swarming around were the French and the Dutch. The expansionist U.S. Government watched these plans with care. Finally to establish America's presence first, the Administration of Millard Fillmore, in by far its most consequential step, commissioned the Japan Expedition and convinced Matthew Perry to command it. For nearly two and a half centuries, since the great warlord Hideyoshi took steps that led to the policies known as *sakoku,* or "closed country," Japan's officials had isolated themselves from the world—and wondered apprehensively when the isolation might end.

In 1549 a Portuguese Jesuit, Francis Xavier, had come ashore on the island of Kyushu. Initially tolerated, even supported by some local noblemen, the Jesuits had in the next 50 years made tens of thousands of Japanese converts. By the end of the century Hideyoshi, weakened by a costly and failed attempt to conquer Korea, and chastened to learn that savage conquistadors had often followed the cross in Latin America, had expelled all missionaries. Soon, the Tokugawa shogunate launched its radical policy of seclusion. As far as possible, Japan and its leaders would function as if there were no world beyond Japan's seacoast. "So long as the Sun shall warm the earth, let no Christian dare to come to Japan," said the shogun's expulsion order of 1638. If contact with foreigners was unavoidable, it would be handled through an enclave of Dutch traders, concentrated in an island ghetto called Deshima, near Nagasaki in the far southern extreme of the country—hundreds of miles from the great, protected centers of Kyoto and Edo.

The sakoku policy worked for a while—indeed, for as many years as the United States has now existed as an independent country. Yet in the early 1800s, as Japan began its third century of near-total isolation, the strains were evident. "In 1642, the year Isaac Newton was born, the last Japanese priest had been crucified and Japan had closed like an oyster," one American historian has written. But the leaders who made the decision "could hardly guess that Japan, which went into seclusion as one of the two or three strongest nations on the globe, would emerge from it, centuries later, as a distinctly second-class power."

The same whalers and fishermen who were inconvenient when washed onto Japanese shores inevitably brought news of the Industrial Revolution and other advancements outside Japan. A young Japanese fisherman named Manjiro Nakajima was himself shipwrecked and picked up by an American whaler in 1841. Under Japan's seclusion law, it was a capital offense to leave the country—or to come back, if one had escaped. But after spending a decade in New England, under the name John Mung, Manjiro decided to risk returning to Japan.

The *daimyo*, or lord, of the southern province of Satsuma realized, as Samuel Eliot Morison puts it, that decapitating Manjiro would not only sever his head but also "would cut off an important source of information." Instead, the daimyo sent him to Nagasaki, "where officials pumped Manjiro dry of everything he knew about the United States." Among the facts Manjiro revealed (as Walter McDougall wrote in *Let the Sea Make a Noise . . .*) was that Americans were lewd by nature, and that in their country "toilets are placed over holes in the ground. It is customary to read books in them."

Officially the Japanese rulers faced news of foreign developments with redoubled sternness. In 1825, as whaling traffic increased, the shogun issued an edict forbidding any foreign ship to land. When a foreign ship came into view, the order read, it was crucial to shoot at it first and ask questions later. "Have no compunctions about firing on [the Dutch] by mistake," the order went on. "When in doubt, drive the ship away without hesitation. Never be caught off guard."

Behind this bravado was a debate, based on very little information but heated because the Japanese felt the very survival of the nation was at stake. In the town of Mito, a day's walk to the northeast of Edo, the "Mito School" of theorists said that an increased threat required increased determination to resist. Japan must shore up its coastal defenses, girding itself for the inevitable battle to the death that would keep the foreigners away. "Today the alien barbarians of the West, the lowly organs of the legs and feet of the world, are . . . trampling other countries underfoot, and daring, with their squinting eyes and limping feet, to override the noble nations," one such scholar wrote in 1825. With such a foe, no compromise could be possible.

COULD JAPAN BEND WITHOUT BREAKING?

In the other camp were the Rangakusha, or "masters of Dutch learning," so called after Holland's role during the closed-country years as the vehicle for all learning from overseas. A realistic assessment of the circumstances, said members of this camp, required Japan to bend so as to avoid being broken. They had evidence of weakness inside the country. Taxes, levied in rice, were becoming oppressive. In several centuries of peace the samurai class had grown large and dependent; in 1850 Edo alone supported some 17,000 bureaucrats, compared with 1,500 in Washington, D.C.

Evidence of the strength of potential invaders was even more dramatic. In 1846, seven years before Matthew Perry's arrival, Commodore James Biddle of the U.S. Navy had reached the mouth of the Uraga Channel. He had retreated with humiliating loss of face, after letting Japanese sightseers and officials inspect every inch of his ship and after accepting a letter from the shogun telling him never to return. Yet the shrewder Japanese officials of the era carefully noted the size and power of his ships, and of the American guns. Biddle's vessels represented destructive potential of a sort Japan had barely imagined.

Most of all the Japanese realists noticed what had happened to China—noticed, and were appalled. China was not just another country but the Middle Kingdom, the Central Country. Its emperor had historically referred to Japan's emperor as "your little king." A new China had been carved up by Westerners, debauched by opium and left totally unprotected by either the Ch'ing dynasty or armed force. If the British and French could polish off China, what hope was there for little Japan—against Britain, France, Russia and the United States? Japan could try to enforce its seclusion law, said one of its very shrewdest leaders after the Biddle affair, but if "the foreigners retaliated, it would be a hopeless contest, and it would be a worse disgrace for Japan."

This leader was Masahiro Abe, the senior counselor for the shogun's government. As the shogun was the power that ruled Japan in the emperor's name, so Abe was the strategist who made plans on behalf of the weakened shogun, Tokugawa Ieyoshi, who was in place when Perry arrived. Abe was a generation younger than Perry, only 34 years old as Perry's flotilla of Black Ships neared Edo. Raised in a scholar's family, he had through force of intellect made himself one of the shogun's most influential advisers while still in his 20s.

In the split between the hard-liners and compromisers in the shogun's court, Abe sided initially with the hard-liners. But after extensive consultation among the daimyos of Japan, he and his allies came up with a brilliant compromise. Japan would open itself to the Western traders—but only for a time—placating them just long enough to learn how to rebuild its own navies and arsenals. Naosuke Ii, the most influential of all the daimyos, reminded the shogun that, even as Japan had earlier used Dutch traders as its bridge to the outside world, it was time to use the Americans and other foreigners as another, broader bridge. Across this bridge new discoveries could flow into Japan—providing the country, in the long run, with means to rearm itself, learn from outside tech-

Of gifts given, those from Japanese were more decorative, while Perry's aimed to impress Japan with industrial might. Baby steam engine was biggest hit, but offerings included plow, scythe, grindstone.

nology, and ultimately "gain a complete victory" over the foreigners.

Some of the American politicians promoting the Japan Expedition had cast it in missionary terms, a chance to open the Orient to faith and flag. "I am sure that the Japanese policy of seclusion is not according to God's plan of bringing the nations of the earth to a knowledge of the truth," Samuel Wells Williams, a missionary traveling with Perry as cultural expert and interpreter, wrote in his journal as the expedition neared Edo. Perry himself, pious enough, never described his duties in these terms. Instead he concentrated on how to deploy his men, his ships and himself for maximum effect. Before the trip began, Perry foresaw that his fleet's substantial armament "would do more to command their fears, and secure their friendship, than all that the diplomatic missions have accomplished in the last one hundred years." In a set of "Instructions" for the voyage, Perry said that the Commander

"will be careful to do nothing that may [compromise] his own dignity or that of the country. He will, on the contrary, do every thing to impress them with a just sense of the power and greatness of this country and to satisfy them that its past forbearance has been the result, not of timidity, but of a desire to be on friendly terms with them."

GIFTS TO SHOW A NATION'S STRENGTH

Like Masahiro Abe, Perry had studied the sad history of Commodore Biddle, who had been forced out of Edo Bay in 1846. In Perry's view, Biddle never recovered from setting his first foot wrong with the Japanese: rather than insisting on retaining a mysterious distance, he had let them climb onto his ship and, in effect, imprison it with guard boats. Speaking of himself in the third person, in his memoir of the voyage Perry said,

"The Commodore . . . was well aware that the more exclusive he should make himself, and the more unyielding he might be in adhering to his declared intentions, the more respect these people of forms and ceremonies would be disposed to award him." He would meet only with officials of "the highest rank" in Japan. He would make a threat only when he was absolutely certain he could carry it out.

Power could be demonstrated through generosity as well as reserve. Perry had prepared gifts to demonstrate the range of strengths his nation possessed. Editions of Audubon's *Birds of America* and *Quadrupeds of America* that had cost $1,000 apiece—a decade's earnings for an average American family at the time. Champagne, perfume and mirrors. Whisky, liqueurs, and small weapons from the Colt factory. And, most important, American machines: plows, a telegraph, a crude camera, even a nifty little quarter-scale steam-powered railroad train.

This was the man who appeared in the Uraga Channel in July 1853. He was not one to be driven away by instructions to *"Départez!"* Sweating alone in his cabin, unwilling to present himself prematurely to the crowd of Japanese, he issued his orders. The *Susquehanna* and sister ships were to repel, with all necessary force, any Japanese who attempted to board the boats. They would proceed up the channel, toward Edo, until their wish to meet a truly senior official, one who could speak for the ruler, was fulfilled. After the failure of the French message, a Japanese official had neared the *Susquehanna* and yelled out, in English, "I can speak Dutch!" To him the Americans conveyed their wish to meet someone truly in command.

Throughout Edo, news of the Black Ships' arrival created near-panic. Some citizens fled, carrying their possessions to the countryside, fearing pillage and war. The shogun's council met to consider bleak-seeming alternatives. The usual reflexive responses to outside pressure—asking the foreigners to come back again in a few years, telling them to go on to Nagasaki, the only site where Japan had done business with foreign representatives through the sakoku years—seemed to have lost their potency. The Americans would not retreat—in fact, they kept sending surveying ships farther up the bay, ignoring Japanese assertions that this violated local law and saying that they needed to be sure about anchorages, for "the next time."

As the governing council quarreled, Abe pushed them toward a decision: the Americans must be placated, at least for now. Perry had been asking to meet the emperor; that was out of the question, of course. Indeed, to this point the Americans were not even aware that a real emperor existed, hidden in Kyoto. When they said "emperor," they were referring to the shogun; their official goal was to present him with letters from President Fillmore.

Clearly some meeting was essential, and so on July 14, after elaborate arguments over protocol, Matthew Perry himself came ashore at the town of Kurihama.

In retrospect this result seems inevitable. America was a country on the rise.

Japan could not wall itself off eternally. Each party had a stake in negotiating reasonably with the other: Perry because he was outnumbered on the scene; the Japanese, because other Americans could come back and exact retribution if anything went wrong. But at the time it was very much touch and go. More than once Perry's men came to the brink of violent confrontation. Crewmen on the *Mississippi* had to level a loaded musket at a Japanese official's chest to keep him from climbing aboard. A small American survey boat, commanded by Lieut. Silas Bent, found itself surrounded by three dozen Japanese guard boats. Bent prepared for hand-to-hand combat, instructing his small crew to fix bayonets—until the mighty *Mississippi* steamed into view and the Japanese retreated.

And so, on the night before Perry's scheduled landing in Kurihama, his crew members watched apprehensively from their decks as more and more Japanese troops filled the shore. Perry considered the possibility that the proposed meeting was really an ambush. After his surveyors reported that Kurihama's harbor was deep enough, Perry ordered his gunboats brought in close to shore, where they could bombard the Japanese if anything went wrong. On the long night before the meeting, 250 American sailors were chosen by lot for the dangerous mission of accompanying their commander ashore. The Japanese worked through the night to prepare a pavilion for the meeting—and to increase the boats guarding the entrance to Edo Bay, in case the Americans were planning a sudden, treacherous assault.

On the morning of July 14, the American boats drew near to shore. Members of the landing party, dressed in their formal uniforms, were issued 20 rounds of ammunition apiece and carefully loaded their muskets and pistols. On the shore they saw three new pavilions, covered with the bright flags and standards of Japanese officialdom. Surrounding the pavilions were files and files of soldiers, armed with swords, bows and arrows, and a few antique firearms.

At 10 o'clock barges full of Americans began arriving on the shore. Mis-

calculations at this moment might have had historic consequences; long after the event, one of the Japanese commanders revealed that ten swordsmen had been hiding under the floor of a pavilion, with orders to leap out and slaughter the foreigners if they made the slightest aggressive move.

As their numbers grew on the beach, Perry's men formed a double line, through which their commander, arriving at last, marched toward the waiting Japanese. Ahead of Perry was a Marine officer walking with sword in hand. On either side of him were two of the largest men from his ship, both black stewards, loaded with all the weapons they could carry and towering over every other person on the beach. Once Perry was safe ashore, tension eased a bit. He was met by two Japanese governors, to whom the stewards presented large rosewood boxes. Inside were small solid-gold cases, which in turn contained Millard Fillmore's letters requesting that Japan open itself to the world. The governors, in return, presented Perry with a letter said to be from Japan's ruler. When translated, it turned out to contain warnings that the Americans had broken Japanese law by landing in Kurihama and must not come back. Perry said that, with his mission accomplished, he was leaving Japan—but he would be back the next year to hear the Japanese government's response. With quite as many ships? the interpreter asked. "All of them," Perry replied. "And probably more, as these are only a portion of the squadron."

After the meeting in Kurihama, Perry had compounded Japan's sense of threat by sending surveying parties even deeper into Edo Bay. Then his departing fleet retraced the route it had taken toward Japan, visiting Okinawa and the Bonin Islands before stopping for repairs and refitting in Macao. He studiously ignored suggestions from Washington that he wait and assemble a much larger force before his return trip. Perry knew that French and Russian missions would soon be heading to Japan. He was suffering terribly from arthritis; a winter passage back to Edo would be dangerous and unpleasant. Yet to forestall all other navies and force action from the Japanese, Perry set sail northward from Macao in the middle of January 1854.

Back in Edo everything was still uncertain. What did the Americans really want? What compromise would be enough to make their warships go away? Suppose the shogun's government offered to give the Americans half the trading rights now monopolized by the Dutch? Or dragged out the negotiations themselves over five or ten years; after which time the Americans might lose interest or Japan might come up with a new plan?

FIGHT IT OUT OR FACE UP TO PROGRESS

Masahiro Abe had ordered Japan's coastal defenses fortified as soon as Perry's flotilla headed south after its first visit. He engineered the repeal of a law—enacted at the start of the sakoku era—that prohibited Japanese citizens from building seagoing vessels, and he opened negotiations with the Dutch about buying some steam-powered warships from them. All factions in Japan agreed that negotiations should be strung out as long as possible. Yet when the moment of choice arose, should Japan fight to the death, as influential figures like Tokugawa Nariaki, daimyo of Mito, were advocating? Or should it bow to the reality of superior force and instead plan for long-term survival, and future revenge?

The issue was forced in the middle of February when American ships arrived once more in the Uraga Channel. This time Perry's flotilla numbered three steam-powered frigates, seven ships under sail, and combined crews totaling more than 1,500 men. Overcoming bitter accusations that he was betraying Japan, Abe at last forced through a decision. Japan would greet the Americans with conciliation. It would accept a code of conduct for shipwrecked whalers and seamen. It would let the Americans obtain coal in Shimoda, near Edo, and trade with them at sites other than

the traditional foreigner's ghetto in Nagasaki. It asked only for a transition period of a few years before the full agreement came into effect.

There were still points of detail to be negotiated—how many ports would be open to trade, what tariff the Japanese could impose. But under Abe's guidance Japan had given in. Matthew Perry, confined by disease and dignity to his Black Ship cabin, was ready by early March to deal face-to-face with his Japanese counterparts. On March 8 he came ashore at Yokohama for a detailed, though still touchy, negotiating session.

On March 13 Perry went ashore once again for the first gift-exchanging ceremony. One by one he gave away the marvels of artistry and engineering he had stowed aboard his ships nearly two years before. The Japanese onlookers were entranced by the scale-model locomotive pulling a train. The passenger coach, complete with interior benches and curtains, was too small for human passengers, but samurai and shogun's officials took rides sitting on top of the train. In their turn, the Japanese offered gifts. But because they thought that valuable gifts might be insulting—suggesting the possibility of a bribe or the need to reply in kind—their gifts were modest, though artistic and of fine workmanship. Perry regarded them as trifling. More impressive were their mammoth sumo wrestlers. Perry watched as the *sumotori* strode in, heavy sacks of rice atop their heads. One of the wrestlers approached Perry, who accepted the invitation to punch the immense stomach and feel its strength. Samuel Wells Williams, Perry's missionary-interpreter, who was generally quite admiring of Japan and who despaired of his crewmates' insensitivity to foreign ways, nonetheless wrote in his diary that the spectacle demonstrated the clash of two cultures: the "success of science and enterprise" on the American side, the "brute animal force" on Japan's.

A final disagreement arose over Perry's desire to walk the streets of the capital city. Here the Japanese held firm:

Perry could, if he chose, view Edo from the deck of his ship, but must not come ashore. Perry accepted, sailed to the top of Edo Bay for a look, and then, on April 14, headed south again.

Negotiations between Japan and the United States were just beginning. For most of the next decade an American counsel, Townsend Harris, would accuse Japanese officials of backsliding, dissembling and attempting to evade the treaty's terms. More than a century later in the debate over trading issues, Japanese and American officials have assumed roles very similar to those first played in Uraga and Kurihama, with the Japanese debating the merits of acquiescence or defiance, and the Americans, far less powerful now, attempting to display impressive and intimidating force.

Perry's role in Japan was complete. It was to be a profound role and, though deeply unwished for by the Japanese, in the long run it had quite positive effects. Although Japan had been forced to make concessions and accept "unequal treaties," it had avoided outright defeat—and had prepared for the rapid modernization that began with the Meiji Restoration of 1868. For this progress Japan could, with mixed emotions, thank Perry and the shock he delivered with the Black Ships.

Perry thought he would be lionized by his countrymen on his return, but he was not, in part because his countrymen were preoccupied with tensions over slavery that would lead to the Civil War. Retiring to his town house in New York, the Commodore worked methodically on his *Narrative of the Expedition*, which he submitted to the publisher at the end of 1857. Masahiro Abe, who had skillfully guided Japan through its greatest challenge of the 19th century, died while still in his 30s, a few months before Perry completed the manuscript. On March 4, 1858, shortly before his 64th birthday, Matthew Perry died at home, of rheumatism and heart failure. His cortege was led down Fifth Avenue by the men with whom he had sailed to Japan—the men, that is to say, with whom he had changed history.

Chinese Burns
Britain in China 1842–1900

Robert Bickers shows how the history of British and European imperialism in China helps explain the ferocious Boxer War of 1900.

THE BOXER RISING began in the obscurity of the north-west regions of China's Shandong province in 1899. It finished as an international crisis. The Chinese siege of the foreign legations in the capital city Beijing from June 20th to August 14th, 1900, gripped the world's press. It fed and still feeds a steady stream of memoir and narrative to willing publishers.

The 'Boxer' became an international figure. But the episode began in 1899 when young Shandong farm boys, made idle as drought followed flooding, started practising 'spirit boxing', a martial art which was acquiring new features including individual 'spirit possession' and invulnerability rituals. They then set out to right a world gone wrong. Boxer beliefs, circulated through placards and pamphlets and rehearsed in doggerel and rumour, restated common prejudices and exacerbated long-standing rural tensions by scapegoating Chinese Christian converts and their foreign missionary mentors. They believed that church spires pierced the sky and prevented the rains and that the withdrawal of converts from communal ritual life unbalanced the world. Exterminating the foreign would surely bring the rain and also save their Qing rulers from foreign aggression.

The rains came in early July, but by August 14th, 1900, British and other armed forces had also arrived and were camped in the ruins of Beijing, having

lifted the fifty-five-day siege of the legations and of the city's Roman Catholic Northern Cathedral (the Beitang). The port city of Tianjin, gateway to the capital, was levelled after its own siege. Numerous small towns and villages on the north China plain had seen vicious destructive warfare, and foreign troops launched raids to 'punish' residents living in the sites of alleged Boxer activity deep into 1901. Russian troops would not be evacuated from Manchuria until forced out in a Russo-Japanese war fought mostly on Chinese territory. The Qing court—which had taken the Boxers as allies and declared war on imperialism on June 21st, 1900—fled to China's north-west city of Xian, where it remained until October 1901. At least 220 foreign missionaries were dead, some executed at the order of Qing officials, while hundreds of foreign soldiers and probably tens of thousands of Chinese Christians, soldiers and civilians were killed in battle or cold blood, or died of disease or starvation as the conflict disordered north China. 'Invulnerable' Boxers had been cut down by foreign soldiers (who would not spare any captives) and by Qing troops angry at the impotence of Boxer magic or cynically using them as cannon fodder. The September 1901 Boxer Protocol imposed a huge indemnity on the Qing state and established permanent foreign garrisons in the capital to guard a legation district that was removed from Chi-

nese control and turned into an internationalised enclave.

Popular xenophobia and elite opportunism have often been blamed for the outbreak of what even one sympathetic foreign observer, the Inspector-General of China's Maritime Customs Service, Ulsterman Sir Robert Hart, called 'midsummer madness'. But there was much method and deliberation in such elite and mass 'madness', and while attention in recent years has focused on understanding the anthropology of the Boxer movement and its roots in Shandong popular culture, research is in progress on the rational deliberations which led a powerful coalition at the Qing court to align itself with a mass movement in a bid to be rid of the foreign peril. It is as well, then, to focus on the history of foreign intrusions which fed Chinese worries. After all, British forces had camped out at Beijing before, in 1860, and had first seen Tianjin from their warships in 1840. Popular and elite resistance had cost Britons dearly at times, but British power had always won out. The use of armed force in China was wearisomely familiar to British diplomats, but its origins lay not in any lack of formal relations between the Qing empire and the British state, but in fact from the very intimacy of the relationship.

That intimacy is easily forgotten. The handover of the former British Crown Colony of Hong Kong to the People's

The Shanghai *bund* (waterfront) in the 1850s, dominated by Western-style buildings. By an unknown artist of the Chinese school.

Republic of China in 1997 was accompanied on the Chinese side by an unprecedented barrage of noisy propaganda that stressed the place of Hong Kong in the imperialist assault on China after 1840. Where British observers stressed the triumphs of the Hong Kong economy and its legislative and legal foundations as legacies of British rule, the Chinese debate mostly emphasised the illegality of the seizure in the first place, rooted as it was in the 'unequal' 1842 Treaty of Nanjing that ended the First Opium War. There was little common ground. British memories of colonialism tend to be short and roseate, and many Britons were surprised that memories of the nineteenth century were alive and well in China in 1997. The importance for modern Chinese nationalism and the national psyche of what is construed in China as 'national humiliation' is indeed singular. The seizure of the obscure island of Hong Kong was one such humiliation, the occupation of Beijing in 1900 was another.

Hong Kong was just one part of a network of leased territories, British concessions and settlements and international settlements in China. British gunboats patrolled Chinese rivers as part of the Royal Navy's China Station (established in 1844). British steamship companies ran coastal and river services while trading firms operated national business networks. Efficient conditions for foreign trade were guaranteed, as

foreign observers saw it, by the creation after 1858 of a foreign-run Maritime Customs Service. Sir Robert Hart was a servant of the Chinese state, but his ten-

---

Shanghai developed a distinctively militaristic settler culture, which was fiercely protective of its independence.

---

ure of the Inspector-Generalship was rightly seen as an indicator of British control. Missionary organisations made opportunistic use of treaty clauses to set up stations in the Chinese interior and proselytise through a range of evangelical, educational and medical initiatives. Underpinning this British presence was the principle of extraterritoriality, by which British subjects in China came under the jurisdiction of their own consular representatives rather than Chinese law. The system was open to abuse and was extended in practice to include British-owned property and even British goods in the hands of Chinese agents.

By 1900 British interests still formed the largest sector of the overall foreign presence, but the treaty port world was

international, and most favoured nation clauses were granted to all who had signed treaties with China. So when farmers in Shandong started to practise Boxer rituals and then to attack Christian converts, they were in part reacting to the growth in China over the sixty years since the Nanjing treaty of this network of concessions and settlements, as well as to local manifestations of the foreign presence. The direct impact on small rural communities might be minimal but the claustrophobia and fear this foreign web caused was quickly communicated throughout the country to all levels of society.

The foreign impact was most visible and potent in the coastal cities. Although the British Minister was based in Beijing, and Hong Kong was formally incorporated into the British empire, the capital city of the British presence in China was Shanghai. By 1900 2,691 Britons (half of those resident in China outside Hong Kong) lived in the city's British-dominated International Settlement, which formed one of its three administrative units, the others being a French concession and the Chinese-administered city and suburbs. The Shanghai Municipal Council, which administered and policed the settlement, was staffed mostly by Britons and answered to nine representatives (seven Britons, one American and one German) elected by the foreign ratepayers. In 1900 the council was chaired by Edbert

Ansgar Hewett (P & O), and contained representatives of such China interests as Jardine Mathesons, E.D. Sassoon and the Chartered Bank, and local British settler interests including the waterworks and a dockyard firm. A Chinese population of 352,000 (out of about 900,000 in the city as a whole) effectively lived under foreign rule. In 1899 the council had extended its territory from 2.75 to 8.35 square miles, bringing more Chinese residents into the settlement, and some hothead local lobbyists wanted to see further extensions, preferably in the context of a British-dominated Yangzi protectorate.

In the International Settlement British residents mixed the pan-imperial pomp of Britain's eastern empire (Sikh policemen, colonial architecture) with institutions of local administration imported directly from the UK. Like colonial communities elsewhere they laid out a *bund* (a raised riverside embankment), built clubs, schools, hospitals and a cathedral (Holy Trinity), marked out race tracks, patronised theatres, joined Masonic lodges, walked in their public gardens and listened to the municipal band. The city had the headquarters of the China Inland Mission, as well as leading commercial firms and the Hong Kong and Shanghai Bank. It had its newspapers (the *North China Herald*, founded 1850), a library, commercial publishers such as Kelly and Walsh, cultural societies and sports clubs. In its learned societies there were discussions and debates on Chinese history and culture, while for those less academically-minded the Amoy Road gaol (built in 'solid lasting British style') could hold 140 prisoners. There were foreign department stores (Lane, Crawford and co., Hall & Holtz), watchmakers, restaurants, dairies and a full range of service industries (law, insurance). Shanghailanders organised a Shanghai Volunteer Corps, a local militia charged with the task of protecting the settlement if need be until British forces could be landed from naval vessels or dispatched from Hong Kong. They were inspected annually by a representative of the commanding officer of British forces in China and Hong Kong, who found them in April 1900 to be 'a fine body of citi-

zen soldiers in whose hands the great mercantile interests of Shanghai are in good keeping'. A distinctive settler culture, typical of that created by overseas Britons, developed—militaristic and fiercely protective of its independence.

As the population figures suggested, however, Shanghai remained a Chinese city. On the surface there was much that was European, especially the buildings reflecting the variegated nature of the foreign community, but appearances were deceptive. The International Settlement was built on Chinese labour, expertise and capital. Shanghai was a lively and important centre of Chinese cultural and commercial innovation. Foreign trading firms sought access to supplies and markets by establishing alliances with Chinese businessmen. Other foreign entrepreneurs—such as Briton Ernest Major, who founded Shanghai's first Chinese newspaper the *Shenbao* (1872) and the illustrated magazine the *Dianshizhai huabao* (1884)—created and fed new Chinese markets. Real estate firms made fortunes from Chinese residents or for Chinese investors. Foreign companies sought capital as well as market expertise and raised finance through share issues. It gets difficult in fact to distinguish between British and Chinese interests. Yet such intimacies often co-existed with informal social segregation and, quite frequently, there was an absence of meaningful communication between Chinese and Briton. Meanwhile the British-dominated authorities discriminated against its Chinese residents by denying them access to municipal parks and gardens, and by refusing them the right to vote or stand for election to the council. The International Settlement prided itself on being a 'model settlement', and Chinese observers looked to it for demonstrations of the practices of Western municipal administration, but the relationship between the foreign and the Chinese was uneasy. 1900 passed off peacefully in Shanghai, but local tensions over the settlement erupted into violence in 1905.

Shanghai's lobbyists talked loosely about their ambitions for greater autonomy, and their actions and words rightly worried Chinese observers. But the for-

eign danger was not confined to the coastal cities. Mission societies were active in treaty ports such as Shanghai, but their chosen field was rural China, and the impact of the missionary sector of the British presence was felt most strongly there. The modern mission presence in the country dated back to September 1807 when the Protestant missionary Robert Morrison arrived in Canton. His twenty-seven years in China produced a path-breaking Chinese-English dictionary but no more than a dozen converts. Yet the treaty of Nanjing facilitated the extension of Protestant and Catholic activities. Missionaries set up operations (including churches, schools and printing presses) in the newly opened treaty ports. The Qing state was forced to accept toleration of Christianity in 1858, while under a clause in the 1860 Sino-French treaty missionaries acquired the right to reside in the interior and purchase land and buildings. By the end of the century there were around 530,000 Catholic and some 80,000 Protestant converts. These numbers were insignificant in relation to the population of the Qing empire, but the impact was intense.

In the twenty years before 1900 Protestant missionary activity greatly intensified as 272 new centres were opened, while the number of stations rose from 132 to 498. Few parts of China were without some form of mission presence, or without some form of resistance, sometimes bloody, to that presence. Reports of 'mission cases' bedevilled smooth diplomatic relations. In the most spectacular incident—the Tianjin massacre of 1870—ten French nuns, one priest, the French consul, his deputy and sundry other French and Chinese unfortunates were killed in an incident related to local rumours about child kidnapping and the removal of eyes by the nuns at a Catholic orphanage. British and French churches were destroyed and gunboats quickly despatched. War with France was feared, and the Qing court was soon riven by divisions over how to deal with the incident, which was eventually settled by a mission of apology to France. Most incidents were smaller in scale and in implications, and the majority involved tensions between

Rapid response force: the Royal Marines Light Infantry monument in the Mall, London, includes a bas-relief of the siege of Tianjin.

converts and their local communities. In fairness, it should be said that the mission record was hardly uniformly negative, and Chinese converts were not all 'rice-Christians' seeking economic or other benefit from their relations with Westerners. Most missionaries did not see themselves as agents of broader British interests in China; but it was impossible to disentangle their activities and impact from that of the broader British and foreign presence.

The British establishment in China, then, was multifaceted and divided. It included official representatives in the consular service and armed forces, missionaries and the traders, bankers and landlords who filled the ranks of the Shanghai oligarchs, together with their servants of empire: shop clerks, engineers and police constables. Baghdadi Jews from India, overseas Chinese from the Straits Settlements, Sikh policemen and Eurasians from Hong Kong all lived and worked under British protection in China. There was a confident sub-imperialism, articulated and served by such aggressive all-rounders as J.O.P. Bland (1863–1945), who worked in the Customs, for settler imperialism through the Shanghai Municipal Council, and later for finance imperialism through the British and Chinese Corporation. Bland also worked from 1896 to 1910 as a

contributor to *The Times*, and as a freelance author and commentator thereafter. He lobbied for a British 'forward policy' on the Yangzi in the 1890s, noting the movements and gains of Britain's European rivals, but was on leave during much of the Boxer crisis: otherwise his shrill voice might have been heard arguing for further settlement extension in Shanghai, bent as he ever was on 'stratagems and spoils for the glory of the Raj'. There was also fear and uncertainty about the British position of course, but in the first fifty years of the

British presence in China there seemed little limit to potential spoils for such Shanghai adventurers.

These British certainties as well as the nineteenth-century treaty settlement were destabilised by the entry of aggressive new actors onto the scene in the 1890s: firstly Japan, and then Russia and Germany. In the aftermath of the 1894–95 Sino-Japanese war, a punitive indemnity imposed on China set off a scramble among European loan consortia to lend China the funds it needed. The lobbying support of national governments was earnestly sought, and to British surprise a Franco-Russian group was awarded the first such loan in 1895, although an Anglo-German group at least secured the second. Such loans threatened the British status quo. Competition intensified in late 1897. On November 1st, two German Catholic missionaries were hacked to death by Chinese assailants in an incident rooted in local ill-feeling towards the mission presence in that part of Shandong. The Kaiser happily seized this opportunity to order German warships to occupy the port of Jiaozhou. A Sino-German treaty of March 6th, 1898, confirmed the seizure and granted preferential rights in Shandong to Germany. German expansion thereafter was effectively stymied by the local Chinese authorities, but with the German navy-administered colony of 'Kiautschou' (Jiaozhou) another slice of the Chinese melon had been

Bloodied but unbowed: part of the British legation building in Beijing in 1900. The invocation of Kipling remained for almost fifty years.

Chinese intellectuals in 1900 feared that the hour of national extinction had arrived.

taken. Before too long Russia had seized Dalian (Port Arthur), and Britain the port of Weihaiwei, which was ruled as a leased territory until 1930. These moves also accelerated the feeding frenzy for railway and other concessions. Chinese intellectuals feared that the hour of national extinction had arrived.

This was the situation into which the Boxers emerged. It explains the vacillations and hesitancies of the official Qing response—and the ultimate decision of the court to try to use the opportunity presented by the popular rural movement to strike back at foreign aggression. But it also explains why British military personnel were already on the spot, why they had few qualms about storming and seizing the Dagu (Taku) forts which protected the route to the capital, and why Britain's Admiral Seymour launched his expedition to relieve the legations on June 10th, thereby effectively invading China's sovereign territory and giving the Qing a perfectly legitimate *casus belli*. Seymour provided the immediate reason for the formal Boxer war, but the treaty system itself and the pressures exerted by Shanghai settlers and foreign diplomats alike had served to raise tensions. Regardless of the established practice of the Qing state and its predecessors of making foreigners administer them-

selves, it is impossible to argue that the establishment of foreign-controlled enclaves on Chinese soil was anything but derogatory to its sovereignty and increasingly to its dignity. The men and boys from Shandong who targeted the foreign legations certainly did not have the treaty establishment in mind, but the overall impact of such encroachments, and latterly the heightened activities of concession hunters and diplomats, was profoundly unsettling for the local and national Chinese elites who took the Boxers as allies.

The robustness of the identities of these British communities was underlined by the ways in which the Boxer events became integral parts of the communal myths they lived by until their demise after the Second World War. 1900 seemed to give the China-British an imperial legitimacy, and it was taken as their own equivalent of the 1857 Sepoy mutiny. One telling event took place on June 17th, 1931, when a memorial service was held at the Canton Road cemetery in Tianjin. Military officials, consular representatives, military detachments and a band gathered together with other foreign residents in the city for a ceremony: the playing of Chopin's *'Marche Funèbre'* was followed by the recital of a 'Memorial Prayer', the singing of Rudyard Kipling's poem 'Lest We Forget' and the decoration of gravestones with potted flowers by Boy Scouts and Girl Guides. What was not being forgotten was the siege of the Tianjin foreign concessions by Boxer forces and regular Chinese troops between June 17th and July 13th, 1900. This act of communal remembrance was in itself hardly striking or unusual, but noting it reminds us that British relations with China were more than ab-

stract or confined merely to diplomatic exchanges.

In Beijing, British diplomats maintained one bullet-riddled wall in the legation, on which someone had daubed that ubiquitous injunction 'Lest We Forget' as a physical memorial of the siege. The motto was carefully tended and periodically repainted until, in the interests of diplomacy, it was removed in 1947. At least one public British memorial remains. Towards the Admiralty arch end of the Mall in London is a statue dedicated to Royal Marines Light Infantry casualties in South Africa and China. On the sides are bas-reliefs of fighting during the siege of Tianjin. Like many such British memorials it is submerged into the London background. We are perhaps more conscious of the empty plinth in Trafalgar Square than of the mute mementoes that surround us and remind us of the colonial centuries. In China the emphasis lies squarely with remembrance, in Britain with forgetting.

FOR FURTHER READING:

Robert Bickers, *Britain in China: Community, Culture and Colonialism, 1900–49* (Manchester University Press, 1999); Sabine Dabringhaus, 'An Army on Vacation? The German War in China, 1900–1901', in Manfred F. Boemeke, Roger Chickering and Stig Förster (eds), *Anticipating Total War: The German and American Experiences, 1871–1914* (Cambridge University Press, 1999); Jürgen Osterhammel, 'Britain and China 1842–1914' in Andrew Porter (ed), *The Oxford History of the British Empire, Volume III: The Nineteenth Century* (Oxford University Press, 1999); Frances Wood, *No Dogs and Not Many Chinese: Treaty Port Life in China, 1843–1943* (John Murray, 1998); Peter Fleming, The Siege at Peking (Rupert Hart-Davis, 1959).

Robert Bickers is Lecturer in History at the University of Bristol.

The Zulus and the Boer War

Jabulani Maphalala recalls the calamitous effects of a white man's war on the Zulu people caught between them.

The ANGLO-BOER WAR is often described as 'a domestic quarrel of the white people', as the two independent Boer republics (the South African Republic or Transvaal and the Orange Free State Republic) in the north fought against Great Britain and its two colonies (the Cape Colony and Natal) in the south of what in 1910 became known as South Africa. The African people, including the Zulu people, had long been subjugated. They had no right to vote, and resided in the 'native reserves', on farms of the white people and on Crown land in Natal. Their involvement in the hostilities was not of their own choosing.

In December 1838 Boer Voortrekkers, or emigrants from the Cape Colony, had defeated the Zulu King Dingane at Ncome or Blood River, and established the Republic of Natalia, with Pietermaritzburg as its capital. They enslaved the Zulu people, used their children as slaves on the farms and forcibly evicted hundreds of Zulus from arable land. The British government was concerned about possible disturbance of the peace in the eastern frontier of the Cape Colony caused by fleeing Zulu people, and in May 1842 British forces defeated the Boers at the Battle of Khangela (Congella). The Boers then went across the Khahlamba (Drakensberg) mountains and the Republic of Natalia became the British colony of Natal in 1843, with its boundaries as the Thukela river in the north, the Indian Ocean in the east, the Mthavuna river in the south and the Khahlamba Mountains in the west. North of the Thukela river there was a sovereign Zulu state under King Mpande (r.1840–72) and later Cetshwayo (r.1873–79).

The British handled the land issue in Natal less brutally than the Boers had done. In 1846 the Land Boundary Commission was instituted by Governor West. This recommended the establishment of 'native reserves' for the Zulu people under *amakhosi* (chiefs or traditional leaders), while the rest of the land was mainly set aside for the white colonists. In the reserves the Zulu governance was left intact. *Amakhosi* were even allowed to try civil and criminal cases. But the reports of these cases had to be presented to the magistrates and appeals against *amakhosi* judgements were permitted. The native reserves therefore combined the traditional Zulu system of governance with the general British law affecting the whole colony.

The traditional authority of the Zulu king was incorporated into a chain of authority that reached from the British governor, through the minister for native affairs, secretary and under-secretary for native affairs and magistrates to the *amakhosi*, the *izinduna* (headmen) and *imindeni* (extended families). The boers had introduced no equivalent structures, and were only greedy for arable land and livestock. The British also undertook missionary activities which resulted in the establishment of mission stations at Groutville (Stanger), Driefontein (Ladysmith), Edendale (Pietermaritzburg) and several other places in the colony. Mission schools were made available for Christian Zulus. It can therefore fairly be argued, that at least in terms of 'Western civilisation', the Zulu people in the Natal colony were ahead of their compatriots under the independent kings Mpande and Cetshwayo.

Following the annexation of Transvaal by the British in 1877, an increase in tension between the British, the Boers and Zulus led to the Anglo-Zulu War. Despite the dramatic Zulu victory at Isandhlwana, the British defeated their army at Ulundi and Cetshwayo was captured. On September 1st, 1879, the Zulu leaders surrendered. The Zulu people were placed in reserves and most arable land was given to the white people. Adopting a classic policy of divide-and-rule, the British established thirteen subkingdoms; Cetshwayo himself was banished. The Zulu people lost their unifying figure and were divided into warring factions, and from 1880 to 1889 the Zulu people north of the Thukela river were engaged in a civil war. Cetshwayo, having visited Britain and met Queen Victoria the previous year, was allowed to return in January 1883, but was given only a small portion of his old kingdom; the largest part was controlled by Prince Zibhebhu, leader of the Mandlakazi. Zibhebhu, whom the British supported, burned Cetshwayo's palace in July 1883, inflicting wounds on the King, who died a few months later.

In 1884, however, a group of about 200 Boers under Lucas Meyer supported the uSuthu faction under King

---

Hundreds of Zulus were forcibly evacuated from their land by the Boers.

Dinuzulu; this defeated Zibhebhu at the Battle of eTshaneni, north of the Mkhuze river, on June 5th, 1884. The Boers used this as an excuse to take most of the best Zulu grazing land of eBaqulusini and establish the so-called New Republic. They produced a 'treaty', signed by Dinuzulu, ceding the territory. This action was condemned by the British government, which knew from its land commission of November 1878 regarding the disputed Zulu-Boer territory west of Mzinyathi (Buffalo) and Ncome (Blood) rivers, that the Zulu king was only the custodian of the land and had no right in Zulu law to cede it. But the British did not immediately intervene, as they saw the Boer-Zulu land issue as one of Christianity against paganism. Instead, on October 22nd, 1886, they recognised the New Republic, and the following year Britain also annexed the Zulu territory north of the Thukela river, establishing magistracies for its administration.

Following the annexation of what remained of the Zulu territory north of the Thukela river and the defeat of the Zulu uprising led by Dinuzulu in June 1888, Dinuzulu was tried for high treason in eShowe and found guilty. In 1890 he was banished to St Helena by the British, together with his uncles, princes Ndabuko and Shingana. In January 1898 Dinuzulu was released from exile but demoted to local government *induna* with a small reserve of his own in the Ndwandwe magisterial division. His status was similar to that of all Zulu *amakhosi* in the areas under British rule; he was allowed to try civil and criminal cases but had to present his reports to white magistrates.

In the New Republic, though, hundreds of Zulus were forcibly evicted from their land by the Boers who, unlike the British, did not first establish land commissions to investigate the issues. Thus, six *amakhosi* who remained in the

New Republic lived on Boer farms and had no rights to treat civil and criminal cases. The Zulu people worked on the farms like slaves (according to Colonel G. A. Mills's Commission of October–December 1902). Tension between the Zulu people and the Boers in the New Republic was very high by the outbreak of the Anglo-Boer War in 1899. The attitude of the British government to Zulu involvement in the coming conflict was clear as early as September 1899. Mr C. Bird, principal under-secretary for native affairs, made it known that, if war broke out between the British and the Boer republics, the British government wished the Zulu people to remain neutral. They were to defend themselves only if attacked by the Boers.

Shortly after the outbreak of hostilities, the Boers sent Coenraad Meyer to Dinuzulu's oSuthu *umuzi waseBukhosini* (palace), requesting the Zulu people to be passive in the war and let the white people fight each other. Thus both white cultural groups agreed that the Zulu people should be neutral. They also agreed, however, that the Zulu people could be used as non-combatants, as scouts, drivers of wagons and leaders of teams of oxen. The numbers involved in the war are not known, but casualties were certainly far higher than the figure of thirty Zulu dead officially given to Dinuzulu.

Many *amakhosi* from the New Republic fled to Dinuzulu's palace in oSuthu at the outbreak of war, returning only in March 1902. The British military authorities now wanted to restore Dinuzulu to the status he had enjoyed as Zulu king, seeing this as a way of extending his activities beyond his small uSuthu reserve and helping to bring the war to a speedy end. This was not done, however, until after March 1901 when British military law was imposed on the region and the Zulu people were armed by the British.

In June 1900 the British forces occupied the town of Vryheid, capital of the New Republic. A.J. Shepstone, patriotic son of Sir Theophilus Shepstone, the former secretary for native affairs in Natal, was shortly afterwards stationed there, where he worked closely with J. Roberts, the assistant British military intelligence officer. Shepstone and Roberts carefully selected Zulu scouts among the aBaqulusi people and armed them with guns. The Zulu scouts had strict orders to report only to Shepstone and Roberts. Subsequently the Zulu scouts became an effective component in the British war machine. In confrontation with Boer fighters in Schurweberg, near Vryheid, they injured two Boers and brought them back as prisoners of war. Thus, even before March 1901 when the British declared martial law in the region, Zulu scouts were already armed with guns and militarily engaging Boer fighters.

In fact, the British had broken the agreement concerning Zulu neutrality before the occupation of Vryheid. *Funamalungelo,* the first Zulu political organisation, had been set up demanding the franchise and equal political rights with white people in the colony. Though Christian, it seems to have been behind an incident at Krantzkloof near Pinetown, south of the Thukela river in February 1900, in which Zulus, who were already in possession of British arms, dug trenches and fired on British troops. Then, when the Boer troops captured the Nquthu district in January 1900, they captured armed Zulu policemen who had been guarding the Nquthu magistracy. Boer president Paul Kruger ordered their release, and he sent three of them to King Dinuzulu with a message that if the Boers had confiscated Zulu property they would always return it.

Following these incidents, Governor H.E. McCallum asked the Natal government to consider arming the Zulu people north of the Thukela river as active combatants under 'white officers'. He was concerned that Kruger's propaganda message would be detrimental to the British military position. He pointed out that the fact the Zulu people had fired on British troops at Krantzkloof showed that they needed military control, and that the abaThembu (who were related to the Zulu people) had been armed as active combatants in the Transkei since January 1900 or earlier, and had succeeded in warding off a Boer invasion of that territory.

The Natal government turned down this request, arguing initially that Zulu methods of warfare since the days of King Shaka in the 1820s had been savage, and that women and children were always killed. This was inaccurate since warriors who surrendered were spared in Zulu warfare and the term *Malushu!* means 'I surrender!' The elders, women and children were never killed, as is illustrated in Shaka's poem:

> The old women will remain in residential sites. The old men will remain in battle route

The Natal government feared that the arming of the Zulus would have dangerous consequences for the whites after the Boers were defeated, since the Zulu people would no longer fear British might. They also argued that the Zulu people south of the Thukela river were more 'civilised' and 'Christian' and could understand methods of civilised warfare. These Zulu, the Natal government reiterated, would feel offended by being left out when their 'uncivilised' compatriots north of the Thukela were armed. There was some truth in this since 'Zulu Christians' had been used against iNkosi (traditional leader) Langalibalele in 1873 and against Cetshwayo in January 1879. The Natal government was also convinced that the arming of Zulu people as active combatants would be a deviation from the agreement with the Boers before the outbreak of the war.

Towards the end of 1900 the Boer troops launched their campaign of guerrilla warfare. The British forces found it difficult to pin them down, especially in the Vryheid district, which was regarded as the best grazing land in KwaZulu-Natal. To bring the war to a speedy end the British military authorities declared martial law north of the Thukela river on March 25th, 1901. All the Zulu people residing in the magisterial districts adjoining the Vryheid district—Nquthu, Nkandla, Mthonjaneni, Mahlabathini, Ndwandwe, Bombo and Ngwavuma—were ordered to arm under the command of Col. H.B. Bottomley of the Imperial White Horse, and his 'white officers'. The Zulu warriors were to go across the Zulu-Vryheid border, raid Boer stock, force the Boers to surrender their arms and drive the livestock to the Zulu side of the border. They were promised ten per cent of the stock looted; the British government was to get twenty-five per cent of the stock while the remaining sixty-five per cent was to be taken by Bottomley and his agents. These last were described by Charles Saunders, chief magistrate and civil commissioner, as the 'dregs of humanity': some were ex-convicts.

For the military operation to succeed, the Zulu people had to be provided with guns and ammunition. Saunders argued that it would be unfair to expect the brave Zulu fighters to face Boer marksmen, while armed only with *assegai* spears and shields. Guns and ammunition were therefore supplied. A fortress was built about a kilometre from oSuthu. It served as a military storage depot and armoury for King Dinuzulu, and was guarded by British troops.

Dinuzulu was also issued with 3,000 rifles and revolver ammunition. The British elevated his status to that of a king for the sake of defeating their foe. He was advised to create a small western-trained military group of Zulu people known as *iNkomendala.* The members of this group were selected from among trusted Zulu princes and carefully chosen Zulu warriors.

A Zulu force of 6,000 men was assembled by Dinuzulu and Bottomley at oSuthu on April 4th. It was ordered to advance against the Boers who had fled with their cattle to the Dleke hill about forty kilometers from Nongoma magistracy northwards towards the Nkunzana river. The military engagement lasted for a week, April 4th–9th, and ended in a Boer defeat. Thousands of cattle, guns and ammunition left on the wagons by the fleeing Boers were captured.

The arming of the Zulu people was called off on June 2nd, 1901. But Dinuzulu was ordered to keep 3,000 armed Zulu men oSuthu in case the military situation changed. Thus, on March 8th, 1902, the King was again ordered to send 250 armed men into the Vryheid district to assist General Bruce Hamilton remove Boer cattle from the bush. By the time the Zulu army reached Vryheid on March 22nd, 1902, its numbers had increased to 1,000 men. A

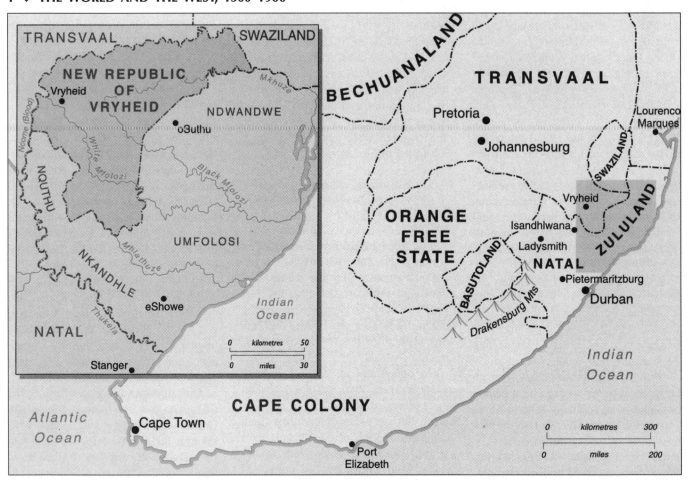

The Zulu territory north of the Thukela formed a buffer zone between the competing white communities of Transvaal and Natal, and was inevitably drawn into the conflict between them.

force of aBaqulusi men under Sikhobobo Sibiya took up arms and joined the British against the Boers. The three-pronged attack resulted in hundreds of head of cattle collected and some Boers surrendering their arms.

Under South African Republic (Transvaal) law, any Zulus who joined the British were liable to have their property confiscated and their families sent to the British lines. There was, however, no mention in this law about the burning of *imizi* (thatched huts). On April 23rd, 1902, in exasperation at the prospect of losing the war and before his departure for the peace negotiations at Vereeniging, the Boer General Louis Botha ordered General M.W. Myburgh and C.F. Meyer to burn down all the huts of the aBaqulusi people under Sikhobobo and Sidunge, confiscate their cattle and send women and children to Vryheid. Thus at midnight on May 1st, 1902, Zulu women and children were

dragged out of their huts to witness them razed to the ground. Their grain was burnt or confiscated and their livestock driven to Mthashan (Holkrantz).

When the half-naked women and children arrived in Vryheid, where Sikhobobo and the aBaqulusi men were accommodated at the Station Building, Sikhobobo's men vowed to teach the Boers a lesson. Shepstone and General Bruce Hamilton did not prevent Sikhobobo from recapturing his stock from Mthashana. Then on May 6th, 1902, a pitched battle took place between the Boers and Sikhobobo's men, which resulted in fifty-six Boers killed and three taken prisoner. On the Zulu side, fifty-two men died while forty-eight were wounded.

After the war ended, the British government's primary concern was reconciliation with the Boers. This is understandable in cultural terms. The New Republic was renamed 'New Ter-

ritories, Vryheid District', and so on. An effort was made to help the Boers rebuild their farms, while the Zulu people—who had suffered untold misery in that district—were told to work on the farms as they had been doing, and were given no financial assistance to rebuild their homes. The Boers objected to working with *amakhosi* who had taken up arms against them on the British side. The British therefore demoted the most militant *amakhosi* (for example Sikhobobo and Mabhekeshiya) and replaced them with more acceptable ones. There was no compensation for the aBaqulusi *imizi* which had been burned by the Boers.

King Dinuzulu was given a hundred head of cattle as a reward for having sent 250 armed men to assist General Bruce Hamilton. All guns and ammunition supplied to him were seized. He was prohibited from visiting the Vryheid district and restricted to his uSuthu district and subjected to the same demotion as the local government induna. From 1903 onwards rumours were circulated by government agents that he had not surrendered all the guns and that he wanted to take up arms against the Natal government. This, combined with the Bhambatha or Poll Tax uprising in 1906, resulted in his arrest in December 1907. Though released after the formation of the Union of South Africa in 1910, he was stigmatised as a troublemaker by the whites and he died in banishment on the Farm Uitkyk on October 18th, 1913. No other *amakhosi* in Natal was ever compensated, despite having been promised ten per cent of the livestock that their subjects looted under the orders of Colonel Bottomley. The Zulu Christians also lost out, because they were refused silver medals for their military sacrifices. The fort built by the British near oSuthu as Dinuzulu's armoury remained until April 1910, when it was finally demolished by the Natal government.

As a result of these grievances, when the Poll Tax uprising occurred in 1906 most Zulu people were determined not to be conciliatory to the English-speaking community, feeling they had been cheated.

The Zulu desire to see the Boers defeated was primarily motivated by resentment at their cruel treatment at the hands of the Boers and by hopes for the return of their ancestral land under Boer occupation. Yet the *amakhosi* who fought on the British side in the Vryheid district were repaid by betrayal. Reconciliation between the Boers and British was speeded up, but for the Zulu people and their king, Dinuzulu, the oppressive *status quo ante* was reestablished. Ultimately, the Zulu people were in a worse position than before the outbreak of the war.

FOR FURTHER READING

J F Maurice, *History of the War in S.A. 1899–1902.* (London, 1906.); R. Kruger, *Goodbye Dolly Gray: The Story of the Boer War,* (London, 1960.); J. Selby, *The Boer War: A Story in Cowardice and Courage,* (London, 1969); L.S. Amery, *The Times History of the War in S.A.,* (Vols. 1–VIII, London, 1900–1909).

S. J. Maphalala is Professor in the Department of History, University of Zululand.

Unit Selections

Key Points to Consider

❖ What is a "feminist"? Does Mary Wollstonecraft fit the definition?

❖ Was George Mason a fool for not signing the Constitution? Explain.

❖ Why did the United States not just simply select George Washington as king and forget all the wrangling of the politicians?

❖ What is "free trade"? How does it contrast to mercantilism?

❖ Explain why the value of money is based upon what people believe it to be? Is this foolish? Would we not be better off to be paid in gold?

❖ What is so important about a dictionary? Is it not a conservative device to keep the language from changing?

 **Links**   **www.dushkin.com/online/**

These sites are annotated on pages 4 and 5.

The European voyages of exploration in the fifteenth and sixteenth centuries are representative of the spirit of adventure, curiosity, and greed that carried Western civilization to the ends of the earth. This unique character of the civilization was formed by many events, ideas, and characters. Adam Smith, for example, gave definition and analysis to the ongoing industrial revolution. Smith, the first great economist, argued that *laissez-faire* and the "invisible hand" of the marketplace would work to supply all the goods that people wanted. If left alone without governmental interference, manufacturers would produce what was

Das Leben Martin Luther's und die Helden der Reformation!

needed and in the correct amount—a case of supply and demand. His concepts of capitalism have been modified by subsequent conditions, such as social welfare and large multinational corporations, but capitalism was not destroyed by oppressed workers, as predicted by Karl Marx. It turned out to be a flexible economic system that at present has triumphed over the socialism of communism.

Still, the world has not turned to pure free trade as advocated by Smith. Jean-Baptiste Colbert, finance minister for Louis XIV, successfully brought wealth to France by policies of mercantilism, whereby France enjoyed a favorable balance of trade. Even today, countries like to protect their industries with tariffs and groups protest about free trade at the meetings of the World Trade Organization. The contrast of these economic theories is explored in "From Mercantilism to 'The Wealth of Nations.'" Mercantilism called for the accumulation of bullion—gold and silver—as the mark of a great nation. Our current ideas of wealth are not so simple today, and gold is not even used as a form of money. "As Good As Gold?" explores the evolution of our ideas about money. Increasingly, paychecks and bills are paid electronically, so that actually our money is in the form of an electric current.

One of the greatest ideological political struggles occurred at the end of the eighteenth century in a peripheral frontier nation: the United States. The victory over Britain unleashed a vigorous, capitalistic, argumentative people determined to make democracy function. Yet, it is a bit of a wonder that it worked at all, since the founders

were given to backstabbing and insult, as Jay Tolson points out in "Founding Rivalries." George Mason, who participated in the writing of the Constitution, broke his friendship with George Washington because the Constitution did not contain a bill of rights. He sacrificed his own public life by refusing to endorse the document. Shortly after the signing of the Constitution, politicians enacted a Bill of Rights as Mason had envisioned and those rights have been emblazoned as a political standard ever since that time for citizens and groups around the world.

Mary Wollstonecraft raised another standard of freedom in this same period. She thought that the female mind was as good as the male mind and that women should be treated in reasonable fashion. She did not deny the traditional roles of women, but she made a career of writing and lived an emancipated life at a time when most women were not free. She was the first feminist, but the struggle for equality has not yet ended. It is an ongoing battle around the world, including the West.

A much more quiet endeavor, but one also of importance for the intellectual world, was the compilation of the first Oxford English Dictionary. It provided not only the meanings of words but also their origins and early usage. The dictionary, with its subsequent editions, still stands as the preeminent authority for the English language that is now the *lingua franca* of the world. Strangely, one of the chief contributors of information was a madman living in an insane asylum, as explained in "The Strange Case of the Surgeon of Crowthorne."

The First Feminist

*In 1792 Mary Wollstonecraft wrote a book to prove that her sex
was as intelligent as the other: thus did feminism come into the world.
Right on, Ms. Mary!*

Shirley Tomkievicz

The first person—male or female—to speak at any length and to any effect about woman's rights was Mary Wollstonecraft. In 1792, when her *Vindication of the Rights of Woman* appeared, Mary was a beautiful spinster of thirty-three who had made a successful career for herself in the publishing world of London. This accomplishment was rare enough for a woman in that day. Her manifesto, at once impassioned and learned, was an achievement of real originality. The book electrified the reading public and made Mary famous. The core of its argument is simple: "I wish to see women neither heroines nor brutes; but reasonable creatures," Mary wrote. This ancestress of the Women's Liberation Movement did not demand day-care centers or an end to women's traditional role as wife and mother, nor did she call anyone a chauvinist pig. The happiest period of Mary's own life was when she was married and awaiting the birth of her second child. And the greatest delight she ever knew was in her first child, an illegitimate daughter. Mary's feminism may not appear today to be the hard-core revolutionary variety, but she did live, for a time, a scandalous and unconventional life—"emancipated," it is called by those who have never tried it. The essence of her thought, however,

is simply that a woman's mind is as good as a man's.

Not many intelligent men could be found to dispute this proposition today, at least not in mixed company. In Mary's time, to speak of *anybody's* rights, let alone woman's rights, was a radical act. In England, as in other nations, "rights" were an entity belonging to the government. The common run of mankind had little access to what we now call "human rights." As an example of British justice in the late eighteenth century, the law cited two hundred different capital crimes, among them shoplifting. An accused man was not entitled to counsel. A child could be tried and hanged as soon as an adult. The right to vote existed, certainly, but because of unjust apportionment, it had come to mean little. In the United States some of these abuses had been corrected—but the rights of man did not extend past the color bar and the masculine gender was intentional. In the land of Washington and Jefferson, as in the land of George III, human rights were a new idea and woman's rights were not even an issue.

In France, in 1792, a Revolution in the name of equality was in full course, and woman's rights had at least been alluded to. The Revolutionary government drew up plans for female education—to the age of eight. "The education of the

women should always be relative to the men," Rousseau had written in *Emile*. "To please, to be useful to us, to make us love and esteem them, to educate us when young, and take care of us when grown up, to advise, to console us, to render our lives easy and agreeable; these are the duties of women at all times, and what they should be taught in their infancy." And, less prettily, "Women have, or ought to have, but little liberty."

Rousseau would have found little cause for complaint in eighteenth-century England. An Englishwoman had almost the same civil status as an American slave. Thomas Hardy, a hundred years hence, was to base a novel on the idea of a man casually selling his wife and daughter at public auction. Obviously this was not a common occurrence, but neither is it wholly implausible. In 1792, and later, a woman could not own property, nor keep any earned wages. All that she possessed belonged to her husband. She could not divorce him, but he could divorce her and take her children. There was no law to say she could not grow up illiterate or be beaten every day.

Such was the legal and moral climate in which Mary Wollstonecraft lived. She was born in

London in the spring of 1759, the second child and first daughter of Edward Wollstonecraft, a prosperous weaver. Two more daughters and two more sons were eventually born into the family, making six children in all. Before they had all arrived, Mr. Wollstonecraft came into an inheritance and decided to move his family to the country and become a gentleman farmer. But this plan failed. His money dwindled, and he began drinking heavily. His wife turned into a terrified wraith whose only interest was her eldest son, Edward. Only he escaped the beatings and abuse that his father dealt out regularly to every other household member, from Mrs. Wollstonecraft to the family dog. As often happens in large and disordered families, the eldest sister had to assume the role of mother and scullery maid. Mary was a bright, strong child, determined not to be broken, and she undertook her task energetically, defying her father when he was violent and keeping her younger brothers and sisters in hand. Clearly, Mary held the household together, and in so doing forfeited her own childhood. This experience left her with an everlasting gloomy streak, and was a strong factor in making her a reformer.

At some point in Mary's childhood, another injustice was visited upon her, though so commonplace for the time that she can hardly have felt the sting. Her elder brother was sent away to be educated, and the younger children were left to learn their letters as best they could. The family now frequently changed lodgings, but from her ninth to her fifteenth year Mary went to a day school, where she had the only formal training of her life. Fortunately, this included French and composition, and somewhere Mary learned to read critically and widely. These skills, together with her curiosity and determination, were really all she needed. The *Vindication* is in some parts long-winded, ill-punctuated, and simply full of hot air, but it is the work of a well-informed mind.

Feminists—and Mary would gladly have claimed the title—inevitably, even deservedly, get bad notices. The term calls up an image of relentless battle-axes: "thin college ladies with eye-glasses, no-nonsense features, mouths thin as bologna slicers, a babe in one arm, a hatchet in the other, grey eyes bright with balefire," as Norman Mailer feelingly envisions his antagonists in the Women's Liberation Movement. He has conjured up all the horrid elements: the lips with a cutting edge, the baby immaculately conceived (one is forced to conclude), the lethal weapon tightly clutched, the desiccating college degree, the joylessness. Hanging miasmally over the tableau is the suspicion of a deformed sexuality. Are these girls man-haters, or worse? Mary Wollstonecraft, as the first of her line, has had each of these scarlet letters (except the B.A.) stitched upon her bosom. Yet she conformed very little to the hateful stereotype. In at least one respect, however, she would have chilled Mailer's bones. Having spent her childhood as an adult, Mary reached the age of nineteen in a state of complete joylessness. She was later to quit the role, but for now she wore the garb of a martyr.

Her early twenties were spent in this elderly frame of mind. First she went out as companion to an old lady living at Bath, and was released from this servitude only by a call to nurse the dying Mrs. Wollstonecraft. Then the family broke up entirely, though the younger sisters continued off and on to be dependent on Mary. The family of Mary's dearest friend, Fanny Blood, invited her to come and stay with them; the two girls made a small living doing sewing and handicrafts, and Mary dreamed of starting a primary school. Eventually, in a pleasant village called Newington Green, this plan materialized and prospered. But Fanny Blood in the meantime had married and moved to Lisbon. She wanted Mary to come and nurse her through the birth of her first child. Mary reached Lisbon just in time to see her friend die of childbed fever, and returned home just in time to find that her sisters, in whose care the flourishing little school had been left, had lost all but two pupils.

Mary made up her mind to die. "My constitution is impaired, I hope I shan't live long," she wrote to a friend in February, 1786. Under this almost habitual grief, however, Mary was gaining some new sense of herself. Newington Green, apart from offering her a brief success as a schoolmistress, had brought her some acquaintance in the world of letters, most important among them, Joseph Johnson, an intelligent and successful London publisher in search of new writers. Debt-ridden and penniless, Mary set aside her impaired constitution and wrote her first book, probably in the space of a week. Johnson bought it for ten guineas and published it. Called *Thoughts on the Education of Daughters,* it went unnoticed, and the ten guineas was soon spent. Mary had to find work. She accepted a position as governess in the house of Lord and Lady Kingsborough in the north of Ireland.

Mary's letters from Ireland to her sisters and to Joseph Johnson are so filled with Gothic gloom, so stained with tears, that one cannot keep from laughing at them. "I entered the great gates with the same kind of feeling I should have if I was going to the Bastille," she wrote upon entering Kingsborough Castle in the fall of 1786. Mary was now twenty-seven. Her most recent biographer, Margaret George, believes that Mary was not really suffering so much as she was having literary fantasies. In private she was furiously at work on a novel entitled, not very artfully, *Mary, A Fiction.* This is the story of a young lady of immense sensibilities who closely resembles Mary except that she has wealthy parents, a neglectful bridegroom, and an attractive lover. The title and fantasizing contents are precisely what a scribbler of thirteen might secretly concoct. Somehow Mary was embarking on her adolescence—with all its daydreams—fifteen years after the usual date. Mary's experience in Kingsborough Castle was a fruitful one, for all her complaints. In the summer of 1787 she lost her post as governess and set off for London with her novel. Not only did Johnson accept it for publication, he offered her a regular job as editor and translator and helped her find a place to live.

Thus, aged twenty-eight, Mary put aside her doleful persona as the martyred, set-upon elder sister. How different she is now, jauntily writing from

London to her sisters: "Mr. Johnson . . . assures me that if I exert my talents in writing I may support myself in a comfortable way. I am then going to be the first of a new genus. . . ." Now Mary discovered the sweetness of financial independence earned by interesting work. She had her own apartment. She was often invited to Mr. Johnson's dinner parties, usually as the only female guest among all the most interesting men in London: Joseph Priestley, Thomas Paine, Henry Fuseli, William Blake, Thomas Christie, William Godwin—all of them up-and-coming scientists or poets or painters or philosophers, bound together by left-wing political views. Moreover, Mary was successful in her own writing as well as in editorial work. Her *Original Stories for Children* went into three editions and was illustrated by Blake. Johnson and his friend Thomas Christie had started a magazine called the *Analytical Review,* to which Mary became a regular contributor.

But—lest anyone imagine an elegantly dressed Mary presiding flirtatiously at Johnson's dinner table—her social accomplishments were rather behind her professional ones. Johnson's circle looked upon her as one of the boys. "Wollstonecraft" is what William Godwin calls her in his diary. One of her later detractors reported that she was at this time a "philosophic sloven," in a dreadful old dress and beaver hat, "with her hair hanging lank about her shoulders." Mary had yet to arrive at her final incarnation, but the new identity was imminent, if achieved by an odd route. Edmund Burke had recently published his *Reflections on the Revolution in France,* and the book had enraged Mary. The statesman who so readily supported the quest for liberty in the American colonies had his doubts about events in France.

Mary's reply to Burke, *A Vindication of the Rights of Men,* astounded London, partly because she was hitherto unknown, partly because it was good. Mary proved to be an excellent polemicist, and she had written in anger. She accused Burke, the erstwhile champion of liberty, of being "the champion of property." "Man

preys on man," said she, "and you mourn for the idle tapestry that decorated a gothic pile and the dronish bell that summoned the fat priest to prayer." The book sold well. Mary moved into a better apartment and bought some pretty dresses—no farthingales, of course, but some of the revolutionary new "classical" gowns. She put her auburn hair up in a loose knot. Her days as a philosophic sloven were over.

Vindication of the Rights of Woman was her next work. In its current edition it runs to 250-odd pages; Mary wrote it in six weeks. *Vindication* is no prose masterpiece, but it has never failed to arouse its audience, in one way or another. Horace Walpole unintentionally set the style for the book's foes. Writing to his friend Hannah More in August, 1792, he referred to Thomas Paine and to Mary as "philosophizing serpents" and was "glad to hear you have not read the tract of the last mentioned writer. I would not look at it." Neither would many another of Mary's assailants, the most virulent of whom, Ferdinand Lundberg, surfaced at the late date of 1947 with a tract of his own, *Modern Woman, the Lost Sex.* Savagely misogynistic as it is, this book was hailed in its time as "the best book yet to be written about women." Lundberg calls Mary the Karl Marx of the feminist movement, and the *Vindication* a "fateful book," to which "the tenets of feminism, which have undergone no change to our day, may be traced." Very well, but then, recounting Mary's life with the maximum possible number of errors per line, he warns us that she was "an extreme neurotic of a compulsive type" who "wanted to turn on men and injure them." In one respect, at least, Mr. Lundberg hits the mark: he blames Mary for starting women in the pernicious habit of wanting an education. In the nineteenth century, he relates, English and American feminists were hard at work. "Following Mary Wollstonecraft's prescription, they made a considerable point about acquiring a higher education." This is precisely Mary's prescription, and the most dangerous idea in her fateful book.

"Men complain and with reason, of the follies and caprices of our Sex," she writes in Chapter 1. "Behold, I should

answer, the natural effect of ignorance." Women, she thinks, are usually so mindless as to be scarcely fit for their roles as wives and mothers. Nevertheless, she believes this state not to be part of the feminine nature, but the result of an equally mindless oppression, as demoralizing for men as for women. If a woman's basic mission is as a wife and mother, need she be an illiterate slave for this?

The heart of the work is Mary's attack on Rousseau. In *Emile* Rousseau had set forth some refreshing new ideas for the education of little boys. But women, he decreed, are tools for pleasure, creatures too base for moral or political or educational privilege. Mary recognized that this view was destined to shut half the human race out of all hope for political freedom. *Vindication* is a plea that the "rights of men" ought to mean the "rights of humanity." The human right that she held highest was the right to have a mind and think with it. Virginia Woolf, who lived through a time of feminist activity, thought that the *Vindication* was a work so true "as to seem to contain nothing new." Its originality, she wrote, rather too optimistically, had become a commonplace.

Vindication went quickly into a second edition. Mary's name was soon known all over Europe. But as she savored her fame—and she did savor it—she found that the edge was wearing off and that she was rather lonely. So far as anyone knows, Mary had reached this point in her life without ever having had a love affair. Johnson was the only man she was close to, and he was, as she wrote him, "A father, or a brother—you have been both to me." Mary was often now in the company of the Swiss painter Henry Fuseli, and suddenly she developed what she thought was a Platonic passion in his direction. He rebuffed her, and in the winter of 1792 she went to Paris, partly to escape her embarrassment but also because she wanted to observe the workings of the Revolution firsthand.

Soon after her arrival, as she collected notes for the history of the Revolution she hoped to write, Mary saw Louis XVI, "sitting in a hackney coach . . . going to meet death." Back in her room that evening, she wrote to Mr. Johnson of seeing "eyes glare through a glass door opposite my chair and bloody hands shook at me. . . . I am going to bed and for the first time in my life, I cannot put out the candle." As the weeks went on, Edmund Burke's implacable critic began to lose her faith in the brave new world. "The aristocracy of birth is levelled to the ground, only to make room for that of riches," she wrote. By February France and England were at war, and British subjects classified as enemy aliens.

Though many Englishmen were arrested, Mary and a large English colony stayed on. One day in spring, some friends presented her to an attractive American, newly arrived in Paris, Gilbert Imlay. Probably about four years Mary's senior, Imlay, a former officer in the Continental Army, was an explorer and adventurer. He came to France seeking to finance a scheme for seizing Spanish lands in the Mississippi valley. This "natural and unaffected creature," as Mary was later to describe him, was probably the social lion of the moment, for he was also the author of a best-selling novel called *The Emigrants,* a farfetched account of life and love in the American wilderness. He and Mary soon became lovers. They were a seemingly perfect pair. Imlay must have been pleased with his famous catch, and—dear, liberated girl that she was—Mary did not insist upon marriage. Rather the contrary. But fearing that she was in danger as an Englishwoman, he registered her at the American embassy as his wife.

Blood was literally running in the Paris streets now, so Mary settled down by herself in a cottage at Neuilly. Imlay spent his days in town, working out various plans. The Mississippi expedition came to nothing, and he decided to stay in France and go into the import-export business, part of his imports being gunpowder and other war goods run from Scandinavia through the English blockade. In the evenings he would ride out to the cottage. By now it was summer, and Mary, who spent the days writing, would often stroll up the road to meet him, carrying a basket of freshly gathered grapes.

A note she wrote Imlay that summer shows exactly what her feelings for him were: "You can scarcely imagine with what pleasure I anticipate the day when we are to begin almost to live together; and you would smile to hear how many plans of employment I have in my head, now that I am confident that my heart has found peace. . . ." Soon she was pregnant. She and Imlay moved into Paris. He promised to take her to America, where they would settle down on a farm and raise six children. But business called Imlay to Le Havre, and his stay lengthened ominously into weeks.

Imlay's letters to Mary have not survived, and without them it is hard to gauge what sort of man he was and what he really thought of his adoring mistress. Her biographers like to make him out a cad, a philistine, not half good enough for Mary. Perhaps; yet the two must have had something in common. His novel, unreadable though it is now, shows that he shared her political views, including her feminist ones. He may never have been serious about the farm in America, but he was a miserably long time deciding to leave Mary alone. Though they were separated during the early months of her pregnancy, he finally did bring her to Le Havre, and continued to live with her there until the child was born and for some six months afterward. The baby arrived in May, 1794, a healthy little girl, whom Mary named Fanny after her old friend. Mary was proud that her delivery had been easy and as for Fanny, Mary loved her instantly. "My little Girl," she wrote to a friend, "begins to suck so manfully that her father reckons saucily on her writing the second part of the Rights of Woman." Mary's joy in this child illuminates almost every letter she wrote henceforth.

Fanny's father was the chief recipient of these letters with all the details of the baby's life. To Mary's despair, she and Imlay hardly ever lived together again. A year went by; Imlay was now in London and Mary in France. She offered to break it off, but mysteriously, he could not let go. In the last bitter phase of their involvement, after she had joined him in London at his behest, he even sent her—as "Mrs. Imlay"—on a complicated

business errand to the Scandinavian countries. Returning to London, Mary discovered that he was living with another woman. By now half crazy with humiliation, Mary chose a dark night and threw herself in the Thames. She was nearly dead when two rivermen pulled her from the water.

Though this desperate incident was almost the end of Mary, at least it was the end of the Imlay episode. He sent a doctor to care for her, but they rarely met again. Since Mary had no money, she set about providing for herself and Fanny in the way she knew. The faithful Johnson had already brought out Volume I of her history of the French Revolution. Now she set to work editing and revising her *Letters Written during a Short Residence in Sweden, Norway, and Denmark,* a kind of thoughtful travelogue. The book was well received and widely translated.

And it also revived the memory of Mary Wollstonecraft in the mind of an old acquaintance, William Godwin. As the author of the treatise *Political Justice,* he was now as famous a philosophizing serpent as Mary and was widely admired and hated as a "freethinker." He came to call on Mary. They became friends and then lovers. Early in 1797 Mary was again pregnant. William Godwin was an avowed atheist who had publicly denounced the very institution of marriage. On March 29, 1797, he nevertheless went peaceably to church with Mary and made her his wife.

The Godwins were happy together, however William's theories may have been outraged. He adored his small stepdaughter and took pride in his brilliant wife. Awaiting the birth of her child throughout the summer, Mary worked on a new novel and made plans for a book on "the management of infants"—it would have been the first "Dr. Spock." She expected to have another easy delivery and promised to come downstairs to dinner the day following. But when labor began, on August 30, it proved to be long and agonizing. A daughter, named Mary Wollstonecraft, was born; ten days later, the mother died.

Occasionally, when a gifted writer dies young, one can feel, as in the example of Shelley, that perhaps he had at any rate accomplished his best work. But so recently had Mary come into her full intellectual and emotional growth that her death at the age of thirty-eight is bleak indeed. There is no knowing what Mary might have accomplished now that she enjoyed domestic stability. Perhaps she might have achieved little or nothing further as a writer. But she might have been able to protect her daughters from some part of the sadness that overtook them; for as things turned out, both Fanny and Mary were to sacrifice themselves.

Fanny grew up to be a shy young girl, required to feel grateful for the roof over her head, overshadowed by her prettier half sister, Mary. Godwin in due course married a formidable widow named Mrs. Clairmont, who brought her own daughter into the house—the Claire Clairmont who grew up to become Byron's mistress and the mother of his daughter Allegra. Over the years Godwin turned into a hypocrite and a miser who nevertheless continued to pose as the great liberal of the day. Percy Bysshe Shelley, born the same year that the *Vindication of the Rights of Woman* was published, came to be a devoted admirer of Mary Wollstonecraft's writing. As a young man he therefore came with his wife to call upon Godwin. What he really sought, however, were Mary's daughters—because they were her daughters. First he approached Fanny, but later changed his mind. Mary Godwin was then sixteen, the perfect potential soul mate for a man whose needs for soul mates knew no bounds. They conducted their courtship in the most up-to-the-minute romantic style: beneath a tree near her mother's grave they read aloud to each other from the Vindication. Soon they eloped, having pledged their "troth" in the cemetery. Godwin, the celebrated freethinker, was enraged. To make matters worse, Claire Clairmont had run off to Switzerland with them.

Not long afterward Fanny, too, ran away. She went to an inn in a distant town and drank a fatal dose of laudanum. It has traditionally been said that unrequited love for Shelley drove her to this pass, but there is no evidence one way or the other. One suicide that can more justly be laid at Shelley's door is that of his first wife, which occurred a month after Fanny's and which at any rate left him free to wed his mistress, Mary Godwin. Wife or mistress, she had to endure poverty, ostracism, and Percy's constant infidelities. But now at last her father could, and did, boast to his relations that he was father-in-law to a baronet's son. "Oh, philosophy!" as Mary Godwin Shelley remarked.

I f in practice Shelley was merely a womanizer, on paper he was a convinced feminist. He had learned this creed from Mary Wollstonecraft. Through his verse Mary's ideas began to be disseminated. They were one part of that vast tidal wave of political, social, and artistic revolution that arose in the late eighteenth century, the romantic movement. But because of Mary's unconventional way of life, her name fell into disrepute during the nineteenth century, and her book failed to exert its rightful influence on the development of feminism. Emma Willard and other pioneers of the early Victorian period indignantly refused to claim Mary as their forebear. Elizabeth Cady Stanton and Lucretia Mott were mercifully less straitlaced on the subject. In 1889, when Mrs. Stanton and Susan B. Anthony published their *History of Woman Suffrage,* they dedicated the book to Mary. Though Mary Wollstonecraft can in no sense be said to have founded the woman's rights movement, she was, by the late nineteenth century, recognized as its inspiration, and the *Vindication* was vindicated for the highly original work it was, a landmark in the history of society.

George Mason

Forgotten Founder, He Conceived the Bill of Rights

By Stephan A. Schwartz

I T HAD RAINED OVER THE WEEKEND, breaking the sweltering heat that had made Philadelphia a cauldron for most of the summer of 1787. The air was cool and fresh on the Monday morning the delegates to the Constitutional Convention gathered for a last time at the war-worn State House (now Independence Hall). They had argued among themselves up to the last minute, and even now not one of them was entirely happy with the results they had achieved.

The new Constitution, professionally copied out on parchment, lay on a small baize-covered table at the front of the room. Next to it was a silver inkstand and a newly trimmed goose quill. The delegates sat in silence as the fruit of their summer's labor was read to them. Then Benjamin Franklin, knowing how fragile the consensus for acceptance was, rose to try to explain why he was prepared to sign. At 81, he was not up to the physical task, though, and his younger colleague James Wilson had to read his words. Franklin confessed there were several parts of the Constitution "which I do not at present approve."

Nathaniel Gorham of Massachusetts immediately asked to speak, offering at this final hour an amendment that would increase the size of the House. The meeting stood at a parlous point; it could easily spiral back into acrimonious debate. George Washington, one of

---

This wise Virginian was a friend to four future presidents, yet he refused to sign the Constitution

---

the seven delegates from Virginia, stood to speak for the first and only time. Through the weeks of the debate, although the presiding officer, he had sat silently in front of the assembly. By his silence he had made himself the vessel of their commitment to integrity. His request that Gorham's change be approved, and that events move on, was irresistible. Finally, they lined up by state, with the New Hampshire delegation at the head. Franklin had to be helped to the small table and was said to be silently weeping as he wrote his name. Washington signed with almost unapproachable dignity, knowing, as they all did, that he would be the first President.

Only three present refused to sign. One of them was George Mason who, more than any other individual, would influence all three American documents: the Declaration of Independence, the

Constitution and the Bill of Rights. Sixty-two, of moderate height, with a round face and chestnut hair, this gouty and irascible militia colonel with large Virginia landholdings had been a slaveholder for most of his life. Yet now, because the Constitution created a federal government he felt might be too powerful, and because it did not end the slave trade and did not contain a Bill of Rights, he withheld his support from the document he had played so large a role in crafting.

His decision not to sign baffled some and alienated others, as he must have known it would. We will never know whether he appreciated what his refusal would cost him, but it is hard to believe that a man so aware of nuance in so many other public matters would have been unaware of what his stand would mean.

He had been born to George and Ann Thomson Mason in 1725, on a Potomac River plantation in what is now Fairfax County, Virginia, near today's Washington, D.C. His father drowned in a boating accident when George was 10, and the responsibility for his upbringing from then on was shared by his mother and his uncle, John Mercer.

In the 18th century, books were rare and valuable. Most families owned only a Bible and perhaps two or three other books, and even wealthy gentry might have no more than a few dozen. Mercer

Somewhere along the line, they discussed with Mason the latest information on events in the country.

possessed more than 1,500 at the time of his death. Being given the run of such an extraordinary library afforded young Mason a significant opportunity. Mason, like his friend George Washington, would receive little formal training. Mercer's library was his real education.

In 1746, when he was 21, Mason assumed control of approximately 20,000 acres of prime land, broken into farms scattered across several counties in Virginia and Maryland. He proved to be successful at running colonial plantations, and his neighbors soon knew it. At his death he owned 80,000 to 100,000 acres, and unlike many planters of the Revolutionary era, he was not crippled by debt.

Four years after taking control of his legacy, Mason married Ann Eilbeck, a planter's daughter. In an age when marriage was still largely seen through the prism of connections, theirs was a love match that lasted until Ann's death, 23 years later. They had 12 children together, nine of whom lived past childhood: five sons and four daughters. Although he was considered by many to be a difficult man, George's love for Ann was passionate, tender and unwavering. Years later he chose to be buried next to her even though he had remarried.

Midway through their first decade together, Ann and George began the construction of a new home. Mason's Gunston Hall, like Jefferson's Monticello and Washington's Mount Vernon, became an extension of the man. Given Mason's wealth and station it is surprisingly small—simple and restrained on the outside and very well appointed and elegant on the inside.

Mason's choice of the location for the new house also says a lot about the man. He could have sited Gunston Hall

anywhere on his thousands of acres. He chose to put it near the main road that ran between Williamsburg—Virginia's colonial capital and most important urban center—and Philadelphia, then America's leading and most cosmopolitan city. Turning aside from their journeys, colonial leaders rode up the drive to spend a day or a week sitting in his gardens looking out at the Potomac, riding over his land, eating at his well-stocked table or gambling at loo or whist in his drawing room. Somewhere along the line, they discussed with Mason the latest information on events in the country. Jefferson, greatly influenced by him, called Mason "a man of the first order of wisdom." "My private intercourse with him," James Madison said, "was chiefly on occasional visits to Gunston when journeying to & fro from the North, in which his conversations were always a feast to me."

What may have made the advice Mason offered acceptable to many of the other Founding Fathers was not only its wisdom but that it came from someone who, unlike most of them, was not a competitor for office or public notice. Mason loved the philosophy of governance, and liked shaping it, but acknowledged that he had no tolerance for the jostling camaraderie of public political life, describing some officeholders as "Bablers."

Consulting Mason, however, was not for those put off by plain speaking. Fellow Virginian Edmond Randolph said, with some irony, that Mason was not "wantonly sarcastic," but Jefferson was blunter; "His elocution was neither flowing nor smooth; but his language was strong, his manner most impressive, and strengthened by a dash of biting cynicism, when provocation made it seasonable."

One person who didn't seem to mind was Mason's near neighbor, George Washington. When they got together they and their wives talked about farming, and fashion, and about the slaves, whose presence was inextricably intertwined with their lives. It is hard for us today to understand slavery; the concept is so repugnant that even educational reenactments at living historic sites such as Williamsburg excite controversy. But

200 years ago slavery seemed a fixture of life. By the mid-18th century, however, some in the colonial elite to which the Washingtons and Masons belonged held deeply conflicting feelings about it.

Washington's final views on slavery were still forming, but even early on Mason's had become clear and characteristically acerbic: he had grown to loathe what the next century would call "the peculiar institution." In his typically blunt style he wrote, ". . . that slow Poison, [slavery] . . . is daily contaminating the Minds & Morals of our People. Every Gentleman here is born a petty Tyrant. Practical in Acts of Despotism & Cruelty, we become callous to the Dictates of Humanity. . . . And in such an infernal School are to be educated our future Legislators & Rulers."

For all their inner conflict, though, neither man had any clear idea what to do about slavery. To the 21st-century mind the answer is easy: free your slaves! But the 18th century was a different world, with different values. Even simple human considerations were complex on this issue. Freed slaves often had to leave the state, tearing apart lifelong relationships. Freeing them in the slave culture of Virginia, and its surrounding states, also meant making them vulnerable to, at best, exploitation and, at worst, recapture and re-enslavement. For the plantation owner, mass manumission also meant financial, and thus social, suicide.

As the years passed, the issue for Mason grew more and more intolerable. He came to believe that the importation of slaves should be stopped immediately. At the same time, according to one source, he felt that before emancipation could even be considered, a program of education should be begun so that the slaves could at least read and write.

Both Georges saw public service as a responsibility, but their approaches were very different. Washington, who was both ambitious and physically commanding, viewed public office as part of his life's plan. Mason, by disposition, was a backroom man. While Washington was careful in his choice of words, famously in control of himself and rarely offended, Mason never shied away from controversy and was an early proponent of the separation of church and state, and a firm opponent of taxation without representation.

In 1773, when he was 48 his wife Ann died, leaving Mason devastated, and he tried to withdraw even further from public life. But a year later, Mason went up to spend the night at Mount Vernon. The invitation from Washington was more than social. The port of Boston had been closed, and the Virginia colonists felt a powerful need to somehow support the people of Massachusetts. To meet that need Mason and Washington got together at Mount Vernon and wrote the Fairfax Resolves, outlining the colonists' constitutional grounds for their objections to the Boston Port Bill. It was the beginning of Mason's public writing on constitutional issues.

When Washington was named Commander in Chief of the Continental Army in 1775, the Virginia Legislature asked Mason to take Washington's seat in that body. Almost immediately he was an "elder" to whom other members turned. Constant consultation, plus his natural affinity and passion for the subject, forced Mason to grapple in earnest with the relative rights of citizens and government, and how this might play out in the sweaty compromises of politics.

In 1776, Virginia delegates met at a convention whose purpose was to replace the House of Burgesses, the colonial legislature. Mason, now 51, was among those selected that year, and he felt he could not decline. Arriving late at the convention, he found himself already appointed to a committee charged with drafting a "Declaration of Rights" and a constitution.

On Saturday, May 4, little Rhode Island seceded, the first colony to declare its freedom from England. The news electrified the Virginians. Mason began work on May 18 filled with enthusiasm, but it didn't last. He complained to one of his closest friends, Richard Henry Lee, that the committee was "overcharged with useless Members ... [who would draft] a thousand ridiculous and impracticable proposals...." By the end of the first week, he had more or less pushed most of them aside. It is a measure of the respect in which he was

Madison and Jefferson were close, both seeing Mason, for all his crankiness, as a man of wisdom.

held that the other delegates went along with this.

Edmund Pendleton, president of the Virginia Convention that year, wrote to Jefferson, then in Philadelphia representing Virginia at the Continental Congress. "The Political Cooks are busy in preparing the dish, and as Colo. Mason seems to have the Ascendancy in the great work, I have Sanguine hopes it will be framed so as to Answer it's end ... but I am yet a stranger to the Plan."

The Plan began with the Enlightenment philosophy of the Englishman John Locke (1632–1704), whose work Mason had likely first encountered in his uncle's library. Locke argued that government's sole purpose was to protect the natural rights—life, liberty and property—of the people. And he enumerated most of the rights Mason would later list. But it was Mason who saw why it was important to make Locke's abstractions law. He had come to a then-radical insight: that a republic had to begin with the formal, legally binding commitment that individuals had inalienable rights—rights that came from the Creator and were superior to any government.

One other committee member did play a significant role: James Madison, just 25 and beginning his public career. At first glance he made an odd contrast with the stout, acerbic Mason, twice his age. Madison, slight of stature, was a university-educated, bookish man of modest means who spoke with a soft voice. Yet, like Mason, Madison did his homework, knew his citations and could marshal his thoughts into a compelling argument. And he never babbled.

That summer spent working with Mason on Virginia's Constitution and Declaration of Rights would become the precursor event upon which Madison

would build his own place in history 11 years later when, only 36, he would be the principal architect of the U.S. Constitution.

But that wasn't all. Madison and Jefferson were close, communicating regularly and candidly, both seeing Mason, for all his crankiness, as a man of wisdom. Madison understood the implications of what Mason was doing and kept Jefferson apprised of their work. Virginia's Declaration of Rights would be an unprecedented political statement; nowhere in modern times had a government acknowledged such a concept as individual inalienable rights, let alone formalized it as a limitation on its own power.

Events, however, were moving almost faster than their correspondence. In the midst of Madison and Mason's work in Williamsburg, the Virginia Convention sent Richard Henry Lee to Philadelphia, where he introduced a measure declaring the colonies' independence. It was well received, and with the usual legislative courtesy of the day, Lee would have been made the chairman of the committee charged with drafting the declaration. But Lee learned his wife was sick, and asked permission of the Congress to return home. In his place that Tuesday, June 11, Thomas Jefferson was appointed. Jefferson, only 33, thought John Adams, as the more senior member of the committee, should draft the declaration. Adams soon made it clear that he felt Jefferson was the man for the job.

"Why will you not [write the declaration]?" Jefferson asked of Adams. Replied Adams, "First, you are a Virginian, and a Virginian ought to appear at the head of this business. Second: I am obnoxious, suspected and unpopular. You are very much otherwise. Third: You can write ten times better than I can."

But what to write, and how to write it? Part of the answer would soon arrive by courier from Williamsburg. The day after Jefferson was appointed, Mason's Virginia Declaration of Rights was adopted in Williamsburg on Wednesday, June 12. The first article of the work began, "That all men are by nature equally free and independent, and have certain inherent rights ... namely, the enjoy-

We credit Jefferson, but the impulse and content were clearly formed by George Mason.

ment of life and liberty, with the means of acquiring and possessing property, and pursuing and obtaining happiness and safety." Jefferson's Declaration of Independence, with minor corrections from Franklin, Adams and others, came to include the immortal words that make up what may be the most famous political statement in history: "We hold these truths to be self-evident, that all men are created equal, that they are endowed by their Creator with certain unalienable Rights, that among these are Life, Liberty and the pursuit of Happiness." We credit Jefferson, but the impulse and content were clearly formed by George Mason.

On June 29 the Virginia Constitution Mason had principally authored was adopted, freeing him to return to Gunston Hall. The war, however, soon made any hopes for a private life impossible. During the Revolutionary War years, in addition to serving in the Virginia House of Delegates, Mason raised the funds for equipping a county militia. (He had been a militia colonel before the war, which fixed the rank to his name; thereafter, he was known as Colonel Mason).

Throughout the war, Mason had watched Washington's struggles with the Continental Congress and Robert Morris' attempts to raise money, and seen everything he despised about politicians confirmed. Still planning to spend time at home, he proposed to Sarah Brent, also in her 50s, of the nearby wealthy Brent planter family. It was to be a marriage of friendship and mutual comfort, but not the passionate romance he had had with Ann.

Mason found once again, however, that a completely private life was not to be his. A consensus had emerged that something had to be done about the Articles of Confederation, and a Constitu-

tional Convention was planned. Franklin, who had deep respect for Native American cultures, called it the "Great Council Fire." It would be held in Philadelphia, and seven Virginians agreed to represent their state: Washington, Madison, George Wythe, Edmund Randolph, Dr. James McClurg, John Blair—and Mason. And so, at 62, he rode down his drive and onto the road as it snaked through the loblolly pines on a May morning in 1787. It was the longest trip Mason had ever made.

Many of the delegates, and certainly their appointing state committees, believed the purpose of the convention was to jigger with the Articles. But Madison had something very different in mind: he wanted to write an entirely new national constitution. Convincing his fellow Virginians to support him in this was not a trivial undertaking, and convincing the entire convention, even harder. One of the first people Madison turned to was Mason.

Mason's positions throughout the summer were consistent with his principles, even when, as was sometimes the case, they were against his own self-interest, or the interests of his Virginia. He argued against the interests of the rich when they abrogated the rights of the individual. He supported the power of the common man against the elite, arguing for popular elections. He fought his fellow delegates who sought to hold on to power, arguing for the admission and full equality of any new Western states. He worried about the power of a federal form of government, and argued against the slave trade.

The unwillingness of the delegates to deal with slavery was only one of Mason's disappointments. By August, he was saying he would "rather chop off my right hand than put it to the Constitution as it now stands."

Toward the end of the convention, he proposed that a bill of rights preface the Constitution, but when the state delegations caucused—each state had only one vote—it quickly became evident that most of the delegates did not get his point. When his proposal was defeated ten states to none, it was a dreadful blow.

Mason made a last effort to explain his reasons for the positions he had taken, sending to some friends 16 written objections. When his objections were still ignored, he turned his face against the new Constitution, and refused to sign it. Because of his active involvement throughout the convention, and his long association with constitutionalism, this refusal caused disappointment and consternation to the signers.

Assent of 9 of the 13 states was needed for ratification of the Constitution. Virginia cast the tenth affirmative vote. Among the Anti-Federalists in Virginia were Mason, Richard Henry Lee, future President James Monroe and Patrick Henry. Among the Federalists, or supporters of the Constitution, were Washington, Madison, George Wythe and John Marshall. After an unusually bitter debate, Virginia ratified the Constitution by an 89-79 vote. On "the first Wednesday in March"—March 4, 1789—the Constitution went into effect.

For Mason, his rejection of it had been a calculated act of public sacrifice; particularly painful to him was the effect his action had on Washington, who would be governing under the new Constitution. We do not know Washington's exact feelings, but his actions make it clear he felt betrayed. If Franklin could sign, why not Mason? But Mason could see no way to avoid what he believed must be done: "You know the friendship which has long existed (indeed from our early youth) between General Washington and myself," he would write, " . . . [but] I would not forfeit the approbation of my own mind for the approbation of any man or all the men upon earth."

He and Washington never visited each other again. Shortly before Mason's death five years after the convention, Washington referred to him as his former friend.

Mason retired to Gunston Hall for the last time, even as the perspective about him was changing—at least within the state and national leadership. He was invited to become one of Virginia's senators in the first U.S. Senate, but he declined. During the months since the convention, Mason's sacrifice had had its effect. At the first session of the first

"I have received much Satisfaction from the Amendments to the federal Constitution. . . . "

Congress, Madison introduced a bill of rights that paralleled Mason's Virginia declaration. Mason commented from Gunston Hall: "I have received much Satisfaction from the Amendments to the federal Constitution, which have lately passed. . . . With two or three further Amendments . . . I cou'd chearfully put my Hand & Heart to the new Government."

Sometime in late September Mason contracted what was called "the fever of the Season," probably malaria, which was endemic in Virginia during the late summer and early fall each year. He died at home on October 7, 1792. In his will he did not free his slaves, as Washington would several years later. Although it would be hard to prove, it is interesting to speculate as to whether Mason's views influenced Washington. Born into a slave-owning world, he did not initially question its order. By the time he became President, however, Washington had begun to see slavery as wrong. He made provision in his will for the freeing of his slaves, and made arrangements for the elderly among them.

Why Mason did not do this we will never know, but if he remained true to his convictions, and it is hard to imagine Mason doing anything else, perhaps he did not free them because he could not see how a single planter acting alone could effect a solution in a matter the nation as a whole should address. In the end it may have been as simple as this: family was more important even than principle. Mason was unwilling to bankrupt his children. It cannot have been an easy decision. Washington, who had no children, did not have to face that choice.

Although recognized by his fellow Founding Fathers, Mason never overcame the public's disregard for him as the result of his stand at the Constitutional Convention, and the events that flowed out of it. His obituaries were small, and as time passed he was largely forgotten, except as a name on high schools and a university in Virginia.

But to those few who have looked deeply into America's democracy, Mason's star has never dimmed, nor has his influence waned. In the House chamber his marble relief hangs with those of other great lawgivers: Moses, the Babylonian king Hammurabi and Thomas Jefferson. When the United Nations was founded his ideas were echoed in its Universal Declaration of Human Rights. In October 1949, President Harry S. Truman wrote to a correspondent, "Too few Americans realize the vast debt we owe [George Mason]. His immortal Declaration of Rights in 1776 was one of the finest and loftiest creations ever struck from the mind of man. . . . Our matchless Bill of Rights came directly from the amazing wisdom and farseeing vision of this patriot. . . . That is why I say that George Mason will forever hold a special place in our hearts."

Virginia-based writer Stephan A. Schwartz plans a book on George Mason.

Founding Rivalries

More like squabbling brothers than 'fathers,' how did they succeed?

By Jay Tolson

Intrigue, duplicity, back-stabbing, and character assassination. Think it sounds like American politics today? Try the 1790s, a decade that saw Thomas Paine—famous pamphleteer for the revolutionary cause—denounce President George Washington as a "hypocrite in public life" for signing a treaty with England. And earlier in the same decade, you'll find the recently retired secretary of state, Thomas Jefferson, telling his crony James Madison to get busy destroying the good name of Treasury Secretary Alexander Hamilton. Yes, the same Hamilton whom Madison had collaborated with only a few years before in writing the famous articles in support of the Constitution.

And back-stabbing? Well, there's the fine case of Ben Franklin penning a secret missive to Congress accusing fellow emissary John Adams of behavior "improper and unbecoming" for refusing to truckle to ally France's every whim. Not nasty enough? Try Vice President Jefferson telling a French diplomat that President Adams is "a vain, irritable, stubborn" man. If that's not quite treasonous, then what about the same vice president urging the French to drag their heels on signing a treaty that his president is earnestly trying to conclude? Given such a climate of slander and treachery, should we be surprised at the 1804 duel between the vice president of

Alexander Hamilton
A self-made man, energetic, forthright, and blunt to the point of arrogance, he was physically and intellectually bold, and extremely loyal.

the United States and the former secretary of the Treasury, a duel in which the latter was killed? More is the mystery that Aaron Burr and Alexander Hamilton were the only two founders who came to such a deadly impasse.

Americans who think they live in politically divisive times might do well to look back at the first decades of their republic's history. And many are already doing just that. Benefiting from a surge of new writing and thinking about the founding generation, they are discovering that the period from 1776 through the early 1820s was racked by political disagreements and rivalries that make ours today look picayune. While denying that they were engaged in anything

so divisive as partisan politics, leaders of what came to be the Federalist and Republican parties strained the bonds of the new union over a number of issues, including the role of the central government, states' rights, foreign policy, the handling of the debt, and slavery. To read of these struggles in such books as Joseph J. Ellis's *Founding Brothers: The Revolutionary Generation* is to wonder how the new nation managed to hold together. "I was out to recover a sense of the real threat to the survival of the American enterprise," Ellis says. "We still don't understand that."

We don't because earlier versions of the founding era presented a very different picture. Both the romantic histories of the 19th century and the more scientific, Progressive histories of the 20th century endowed the founding enterprise with an air of inevitability. According to the former, mysterious forces, even a divine hand, guided the Founding Fathers as they led the colonies to independence and, then, from a loose confederation of states, into a "more perfect Union," while the latter held that economic forces drove the founding down its inevitable course.

To some degree, that picture reflected the vision of Thomas Jefferson. Convinced that the march of history was inevitable and that he and his fellow Republicans were in step with it, he

Thomas Jefferson

*Idealistic and ideological,
he saw himself as
the guardian of the
revolutionary spirit.
Politically cunning,
he was backhanded
and ambitious.*

Benjamin Franklin

*Clever, industrious, and
witty, he was also a ladies'
man and bon vivant who
championed the
abolitionist cause near
the end of his life.*

managed through both his political successes and his rhetorical power to insinuate his view into many of the subsequent historical interpretations of his era. Not surprisingly, it cast him in a very favorable light, "in part," Ellis explains, "because the moralistic categories that shaped all his political thinking fit perfectly the romantic formula that history writing seemed to require."

There have been doubters of the formula, of course. For more than a century, historians have been pointing out the inconsistencies and veiled motives of the founders. And when not debunking them, most academic historians of the past 30 years have ignored them, focusing on the marginalized and downtrodden and stressing social history rather than the grand political narrative. But political history of the founding generation is making a comeback, thanks partly to journalists and other writers outside the academy. Richard Brookhiser, Roger Kennedy, and Bernard Weisberger are just a few who have recently produced biographies and narrative histories focused on the founding era. Coming soon is David McCullough's biography of John Adams, a work that some say will boost that founder's reputation as much as McCullough's earlier biography bolstered Truman's.

Also contributing to this recovery is the convergence of work by a number of established academic historians—Ellis, John Ferling, and Gordon Wood, among others—with that of younger scholars such as Joanne Freeman, David

Waldstreicher, Catherine Allgor, and Rosemarie Zagarri. What distinguishes this new political history is what Wood calls "a greater sense of irony and skepticism about the founders," an effort to show how things turned out quite different from what the founders intended—and could easily have turned out far worse.

Wood, for one, argues that America's leaders knew they were bringing about social as well political change when they broke loose from the English monarchy and created a republic. Indeed, as he contends in *The Radicalism of the American Revolution*, America's upheaval ended up being at least as radical as the revolutions of France and Russia. Committed to liberty and equality, the revolution's leaders hoped to root out hierarchical social rankings, hereditary privilege, patriarchy, paternalism, and patronage. But they also believed that a principled, disinterested leadership was essential to a true republic. Drawn from the aristocracy of talent, not birth, the republican leaders had to be free themselves, Wood writes, "from dependence and from the petty interests of the marketplace."

But the energies unleashed by the ideas of liberty and equality made it hard to hold fast to the ideal of the virtuous republic. Once people were free to pursue their own interests, they began to ignore the greater national good—and those leaders who claimed to stand for it. The competitiveness and individualism released by the Revolution began to produce something quite different from a genteel republic: a rough-and-tumble democracy with a vigorous capitalist economy.

The founders recognized the problem almost immediately after the Revolutionary War. Indeed, the drafting and ratification of the Constitution in 1787–88—the "second founding"—was partly an attempt to contain the excesses of narrow localism and interest-based politics. Hamilton and Madison, two vigorous champions of a new national charter to supplant the weaker Articles of Confederation, repeatedly made that point in their *Federalist Papers*. But the founders' dream

that the national government might serve as a bulwark of disinterestedness against the powerful tide of interest-group factionalism was soon dashed by the realities of politics, including clashes among the founders' own interests. Having decried the factionalism that they saw rampant at the state level, they created it at the national level. Indeed, says historian Zagarri, "almost as soon as the Congress met, profound differences emerged." And by the mid-1790s, these differences were fueling a two-party struggle for power.

Not that anyone would admit it. For it was a peculiar politics of denial and indirectness that the founders practiced, in which politicians denied that they were interested in officeholding, denied that they belonged to a party, or even denied that their party was a party. These politicians were also skilled in disguising what was really at stake in the positions they took, particularly if it was their own interests or ambition. In her forthcoming book, *Affairs of Honor*, Freeman shows how politicians used assaults on their opponents' character, reputation, and honor as a backhanded means of pursuing their highly partisan goals. George Washington grew so fed up with character assassination, Freeman explains, that he begged his cabinet members and others to put an end to the "wounding suspicions, and irritating charges." Personal attacks in pamphlets, broadsides, and newspaper articles, political gossip, and duels (most of which did not end in shooting) were all ways in which, says Freeman, "the founders

Aaron Burr

The most self-assured and aristocratic of the founders, he was also the most like a modern politician, openly working for his own interests.

used the code of honor to regulate their political combat on the national stage."

Just as important as the political style, though, is the role of personality and character, because it was the human element that gave this peculiar politics its messy, improvised quality—and, in the end, made the founders' achievement all the more remarkable. "It was the way they collided and found characterological checks and balances," says Ellis. "Instead of killing each other off, they worked through their differences and constructed institutions."

George Washington's character made him something of an exception to the dominant political style. He held more truly to the ideal of disinterested, principled, and nonpartisan leadership than any other founding brother. (Maybe, in his case, the sobriquet of *father* is just.) This Virginian of little formal schooling made the formation of character the core of his self-education, having copied out the 110 "Rules of Civility and Decent Behavior in Company and in Conversations" at age 16. Although he could be stern, hot tempered, and unforgiving, as deserters from the Continental Army learned with their lives, he was unfailingly a man of principle. And though his own experiences and inclinations aligned him with the Federalist faction, the party championing strong central government, his adherence to nonpartisanship remained firm.

Before Washington sought a second term, Jefferson, his secretary of state, urged him on, saying, "North and South will hang together if they have you to

hang on." But Jefferson was already doing more than his share to stoke the flames of partisanship that would singe even Washington. It was around this time, McCullough writes, that Jefferson, Madison, and other allies provocatively began "calling themselves Republicans, thus implying that Federalists were not, but rather monarchists, or monocrats, as Jefferson preferred to say."

Jefferson has long been recognized as the great idealist among the founders, the man whose soaring republican rhetoric was ideally suited to crafting the Declaration of Independence. But the new historical reading of the Sage of Monticello emphasizes his dangerous and devious qualities. It reveals even a certain reckless disregard for the national good in his devotion to revolution and extreme liberty and in his increasingly strong stand on the principle of states' rights (a stand that protected his, and his home state's, dependence on the "peculiar institution" of slavery). Jefferson's rivalry with his nemesis, Hamilton, is well known. Washington's brilliant former aide-de-camp, the first secretary of the Treasury, and the highest of High Federalists, Hamilton stood for everything Jefferson despised, including a powerful central government and English sympathies. Jefferson, the devout Francophile who became more avid after the French Revolution of 1789, even condoned the massacres of France's Reign of Terror, identifying the Jacobins with America's "Republican patriots." But what we now appreciate more clearly is how ruthlessly Jefferson advanced his own ambitions, even when that meant undercutting the two presidents, Washington and Adams, in whose administrations he served. Jefferson was a master of the politics of denial, planting gossip, writing anonymously in newspapers, or having others—Madison or the journalist Philip Freneau—engage in the dirty business of character assassination for him. To get at Hamilton, for instance, he ordered Madison to "take up your pen, select the most striking heresies, and cut him to pieces in the face of the public." He would orchestrate similar campaigns against Adams while serving as vice president.

John Adams

A shrewd judge of character, he was a hands-on committeeman. Though more practical than Jefferson, he also wanted to be seen as a gentleman.

Jefferson, in fact, did such a good job of depicting Adams as a monocrat and reactionary that historians have been slow to give Adams his due. Adams's accomplishments were legion: fearless advocate of independence in the Continental Congress; author of the Massachusetts Constitution; ambassador at large in Europe during the Revolutionary War; loyal vice president during both of Washington's terms. But what is underappreciated is how often he did the hard or unpopular thing when he thought it was for the good of the country. A perfect example is the course he steered during his presidency, when French hostilities had many Americans screaming for war. Adams's response—to press for peace even while he prepared a navy and an army for war—satisfied neither the Federalists, who were scrapping for a fight, nor the Republicans, who thought that Adams had aggravated tensions through botched diplomacy and war preparation.

Adams made mistakes during his presidency, none worse than supporting the Alien and Sedition Acts of 1798, which, among other things, made criticism of the government a crime. But perhaps his most self-destructive mistake was honorably intended: Trying to maintain the nonpartisanship that Washington had upheld, he lost the steady backing of many of his natural political allies in the Federalist faction. That would have made things hard enough, but Adams had to run an administration with Jefferson as his vice president. (With a vice president like that, one might say, who needed enemies?) Adams appreciated Jefferson's virtues and had long considered him a friend. But even during Washington's first administration, Adams came to see Jefferson's treachery, ambition, and fierce partisanship. Shortly after Jefferson resigned as secretary of state at the end of 1793, Adams wrote to Abigail, his wife and wisest political adviser, "Jefferson went off yesterday, and a good riddance of bad ware."

But the bad goods would return from Monticello in 1797, when Adams was elected president and Jefferson, as runner-up, the vice president. Instead of supporting the president, Jefferson fed the opposition press and even covertly counseled the French to draw out peace negotiations as long as possible, a delay that probably ended up costing Adams the next election. If that weren't mischief enough, after the Alien and Sedition Acts were passed, Jefferson secretly wrote the Kentucky Resolutions arguing that states had a right to nullify federal actions.

With rivalrous back-stabbing such as this, how *did* the nation hold together? That is the question that Ellis answers in the six essays of *Founding Brothers*. In one, for instance, he tells how in 1790 Jefferson brought Madison and Hamilton together to broker a deal over two issues that divided the nation: whether the federal government should assume all of the states' war debts, and where the nation's capital should be permanently located. Ellis writes that the former nationalist Madison had become wary of Hamilton's argument for assumption even before Jefferson converted him into a Republican. Madison, as a representative from Virginia, believed that assumption would punish Virginia unduly, forcing it to pay in federal taxes more than it owed in debts. Then why did Jefferson nudge him in the direction of a compromise that both would later regret? Because Jefferson believed that locating the capital on the Potomac would give the Southern states greater influence over the national government—and, at the same time, lessen the influence of Northern bankers and financiers in whose interests he thought Hamilton served.

George Washington
Solid, principled, and loyal, he was an officer and a gentleman. A confident delegator, he was also a stern and sometimes unforgiving leader.

Ellis—who joins other recent historians in giving the Federalists a far more sympathetic hearing—says that Hamilton engineered assumption and other federal initiatives not to "enrich the commercial elite" but to "channel their talent and resources into productive activities that served the public interest." But Ellis's more important point about the compromise of 1790 is that it showed that the Constitution had not really settled the question of what the American Revolution had been intended to create. Instead, Ellis writes, "it only provided an orderly framework in which the arguments could continue."

The one argument that got cut short, with tragic consequences, was that over slavery. Congress effectively removed itself from a constructive role in the debate in 1790. In that year, two Quaker delegations petitioned Congress to bring an end to the slave trade, petitions that prompted outrage among many legislators, who pointed out that the Constitution expressly forbade discussion of slave trade until 1808. The petitions would have been ignored, in fact, had they not come with the endorsement of Benjamin Franklin. Franklin, who himself had once owned slaves, in the last three years of his life became an ardent abolitionist, turning his eloquence and wit to the cause. Acknowledging the weight of his endorsement, a committee of the whole Congress argued the question for at least four hours. But their report helped set the nation on the way to civil

strife. Masterminded by Madison, the report made it unconstitutional for Congress to attempt to manumit slaves at any time in the future, a precedent that would be invoked repeatedly in the years ahead. "What had begun as an initiative to put slavery on the road to extinction had been transformed," Ellis writes, "into a decision to extinguish all federal plans for emancipation."

Perhaps the final irony is that though slavery would eventually bring about a civil war, it never occasioned a duel among the founding brothers. Instead, the only duel that resulted in fired shots and a founder's death was a duel over honorability itself. Hamilton, as Freeman has discovered, made a minor career of dueling, having been involved in 10 other "affairs of honor" before the last one with Burr. But the last was the only one that concluded with what was euphemistically called an "interview," or actual shootout—and a death. Hamilton was pushed to this drastic end because he could not in good faith take back what he believed: that Burr was a man without real principles. Many have tried to rehabilitate Burr, pointing out that he was an abolitionist and a proto-feminist, among other things. But what Hamilton (also an abolitionist) meant by unprincipled was that Burr was a creature of unveiled ambition who would do whatever suited him, including changing parties, to attain power. In other words, he behaved not like a politician of the founding era but a politician of the Jackson era and beyond—a true democratic politician. That behavior inspired Hamilton to do everything in his power to block his ascent. In fact, when the election of 1800 was thrown into the House of Representatives because of a tie between Burr and Jefferson, who were both on the same Republican ticket, Hamilton got his Federalist allies to back Jefferson, despite his abhorrence of Jefferson's ideas. Supporting Burr was inconceivable.

Hamilton's death would destroy Burr's career, and so one could say that the famous duel of 1804 resolved in Hamilton's favor. But the duel would not stop the direction of American politics. Burr's time—if not Burr himself—was arriving.

From Mercantilism to 'The Wealth of Nations'

The Age of Discovery gave rise to an era of international trade and to arguments over economic strategies that still influence the policies of commerce.

By Michael Marshall

We live in an era when continual economic growth is almost considered a birthright, at least in the developed world. It has become the benchmark of the health of a society, guaranteeing an ever-expanding prosperity. The current president of the United States even finds that his extensive misbehavior is overlooked by a majority of Americans because he happens to be presiding over an extended period of economic growth and optimism.

If annual growth drops below about 2 percent, planners and politicians start to get nervous, while a recession (negative growth) is considered a serious crisis. Where will it all end? Can such growth continue—with periodic setbacks, of course—indefinitely? We do not know and usually do not care to ask.

One thing is clear, however. It was not always so. For most of human history it has not been so. In western Europe in the period 1500–1750, output increased by a mere 65 percent, by one estimate, or an average of 0.26 percent a year, even though the population grew about 60 percent. For most of this period, 80 percent or more of the population worked the land. Studies of wage rates in England and France suggest that the working poor had to spend a full four-fifths of their income on food alone.

So this was not an economically dynamic society. There was relatively little disposable income, that being enjoyed by the prosperous elite of landed aristocracy and, increasingly in this period, merchants. Consequently, there was no prospect of creating a mass domestic market for new products. Most wealth was still tied up in the relatively static commodity of land, and agriculture was the major measure of a country's wealth.

Yet in the period from the voyages of discovery in the late fifteenth and early sixteenth centuries [see "Columbus and the Age of Exploration," THE WORLD & I, November 1998, p. 16] up till the Industrial Revolution there occurred what has been called a "commercial revolution."

The story of that revolution, which I will tell here, weaves together a number of significant themes. The upshot of the Age of Discovery was the emergence of a network of global trade. The consequences of that trade, and the measures taken by increasingly centralized European governments [see "The Ascent of the Nation-State," THE WORLD & I, March 1999, p. 18] to control and direct it, produced the system later labeled, most notably by Adam Smith, mercantilism. This was the practice of imperial rivalry between European powers over global trade, and it gave impetus to the disagreements between Britain and its

American colonists that led to the American Revolution. Critical consideration of these issues gave birth to Smith's theoretical study of economics, which culminated in the publication of his masterwork *The Wealth of Nations.*

PROTECTING BULLION RESERVES

Smith wrote: "The discovery of America and that of a passage to the East Indies are the two greatest and most important events recorded in the history of mankind." No doubt he exaggerated, but nothing was more important in the unfolding of this story. The Spanish conquistadores went to the New World in search of El Dorado. They found little gold but plenty of silver at Potosi in Peru and in northern Mexico. This silver became the lubricant of the machinery of an emerging global economy.

It flowed into Spain, from where much of it went to the rest of Europe, especially Holland, to pay the debts the Hapsburg rulers had incurred through the religious and dynastic struggles in their German possessions and in the Spanish Netherlands. Some of it then flowed to the Baltic to pay for the timber, rope, and other shipbuilding materials that the region supplied, especially to Holland and Britain. The bulk of it,

This article appeared in the May 1999 issue, pp. 18-31, and is reprinted with permission from *The World & I,* a publication of The Washington Times Corporation. © 1999.

The Commercial Revolution

Voyages of discovery in the fifteenth and sixteenth centuries resulted in a growing network of international trade.

Silver from the New World became the lubricant for the machinery of an emerging global economy.

Fearing the success of their rivals, European governments imposed trade restrictions to protect their national interests.

Viewing commerce as an arena of conflicting national interests at times thrust competing European powers into war.

Advocates of free trade criticized mercantilist policies, suggesting peace could arise from mutually beneficial terms of trade.

Clashes over trade were significant factors in the antagonisms that led to the American Declaration of Independence.

The growth of economic relations between America and Britain after the Revolutionary War suggests that the free traders were right.

though, went to Asia to satisfy the growing European demand for spices, silk, Indian calico, and later, Chinese tea.

Without the silver that demand could not have been satisfied: Europe had nothing that Asia wanted to import in exchange. That situation would not change until after the Industrial Revolution, when clothing from the Lancashire cotton industry in the north of England found a market in Asia. Even then problems remained. The economic reason for the shameful opium trade in the early and mid-nineteenth century, when opium grown in India was exported illegally to China, was to earn exchange to pay for tea without having to export silver.

Silver was not without problems. So much of it flowed into Europe in the sixteenth century that it caused serious price inflation. The Spanish economy, in particular, was considerably disrupted, a significant factor in Spain's gradual decline. During the seventeenth century, from a peak around 1600, the supply of silver began to decrease. The demand for goods from Asia, however, did not. The result was a net outflow of silver bullion from Europe, a shrinkage of the money supply, and as a result, economic recession.

No economic theory existed at the time, and no contemporary thought argued that governments should not regulate such matters affecting national wealth in the national interest. So they did. The ad hoc system of tariffs and other measures influencing trade and manufactures that came to be known as mercantilism began to emerge.

The context in which this happened was one of increasingly centralized emerging nation-states that were spending a greater portion of the total national income than in the past, especially in the frequent times of war. They exercised closer control over more aspects of life in pursuit of national policy than in the past, especially through the taxation needed to fund wars. Trade with the New World nurtured the idea that commerce could be a source of national wealth and strength just as much as agriculture and should be developed to that end.

Spain, Britain, and France all banned the export of gold or silver bullion, but this proved to be like trying to stop water from running downhill. The belief was that bullion represented the national wealth or treasure, and that trade should be conducted so as to amass a surplus of it. A country would then have a reserve to cushion itself from the economic effects of adverse fluctuations in the supply of gold and, especially, silver.

Underlying this thinking was the assumption that markets and the amount of trade were relatively fixed, and that gaining a larger share of the pie necessarily meant depriving another country of part of its share. Trade was thus conceived as an arena of national competition and even conflict, a form of war by other means.

COLBERT AND FRENCH MERCANTILISM

Advocates of free trade in the late eighteenth and the nineteenth centuries strongly criticized this aspect of mercantilist policy. They proposed that peace was one of the benefits of free trade, since it tied trading partners in mutually beneficial exchanges that could only be lost through war. Neither side was totally right. Circumstances always affect cases, and the mercantilist policymakers were pragmatists who reacted to the situation before them.

The most systematic practitioner of mercantilist policies was undoubtedly Jean-Baptiste Colbert, finance minister for France's Louis XIV in the later seventeenth century. Colbert used the considerable power of the Sun King's state to increase its wealth through the promotion of French trade and manufactures. He certainly banned the export of bullion, but his policy was aimed at replacing bullion as the means of payment for necessary imports with the earnings from the export of French manufactures.

To that end he developed selected industries by state subsidies and bringing in skilled foreign artisans. He particularly encouraged high-value products such as quality furniture, glass, and tapestries, and the quality of French workmanship in these areas became legendary throughout Europe. He used tariff barriers to protect industries that faced serious foreign competition. Wanting to develop the French cloth industry in the face of the well-established British cloth trade, he doubled the duty on imports.

Thus emerged the classic mercantilist pattern that, because it came about in a piecemeal, pragmatic manner, has only existed in its complete form in the writings of historians. The export of domestic raw materials was largely discouraged, so that domestic manufacturers could enjoy their use. The export of sheep and raw wool from Britain, for example, was heavily regulated for the benefit of the domestic textile industry. The export of manufactures was encouraged as the means to a favorable balance of trade and the bullion inflows that came with it.

The import of foreign manufactures was restricted since this adversely affected the balance of trade. Raw material imports were looked on favorably to the degree that they could be used in or support domestic manufactures, although a large agricultural country like France, under Colbert, aimed at as much self-sufficiency as possible.

Colbert realized that encouraging French industry had little point if its products could not then be exported. That meant commercial shipping and a navy to protect it. Colbert had before him the example of the Dutch. They were the dominant economic power in Europe in the early and mid-sixteenth century through their skills in trade and shipping.

The Dutch dominated North Sea fishing, annoying the British by taking huge catches of herring from Britain's east coast, developing a factory-style industry for salting the catch, and then exporting it throughout Europe. They dominated the carrying trade from the Baltic to western Europe, were major carriers of imports to Europe from the Americas and from the East, and grew rich through their control of the lucrative reexport of those imports throughout Europe from their initial port of entry in Amsterdam.

To support these efforts the Dutch dredged and improved their rather shallow harbors and developed specialized forms of shipping, both for fishing and for moving bulk materials. They also developed financial instruments to ease the flow of trade and extend the use of credit. Most notably, they established the Bank of Amsterdam, a public bank that offered a source of capital very different from the government funding of chartered companies that had marked the enterprise of discovery and trade in the sixteenth century.

Colbert built up a merchant marine to rival that of the Dutch and ensure that French trade was carried in French ships. Under his direction the merchant fleet grew from a mere 60 ships of 300

tons or more to over 700 ships of that size. He provided for the protection of French maritime commerce by building up the French navy from 20 ships to 250 by the time of his death in 1683.

He always viewed commerce as an instrument of national policy, and merchants had little say in his decisions. This was unlike the situation in England, where various merchant groups formed influential lobbies on the Crown's commercial policies. The prizes of commerce remained for him a zero-sum game: France's gain must be someone else's loss. He created a successful glass industry in Paris by inviting Venetian glassblowers to teach their skills. He later boasted that the successful royal mirror factory that resulted was depriving Venice of one million livres a year.

COMMERCE AND CONFLICT

Colbert's attitude was much derided by the later free-trade economists, most notably Smith. The Scottish philosopher David Hume, a contemporary and good friend of Smith's, wrote on the subject: "I shall therefore venture to acknowledge that, not only as a man, but as a British subject, I pray for the flourishing commerce of Germany, Spain, Italy and even France itself."

It was an irony, too, and one that later critics did not fail to point out, that a considerable contribution was made to the growth of French transatlantic exports by industries that did not receive Colbert's nurturing support. Iron and coal, hardware, and the cheaper cloths produced by the textile industry in Normandy all developed through their own enterprise.

Nevertheless, Colbert's legacy was a foundation for rapid and successful French commercial development in the eighteenth century. Between 1715 and 1771 the total value of French foreign trade grew eightfold until it almost matched British trade. The value of French exports multiplied more than four times between 1716 and 1789. Colbert must have been doing something right.

Advocates of free trade proposed that peace was one of its benefits.

Nor were the policymakers of the time completely wrong in their view of commerce as conflict to gain the largest share of a fixed prize. It is certainly true that bilateral trade is mutually beneficial. If a country wants to export its goods, its potential trading partners must have the means to pay for those goods. So it is in the exporter's interest that partners have their own successful export markets, perhaps in the original country's own home market, to generate the revenue needed to buy its exports.

This is not true of the carrying and reexport trade, however. The Dutch had grown rich on this trade, and the British and French set out to take it away from them. Both ended up fighting trade wars with the Dutch over the issue. In the second half of the seventeenth century, Britain passed a series of Navigation Acts, which required that goods shipped in and out of British ports, and to and from British colonies, had to be carried in British ships.

This struck at the heart of the Dutch trade, hence the tensions that led to war. At issue was who would distribute the new colonial imports throughout the rest of Europe. The Dutch gradually lost out to the French and British. Between the 1660s and 1700 British exports grew by 50 percent. Half of that increase came from the reexport of colonial imports, mostly to Europe.

As a result, the eighteenth century was the Anglo-French century in terms of commerce. I have already mentioned the spectacular growth in French trade. The value of British trade grew threefold between 1702 and 1772, and British shipping grew at a similar rate, reaching over one million tons by 1788. This phenomenal growth represented a tremendous amount of new wealth, most of it associated with colonial trade, especially that of the New World.

The bulk of British trade in 1700 was still with Europe, but by 1776 two-thirds of its overseas trade was outside Europe. Between 1700 and 1763 the value of British exports to America and the West Indies multiplied fivefold, while the value of imports from those areas grew fourfold. Anglo-French rivalry resulted in a number of wars throughout the century. It is small wonder, given the importance of colonial trade, that parts of those wars were fought in North America and in India, over strategic control of its sources.

'BADGES OF SLAVERY'

The Atlantic trade not only was the most substantial but it also formed an interlocking network. From the plantations of the southern colonies of America, the Caribbean, and the Brazilian coast, tropical staples—tobacco, cotton, sugar, coffee, cocoa, rice—flowed to Europe. European manufactures flowed back west, supplying the plantation economies with necessities they did not produce themselves. European cities, especially those on the Atlantic, grew and prospered on this trade. From Cadiz and Lisbon in the south, through Bordeaux and Nantes in France, to Bristol, Liverpool, Glasgow, and the burgeoning entrepôt of London in England, they all became part of the Atlantic economy.

A city like Liverpool benefited from importing, refining, and reexporting sugar and tobacco. It also benefited from a new and increasingly significant part of the Atlantic economy—slavery. Plantation agriculture is labor intensive, and the plantations of the Americas looked to West Africa to supply that need. Ships from Liverpool or Bristol, or Lisbon for that matter, would sail to West Africa and trade cheap manufactured items to local chiefs in return for live bodies.

These were then shipped across the Atlantic—the Middle Passage—to the Caribbean or the American South, where those still alive after the horrors of the voyage were sold. The ships then returned home laden with cotton, tobacco, or sugar. In the case of Portuguese ships, they would sail to Brazil and return with Brazilian produce.

LIBRARY OF CONGRESS

Slaves on the deck of the bark *Wildfire*, brought into Key West, Florida, on April 30, 1860. Carrying 510 slaves, the ship violated the 1809 slave trade law that prohibited slave importation. This engraving was made from a daguerreotype for *Harper's Weekly*, June 2, 1860. Blacks were rarely allowed on deck except for occasional "exercise."

European manufactures were also exported to the settler societies of the Americas. The half million Spanish settlers in Mexico and Peru paid for these with silver. As the supply of silver slackened and Latin American society became increasingly self-sufficient, this trade became less important.

The North American trade continued to burgeon. European manufactures were paid for by the products of the region. The question arose as to what those products were to be, and who should determine that: the colonists or the government in London? At this point,

questions of mercantilist policy become questions about the future of the American colonies, in other words questions about independence. Adam Smith addressed both sets of questions in The Wealth of Nations.

He described the regulations by which London sought to control the American economy as "impertinent badges of slavery." They were intended to ensure that the American economy would complement the British economy, but that, of course, also meant subordinating the one to the other. The American colonies were viewed as a supplier of those staples mentioned above and a protected market for British manufactures.

The colonies were by no means expected to develop industries that might compete with those in Britain. In 1699, Britain sought to ban the woolen industry in America and prevent any inter-colony trade in woolen goods. In 1750 a similar ban was applied to steelmaking and the manufacture of finished products from iron.

The role of the New England colonies was to reduce British reliance on the Baltic region for naval materials and certain types of shipbuilding timber. Thus, these strategically sensitive materials—essential for building the ships of the Royal Navy that protected British commerce—would be under British political control. These products were allowed into Britain duty-free, as was pig iron, in that case to reduce British reliance on Swedish and Russian sources. But the pig iron was not to be any further refined in the colonies, lest it compete with the British iron industry.

Being true Englishmen jealous of their liberties, the colonists chafed under these restrictions. Political conflict inevitably resulted, and many commentators in Britain considered that the costs of that conflict outweighed any economic benefit from trying to restrict the natural economic development of the colonies. Matters came to a head in 1776, the year in which both the Declaration of Independence and *The Wealth of Nations* were published.

NEW ECONOMIC DIRECTIONS

Smith had definite views on the American economy and on the system of tariffs and trade regulations that had helped produce the conflict. Unlike the views advocated by other contributors to the debate, however, his arose from the context of an extensive theoretical consideration of how wealth is created. It is only a slight exaggeration to say that he invented economic theory.

He can certainly be considered the originator of classical economics. It was his ideas that were first developed and interpreted by David Ricardo and then by John Stuart Mill in *Principles of Political Economy*. At the end of the nineteenth century they were revived and revised as "neoclassical" economics by Alfred Marshall. Even the economic ideas of Karl Marx and, in this century, John Maynard Keynes, started from the principles first enunciated by Smith, although they then moved in very different directions.

His book discusses systematically the basic economic questions: a theory of price or value; wages, profits, and rents; the role of labor; how wealth is distributed among owners of the different factors of production; the role of capital, money, and the banking system; and taxation and the national debt. He famously introduced the concept of the division of labor, explaining how it increases productivity and also is limited by the extent of the market.

He held a dynamic view of the economy. National wealth resulted from the flow of income over time rather than from the size of the stock of capital held. His theory anticipated the actuality of burgeoning economic growth produced by the Industrial Revolution. It differed significantly from the assumptions that lay behind mercantilist policies.

Smith and his good friend Hume refuted the argument that trade should be managed in such a way as to maintain a positive balance so as to earn bullion. Hume pointed out that if bullion flowed out of a country its prices would fall, which would render its exports more competitive, thus increasing the flow of export earnings into the country until balance was restored. In other words, Hume and Smith thought of the economy as a dynamic self-regulating system. In Smith's most famous phrase, it was as if an "invisible hand" harmonized individual economic actions pursued out of self-interest into an overall balance that served the public good. It worked best without government interference.

Economic historian Peter Mathias sums up Smith's arguments on this topic admirably, saying that

a system of freely operating market prices, under naturally competitive conditions, would ensure the lowest effective prices to the consumer and produce the most efficient allocation of resources between the different branches of economic activity. The ultimate test of efficiency and welfare thus became a freely moving price level not distorted by legislative interference.

On the basis of this argument, Smith launched into a critique of tariffs, subsidies, and monopolies, all the tools of the commercial policy of the era that he dubbed mercantilism. "Consumption," he argued, "is the sole end and purpose of all production," yet under the mercantilist system the consumers' interest was sacrificed to that of producers, who sought special favors from the government for their particular industries.

With such views he could not help but be critical of contemporary British policy toward the American colonies. He thought that Britain could rightly impose its own taxation system on the colonies but only in the context of colonist representation at Westminster. (He was, incidentally, a friend of Benjamin Franklin's, and the two discussed these issues when Franklin was in London.) He thought, too, that Britain could extend its customs laws to America provided that *all* internal barriers to trade were abolished.

Smith thus conceived of the British Empire as a vast and free internal market for each and all of its component regions. He even envisaged that the seat of the empire should not remain fixed in London but should move "to that part of the Empire which contributed most to the general defense and support of the whole."

THE DISCUSSION CONTINUES

Economic relations between Britain and America after the Revolutionary War suggested that the free-trade arguments promoted by Smith and his fellow critics of the system of colonial regulation were right. After 1782, British exports to the United States began to grow more rapidly than those to any other region. By 1836 about a quarter of Britain's total exports went there, while the

"Consumption," Smith argued, "is the sole end and purpose of all production."

United States provided 80 percent of Lancashire's cotton.

Such evidence boosted free-trade ideas, which became increasingly influential in the nineteenth century, especially in Britain—whose manufacturers, of course, stood to gain the most by them. But the argument that Smith first articulated against mercantilist policy is still going on today. Countries still remain very sensitive about their balance of trade. In the United States, a Republican presidential candidate, Pat Buchanan, argues for greater protection for American industry, in the face of widespread free-trade thinking in both parties.

Back in the 1970s, the Carter administration bailed out Lee Iacocca's Chrysler Corporation because it was thought that the damage to the economy as a whole and the social cost of the resulting unemployment were worse than paying the cost of a bailout. Right now the United States is entering into a tariff war with western Europe over Caribbean bananas. The Europeans want to reserve 25 percent of their banana market for producers in their former colonies. Without that guaranteed market those producers probably could not survive. The United States is arguing for unrestricted free trade in bananas, which would benefit the mighty Dole Corporation. Whoever is right in the argument, its roots lie in the system of Atlantic trade and colonies that developed in the seventeenth and eighteenth centuries.

The "commercial revolution" of the eighteenth century generated a huge increase in trade and wealth. This all happened under a system of mercantilist policy. Whether that policy nurtured the development or, as Smith argued, it took place despite the policy is a question that can probably never be resolved.

What can be said is that the commercial revolution was an important prelude to the Industrial Revolution. Some of the capital generated from trade found its way into the new manufacturing industries. Perhaps more important was the development of extensive new global markets, for it is questionable whether in the absence of those markets European domestic demand could have grown enough to sustain the rapid growth of the new industries. As it was, those industries found an already established international network of markets through which their new products could flow.

Michael Marshall is executive editor of THE WORLD & I.

As Good As Gold?

Not always. Money in America has gone from crops to bullion to greenbacks to electronic markers—igniting political and economic crises along the way

By T. J. Stiles

IT'S A TYPICAL FRIDAY FOR A TYPICAL American—and that means payday. Over her lunch hour, she makes a pilgrimage to the bank; on the screen of an automatic teller machine, she sees the reassuring numbers: her employer has deposited her wages into her checking account. She spends the rest of the hour paying her bills—settling some through the Internet, by authorizing deductions from her bank balance. Her employer has automatically subtracted her health-insurance premium, her retirement-plan contribution and her taxes.

In a few hours she has participated in numerous transactions involving thousands of dollars, yet she has not handled one slip of physical currency. She organizes her entire life around this day—and she never gives a thought to the invisibility of her money. A few numbers on a computer screen, a poorly printed ATM receipt and a computerized voice on the phone are all the evidence she needs that the money is there.

So what exactly *is* money? It's a question that has become harder to answer, as we use less and less actual cash. Maybe one place to go for a solution is 80 feet beneath the steel and concrete forest of Manhattan's financial district, inside the international gold vault. Maintained by the Federal Reserve Bank of New York, it contains the largest hoard of monetary gold on the

planet. A quarter of the world's reserves lie there, stacked floor to ceiling, bar after very heavy bar, in dozens of locked cages according to country.

Impressive as this pile may be, it suffers from a serious problem: it really isn't money anymore. Today, we cannot walk into a store, plunk down a chunk of gold and buy something. A debit card will do, but not bullion. It is not, as the economists say, a generally accepted means of payment.

And those two little words, "generally accepted," hold the secret meaning of money—and how it has melted from some of the heaviest of metals to mere electronic markers. Money is not merely a measuring system for value; it is also a thing that everyone is willing to accept for payment for everything else, all the time.

But what happens when a large proportion of the public remains on the ledge, refusing to make that leap of faith? The answer is crisis—and just such a crisis dominated much of American history, shaping politics and tearing apart communities. The fight over how to define money created political parties, made and destroyed Presidential candidates and rang in depressions.

This long debate tells us a great deal about the nature of money, because at the center of the argument was the question of how abstract it should be. A sub-

stance intrinsically valuable, or an item we invent as needed? The issue dogged Americans for some 300 years, because we faced a critical problem: a drastic, ongoing shortage of cash.

Consider Gov. Thomas Dudley of Massachusetts Bay. In 1624 he met with two ambassadors from the Pequots, the colony's powerful Native American neighbors, who came to discuss reparations for the recent murder of an Englishman by the tribe. Dudley's demands: a few dozen furs and a large cash payment—specifically, some 2,400 feet of wampum.

Wampum—strings of shell beads—served an important ceremonial function among the Native American nations of the Northeast. And when the Indians began to ask for it as payment for their furs, it became almost as important to the colonists. Soon after Governor Dudley's talks with the Pequots, Massachusetts made wampum legal tender.

Wampum was not the colonists' first choice for cash. In the world they left behind, money was mostly gold and silver coin. But throughout the colonial era, the British government banned the export of coin across the Atlantic. Even when colonists began to acquire Spanish silver through trade with the West Indies, much of it went straight to England to pay for imports. Colonists made a few attempts to establish their own mints,

Originally appeared in *Smithsonian*, September 2000, pp. 106-119. © 2000. Reprinted with permission of the author.

but London quickly quashed them. The result was an often catastrophic shortage of money.

"We were in the Years 1721 and 1722," declared the Pennsylvania legislature, "so effectually drained of our Coin ... that the Inhabitants of every Degree were reduced to the greatest Straits; Debts could not be discharged, nor Payments be made; the Rents of Houses fell, many whereof were deserted; Artificers and Traders were obliged to quit the Country."

In desperation, the colonies began to invent money for themselves. At first, they made existing commodities the official standard. In South Carolina, rice, peas, beef and even pork were used as monetary commodities; Virginia began to set prices in terms of tobacco as early as 1619, and shortly afterward made it legal tender. The colony established warehouses where it stored bales of tobacco; it settled bills by paying out receipts for the leaf deposited there. Taxes, even salaries were paid in these "tobacco notes," which circulated publicly and privately as a kind of paper money.

Some colonies turned to paper currency or bills of credit. Generally speaking, the issuing government would make the bills legal tender, set a terminal redemption date (usually five years or so) and establish a special tax to build a fund to pay off the notes in coin at that time.

In the Western world, legal-tender paper money (first issued by Massachusetts in 1690) was an American innovation. Despite plenty of problems, the coin-poor public loved it. In fact, one of the lesser-known provocations leading to the Revolution was an act of Parliament in 1764 that banned the issuance of paper currency in all the colonies (a band had been issued for New England in 1751). Many colonists saw the law in the context of the Sugar Act, the Stamp Act, the Quartering Act and the Townshend duties—which seemed to be a determined program by Parliament to suppress American autonomy.

Once the colonies organized the Second Continental Congress in 1775, Americans got more paper money than they ever wanted. Congress tried to finance the war of independence by issuing notes called continentals. It pledged to print no more after the first batch—then proceeded to flood the economy with more than $200 million by 1780. These legal-tender bills became virtually worthless. In desperation, Congress turned to one of the wealthiest—and shrewdest—men in the new Republic, Robert Morris of Philadelphia.

Almost from the beginning, Morris served as the financial godfather of the Revolution. In early 1777, for example, right after George Washington won a great victory at Trenton, New Jersey, the general saw a chance to strike a second blow against the British—but many of his troops had reached the end of their terms of enlistment. Washington promised a $10 bounty to each man who stayed on for six more weeks; then he wrote a frantic appeal to Morris for the money. "I am up very early this morning to despatch a supply of $50,000 to your Excellency," Morris wrote back. The general scored another success at Princeton.

Morris accomplished a similar feat in 1781, during the critical Yorktown campaign. This time Washington was desperate for supplies. Morris mobilized his wealthy friends, pledging his personal fortune as security for purchases of flour, cattle and boats.

By the time Washington won that final victory of the war, Congress had named Morris the Superintendent of Finance. Once again, he put his own good credit to work as he rebuilt that of the government. At one point, he even circulated his own notes, backed by his personal wealth. His bills were considered as good as precious-metal coin in the marketplace (thanks to Morris' vast fortune).

But Morris had no intention of bankrolling the new nation. He persuaded the Continental Congress to begin construction of a financial infrastructure. In 1781 Congress established the Bank of North America—the first federally chartered bank on these shores. It made loans to Congress, to be redeemed at specific intervals, allowing Morris to anticipate revenues and maintain sufficient cash flow.

After the disastrous experience with continentals, the Founders got out of the legal-tender business. They wrote a prohibition on state-issued currency into the Constitution, and Congress rested content with minting gold and silver coins. Paper money was left to banks. Usually banks would take deposits in gold and silver coin (or "specie," to use the technical term) and make loans by issuing paper notes. The public paid each other with these privately printed bills, assuming they could be redeemed at the issuing bank for precious-metal coin (or cash—as in "cold, hard cash"). Banks multiplied the supply of money; they issued paper worth two or three times their specie reserves, since it was unlikely all their notes would be returned at once.

All this raised the abstraction of money to bewildering proportions. Gold and silver coin was still there at the heart of the system, tangible and real. But it tended to settle in the bellies of banks, which digested it and regurgitated paper notes. All kinds of notes. By 1860 there were no less than 1,562 state-chartered banks, and almost every one distributed its own variety of bills.

When that private-enterprise paper hit the marketplace, it fluctuated in value depending on how easily the notes could get "real" money (that is, specie). A merchant might insist on steeply discounting a note, when taking it as payment, because of the issuing bank's reputation. Distance mattered too: the farther away the bank, the harder to return its notes for coin.

This diverse, ad hoc currency aroused distrust and distaste—a sentiment expressed most belligerently by Andrew Jackson. No one better expressed American belligerence itself, for that matter: he once killed a man in a duel, and he was undoubtedly the only President who took the oath of office with two bullets in his body and then had one of them removed (without anesthesia) while in office. In one of his most famous acts as President, he crushed the Second Bank of the United States, a federally chartered giant that towered over the nation's financial structure.

But Jackson hated the entire currency system. He saw paper bills as a lot of mysterious mumbo jumbo, and bankers as a bunch of unproductive thieves who lived by other men's sweat. In 1836 Jackson drew up the Specie Circular, which decreed that federal lands would be sold only for coin—not the banknotes used by most westward-marching migrants. When consumers rushed to get specie for their notes, banks went down like dominoes, ushering in a stark depression that lasted until 1843.

That crisis was merely a bonfire compared with the firestorm of the Civil War—a conflagration that consumed everything in its path, including the country's currency. As the military and financial situation worsened in 1861, panicked note holders rushed to banks and demanded gold. By December, banks had stopped redeeming their notes. With previous metals hoarded and hidden, paper money depreciated radically.

It fell to Congressman Elbridge G. Spaulding, a banker, to solve the crunch. He authored an act for a national paper currency that became known as legal-tenders, or, more commonly, greenbacks. After July 1, 1863, these notes were used for all debts except customs duties, and they could not be redeemed for specie.

The immensity of this innovation can easily be missed, as we look back from our specie-free society. But at the time it was stunning. Unlike virtually every other paper note in American history, the greenback did not represent an underlying commodity. It could not be redeemed in gold or silver—or tobacco, or wampum—then or in the future.

Probably the first thing the greenback purchased was outrage. "Gold and silver are the only true measure of value," one influential banker thundered. "These metals were prepared by the Almighty."

"I prefer gold to paper money," agreed Senator John Sherman. "But there is no other resort. We must have money or a fractured Government." But critics found plenty of ammunition in a rather peculiar market in New York City that the greenback created, known as the Gold Room.

For the first time, gold had a price. The law recognized the greenback and the old gold dollar as equals, but in the Gold Room (officially established in

He took the oath of office with two bullets in his body— and had once killed a man in a duel.

1864), traders exchanged the two kinds of money, paying extra greenbacks for the rarer gold. The market, in fact, was an economic necessity, since international purchases were made in the yellow metal, while the domestic economy used paper money almost exclusively.

For Jay Gould, the market would be a hunting ground. In 1869 the famed financier and his friend and partner, James Fish, Jr., had just made their mark on Wall Street by besting Cornelius Vanderbilt in a fight for the Erie Railroad. Now Gould led his friend to the Gold Room.

On the surface, Gould's plan was simple: he would corner the market. That is, he would create a general craze for gold by purchasing massive quantities and convincing brokers and the public that the price would keep climbing. As buyers joined the frenzy, the price of gold would shoot up.

The primary threat to Gould's scheme was the U.S. Treasury, the biggest player in the market. It could undercut the price of gold through its large sales of the specie it acquired through customs duties. So Gould spun a web of intrigue around the new President, Ulysses S. Grant. The financier bribed Grant's brother-in-law, Abel Corbin, to argue for a freeze on U.S. gold sales. Gould corrupted Daniel S. Butterfield, the assistant treasurer in New York, for inside information.

On June 15, 1869, Gould and Fish lobbied Grant himself on a passage to Boston aboard one of Gould's steamships. "We went down to dinner about nine o'clock," Fisk recalled, "intending while we were there to have the thing pretty thoroughly talked up, and, if possible to relieve him of any idea of putting the price of gold down." They came in for a shock: Grant was not interested.

But Gould knew that perception was as important as reality in the markets, so he created the impression that Grant was solidly behind them. Apparently, Gould even set up an account for First Lady Julia Dent Grant. "Mr. Gould," Fisk later told Congress, "sold $500,000 of gold belonging to Mrs. Grant . . . leaving her a balance of about $27,000." In September, the price of the precious metal went up, thanks in part to the two financiers' purchases and shrewd use of the press. Desperate to drive the market still higher, the conspirators pressured Abel Corbin to send the President one last plea for a moratorium on Treasury gold sales.

Gould had gone too far. Grant, too, had heard the rumors of his own complicity; when Corbin's note interrupted a croquet game, Grant angrily ordered his wife to write back and tell Corbin, "My husband is very much annoyed with your speculations. You must close them as quick as you can!"

"Mr. Corbin, I am undone if that letter gets out," Gould said. "If you will remain in and take the chances of the market I will give you my check for $100,000." Then the mogul left for the Gold Room, where he bid the price to new heights.

Then, unknown to everyone—even his partners—Gould began selling the bulk of his gold. And for good reason: Grant quickly ordered his Treasury secretary to dump gold on the market to stop the craze. A sale of $4 million in government specie was all it took to shatter the confidence of speculators. The market crashed on September 24, 1869, a day immediately dubbed Black Friday. Fisk later summed up the disaster succinctly: it was "each man drag out his own corpse." Gould, however, strolled away, very much alive, with a rumored $11 million in profits.

Black Friday added to a growing sense that America's money had become too abstract, too detached from the physical and metaphorical weightiness of precious metals. Congress suffered from nagging worries that the greenback was somehow dishonest—that, with the war over, a proud nation should redeem its currency in gold. The debate had even permeated the impeachment trial of

Personnel inside the international gold vault at the Federal Reserve Bank of New York, which stores more than 600,000 bars of bullion from 60 countries, tally up a shipment.

Money was now largely a matter of ledger books, not stacks of gold or even paper notes. The establishment of the Federal Reserve System (known as the Fed) in 1913 confirmed this trend. Its 12 regional banks held the reserve accounts for member institutions; when checks cleared between banks, the Fed would make a ledger entry, deducting one reserve account and crediting another.

The Fed also controlled the supply of paper currency: the new Federal Reserve note, the first version of the bills we use today. More importantly, the Fed could make it more or less costly for banks to expand their reserves and thus their loans. This system is still largely in place today.

But the cable that held the drifting supply of money to the deadweight of gold had not yet been cut. Each bank still had to maintain a fund for redeeming notes in specie; the amount of gold set an absolute limit on the number of dollars in circulation—as the nation would soon learn.

On October 24, 1929, the greatest financial panic in American history rolled across the economy like a tsunami, leaving behind a wrecked and desolate country. Endless debates have raged over the causes of the crisis, but the results were all too clear: the money supply simply shriveled. Frightened depositors emptied their accounts to get cash; frightened banks called in loans. For many, even Federal Reserve notes weren't good enough: they handed them over for gold, which they hoarded. By 1933 the money supply had shrunk by at least a quarter; more than 5,000 banks had come crashing down.

As Franklin Delano Roosevelt entered the White House that March, he realized that the currency had to be freed from the anchor of gold. Soon after taking the oath of office, he issued an extraordinary executive order that nationalized the nation's coin and bullion: gold was to be handed over to the Treasury, in return for Federal Reserve notes (which were more likely to circulate). With Congress's help, Roosevelt made it illegal to own gold (except for industrial and artistic purposes); he also stopped minting gold coins and redeeming paper dollars for gold.

Andrew Johnson in 1868. Many Republican senators had been reluctant to convict him because his designated successor, Senator Benjamin Wade, was a "soft money" man who wanted to print more greenbacks.

But to cash-starved Westerners and Southerners, legal tenders meant relief. When the Supreme Court declared the legal-tender laws (and thus greenbacks for certain debts) unconstitutional in 1870, Grant won popular acclaim by adding two new appointments to the Court to overturn the decision in 1871.

The fight between hard money and soft money dominated politics, due to the continuing money shortage after the Civil War: in 1879 there were only $72 per person in existence. While hard-money men pleaded for the honesty of the gold standard, soft-money advocates believed that there just wasn't enough specie to keep up with economic expansion.

Such conditions led to the rise of the descriptively named Greenback party. It briefly proved to be one of the most successful third-party movements in history: it won a million votes in 1878,

electing 14 Congressmen. Nevertheless, the nation went back on the gold standard in 1879. Then a strange thing happened: the debate suddenly ended. The former Greenbackers gave in to the idea that paper currency had to be backed up by precious metals. True, they still wanted to expand the money supply; but now they argued that silver should be added to gold as the specie basis of the currency—an idea called bimetallism. William Jennings Bryan, for example, won the Democratic nomination for the Presidency in 1896 with his "Cross of Gold" speech, which summed up Western and rural fury with Eastern gold-standard purists. But despite the intensity of the debate, the real war of ideas was over: the dollar, they agreed, had to be intrinsically valuable.

Ironically, money was simultaneously becoming more and more abstract in actual practice. The culprits were the banks, which spread rapidly into even rural areas after the Civil War. Banks, in fact, were becoming the medium of the medium of exchange, as the checking account began to replace actual notes.

But behind the scenes more subtle and much farther-reaching plans were being prepared. For all of the psychological importance of specie and Federal Reserve notes, the real job of making new money fell not to government printing presses but to the loan offices of banks.

In earlier times, consumers needed to trust in specie redemption before they would accept paper notes; now they had to trust in the durability of banks before they would make deposits, take out loans, or write and accept checks. So the federal government quietly poured a billion dollars into bank stocks and established the Federal Deposit Insurance Corporation (which reassured consumers that they would not lose their savings if a bank went belly-up).

As a result of the New Deal reforms, American money is more abstract than ever before. It also works better than it ever has. Since the end of the Great Depression, the United States has not suffered a single financial panic—a stretch of more than 60 years, the longest in history.

Most dollars today have no physical existence. Even ledger books began to disappear in the 1960s and '70s, replaced by computer records. The Federal Reserve System processes an average of $2.1 trillion each day through an electronic network known as Fedwire. Meanwhile, credit card companies, insurance companies, mortgage firms and retirement funds (among others) compete with banks to generate loans.

As a result of the New Deal reforms, American money is more abstract than ever.

The gold standard has sunk without a trace in this vast and complex sea of financial institutions—but it did not immediately die off in 1933. Under the Bretton Woods accord of 1944, the value of the dollar was set at $35 per ounce of gold, but only dollars held by foreign officials could be redeemed for U.S. specie (most of which was, and is, kept at Fort Knox, Kentucky). At the gold vault under the Federal Reserve Bank of New York, countries could pay each other simply by shifting so many bars from one cage to another. But a severe drain on American gold reserves caused the United States to restrict and ultimately halt specie payments, leading to the end of the international gold standard in 1971.

Today, the New York gold vault sits mostly in silence. Although individual transactions are kept secret, those that occur are generally withdrawals, as nations sell bullion on the open market. A lot of its daily activity consists of visits by tourists—a fitting reminder that the vault is essentially a curiosity, a throwback to the age when Americans believed that money had to be something valuable in and of itself. Now money is largely a unit of account—it exists simply because we say it is there. And gold is just another asset like stocks, bonds or real estate—except it is less popular as an investment.

In American history, money has gone from tobacco to gold to greenbacks to ledger books to electrons. Today our institutionalized, interconnected economy resembles an electronic circuit, with money constantly flowing through it like an electric current. No, not *like* an electric current—it *is* an electric current, powering our globally wired world.

T. J. Stiles began the study of money and banking as part of his research for his forthcoming biography of Jesse James.

The Strange Case of the Surgeon at Crowthorne

"I am Dr. James Murray of the London Philological Society and Editor of the New English Dictionary. *It is indeed an honor and a pleasure to at long last make your acquaintance—for you must be, kind sir, my most assiduous helpmeet, Dr. W. C. Minor?"*

By Simon Winchester

POPULAR LEGEND HAS IT THAT A most remarkable conversation took place on a misty autumn afternoon in 1897, in the small English village of Crowthorne. One of the parties to the colloquy was the formidable James Murray, the then editor of the *Oxford English Dictionary,* or, as it was called in its early days, the *New English Dictionary.* On the day in question Murray had traveled 50 miles by train from Oxford to meet an enigmatic figure named Dr. W. C. Minor, who was among the most prolific of the thousands of volunteer contributors whose searches into word origins and meanings were crucial to the dictionary's creation. For very nearly 20 years these two men had corresponded regularly about the finer points of English lexicography. But, so the story goes, they had never met. Dr. Minor never seemed willing or able to leave his home at Crowthorne, never willing to come the 50 miles up to Oxford. He was unable to offer any kind of explanation, nor do more than offer his regrets.

Murray, who himself was rarely free from the burdens of his work at his dictionary headquarters, the famous Scriptorium in Oxford, had long wished to see and to thank his mysterious and intriguing helper, particularly so by the late 1890s when, with the dictionary well under way, official honors were being showered upon all its creators. Murray wanted to make sure that all those involved—even one so apparently bashful as Dr. Minor—were fully recognized for the demanding work they had put in. Murray decided that he would pay a visit. "If the mountain would not come to Mahomet, then Mahomet would go to the mountain."

Accordingly, he telegraphed his intentions to Dr. Minor, noting that he would find it most convenient to take a train that arrived at Crowthorne Station just after 2 o'clock on a certain Wednesday in November. By return wire, Dr. Minor said that would be fine; the great lexicographer was indeed expected and would be made most welcome.

At the railway station a polished brougham and a liveried coachman were waiting, and with James Murray aboard they clip-clopped back through the lanes of rural Berkshire and at last drew up outside a huge and rather forbidding red-brick mansion. A solemn servant showed him into a grand and book-lined study, where behind an immense mahogany desk stood a man of undoubted importance. Murray bowed gravely, and launched into the brief speech of greeting that he had so long rehearsed:

"A very good afternoon to you, sir. I am Dr. James Murray of the London Philological Society, and editor of the *New English Dictionary.* It is indeed an honor and a pleasure to at long last make your acquaintance—for you must be, kind sir, my most assiduous helpmeet, Dr. W. C. Minor?"

Seizing the murder weapon, Tarrant asked, "Whom did you shoot at?" "A man," said Minor.

There was a brief pause, an air of momentary mutual embarrassment. A clock ticked loudly. There were muffled footsteps in the hall. And then the man behind the desk cleared his throat, and spoke:

"I regret, kind sir, that I am not. It is not at all as you suppose. I am in fact the superintendent of the Broadmoor Criminal Lunatic Asylum. Dr. Minor is most certainly here. But he is an inmate. He has been a patient here for more than 20 years."

William Chester Minor, the man whom Murray visited at Crowthorne, was an American. In 1897 he was 63. Born of American missionary parents on the island of Ceylon, he had spent his teenage years in New Haven, Connecticut, gone to Yale, and later qualified as a surgeon. But a distinctly unkind fate eventually brought him to England and placed him in Broadmoor—a grim place still standing today—which had been built shortly before he arrived. It was then the pride and joy of those doctor-scientists who were still called "alienists," eventually to be restyled as clinical psychiatrists. Minor was in Broadmoor because he was quite mad, and because he had committed a murder in London in February 1872.

The crime was as shocking as it was unprecedented, for it was one of the few murders in London to involve the use of a firearm. The killing, trial and punishment also provide an astonishing early look at a subject that has lately much preoccupied American courts: the relation between murderous intent, high intelligence and insanity. The killing actually took place around 2:30 one moonlit Saturday night in the run-down Lambeth section of London. Three or perhaps four shots rang out. They were loud, very loud, and they echoed through the cold and smokily damp night air. They were heard and instantly recognized by a young police constable named Henry Tarrant.

When Tarrant heard them he ran toward the sound and met Minor, who was holding a gun. Seizing the murder weapon Tarrant asked, "Whom did you shoot at?" "A man," said Minor. "You don't suppose I would be so cowardly as to shoot a woman?" Two other policemen appeared, and were sent to look after the dying man. A few onlookers began to collect. Blood was gushing onto the pavement—staining a spot that for many months afterward would be variously described in London's more dramatically minded papers as the location of a "Heinous Crime," a "Terrible Event," an "Atrocious Occurrence" and a "Vile Murder."

The man who died, a Wiltshire farm laborer named George Merritt, has since been almost obliterated by the wash of history. He was one of many country folk who had lately been lured to industrialized London in search of work. He was married to a farm girl named Eliza and had seven children. (Eliza was pregnant with an eighth). He worked in Lambeth as a night stoker at the Lion Brewery (the landmark lion of which still stands today, outside Waterloo Station). It was pure accident that walking to work so early on that cold morning, he came across, of all people, an American with a gun—an American tormented by a curiously insane belief.

Dr. Minor takes the red hot branding iron and presses the glowing metal onto the deserter's cheek.

The American was William Minor. In his deranged mind, he thought George Merritt, an utterly innocent stranger, was actually a vengeful Irishman bent on doing him sinister, even unspeakable, harm—an Irishman, as he saw it, who needed to be shot dead in self-defense. To understand these grim and bizarre doings requires taking a look back into William Minor's own tragic history, as the English courts promptly did.

Minor appeared, at first, to be one of fortune's favorites, rich, intelligent and of good family. After Yale he joined the Army—the Union Army, which, the year being 1864, was fighting the Civil War. After a few months' training in a Connecticut hospital, he served as an assistant surgeon in the Northern army, and was sent into battle against the Confederates.

He was by all accounts a sensitive man. He read a good deal, painted in watercolors, played the flute. Perhaps not the ideal candidate to handle the rough and bloody work of war, he was particularly ill-prepared to deal with the dreadful slaughterhouse known as the Battle of the Wilderness.

The battle began when General Grant's army crossed the Rapidan River and ended, after just 50 hours, with 25,000 dead and wounded. The rifle fire was so thick and so close that it not only killed men but cut off whole trees at shoulder height and set the Virginia underbrush afire. Hundreds and hundreds of men, the wounded as well as the fit, were burned to death.

The "ammunition trains exploded," one soldier wrote; "the dead were roasted in the conflagration; the wounded . . . dragged themselves along with their torn and mangled limbs, in the mad energy of despair, to escape. . . . It seemed as though Christian men had turned to fiends, and hell itself had usurped the place of earth."

Many of the men caught up in the battle happened to be Irish—men who, suffering from famine across the Atlantic, migrated to America and got work as soldiers in the Union Army for $13 a month.

Scores of soldiers had begun to desert. Desertion, the high command decreed, must be stopped. Not by execution; the ranks were too thin to permit so many men to be literally stricken from the rolls. Instead, deserters were to be humiliated, then returned to the line; punished, and sent back into the fight.

Anyone leaving his post would be subjected to savage official abuse, the aim being to make sure he didn't desert again. A deserter could, for example, be gagged with a bayonet, the blade tied across his open mouth with twine, or be suspended by his thumbs.

In some cases—and this was deemed a perfect combination of pain and humiliation—deserters were branded, the letter *D* seared into a cheek, or chest or buttock. Regulations became quite specific on this point—a letter an inch and a half high could either be burned on with a hot iron, or cut with a razor and the wound then filled with black powder, to cause irritation and indelibility.

Branding, it was claimed at William Minor's London trial, was what the young doctor had been forced to do. It is easy to imagine the situation. An Irish deserter, convicted by a drumhead court of running from the terrors of the Wilderness, is sentenced to be branded. The officers of the court decide that the new acting assistant surgeon, this fresh-faced and genteel-looking Yalie, should carry out the punishment. It will be as good a way as any, the older, war-weary officers imply, to introduce Dr. Minor to the rigors of war. And so the Irish deserter is brought to him, arms shackled behind his back.

He is exhausted and frightened. He is dirty and unkempt. His uniform is torn to rags by a frantic, desperate run through the brambles. He wants to go back home to Ireland. He begs for a chance to see his family again. He may expect one day to use what soldiering skills he has learned in Grant's army to fight against the British occupiers of his homeland.

Doubtless he pleads with the court; he pleads with his guards. He cries, he screams, he struggles. But the soldiers hold him down, and Dr. Minor takes the red-hot branding iron from a basket of glowing coals hastily borrowed from the brigade farrier. Minor hesitates for a moment—a hesitation that betrays his own reluctance. The officers grunt for him to continue—and he presses the glowing metal onto the deserter's cheek. The flesh sizzles and steams, the prisoner screams and screams.

And then it is over. The wretch is led away, holding to his injured cheek the alcohol-soaked rag that Minor has given him. Perhaps the wound will become infected, will fill with the "laudable pus" that other doctors have said hints at cure. Perhaps it will fester and crust with sores. Perhaps it will blister and burst and bleed for weeks.

By any accounting such a man would have ample reason to want, one day, to wreak his revenge on the man who tortured him.

As for William Chester Minor, the vision of this Irishman would haunt him for the rest of his life, filling his nights with waking nightmares, paranoid visions of vengeful spirits bent on exacting horrible retribution. He grew fearful of all Irishmen—imagining that not only his branded victim but the man's friends and relations and colleagues were after him. Indeed, he thought every Irish man jack in creation would come in the night, find him and, as he put it, "abuse him shamefully." All because he had been ordered to inflict so cruel a punishment on one of their number in America.

If that seems far-fetched, it was suggested during his trial that sometime after the branding, William Minor began to spiral downward into madness. He was steadily to become a sufferer from what in those days was called dementia praecox, what modern-day medicine defines as schizophrenia—though whether a branding would exacerbate this condition long term, is doubtful. In any case, he became delusional, violent, suspicious. He began to have horrible dreams in which, night after night, "people" would wake him and transport him to distant seraglios where he would be forced to perform unnatural acts with men, young children, animals. Today he could go into therapy, or be treated with sophisticated, psychotropic drugs, such as risperidone, which allow some schizophrenics to function with fair normality in society. Back then there was almost nothing that could be done for him.

In the end Murray accumulated a ton of such paper contributions —millions of small cards.

He retired from the Army, though not before fighting for and winning a lifetime pension from the authorities—fellow officers who, in a kindly way, agreed that his illness doubtless had been contracted in the line of duty, as a result of war. So Minor became a veteran, sickly and with shattered nerves, because of service to his country. It was in this sadly afflicted condition that Minor was sent by his parents to England. They wanted him to settle down, to live life at a slower and more untroubled pace, to paint, to mingle with great minds, to try to redeem himself. They had a friend who knew the great art critic and drawing master John Ruskin, and they equipped their son with a letter of introduction to him, the better to gain entry to the English capital's beau monde.

Instead, for reasons that no one was able to elucidate, Dr. Minor took rooms in the lowest and meanest parts of London, possibly to gain easy access to

women of the night. And when he killed a man, he said that the man was one of the Irish who loomed so large in his persecutional delusions. George Merritt was the soon-forgotten victim; his murderer, the court decided, was a man who must be put away for the rest of his life in Broadmoor Asylum, locked up in a cell overlooking the green Berkshire countryside. He was to be detained, the authorities decreed in the sentencing language of the time, "During Her Majesty's Pleasure."

And there Minor would have rotted away for the remainder of a lifetime, except that one day in the summer of 1880, he came across a slip of paper tucked into a book that he had ordered from a library in London. "An Appeal for Readers," the paper was headed. It was an invitation for interested and scholarly people to help in assembling an ambitious publication in progress at Oxford University and eventually to be called the *New English Dictionary,* the biggest expository collection of English words and their senses that had ever been created in the history of the English language.

Minor was intrigued. He had plenty of money and long since had established connections with bookstores by mail. He was himself a considerable reader and book collector. A model inmate during the day, and an inmate of means, he was allowed to occupy two cells in Broadmoor's relatively relaxed Cell Block Two, one of them equipped as a library. (In the other room, in which he slept, he had had the floors covered with zinc—to keep the demons from coming up through the floorboards at night.) A manservant helped him organize his books.

Astonishingly, he had also forged a relationship with young Eliza Merritt, the widow of the man he had shot dead. She said she had forgiven him—not least, it is perhaps cynically appropriate to remark, because, by way of apology and reparation, Minor had settled some money on her and her children.

Eliza was allowed to visit him in his cell every now and then. Minor persuaded her to bring him parcels of antiquarian books from the great dealers in central London. Since he was able to add to his library at will, he surmised after reading James Murray's "Appeal" that he was in an ideal position to become an invisible scholar, a constant contributor to this noble and redeeming dictionary project.

Off went a note to Murray, at the oddly named Scriptorium—the dictionary's headquarters, first in London's Mill Hill district, and then, for the remaining three decades until Murray's death, on the Banbury Road in Oxford. Minor gave his address merely as Crowthorne, Berkshire, and wrote to inquire if he might be able to help. He had a reasonable knowledge of 16th- and 17-century English literature, he said. And he had a fair amount of time on his hands.

Murray said later that the letter from Crowthorne came very soon after the beginning of his work on the dictionary—probably 1880, or perhaps 1881. Dr. Minor, he was to write, "proved to be a very good reader, who wrote to me often. I thought that he must be a retired medical man with plenty of available time."

The work that Murray demanded of some thousands of volunteers was of a kind peculiar to the style of this pioneering dictionary. Murray and his predecessors had decided that each and every word in English, and each and every sense of each and every word, needed to be supported by an illustrative quotation. And that, if possible, the uses would include the earliest known in English and an example from each century thereafter. One of the first uses found of the word "pig," for example, was as a plural noun in Chaucer's *The Reeve's Tale,* from the 14th century: "And in the floor, with nose and mouth to-broke, They walwe as doon two pigges in a poke."

As the work progressed through the alphabet, readers like William Minor were supposed to scour all English literature and send in cards quoting findings and uses, for every meaning, every word, every variant form.

In the end the editors accumulated a ton of such paper contributions—millions of small cards, made up by thousands of volunteers not only from all over England and Ireland and Scotland but in some cases America as well, with handwritten notations and quotations and references culled from English-language books and newspapers and magazines written and edited from every century since the ninth, when a significant number of documents in English had accumulated.

Eliza was allowed to visit him. Minor persuaded her to bring him antiquarian books from London.

William Minor was among the best and most assiduous of the contributors. He sent in cards by the score, by the thousand, eventually by the tens of thousands. Quotations, meticulously written and noted and bundled and annotated, cascaded from large brown manila envelopes out onto the desks of the sub-editors at the Scriptorium, delighting Murray, and proving time and again that he had been right to believe in this strategy of finding volunteers—and especially volunteers of Dr. Minor's quality—as the best and most economical means of assembling his dictionary.

Each time Murray found himself basking in the pleasure of receiving yet another batch of contributions from the surgeon at Crowthorne, he would write back immediately, offering his thanks, suggesting that the good doctor might like to come up to Oxford and receive in person the thanks and admiration that his meticulous and perceptive labors deserved.

But the good doctor, as we know, never came. He dissembled. He made excuses about infirmity, shyness, the physical impossibility of his coming up to Oxford. And for years James Murray accepted it all as eccentricity, and shrugged his shoulders. Lexicographical volunteers were a rum bunch (one, Henry Furnivall, assembled rowing crews of buxom waitresses charmed out of a Hammersmith tea shop); if William Minor was recluse down in Crowthorne, then so be it.

And yet, he was so good, so keen, so energetic—and so tantalizingly close. Murray really wanted badly to see him. The matter came to a head as a result of what has ever since been known as the Great Dictionary Dinner.

It was 1897, a Jubilee Year, the 60th year of Queen Victoria's reign, and Oxford was more than in the mood for a party. The dictionary was going well. The progress, faltering in the early years, had accelerated—the section from *Anta* to *Battening* was finished in 1885, *Battenlie-Bozzom* in 1887, *Bra-Byzen* in 1888. A new efficiency had settled over the Scriptorium. As the crowning glory, Queen Victoria had in 1897 "graciously agreed," as the court liked to say, that the whole dictionary could be dedicated to her. They had just completed Volume III—embracing the letters *D* and *E*.

An aura of majestic permanence had all of a sudden invested the dictionary project. There was no doubt now that it would eventually be completed—for since it had been regally approved, who could now ever brook its cancellation? The queen had done her part, so now Oxford, in high mood for celebration, decided it could follow suit. James Murray deserved to be given honors and thanks, and who more appropriate than the great man's adopted university to bestow them.

The university's new vice-chancellor decided that a big dinner—a "slap-up," to employ a phrase that the dictionary was to quote from 1823—should be held in Murray's honor. It would be staged in the huge hall at Queen's College, where by old tradition a scholar with a silver trumpet would sound a fanfare to summon guests in to dine. It would celebrate what the *Times,* on the day of the dinner, proclaimed to be "the greatest effort probably which any university, it may be any printing press, has taken in hand since the invention of printing. . . . It will not be the least of the glories of the University of Oxford to have completed this gigantic task." The evening would be a memorable Oxford event.

As indeed it was. The long tables were splendidly decorated. The menu might be forthright and English—clear turtle soup, turbot with a lobster sauce, haunch of mutton, roast partridges, Queen Mab pudding, strawberry ice, but like the dictionary itself, it was also flavored generously, but not too generously, with hints of Gallicisms: sweet-breads *á la Villeroi,* grenadins of veal, *ramequins.* There were no fewer than 14 speeches—James Murray on the entire history of the making of the dictionary, the head of the Oxford University Press on his belief that the project was a great duty to the nation, and the egregious Henry Furnivall—as lively and amusing as ever, he had taken time out from re-cruiting waitresses to go a-rowing with him—on what he saw as Oxford's heart-less attitude toward the admission of women.

Among the guests, along with all the great and the good of the academic land, were some of the most capable and en-ergetic of the volunteer readers. But not the most energetic of all, William Minor. He was invited, of course, but he never showed. His absence saddened James Murray, more than at any time before. And so a few days later we approach the scene with which this story begins.

Though they may have met once be-fore—Murray's letters suggest they probably did—according to legend their fateful first meeting occurred after the famous brougham ride through the lanes of Berkshire.

Whenever it happened, for both men in the first sight of each other must have been peculiar indeed, for they were un-cannily similar in appearance. Both were extravagantly bearded. Portraits of Minor have an air of avuncular kindli-ness; Murray looks much the same, but with a trace of the severity that might well mark a lowland Scot from a Con-necticut Yankee.

Each man might have imagined, for a second, that, rather than meeting a stranger, he was stepping toward himself in a looking glass.

Over several years, the two met a number of times. By all accounts they got on famously—a liking that was sub-ject only to Dr. Minor's moods, to which Murray became fully sensible as time passed. Murray often had the foresight before each visit to telegraph, asking how the patient was; if Minor was in

low spirits and angry, Murray remained at Oxford; if he was low and likely to be comforted, then Murray would board the train.

The years passed, the passion for English words uniting the two old men, despite their differences.

When the weather was poor, the two men would sit together in Minor's room—a small and practically furnished cell not too dissimilar from a typical Oxford student's room, and just like the room that Murray was to be given at Balliol College once he was made an honorary fellow. It was lined with book-shelves, all of which were open except for one glass-fronted case that held the rarest of the 16th- and 17th-century works from which much of Minor's dic-tionary research was being done. The fireplace crackled merrily. Tea and Dun-dee cake were brought in—one of the many privileges that the superintendent accorded to his now distinguished patient.

And so the years passed, the passion for English words uniting the two old men, the differing dynamics of insanity and anonymity and distinction dividing them.

But just at the turn of the 20th cen-tury, a terrible tragedy suddenly befell Dr. Minor, a savage self-mutilation, done, he felt, to remove him from sexual exploitation by the demons of the night. This wounding enfeebled him. His work for the great book began slowly to fall away. He seemed to lose interest, at a point meticulously noted by the stern editors at the press as occurring at the time he was gathering quotations for the letter *Q.*

Shocked and deeply concerned, James Murray suggested to members of the government—now that he had been knighted and showered with honors—that the old man ought to be released. Minor was in failing health, he said, and

harmless. Whitehall's bureaucrats and Westminster's politicians should let him go back to America, to die among his own people.

It was not until 1910 that the govern-ment, wearied by Murray's badgering, agreed. It fell to the young Winston Churchill, as Home Secretary, to sign the papers granting Minor's release and, more out of formality than spite, order that he be deported, forever forbidden to reenter the United Kingdom. Back in Connecticut, the family agreed to pro-vide an escort. Sir James Murray went down to Broadmoor to say fond fare-wells. He brought with him a court pho-tographer, who would take a final portrait of the brilliant old volunteer: a sepia image that still speaks of scholar-ship and friendship, of wisdom and pain. It is somehow a very touching pic-ture, cracked and frail and venerable, much like the subject himself.

In April 1910, the steamer *Minne-tonka* left England, bearing Dr. Minor home to New York, in the company of his brother Alfred, who for years had borne up as well as he could under the knowledge that his brother was mad, but clearly not bad, much less danger-ous to know.

It was years before he actually got home. His first stop was Washington, D. C., and what is now St. Elizabeths hos-pital for the insane. The American gov-ernment consigned him there for nearly a decade before letting the family take him back to Connecticut, where he died at age 85 in the spring of 1920. (He is buried in New Haven's fashionable Ev-ergreen Cemetery with a small brown sandstone marker on his grave.)

William Chester Minor's name ap-pears, without a hint of his scandalous secret, in the preface to the *Oxford En-glish Dictionary.*

This story has been adapted from Simon Winchester's new book, The Professor and the Madman, *published by Harper-Collins. Robert Steele lives and works in San Francisco.*

Unit 3

Unit Selections

Key Points to Consider

❖ Why was it important to know about eyes and light? How did this affect later thinking?

❖ Why are science and industry considered unique characteristics of Western civilization? Are they really unique? How so?

❖ Debate the statement, "the only good science is applied science" (science that has a practical result).

❖ Why are information systems important? What happens if information is withheld or censored?

❖ Why should Howard H. Aiken be honored if his Mark I did not lead the way to modern computers?

❖ If information is transmitted instantaneously, as with a telegraph, can it ever be improved? Are we at a communications "dead end"?

❖ Should we bother to spend money on space exploration? What would happen to human accomplishments and history if a meteorite should obliterate life on the planet, as has happened in the past?

 **Links**   **www.dushkin.com/online/**

These sites are annotated on pages 4 and 5.

The purpose of science is to explain natural phenomenon; the purpose of technology is to apply knowledge from any source for the benefit of humankind. Although it was the scientific revolution and the industrial revolution (where technology was used for mechanization and mass production) that gave overwhelming power to the West, it would be arrogant to assume that other civilizations made no contribution. "Eyes Wide Open" illustrates the significance of an observation by an obscure Arab in the tenth century. The people of the West, however, progressed rapidly in science compared to others. With the publication of Isaac Newton's *Principia* in 1687 (see "In God's Place"), the destruction of the Aristotelian paradigm of the cosmos was complete. There were physical rules that human beings had the power to uncover. Humans were no longer at the center of the universe. This had a dramatic impact on human thought and philosophy.

The industrial revolution was not a revolt in the sense of a quick, dramatic overturn like the French Revolution. It was slower than that, with roots that reached back into the Middle Ages. It started in England where favorable economic, religious, and governmental policies prevailed. "The Workshop of a New Society" explains that England possessed the resources, need, and opportunity for the change. Having used up its forest resources, the British turned to coal for fuel. As miners dug deeper for the coal, drainage of water became a necessity. In the early eighteenth century, Thomas Newcomen, therefore, designed a practical steam engine to pump and drain the water. Thus, coal and steam power gave the British portable energy, and people were able to escape the vagaries of wind power and streams.

The success of the British with the industrial revolution contrasts the industrial failures of the Chinese, who had the ideas of mechanization and mass production as early as the eleventh century. As examined in the article, "The X Factor," the ideas did not flourish in China, and the explanation for their failure is not entirely clear. Various reasons are given, but the result was that China fell behind in this important technological development.

A variety of machines contributed to the success of the industrial revolution, such as the steam engine, but there are others that aided the ongoing changes in production. Larry Hoffman, in "The Rock Drill and Civilization," reveals the significance of the changes in mining and metallurgy through time. As industrialization commenced, mining became more sophisticated and mechanized. Communications, in addition, steadily improved with the telegraph, telephone, and wireless radio. An important episode in the history of communications was the laying of a telegraph cable across the Atlantic Ocean in 1866. "The Transatlantic Telegraph Cable" by Gillian Cookson illustrates the technology, resources, and determination of Westerners. According to arcane information theory, it is the flow of information that is most important for the success of business, military, and social systems. Telegraph cables provided instant information about business and other news from Europe and around the world.

With the advent of the Internet and e-mail a new information age has started. The key enabling invention was the computer, which was invented during World War II. "Father of the Computer Age" names Howard H. Aiken as a major pioneer in this technology and describes one of the early computers that measured 51 feet long. These machines, which are essentially an extension of the industrial revolution, made space exploration possible. One example is the stunning achievement of Pathfinder, a small dune buggy that the United States landed upon the surface of Mars. The precision necessary for such exploration would have been impossible without the use of computers. In a broad sense the mission of Pathfinder, as described in the article, "Greetings From Mars," combines the spirit of adventure that propelled the Western navigators across the oceans with the knowledge and capability gained from the scientific and industrial revolutions.

The Industrial and Scientific Revolutions

Eyes Wide Open

When an obscure Arab scientist solved the riddle of light, the universe no longer belonged to God.

By Richard Powers

By any human measure, a millennium is a considerable chunk of time. It is the longest fixed unit of time with a distinct name in common usage. At the beginning of our spent millennium and at frequent intervals throughout it, vexed to nightmare by the calendar, believers have awaited Christ's imminent return to rule over a new heaven and earth in a kingdom that was to run for the unthinkable span of a thousand years. Near the millennium's end, the Nazis, refiners of another one of the period's most persistent concepts, predicted their own third kingdom would last for a thousand years. They were off by 988.

At the start of this millennium, nothing resembling an accurate map of any continent existed. Now a hand-held Global Positioning System satellite receiver can pinpoint its owner's location anywhere on the face of the globe. Trade and enterprise have expanded beyond all reckoning. More volumes are printed each year than existed in the year 1000. The last 10 centuries have also seen global deforestation, a steep falling off in spoken languages and mass extinction on a scale beyond anything since the Cretaceous.

Any search for the millennium's most important concept already dooms itself to myopia. Consider the candidates that spring to mind: parliamentary democracy, the nation–state, free markets, due process, the limited liability corporation, insurance, the university, mandatory formal education, abolition, socialism, the emancipation of women, universal suffrage, universal human rights. The scope of the upheaval in social institutions suggests some corresponding revolution in underlying thought almost too large to isolate.

It lies beyond all reasonable doubt that no single idea has had a more profound or ubiquitous impact on what the human race has become, or what it has worked upon the face of the planet, than the vesting of authority in experiment.

Line up the usual intellectual suspects: the theory of evolution, relativity, the mapping of the unconscious. As cataclysmic as each has been for our own era, they are 11th-hour arrivals, the latter-day consequences of ideas much larger and longer in motion. Push backward to Boyle's Law, Newton's F = ma or the Copernican Revolution, and you begin to close in on that fundamental leap in human conception.

The notion of progress, the invention of the future, might itself be a leading candidate for the most influential idea of the millennium. But the belief in transformation and advancement, in a constantly increasing control over the material world, is still just a symptom of a wider conceptual revolution that lies at the heart of what has happened to the world in these last 1,000 years: the rise of the experimental method.

Say, then, that the most important idea of this millennium was set in motion by a man named Abu Ali al-Hasan Ibn al-Haytham, born around the year 965 in Basra, in what is now Iraq. Even by his Western name, Alhazen, he remains a little-known figure in the history of thought. But the idea that Ibn al-Haytham championed is so ingrained in us that we don't even think of it as an innovation, let alone one that has appeared so late in the human day.

Ibn al-Haytham resolved a scientific dispute that had remained deadlocked for more than 800 years. Two inimical theories vied to explain the mystery of vision. Euclid, Ptolemy and other mathematicians demonstrated that light necessarily traveled from the eye to the observed object. Aristotle and the atomists assumed the reverse. Both theories were complete and internally consistent, with no way to arbitrate between them.

Then Ibn al-Haytham made several remarkable observations. His most remarkable was also the simplest. He invited observers to stare at the sun, which proved the point: when you looked at a sufficiently bright object, it burned the eye. He made no appeal to geometry or theoretical necessity. Instead, he demolished a whole mountain of systematic theory with a single appeal to data. Light started outside the eye and reflected into it. No other explanation was consistent with the evidence.

Ptolemy had appealed to math and reason: Aristotle's position had been mere conjecture. The world, however, answered to neither reason nor conjecture. What argument required was something more than theory, something that would hold up in the court of controlled looking. This empirical insistence lay at the heart of Ibn al-Haytham's real revolution, and while he did not upend the world single-handedly, his influence has spread without limits.

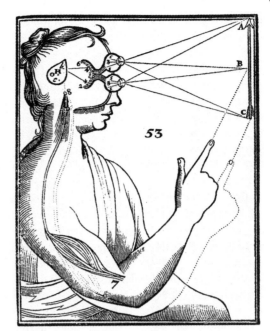

For René Descartes in the mid-1600's, seeing was believing, as underscored by this diagram in one of the mathematician and philosopher's books.

THE SHIFT FROM AUTHORITY to observation seems small, self-evident, almost inevitable. In reality, it is none of these. Over the course of 1,000 years, the conceptual shift would grow catastrophic, and its consequences would transform every aspect of existence.

Ibn al-Haytham made numerous other experimental contributions to optics and physics, part of a surge of Arab science at a time when Europe possessed little science to speak of. His contemporaries, investigators like Ibn Ahmad al-Biruni, Ibn Rushd (Averroes) and Ibn Sina (Avicenna), revived and extended Greek thought, unhindered by Augustine's insistence that the world was an inscrutable riddle invented by God to lead us toward contemplation of a universe beyond this one. While none of these men can be called an experimental scientist in the modern sense, each helped to open up the possibility that the world can be known through its particulars and that direct observation was the best way to know it.

When the Arab cities in southern Spain began to fall in the late 11th century, the contents of their great libraries flooded into Christian Europe. Ibn al-Haytham's works on optics were at last translated into Latin late in the 12th century, enlightening the proto-empiricist Roger Bacon (c. 1220–1292).

Bacon—Dr. Mirabilis, as he came to be known—was a bizarre mixture of old and new mind. Both a philosophical Franciscan and an anti-philosophical experimentalist, he fought to introduce science into university curriculums and became the first European to write down the recipe for gunpowder. He proposed ideas for airplanes, power-driven ships and automobiles. Ibn al-Haytham's optics, which included the invention of a primitive camera obscura, led Bacon to many optical insights.

But optics formed just the visible surface of what Bacon took away from Ibn al-Haytham. "Argument," he asserted in his "Opus Majus" (1267), " . . . does not remove doubt, so that the mind may rest in the sure knowledge of the truth, unless it finds it by the method of experiment. . . . For if any man who never saw fire proved by satisfactory arguments that fire burns . . . his hearer's mind would never be satisfied, nor would he avoid the fire until he put his hand in it . . . that he might learn by experiment what argument taught."

The world was not a vaporous trap but a collection of things with heft and substance, worth the closest scrutiny and palpation. Aristotle failed to see the value of controlled experiment, believing that nature could only be understood whole. With Bacon, through Ibnal-Haytham, there arises the idea of testing for truth through isolated particulars. Bacon's was also the moment in Western sculpture when Mary stops holding her child out in front of her like a pillar of stone and starts to straddle her grasping boy over one load-bearing, sensual hip.

Another three centuries passed before science emerged from its roots in natural philosophy. But the idea of looking had begun to shake the foundations of authority at the base of thought.

Light did not come from the eye, but rather fell into it. The world could be grasped in its particulars.

WILLIAM OF OCKHAM (c. 1285–c. 1347) bolstered empiricism with his own Law of Parsimony, or Ockham's Razor: when multiple ways exist to explain a datum, go with the one that requires the fewest theoretical assumptions. Jan van Eyck (c. 1395–c. 1441) took the zeal for nominal reality to such heights that his Ghent altarpiece depicts more than 40 identifiable plant species. Ibn al-

Haytham's empirical optics traveled down yet another path to trouble the medieval mind into early modernism. If light entered the eye from the outside, then the eye sat at the tip of a visual cone, where the perpendicular ray dominated over all oblique ones. This implied a geometry of seeing, described by Ibn al-Haytham and elaborated on by Witelo (d. after 1281), a Pole connected with the papal court. Through Witelo, the idea of visual perspective spread in Italy.

The new depth of seeing worked its spell on Giotto (c. 1267–1337). The solid spaces hinted at in his frescoes were said to reduce viewers to alarm and ecstasy. The eye of Europe turned itself inside out. Ibn al-Haytham's camera obscura, improved upon by Bacon, set painters loose on the pursuit of light and its reflection off real surfaces.

But only when Brunelleschi, Masaccio and Uccello got wind of the new optical mathematics through their compatriot, the geographer-mathematician Paolo Toscanelli (b. 1397), did Western Europe achieve full liftoff into rectilinear reality. Using the techniques of deep perspective, with its ability to measure the relative size of objects at any distance, Toscanelli assembled a chart that wound up leading Columbus to the New World. The deep spaces of the new painting opened up even deeper spaces on the map, terra incognita that the Age of Exploration rushed to fill in.

Ibn al-Haytham's inexorable idea derives its power from a radical overthrow of what constitutes acceptable demonstration. Nothing, finally, can gainsay the data. Wholeness, harmony and radiance must give way to verifiability and repeatability. With the invention of printing, experimental data could proliferate without limit. Fueled by and fueling the Protestant Reformation, with its universal priesthood of man, skepticism's challenge to received wisdom spread into all quarters.

So did Ibn al-Haytham's optics. His work on refraction and lenses led to the development of the telescope and microscope. Once these devices threw open their portals onto the invisible, there was no looking back. Van Leeuwenhoek's (1632–1723) "tiny animalcules" revealed the living world to be stranger than any natural philosopher could have guessed.

The Lutheran Kepler (1571–1630), in his "Supplement to Witelo," solved the problem of atmospheric refraction and built Ibn al-Haytham's foundation into a full account of vision. Freed up to cast his glance into the heavens, Kepler explained magnification and laid out the laws of planetary motion. And Galileo, the true prototype of the modern skeptical empiricist, looking at the light that fell into his telescope tube and reporting what he saw, defying all theory and common sense, moved the world against the world's wishes. Rising to his feet after recanting to the authorities, as legend has it, he muttered the words that would form the credo of triumphant science: "But it does move." In short order, measurement laid out the calculus behind its every wobble.

"And new philosophy calls all in doubt," John Donne wrote in his poem "An Anatomy of the World: the First Anniversary" (1611). And doubt itself became the engine of the new creation.

Francis Bacon (1561–1626) wrote the user's manual for the new scientific instrument of thought. He banished the "idols of the mind," those habits of reason that blinded you to the evidence. Knowledge depended on suspending belief in anything except the most indifferent measurement. In "The Advancement of Learning" (1605), he wrote, "If a man will begin with certainties, he shall end in doubts, but if he will be content to begin with doubts, he shall end in certainties."

With the Baconian method, knowledge did not stop at the curation and annotation of bygone ideas. Bacon was right: the revolution unleashed in Western Europe in the 17th century represents the sharpest break with the past in history. In the 300 years since the break commenced, modern science and its handmaid, technology, have altered the globe beyond recognition or recall, revising the terms of material existence, not to mention the geopolitical ones. For politics, too, is born in experiment. The rise of a technological Europe produced an era of imperialism from which the continents have yet to recover.

"It is not *what* the man of science believes that distinguishes him," Bertrand Russell said, "but *how* and *why* he believes it. His beliefs are tentative, not dogmatic; they are based on evidence, not on authority or intuition." Out of that tentativeness have flowed the airplane, air pump, anesthesia, aniline dye, antiseptic surgery, aspirin, atomic energy, automobiles and on, ad infinitum.

The most adventurous mind from the year 1000—even Ibn al-Haytham himself—faced with the runaway results of the experimental method, would have no available mental response short of schizophrenia. Ibn al-Haytham's doubt of existing optical theory has led to the certainties of electron microscopy, retinal surgery and robotic vision. Millennial expectation has shifted away from the thousand-year reign of Christ toward the thousand-megahertz personal computer. The universe has progressed from an enigmatic metaphysical emblem to the accidental byproduct of superstrings. An orbiting telescope now extends the cone of vision out to the very edges of creation.

There is something paradoxical in claiming, as the greatest concept of the last millennium, the skeptical rejection of concept in favor of evidence. But there is something paradoxical in the idea of radical empiricism itself. At its purest, science strives to be neither logical nor reasonable, merely suspicious. It claims to begin in the abeyance of theory, but strives to produce a deeper, wider explanation of observable event. It pursues a relentless reductionism in order to erect a single, consistent material theory of everything from the unified cosmological force to the evolution of consciousness, a vastly more comprehensive blueprint than any City of God, yet still a theory, always tentative, and refutable at best.

In fact, in the most fundamental sense, skeptical empiricism may be a contradiction in terms. It has come under attack in recent years by a number of thinkers—from Ludwig Wittgenstein to Thomas Kuhn and beyond—who have no qualms about applying the same skepticism toward the scientific method that Francis Bacon advocated applying to any body of accepted lore. Their objections are many and varied: that fact and artifact may be closer than most empiricists are comfortable accepting. That even pure observation has an agenda. That great empiricists have rejected initial data on hunches, until their observations produced more acceptable numbers. That scientists need pre-existing theory and supposition even to ask the questions that will lead to data. That the shape of a question produces the data that answer it.

A new generation of cultural constructionists similarly maintains that Western science, whatever its technological triumphs, is the product of a certain cultural moment and represents no transcultural truths. But that notion, too, may beg the question of just which forces construct culture. You may well wonder whether any but a culture of high technology could have produced the theories of cultural construction.

Still, it lies beyond all reasonable doubt that no single idea has had a more profound or ubiquitous impact on what the human race has become, or what it has worked upon the face of the planet, than the vesting of authority in experiment. Anyone who looks can arrive at no other conclusion. More urgent, at this moment, is the question of what the greatest idea of the next thousand years will have to be if we are to survive the power unleashed by the last.

Many have noted, here at millennium's end, that our vast increase in technical ability has not been accompanied by a commensurate increase in our social or ethical maturity. A soul in the year 1000, from any region of the globe, knew more about its place in the grand scheme than a body in the year 2000 does. Francis Bacon was right: the program that began in doubt has produced certainties beyond a medieval mind's

wildest dreams. But what was once a certainty now drifts in a gulf of doubt wider than the millennium itself.

The greatest idea of the last 1,000 years has granted us ascendance over matter by asking not how things ought to be but how things are. We have given ourselves to finding out not what we should do with the world, but what we can make the world do. The greatest idea of the next thousand years must make up the difference, returning subtlety and richness and morals and lightness of spirit to the long human experiment, if any part of it is to survive. Light falls into the eye, reflected from the object under observation. But something else, too, must go out from the eye to the things we observe.

Richard Powers is the author of six novels, most recently "Gain."

In God's Place

**With his discovery of gravity, Newton taught that
understanding the cosmos is not confined to the divine.**

By Alan Lightman

Giovanni di Paolo's 15th-century painting "The Creation of the World and the Expulsion From Paradise," which hangs in the Metropolitan Museum of Art in New York, offers an unexpected synthesis of Western art, religion and thought.

The picture has a split-level appearance. On the right is the title scene: a grove of fruit trees, the Garden of Eden and the frail, ashamed figures of Adam and Eve being shoved out by an angel. The left half is dominated by concentric spheres. At the middle is the earth, center of the universe, encircled by the planets and sun. An outermost sphere contains the stars, all straight out of Aristotle's "On the Heavens." Above this cosmic hierarchy floats a divine God, who gravely reaches down with an index finger to spin His heavenly spheres.

This painting presents a doubled portrait of the fierce boundary between human and divine. Aristotle made all terrestrial phenomena out of earth, air, water and fire. For the moon, the sun and the stars, however, he decided he needed to introduce a completely new kind of substance: the *divine* ether. Adam and Eve were banished from Eden for crossing a more local boundary and eating from the tree of knowledge, God's knowledge. As it turns out, the forbidding separations of substance and place in Aristotle's cosmology seem to resonate with the forbidden knowledge, transgression and guilt in Judeo-Christian theology. In both cases, and on both sides of di Paolo's painting, the proper

domain of human existence and understanding is severely restricted.

Indeed, for centuries Western culture was ingrained with the notion that some areas of knowledge are inaccessible, or forbidden, to human possession. In this view, humankind is entitled to comprehend only what God deigns to reveal. Zeus chained Prometheus to a rock for giving fire, the secret of the gods and the wellspring of advanced civilization, to mortal man. St. Thomas Aquinas (1225–74) distinguished between scientific knowledge, discoverable by the human mind, and divine knowledge, "higher than man's knowledge." Divine knowledge could "not be sought by man through his reason, nevertheless, once . . . revealed by God [it] must be accepted by faith." When Dante asks the divine Beatrice about the mysteries of the moon, she replies that "the opinion of mortals errs where the key of sense does not unlock." When Adam, in Milton's "Paradise Lost" (1667), questions the angel Raphael about celestial mechanics, Raphael offers some vague hints and then says that "the rest from Man or Angel the great Architect did wisely to conceal, and not divulge His secrets to be scann'd by them who ought rather admire."

The idea that there are limits to the rightful scope of human knowledge is, of course, partly a cultural belief. Surrounding it is an entire worldview, an understanding of how the cosmos is put together, spiritually and physically, and where we fit into the grand scheme. But the idea is also deeply psychological. It is an introspection, a state of mind

that subtly imprisons individual thinkers as well as societies, and its effects and ramifications cannot possibly be weighed. No one can say how the history of civilization would have changed if God had never forbidden us to taste from that tree. However, a number of developments over the 16th and 17th centuries did succeed in introducing a new belief: that the entirety of the universe, at least its physical parts, was knowable and discoverable by human beings. This new belief, a belief in the unfettered entitlement to knowledge, was the most important intellectual development along the lengthy time line of the past millennium.

Perhaps the most glorious culmination of the new thinking was Isaac Newton's "Principia" (1687). This monumental treatise established fundamental ideas like inertia and force, articulated general laws of motion of bodies under general forces and proposed a specific law for the force of gravity. Newton's book was unprecedented in the history of science and played a pivotal role in the birth of modern science. But what was most important about Newton's work was not his particular law of gravity, great as it is, but the universality and unbounded application of that law. The same gravity that caused an apple to fall from a tree also caused the moon to orbit the earth, and these trajectories, and an infinity of others, could be mathematically calculated from equations that the English physicist and mathematician had discovered on his own. The heavenly bodies were, after all, physical things, like rocks—or inkwells tossed in frustration against a stone fireplace. The "Principia" dealt a mortal blow to Aristotle's strong division between earthly and cosmic phenomena.

Beneath Newton's idea of the universality of gravity, in turn, lay the implicit assumption that the physical universe was knowable by man. This was a new idea in the evolution of human self-awareness, a psychological turning point, a liberation, an empowerment. Without this idea we might never have had Newton. Nor would we have had the intellectual and scientific breakthroughs that followed: Lavoisier's discovery of oxygen and the beginnings of modern chemistry, Mendel's seminal work on genetics, Dalton's concept of the atom, Darwin and Wallace's theory of evolution and natural selection, Maxwell's formulation of the laws of electricity and magnetism, Einstein's relativity, Hubble's discovery of the expanding universe, Watson and Crick's unraveling of DNA and countless other scientific discoveries.

Even Newton's contemporaries realized that the great physicist had achieved something far deeper than his individual laws. Roger Cotes, in his introduction to the second edition of the "Principia," wrote that Newton had reached "discoveries of which the mind of man was thought incapable before. . . . The gates are now set open." Submersed in a scientific and technological culture as we are today—a culture that has been so totally shaped by telephones and microchips, daily reports on the genes of disease or the recession rate of galaxies—it is hard for us to conceive any limitations in knowledge. All things are our province. The universe is our oyster. We are mostly oblivious to the intellectual history that led us to this point. And we take for granted the active part being played by our own psyches.

What produced the new psychology found in Newton's "Principia"? Certainly, changes in religious thought played a role. Martin Luther's proclamations of 1517, which sparked the Protestant Reformation, helped diminish the authority of the church. Despite Luther's vicious anti-Semitism, his argument that

Science can push back the equations of modern cosmology to less than a nanosecond after the 'big bang,' but it cannot answer the question of why the universe came into being. Science can, in principle, explain all human behavior in terms of biochemical processes in the brain, but science can never determine what is ethical behavior.

every person should be able to read and interpret the Bible for herself, without lock-stepping with the priesthood, encouraged a certain freedom of mind. This religious freedom spread. For example, the subject matter of art turned from almost exclusively religious themes to landscapes, still lifes, interiors and other broad explorations of the secular and natural worlds. Compare Masaccio or Michelangelo with Rembrandt or Vermeer.

There were scientific discoveries as well. On Nov. 11, 1572, soon after sunset, the Danish astronomer Tycho Brahe sighted an intensely bright object in the constellation Cassiopeia that he realized had not been there before. Brahe was the first person to prove that such novae lay beyond the orbit of the moon, within the celestial realm. Brahe had discovered an exploding star, and his discovery exploded the centuries-old belief that the stars were eternal and constant. The divine perfection of the heavens was further questioned when the Italian physicist Galileo turned his new telescope to the moon in 1610 and found the surface "to be not smooth, even, and perfectly spherical, as the great crowd of philosophers have believed about this and other heavenly bodies, but, on the contrary, to

be uneven, rough and crowded with depressions and bulges."

Also of enormous influence, in the decades just preceding Newton, were the scientific and philosophical ideas of René Descartes. Most of the great thinkers throughout history have debated the kind of knowledge that is knowable by the human mind, but philosophers before Descartes assumed that at least some certain knowledge already existed. Descartes, for the first time, began a philosophical system by doubting everything, even his own existence. After convincing himself of his own reality ("I think, therefore I am"), he entered a long meditation that eventually established the existence of God.

Descartes helped us to question. He also prefigured Newton's idea of universality of physical law by proposing a universal mechanism himself, namely his "vortices," which swirled here and there through space, like whirlpools in an ocean, directing the motions of planets and other heavenly bodies. Although Descartes's vortices lacked quantitative description and proved finally unworkable, they had the psychological import of explaining and unifying a vast range of terrestrial and cosmic phenomena under one rational system.

One way of looking at these developments is that they altered and clarified the distinction between what one could call a physical universe and a spiritual universe. Little by little, the sacred geography of Aristotle was replaced by a more amorphous and subtle map of the world. In this map, there exists a material universe, which includes all matter and energy: electrons and atoms, light and heat, brains and stars and galaxies. This vast cosmos is subject to the inquiries of science and to rational mathematical laws that we can discover with our minds.

Coexisting with this physical universe is a spiritual one, not quantifiable, not located in space, not made of atoms and molecules but, to believers, pervasive nonetheless. Each universe poses an infinity of important questions. It is the physical universe, not the spiritual, that is the domain of science. Science has everything to say about the physical universe and nothing to say about its spiritual counterpart. Science can push back the equations of modern cosmology to less than a nanosecond after the "big bang," but science cannot answer the question of why the universe came into being in the first place or whether it has any purpose. Science can, in principle, explain all human behavior in terms of biochemical processes in the brain, but science can never determine what is ethical behavior.

These new perceptions did not happen quickly, neatly or with finality. Like all deep psychological seeds, the idea that some areas of knowledge are off-limits to human beings is not easily excised from our consciousness. The scientist in Mary Shelley's "Frankenstein" (1818), a novel significantly subtitled "The Modern Prometheus," laments,

"Learn from me . . . how dangerous is the acquirement of knowledge, and how much happier that man is who believes his native town to be the world, than he who aspires to become greater than his nature will allow." Some of the horror at the first test of the atom bomb in New Mexico was surely that we had unleashed forces greater than our nature. Soon after the Second World War, J. Robert Oppenheimer, the head of the Manhattan Project, told an audience that "we thought of the legend of Prometheus, of that deep sense of guilt in man's new powers." The troubled public reaction to Dolly, the first adult mammal to be cloned, shows that our fear remains. The sheep's human manipulators were described by The New York Times as having "suddenly pried

open one of the most forbidden—and tantalizing—doors of modern life."

Most likely, each new door opened will continue to disturb us and play upon our guilt. We are advanced and we are primitive at the same time. We are Newton's flight of mind and we are Prometheus chained to a rock, we are Watson and Crick and we are Adam and Eve. All of it, all of the centuries of liberation and imprisonment, creation and dread, live together in one house. And each new door opened will disturb us. Yet we will keep opening the doors; we cannot be stopped.

Alan Lightman, the author of "Einstein's Dreams," is Burchard Professor of Humanities and a senior lecturer in physics at M.I.T.

The workshop of a new society

The industrial revolution gave an utterly new shape to Britain's economy, its population, its cities and its society. But not quite as fast as is supposed

1670–1850

BRITAIN'S industrial revolution was more than that. In most senses, it was a revolution of society too. A mainland population of maybe 6m–7m in 1700 was put at 10.7m by the first official census in 1801, 20.9m in 1851 and 37.1m by 1901. A nation of countrymen went to town. Agriculture's share of male employment fell between 1700 and 1850 from about 60% to about 25%; industry's rose from under 20% to around 50%. And as industrialists built steam-powered factories near the markets, the one Briton in six living in town in 1700 became by 1850 one in two.

The industrial change, however, was neither as swift nor as complete as is often thought. Tradition describes a roaring take-off between 1770 and 1830, driven by a handful of technological innovations, such as textile machinery and James Watt's improved steam engines; and, hey presto, Britain is "the workshop of the world". In fact, the process had begun in the 17th century and was still incomplete in the 1830s, by when only a few industries—mining, metal-working, textiles, brewing—had taken to "factory" methods.

Technological change, important as it was, was not the be-all and end-all. Nor yet did it start with the machine-builders. They depended on earlier advances in iron technology that enabled that industry to produce, in quantity, better and cheaper iron goods such as components for the new machines or for structural use. And, from around 1670, other factors were at work.

One was the development of coal as a fuel, as the cost of wood rose. Next, the growth of thriving rural industries, supplementing farm incomes, which laid the basis for a skilled industrial workforce. Third, the increasing commercialisation of manufacturing, to meet rising demand for cheaper cloth and metal goods from the growing urban elites in Britain and mainland Europe, and from British colonies.

Britain was helped too by easy access to the sea, political stability and light regulation of trade, finance and industry. It also developed a highly specialised workforce, speeding up the development of new products and processes. Industrial output, according to one modern estimate, rose by 0.7% a year between 1700 and 1760, by 1.3% in the 1760s and 1770s, 2.0% in the 1780s and 1790s, and 2.8% between 1800 and 1830.

Work changed, and more than that, as manpower and water power gave way to steam and machines, and rural craftsmanship to urban factories manned by unskilled labour. For some, work vanished. Rural weavers put up a desperate fight for their jobs, marching, petitioning Parliament and burning mills and machinery such as Daniel Burton's textile factory in Middleton, Lancashire, in 1812, but all in vain.

The new factory workers who took their place were mostly unskilled, and earned less than the craftsmen had. Yet for the many men, women and children who flocked to the factory gate, the pay on offer was better than they had earned as farmhands or servants. And as one skill died, new ones were needed: those of tool- or machine-builders, or—almost a new class—foremen.

One aspect of factory life was universally hated by the workforce. Considerations of productivity and safety led employers to regulate all aspects of life in the factory: working hours, breaks and movement inside "the works". Many workers resisted what they saw as infringements of individual freedom, and some of the traditions of the small workshops survived for a while. Employers had to fight hard for the demise of "Saint Monday", when men went to the pub after work on Saturday and did not return until Tuesday morning, disrupting production in spite of (or by) their frantic efforts to catch up by the end of the week.

The clergy and the good-hearted middle classes worried much about their inferiors' morality, as men and women in the mass flocked into the new workplaces. Some industrialists tried to prevent workmen entering parts of the factory where women worked—without much success. In time, awkward-squad parts of the middle class began to worry about the employers' social morality too: Mrs Gaskell's "North and South" offers an early illustration.

Outside "the works" too, conditions altered greatly. Overcrowding, in jerry-built housing in the much-polluted new towns, brought ill-health; at its worst, the devastating cholera epidemics of 1831–32, 1848 and 1854–55. Despite efforts by some employers, charities and eventually local authorities, improvement was slow before the end of the 19th century. Yet a new, mass urban society was born, and not all of its life was the misery depicted by writers from Dickens to D.H. Lawrence. Our deprived Victorian ancestors were quite good at enjoying themselves.

The most obvious beneficiaries of the industrial revolution were the new "barons" such as the Whitbreads in brewing, the Guests in iron or the Strutts in the cotton industry. But the landed classes too profited, from mineral royalties, rises in urban land values and their own investment in industrial concerns. The greatest gainers, though, were the working class, whose living standards rose from 1820 onwards, after 70 years of stagnation. This rise accelerated between 1870 and 1900, when real wages, consumption and life expectancy all rose sharply.

Simultaneously, new forms of leisure emerged, which became synonymous with the British working class: football matches, social clubs, seaside resorts. By 1900, the ordinary Briton was better paid, fed, clothed, housed, educated, perhaps amused and certainly better represented in politics, than his forefathers could have dreamed of.

Not everyone was content. Lawrence was soon to pour out his ample bile on the machine world. In 1933, J.B. Priestley lamented that it was "as if the country had devoted a hundred years of its life to keeping gigantic sooty pigs. And the people who were choked by the reek of the sties did not get the bacon." Actually, they got quite a lot. Whether that was a fair share is a separate story.

The X Factor

A thousand years ago, China appeared to have assembled all the pieces for an industrial revolution. What happened?

By Mark Elvin

Early in the 11th century, Chinese government arsenals manufactured more than 16 million identical iron arrowheads a year. In other words, mass production. Rather later, in the 13th century, machines in northern China powered by belt transmissions off a waterwheel twisted a rough rope of hemp fibers into a finer yarn. The machine used 32 spinning heads rotating simultaneously in a technique that probably resembled modern ring-spinning. A similar device was used for doubling filaments of silk. In other words, mechanized production, in the sense that the actions of the human hand were replicated by units of wood and metal, and an array of these identical units was then set into motion by inanimate power.

Common sense thus suggests that the Chinese economy, early in the millennium just coming to a close, had already developed the two key elements of what we think of as the Industrial Revolution: mass production and mechanization. That, nonetheless, nothing much more happened in this direction during the next 600 or 700 years is also a matter of common knowledge. Even the spinning machine went out of use, and survived only in literature and ever less comprehensible copies of copies of diagrams made by artists who had never set eyes on the real thing.

Much later, from the middle of the 19th century on, China had to import, then service, adapt and even at times improve, mechanical engineering from the West. This was done with considerable flair, particularly by Chinese firms in Shanghai, a city which during treaty-port days turned into a nonstop international exhibition of machine building. So Chinese technical capability can hardly be said to have withered in the intervening centuries. But what went wrong the first time? Why did

the first industrial revolution not take place in China, as it seems it should have?

Of course, there is much more to such a revolution than technology alone. It requires a large-scale market economy, and that presupposes cheap transport and communications, extensive commercialization, monetization and credit instruments. China during the Song dynasty (960–1279 A.D.) delivered all of these.

The Song enjoyed the results of an economic revolution that featured the rapid development of wet-field rice farming in the lower Yangtze valley, the burgeoning of a dense network of low-coasts, and a money supply increased by many means, including fiduciary money (some of it the world's first paper money) and credit. A proliferation of petty local markets supported three great market-regions in the north China plains, the lower Yangtze and

From *Far Eastern Economic Review*, June 10, 1999, pp. 66–69. © 1999 by Far Eastern Economic Review, Dow Jones & Co., Inc. Reprinted by permission.

Sichuan. Above these rose a nation-wide market and an overseas commerce so vigorous that taxes on it were the main financial support of the Southern Song (1127–1279) government.

To these we may add a growing literacy, linked with woodblock printing, a growing numeracy and some of what were then the largest cities on the globe, in one or two cases with more than a million inhabitants. Many of these were now also producer cities, not just consumer cities living off administrative revenues. What could be called the "textbook package" of factors that we commonly assume produces an industrial revolution was all in place. And still there was no breakthrough. Why?

The disruption caused by the conquests of the Jurchen in the north during the 12th century, and then the Mongols in the whole of China during the 13th, is the most direct answer, and should not be discounted just because it is obvious. At a deeper level, the economic driving force provided by the expansion of production in the Yangtze valley had diminished. From the late 10th century until about 1100, the 26 prefectures of the lower Yangtze had maintained an average annual growth rate in population of more than 1%. For premodern times, this is impressive, approaching a tripling within a century.

But land fills up, and opportunities once taken cannot be taken again. The coherent pattern fall apart during the Southern Song and, with a few local exceptions, this sustained growth was not maintained. The climate also grew more variable and colder, dropping at times to two degrees Celsius below the annual average at the start of the medieval economic revolution.

Economic vitality returned in the later 16th and early 17th centuries. It was then disrupted again, by internal rebellions, the Manchu conquest, and one of the coldest periods of what in Europe at this time was called the "Little Ice Age." When

growth picked up spectacularly in the warmer 18th century, it had distinctive characteristics.

First of all, it was more quantitative than qualitative. Some diffusion of technology that was new in China occurred, notably food crops, like sweet potatoes introduced from the New World, and some fine-tuning, notably of "intermediate" rices. There was no major innovation or invention. The pattern was more of the same, multiplied over and over again, and greater intensification, based on the input of more labour. Accounts of women working regularly in the fields become much more common at this time.

Second, the growth was environmentally destructive on an unprecedented scale. The stripping of vegetation cover of course had a long history in China. The Qing-period removal of original vegetation and forests, and exploitation of other resources like accessible coal and metallic ores, was on a new scale. China's population reached more than 400 million by 1850, about twice what it had been around the end of the 17th century. The literature is filled with a litany of woes about deforestation, shortage of construction timber and firewood, devastating erosion, loss of fertility in upland soils, salination of unsuitable lands opened for farming, and exhaustion of veins of copper and other materials. It was an ecosystem under a new intensity of attack.

Third, the general style of economic organization was to subcontract, employing commercial relationships instead of management. This can be seen in the production of cotton cloth. A legion of rural spinners bought raw cotton in local markets and sold their thread through intermediaries to another legion of weavers. A pyramid of lesser and greater brokers than purchased the cloth, putting it out to independent workshops for dyeing and, separately, calendering–hardening the cloth with pressure. The best of the cloth ended up with whole-

salers who might have a turnover of a million bolts a year.

In one sense, this was an efficient system, based on pitting basic producers against each other in competition. On the other, it made technical innovation difficult, by separating marketing from production, and leaving producers with minimum reserves or incentives for experiment. Only in a few businesses, where there was a need for large-scale management was there much innovation. An example is some of the mountain timber-cutting organizations that pioneered more technically effective ways of getting timber out of difficult terrain, such as precursors of cable-skidder trackways that used overhead tow-lines to drag cut trunks along rough tracks.

Finally, the productivity of farming, both in per-hectare terms and seed-to-yield ratio (in better areas, about 1:35 for rice), was breathtakingly high in a comparative perspective. But success was beginning to block progress. Without modern science, and modern productive techniques, to draw on, there was a ceiling on further improvement. With usable land largely occupied, there were few if any easy ways to create the surges of extra demand that can have domino effects through an economy, and often prompt invention. And the Chinese economy was now too big for foreign trade to be able to deliver impulses of this sort on the required scale. This was the famous high-level equilibrium trap.

Was there, beyond this, still some "X factor" missing? Two possibilities are worth consideration. The first is that the analytical-experimental aspect of culture that crystallized in the West into modern science, but which often crucially affected technology, too, was much weaker in China. One can see this by comparing Chinese and Western analyses of water-pumping technology, a field located on the interface between science and technology (which it is an error in any case to distinguish too sharply). By the start of the 18th century, the French hydraulicist B.F. de Bélidor was already using formal geometry in his quest for the perfect trough-pump—which consists of a trough up which water is drawn by a continuous chain of pallets at a given slope. Chinese texts of this time merely noted empirically that effective high-angle and low-angle lifts needed trough–pumps with parts of differing dimensions.

The second possibility is democracy as a way of running public business. Jean Baechler at the Sorbonne has recently insisted that this is the aspect of the modern West for which premodern parallels in China are the weakest. The democratic style for safeguarding argument within a stable framework, and facilitating broadly acceptable change, may have helped the West develop new ways of thinking and new types of social organization. If we follow this line of thought, then the fifth modernization—to borrow Chinese dissident Wei Jing-sheng's phrase for democracy—appears as less of a luxury and more of an essential.

The late-imperial decline in inventiveness has also sometimes been ascribed to "Confucianism" or to the heavy hand of the Chinese state. This raises a difficulty. Weren't these exact features also associated in the Middle Ages with China's rise to economic world leadership? Can one rationally have it both ways? At best, these factors, suitably nuanced, might perhaps be included as part of a more complex analysis of the historically changing patterns in later times.

The riddle remains.

Mark Elvin is a research professor of Chinese history at the Australian National University.

The Rock Drill and Civilization

*Rock drilling is one of the world's most ancient technologies—
and a prerequisite for nearly all the others*

By Larry C. Hoffman

THE PROGRESS OF MANKIND CAN be measured by the progress of mining and metallurgy. The successive historical epochs of stone, copper, bronze, iron, steel, and silicon are the steps our species has taken in the quest to control the world rather than simply survive it. Besides adding to humanity's health and material well-being, each of these stages has created the need for an ever-increasing web of laws, rules, and etiquette. The whole complex synergy that we call civilization ultimately depends on mining, and mining depends on rock drills.

The earliest miner was a prehistoric hominid who picked up a loose rock and used it as a tool to increase the advantage of his or her opposable thumb. He or she found glittering gemstones, gold nuggets, and pieces of native copper useful or at least decorative, and when the loose pieces lying close to the surface were used up, mining began in earnest. Salt, too, was an important mined substance in ancient times. Without its use in cooking and food preservation, little advance beyond hunting and gathering would have been possible.

In near-surface deposits, early humans could mine by simply finding loose hard rocks to beat on softer ores. But below a weathered upper layer, ore deposits generally became tougher. Metals were then pursued to incredible depths by artisan miners and slave la-

The first attempts to use machines to drill were complete failures.

borers working in hellish conditions. They built fires next to an ore face to soften it, sometimes quenching the hot rock with water (or vinegar, which was thought to be more efficacious) to break a few pounds of mineral off the surface. Not only mines but other rock openings, such as the tombs of ancient Egypt and the tunnels of the Roman aqueducts, were undoubtedly excavated in this manner. Without forced ventilation, and with only limited comprehension of the gases produced, such work could be deadly.

The arrival of the Iron Age, during the second millennium B.C., improved people's lives in many ways. It led to much more efficient plows, hoes, and other agricultural implements and to great improvements in wheeled vehicles and swords, shields, daggers, and other instruments of advancing civilization. Below the ground, iron metallurgy gave miners picks and bars, wedges and gads, tools hard enough to drive into natural cracks in ore and force them apart. More

mines opened to produce iron, and more slaves were shackled to swing the picks and drive the wedges.

The old thermal-stress methods were retained for some uses, however, even in the most modern and progressive mines. Iron was still expensive and of variable quality, and much skilled labor was required to fashion it into tools and keep them in working condition. The Japanese were still using thermal-stress methods for long tunnels in the 1880s.

It took about three centuries after gunpowder became known in Europe before some resourceful miner, probably in the late 1500s, thought to stuff the powerful little grains into cracks in the rocks, ignite them, and let chemistry do the work of many hands and arms. The deeper the crack, the more gunpowder could be loaded and the more rock broken. Eventually miners realized that they could extract even more if instead of relying on natural cracks they used an iron tool to make a narrow, deep hold with a small outer opening that could be plugged to confine the combustion gases. The first documented use of drilling and blasting for mining was by Martin Weigel in Freiberg, Germany, in 1613.

As gunpowder greatly multiplied the rate at which ore could be removed, mines went deeper and deeper into the earth and metals began their long transition from luxury items to commodities. While great effort went into such problems as keeping the tunnels from collapsing and transporting workers, supplies, and rocks in and out of the mines, the whole process depended first and foremost on the men who drilled the blastholes. For three centuries their powerful arms ceaselessly swung hammers against iron (and later steel) drill rods. Each stroke pulverized a tiny bit of rock under the chisel tip. On the backswing of the hammer, the drill would be rotated (by the hammer wielder himself if he was alone, or else by a workmate) so that the next blow would drive the bit into fresh rock. Swing, turn, swing, turn was the endless rhythm, hour after hour, day after day.

Drilling a narrow, precise hole required much more from the tools, and thus from the toolmakers, than the brute-force methods of the pick-and-wedge era. Blacksmiths used all their energy and skill to keep miners supplied with sharp drills, and a constant stream of rods—sharp in, dull out—was carried through the mines by young boys called nippers. Every good smith had his secret hardening compounds and ritualistic tempering process, for hardness at the cutting edge was everything in the battle against the rock. As with gunpowder, the technology of war served the rock driller well, with blacksmiths adopting many advances from the fabrication of sword steel and armor plate.

In the hand-labor era, which lasted right up to early in this century, there were two kinds of hard-rock drilling: slow and slower, depending on whether it was done by a team of men or by one man working alone. One man swinging a four-pound hammer and holding his own drill rod was called single-jacking. A two-man team was called double-jacking. One man would swing a hammer that might have a nine-pound head while his partner held the drill rod as a steady target and gave it a quick twist while the hammer was going back. If the end of the drill rod wasn't exactly where the driller wanted it on the next blow, the swing could be very hard on the holder. Trust in your partner was everything, and it wasn't a good idea to do anything that might get him mad at you.

When the hammer man tired, they would switch positions, often in mid-stroke without missing a beat. A little water was usually added to downward holes to help flush out the cuttings, keep the dust down, and cool the bit to preserve its temper. With upward holes this was not possible, so they were drilled dry. Over the years the accumulation of dust in a miner's lungs would gradually smother him, as his alveoli became plugged with insoluble silica particles. This was the dreaded silicosis, or miner's consumption, usually just called "the con."

Hand drilling is an extremely slow and grueling process, a severe test of strength and endurance. In very hard rock two strong miners might work 12 hours and make less than one inch of hole. Every old miner claimed to have worked in a place where the rock was so hard that the first shift had to work all day and then leave a man underground with his finger on the spot so the night shift would know where to continue drilling. In average rock one man might drill 8 inches an hour, while a two-man crew might make 2 feet. It would take 20 to 30 holes, 1 to 1½ inches in diameter, to be able to blast away enough rock to advance a 4-by-6-foot tunnel 4 feet. Drilling those 120 feet of hole might use up 200 pieces of sharpened drill rod over several days.

For almost 250 years this method was improved on only in the composition of the drill rods and the methods of tempering them. The cutting edge had to be as hard as possible to chip the rock, but not hard enough to shatter. Similarly, the rod had to be hard enough not to deform from the countless hammerblows, but soft enough not to break. Irons and steels from certain regions, especially in Sweden, gained favor because of naturally occurring alloying elements such as chromium or nickel in the iron ore. As metallurgical knowledge increased, smiths learned to duplicate these materials by adding secret ingredients to their alloys.

This period, the late Iron Age, which actually lasted well into the Industrial Revolution, was the grade school of mankind. Human and animal power, with occasional assists from wind and water, performed most of the labor required for survival. As the Middle Ages and the Renaissance gave way to the early modern era, iron tires and gears, nails and fittings, tools and instruments all were making life easier. Progress in mining was also accelerating the growth of international trade. It did this in several ways: by making travel faster, easier, and safer; by expanding the array of manufacturers that could be used as trade goods; and by increasing the supply of precious metals, which lifted

The first mechanical rock drill, patented by J. J. Couch in 1849, was too big and cumbersome to be a commercial success.

local and world economies beyond the barter system. But those processes of growth and change remained slow, and hand drilling continued to satisfy the needs of mankind's endeavors.

In the first years of the nineteenth century, the steam engine accelerated this calm pace forever. Suddenly one engine could do more work in a day than a small village had done before. The demand for iron and other metals, as well as coal, to feed this industrialization was tremendous, and mines became the vanguard of many new technologies. The world's first practical steam engine was used to pump water from a mine. The first practical locomotive pulled cars in a coal mine. Steam hoisting engines, along with the pumps, allowed miners to reach ores that had formerly been too deep to recover.

These and other aspects of mining saw much progress, but in the end everything still depended on the rock drill. One analysis attributed two-thirds of total mining costs to the drilling of boreholes. And since mine owners found themselves hard pressed to get enough arms swinging hammers to drill all those holes, the search for a mechanical drill began in earnest around the middle of the nineteenth century. The earliest attempts were cumbersome steam-driven machines for drilling holes in canal construction or open-pit mines. They were complete failures. The machinery had to be kept close to the boiler, since steam loses much of its heat and pressure when transported over long distances. No successful high-temperature, high-pressure hoses were available for flexible connections. Open space was also needed to allow for the dissipation of waste heat and water vapor. All these considerations made steam impractical for most underground mining.

Mining wasn't the only industry that needed a good mechanical rock drill. Beginning in the 1830s, railroads gave promise of bringing the United States closer together by spanning the prairies and crossing the mountains. But in order to do so, they needed to maintain moderate grades and curvatures. Mountains would be impassable barriers without long tunnels through solid rock.

The first true mechanical rock drill of record was designed and built in 1848 and patented in 1849 by Jonathan J. Couch of Philadelphia. It was large and unwieldy and far from a commercial success. Couch had been assisted by Joseph W. Fowle, but the two men parted company before the patent was issued, and Fowle patented his own drill within two months. In 1851 Fowle patented a new design that was the seed of the modern rock drill. It was the first to use a flexible hose that made the drill independent from the boiler, and it later pioneered the use of compressed air for power transmission. Unfortunately, while Fowle had imagination and vision, he did not have the financial resources to carry his design forward. Between his 1851 patent and 1866, only 12 U.S. pat-

Mont Cenis would have taken decades to drill by hand.

ents relating to rock drills were issued, including a second (and last) by Couch in 1852.

The first moderately successful rock drills appeared in the 1860s, their development spurred by the agonizingly slow progress that was being made on two major railroad tunnels: the 24,000-foot Hoosac Tunnel in Massachusetts and the 44,100-foot Mont Cenis Tunnel through the Alps between France and Italy. These were monumental projects, greatly exceeding anything that had been attempted before, in rock of unyielding toughness.

In 1854 the Massachusetts legislature passed an act to assist construction of the Hoosac Tunnel in the northwestern corner of the state. (Ground had been broken in 1851). The state lent its credit to the extent of $2 million (the equivalent of about $30 million today) for the projected $3.35 million enterprise, an arched tunnel 24 feet wide and 21 feet high. The tunnel was expected to be finished in a little more than four years.

It wasn't. False starts were made by a number of different contractors, some of whom had to raise the money for the work themselves. After nine years the total progress amounted to 4,250 feet, less than 20 percent of the project, all of it by hand drilling. Several novel machines, both rock drills and full-face boring devices, were tried. One of them was supposed to carve a ring 13 inches wide and 24 feet in diameter into the face, after which explosives would loosen the core. The 75-ton device, powered by a pitiful 100 horsepower, advanced all of 10 feet before finally being scrapped. Like all the other machines that were supposed to make the excavation a snap, it was no match for the tough gneisses and schists of Hoosac Mountain.

In October 1863, after a succession of bankruptcies, the Commonwealth of Massachusetts took over. Partly because of the Civil War, little was accomplished until 1865, when about 550 feet of tunnel was completed. (It is difficult to measure progress precisely because the Hoosac was constructed in stages. First an initial small bore was driven; then it was enlarged to the final cross section; and finally the sections were arched with masonry. In written accounts, progress is usually given as the advance of the pilot hole only. Thus months with no apparent progress may have been spent on enlargement or other work.)

Between 1863 and 1865 the state made several attempts to introduce rock drills into the tunnel, and in June 1865 a flume and penstock were completed to provide waterpower to air compressors. The most successful of these early experiments was the Brooks, Gates, and Burleigh drill, which was developed for the tunnel and first tried when the compressors became available in June 1866. While not a success, it did serve as a steppingstone. The machine weighed 240 pounds and consisted of 80 pieces. It cost $400 in the days when a good Colt revolver could be had for $10 or less. The longest recorded use of such a drill was five days, and even two consecutive days' use was considered exceptional. Nothing on the machine stood up to the abuse of hitting solid rock 200 times a minute. In four months 1,084 drills were sent out of the heading for repairs, or about 10 a day. To keep 5 or 6 drills in the face, 40 were required. One account of the drilling effort said that "the tunnel seemed to be a highway, along which a crowd of people was continually passing, each person carrying a portion of a drilling machine, or tools or materials for repair."

The air compressors were only slightly more dependable. They relied on water injected into the cylinders to cool the heat of compression and seal the pistons and valves. Occasionally excess water demonstrated its incompressibility and the machine spontaneously disassembled itself. Furthermore, compressing air for power transmission is inherently wasteful, and as little as 10 percent of the energy applied to the compressor was delivered at the rock face. But waterpower was plentiful and cheap, and drillers appreciated the constant stream of cool, fresh air—especially when compared with the sticky heat created by steam power.

Charles Burleigh fell out with his partners early in the tests and refined the design on his own, buying the Fowle patent to avoid litigation. (Burleigh had helped build the original Couch/Fowle drill as a machinist in Fitchburg, Massachusetts.) He continued to improve the machine and came up with an entirely new drill that was placed into service on October 31, 1866. The new drill was nearly as complex as the partnership-designed machine, but it transferred the stress to stronger components. The whole assembly was bulked up, weighing 372 pounds. While it drilled at about the same rate as the old model, it was much more durable. One exceptional machine worked two and a half months and drilled a mile of hole without a breakdown. Only two or three machines were needed to keep one in the face. The progress of the tunnel increased from 570 feet in 1866 to 1,187 feet in 1867. (The replacement of black powder with much more powerful nitroglycerin also played a big part.) During 1871 workers drove through 1,743 feet in 10 months with a newer-model Burleigh drill. The headings met in November 1873, and

the tunnel opened to traffic in February 1875.

The Hoosac Tunnel demonstrated that powered rock drilling had crossed from the experimental to the practical. Once it was shown to be possible, everyone started doing it, though the speed of its adoption varied widely by industry. The new technology saved enormous amounts of time but not necessarily money, especially where cheap labor was plentiful. Tunnelers were quicker than miners to adopt the new technology, since speed of completion was generally more important than keeping costs down; mine owners, especially small ones, lagged behind in modernizing their operations. For quarrying and surface extraction, which were conducted in the open air, the simpler and cheaper technology of steam power held sway much longer.

In Europe, meanwhile, work on the Mont Cenis Tunnel progressed slowly with hand drilling from 1857 until 1861, when machine drills designed by Germain Sommeiller, an Italian engineer employed on the tunnel, were put in service. These machines used compressed air provided by hydraulic rams at a pressure of 9 psi (modern drills operate at 100 psi), and 200 drills were needed to keep 20 in the faces. They were heavy, awkward tools mounted on carriages that had to be rolled into and out of the tunnel on rails, but they were still three times as fast as hand drilling (at two and a half times the cost). The Sommeiller drills were used for the entire tunnel until completion nine years later, with modest improvements taking place over that time. By the end the Sommeiller drills were advancing at five times the rate of hand drilling. The tunnel's two headings met on December 25, 1870. Without power drills, they would have taken 40 or 50 years to converge.

European drilling progress stagnated after the introduction of the Sommeiller machines, and by the mid-1870s Continental hardware was years behind that of the United States. American technology was making rapid progress in related fields as well. Metallurgy was shifting from an art to a science, with superior cast iron and steel coming into use. Air compressors became more reli-

Modern drills can have penetration rates of five feet per minute or more.

able, and pressures climbed from 35 to 80 psi. Nitroglycerin was replaced by much safer dynamite, and fans were built to provide fresh air to deep tunnels. In spite of its early dominance, the Burleigh Rock Drill company lagged behind newcomers like Rand, Ingersoll, Sergeant, Wood, Waring, Blatchley, and McKean. Still, for many years miners referred to all piston-style rock drills as "burleys." In 1872 Burleigh sold out to Ingersoll, which in turn merged with Rand into a company that bought out many small firms and continues as a leader in the field to this day.

All these drills were of the piston, or "slugger," type, in which the drill rod was firmly clamped to a piston that traveled somewhere between 2 and 10 inches—the harder the rock, the shorter the stroke. The drill rods were solid, and the cuttings were removed by the plunging action of the drill. After the early 1870s all machines rotated their drill rods with a spiral "rifle bar" at the rear of the piston. At 60 psi of air pressure, these drills ran from 200 to 600 strokes and penetrated two to six inches per minute. All were firmly mounted on columns, tripods, or carriages to support their weight and resist the forces of recoil. Workers made sure to install their drills firmly to keep the mounts from falling on the careless user.

As the appetites of civilization continued to increase, miners were forced to dig deeper for more metals. Electricity for communications, lighting, and power created an unprecedented demand for copper. Iron and steel became the most important materials for suspension bridges, sub-oceanic cables, transcontinental railroads, oceangoing ships, and huge machinery, the showpieces of civilization.

In the 1890s, as metallurgists developed steels that could be heat-treated to resist deformation, a new type of machine evolved: the hammer drill. In this variant—a mechanical analogue of old-fashioned hand drilling—the drill rod slid freely in a chuck while a piston hammer struck its end, either directly or through a tappet. Without having to move nearly as much mass as the piston-type drill, the hammer drill could operate at around 1,400 strokes per minute, delivering sharp, fast blows to the rock. These hammer drills were light-duty machines, best adapted to drilling upward holes. They were not suitable for downward holes because there was no way to get rid of the cuttings, which made a powder that cushioned the blows. Because of their high speed, these drills were known as "buzzies." Later, as the fine dust they produced built up in workers' lungs, they were called "widow makers."

Adapting techniques and metallurgy originally developed for boring gun barrels, hollow drill steel was developed in the late 1890s, primarily by J. George Leyner, a Colorado entrepreneur. He used the latest high-impact steels to build a heavy-duty hammer drill that could work in any direction by evacuating the cuttings with a jet of air through the center of the drill rod. The machine was an immediate success, and Leyner sold about 75 of them.

Unfortunately, high-pressure ejection of extremely fine rock particles compounded the dust problem, and miners refused to use the new machines. Leyner met the problem head-on by recalling every drill his fledgling company had built and retrofitting them all with an ingenious needle through the center of the piston that injected water through the drill steel, wetting down the dust. Still, the episode made mine operators, a habitually conservative bunch, slow to accept Leyner's innovation.

After World War I the hammer-type drill almost completely supplanted the piston drill, as all manufacturers began building them when Leyner's patents expired. The "jackhammer" hand-held pneumatic drill became a fixture at every mine and construction site. These drills were often powered by portable air compressors that were a far cry from the massive, inefficient water-injected machines used at the Hoosac Tunnel. By the 1930s the basic design had become standardized and the major drill makers' machines differed only subtly from one another.

With drilling mechanisms working efficiently at last, the drill stem and bit became the weak link in the system. In a large mine or tunnel job, tons of drill steel still had to be hauled in and out of the workings every day to keep sharp tools at the face. Many attempts were made to build a detachable drill bit so that the long, heavy drill rods could stay at the working face with only the tips being replaced. In 1918 A. L. Hawkesworth, a mechanical foreman for the Anaconda Company in Butte, Montana, developed a bit with a dovetail joint to the drill steel. It was the first successful removable cutting edge. Later versions were threaded together, followed by a simple tapered friction joint for lighter drills.

Post–World War II improvements in hydraulics have led to the jumbo, in which a single miner controls several drills on a wheeled mount.

The Carlton Tunnel, driven at Cripple Creek, Colorado, between 1939 and 1941, shows how much progress had taken place in the 70 years since the Hoosac. The first mile was driven in 121 working days, the second mile in 108. The best single month's advance was 1,879 feet, more than the best year's work under Hoosac Mountain and with less than a third the manpower. Of course, not all the credit goes to drilling science. At the Carlton workers had telephones to order supplies and trucks to deliver them. Electric-powered machinery and mechanical loaders mucked up the blasted rock, and locomotives instead of mules hauled it out. Powerful air compressors and ventilation fans, as well as bigger, healthier workers, all played a part. Within a few years advances of 100 feet a day were being posted in mines and tunnels.

After World War II the hand-held jackhammer was flexibly attached to a light air cylinder and the Jackleg drill was born, allowing a single miner to drill in any direction without a mounted drill. The new machines weighed around a hundred pounds and could drill two or three feet a minute using the new tungsten carbide-tipped drill bits. In larger tunnels improved hydraulics were showing up in the versatile drill "jumbos," which allowed one miner to control several drills on a wheeled mount. In the 1970s hydraulic technology was applied directly in the rock drill itself, instead of being used to create the compressed air that powered the drill. This development made air-powered drills obsolete for most heavy mining and tunneling applications and allowed penetration rates of five feet per minute or more. (There is, of course, a much wider range of rock drilling and boring equipment. Surface mining, tunnel boring, highway construction, well drilling, and geological exploration are but a few of the areas that have developed their own specialized apparatus. But their inclusion here would make a book, not an article.)

Even down to the most mundane items, our world is built on materials taken out of the earth, from talcum powder to diamonds, gravel to silicon. The infrastructure of our cities depends on huge rock tunnels to bring water in and take waste out. Building foundations and sublevels are blasted into bedrock. At some point all transportation, from deeper shipping ports to longer aircraft runways, requires a major modification of the rocky face of the earth. Without advances in rock drilling, which have both fed and been fed by the Industrial Revolution, the cost of our modern civilization would be prohibitive.

Larry C. Hoffman, P.E., is a mining engineer who lives in Butte, Montana.

The Transatlantic Telegraph Cable

Eighth Wonder of the World

Gillian Cookson describes how the first physical link across the Atlantic was finally achieved.

IN 1858 A TELEGRAM of ninety-eight words from Queen Victoria to President James Buchanan of the United States opened a new era in global communication. The Queen's message of congratulation took sixteen and a half hours to transmit through the new transatlantic telegraph cable. After White House staff had satisfied themselves that it was not a hoax, the President sent a reply of 143 words in a relatively rapid ten hours. Without the cable, a despatch in one direction alone would have taken perhaps twelve days by the speediest combination of inland telegraph and fast steamer.

The Atlantic crossing had been achieved only at the third attempt, and until the first messages passed on August 17th, 1858, it was by no means certain that the project was technically feasible. Once its success had become clear, as far as the public was concerned all doubts melted away, to be replaced by huge enthusiasm. The impact of the first telegraphic communication between Europe and America is hard to appreciate now. *The Times* enthused:

More was done yesterday for the consolidation of our Empire than the wisdom of our statesmen, the liberality of our Legislature, or the loyalty of our colonists could ever have effected. Distance between Canada and England is annihilated.

The United States celebrated its new closeness to Europe. City Hall in New York was alight with candles and fireworks. On September 1st, a procession filled Broadway and led to the largest ever fete in Union Square. On both sides of the ocean, songs were written, souvenir editions of newspapers published, sermons preached about the unity of mankind. Cyrus Field, the New York businessman whose vision had driven the project forward against great odds, became a national hero.

But even as the celebrations continued, the line was breaking down. In all, 271 messages, increasingly fragmentary and incomprehensible, passed down the cable before it finally failed on September 18th. The Atlantic Telegraph Company's total investment of around £500,000 on the three attempts was a complete loss. The failure was blamed on manufacturing faults in the copper core and insulation, and on poor electrical management. The company's chief electrician, Wildman Whitehouse, a former surgeon from Brighton, had hastened the cable's end by increasing the voltage as the cable deteriorated.

The sceptics, those who had criticised the Atlantic projectors for being over-ambitious and underqualified for such an enterprise, began to re-emerge. The criticisms had some justification. Yet although it is now clear that Whitehouse was incompetent, at the time there were few engineers with practical experience of electricity, fewer still with a sound understanding of the subject, and no easy means of telling who was best qualified to supervise such a project. Electrical science was in its infancy, and the associated technology for submarine telegraphs—including cable construction, cable laying, and the design of instruments to send and receive signals—was still in the process of development. Field trials were central to this, each expedition experimental, the Atlantic ocean a laboratory from which a new understanding of electricity was growing. Those who were to be leading practitioners of submarine telegraphy during the 1860s, including Charles Bright and William Thomson (later Lord Kelvin), learned their trade by experience through trial and error during the unsuccessful attempts on the Atlantic in 1857 and 1858.

In retrospect, the Atlantic expeditions during the 1850s do appear to have been over-ambitious. The scheme had been launched less than twenty years after Wheatstone's first experimental telegraph, which opened in 1837 between Euston and Camden. While overland telegraphs had become well-established by the 1850s, submarine lines were technically much more difficult. The first working submarine cable had been laid in 1851 between Dover and Calais. Its design formed the basis of future cables: a copper conductor, the cable's core, was insulated with gutta percha, a kind of latex from Malaya which had been found preferable to india rubber for underwater use. The cable was armoured with iron wire, thicker at the

shore ends where extra protection from anchors and tidal chafing was needed. Although this basic technology was in place, there was a world of difference between a cross-Channel line of less than twenty-five miles and a cable capable of spanning the Atlantic, crossing the 1,660 nautical miles between Valentia, on the west coast of Ireland, and Newfoundland in depths of up to two

---

An elaborate procedure had to be worked out to rendezvous and splice the line in mid-ocean.

---

miles. There were difficulties of scale, and also of electrical management. In long submarine cables, received signals were extremely feeble as there was no way of amplifying or relaying them in mid-ocean; there was also a phenomenon of 'smearing', where the sharpness of transmitted signals was lost.

The scale of the enterprise brought more obvious problems. There was no ship in the world large enough to stow the full length of cable. An elaborate

procedure had to be worked out to rendezvous and splice the line in mid-ocean, for while the cable-laying vessel could communicate with the shore; ships out of sight could not communicate with each other. Cables could be laid only during a short summer season, so that cable production was rushed. Quality control was inadequate and other preparations carried out in haste. And even in summer the Atlantic could be cruel. On the 1857 and 1858 expeditions, the ships used were naval sailing vessels. Contemporary engravings of HMS *Agamemnon* and the US frigate *Niagara* at work laying the cable show scenes which rather evoke Tudor sea battles than suggest the dawning of a new age of electrical engineering. The first, unsuccessful, expedition of 1858 almost ended in outright disaster when one of the worst storms ever recorded came close to wrecking the *Agamemnon*.

Given the complexity of the problems, it was a great achievement to have completed a working line in the 1850s, and hardly surprising that it soon failed. Once the cable had expired, many of the public, including some who had suffered large losses, turned against the scheme.

The *Illustrated London News* graphically showed the dangers endured by the *Agamemnon* in June 1858.

It was even suggested that the whole episode had been a confidence trick designed to extract money from gullible investors. Yet while many saw it only as a financial disaster, those closer to events took confidence from the experience. The small group which could be described as fledgling electrical engineers saw that amidst all the faults and difficulties there was the basis of a viable project. These men—such as Thomson, Bright, Fleeming Jenkin and Latimer Clark, who like the telegraph companies and most others involved, were British—saw the expeditions as a glorious opportunity to experiment on evolving technology. Although the 1858 failure had shown that there were still fundamental electrical questions to be answered, the engineers' optimism was undimmed and their confidence actually increasing.

While the electricians had been heartened about the technical possibilities, there were others who continued to back

The *Great Eastern* under construction in 1857; at five times larger than anything else afloat, it was the only ship capable of carrying the miles of cable needed for the whole crossing. Below, storing the cable in the hold, 1865.

the scheme for its potential to transform transatlantic relations. In its short life the cable had carried market information, official despatches, and news which, whatever its content, was exciting for its immediacy. The British government had had a stark lesson in how useful the telegraph could be in ruling its scattered empire. One of the messages passing through the 1858 cable told the 62nd Regiment in Nova Scotia that they were no longer needed to help subdue the Indian mutiny, countermanding previous instructions to embark for London. This nine-word communication alone, it was said, had saved the British government £50,000, the expense of a needless mobilisation.

The government, though, was unwilling to offer any direct support for further attempts on the Atlantic. Their reluctance did not stem simply from a prevailing economic creed which frowned on public money supporting private enterprises. In fact both the British and United States governments had given significant help to the expeditions of 1857 and 1858, carrying out advance ocean surveys, and providing ships and personnel during the laying. Later, in 1868, all British inland cables were nationalised under Post Office control. So there was not an inflexible principle against public involvement in telegraphy. The real reason for the government's unwillingness to invest directly in a transatlantic cable lay in a calamity they had suffered with a projected telegraph to India.

The first British government venture into submarine cables had been encouraging. During the Crimean War in 1855 a temporary, unarmoured cable was laid between Bulgaria and Balaklava, financed, owned and operated by Britain. It served its purpose, functioning until the end of the war the following year. During the next major foreign crisis, the Indian Mutiny of 1857, an emergency request for reinforcements took forty days to reach London from the besieged British community in the city of Lucknow. As a direct consequence Lord Derby's government agreed to underwrite a privately promoted Red Sea cable. The existing arrangements, using an overland route across the Ottoman em-

pire, were unsatisfactory even in times of peace. Telegraphers who did not understand English transcribed Morse code messages at far-flung relay stations, making so many errors that telegrams, delivered days or weeks late, were often impossible to decipher. There was additional anxiety about security when confidential messages passed over foreign territory. An advantage of submarine cables is that they are almost impossible to eavesdrop—which is why they continued to be used in preference to radio for classified despatches during the Second World War. A Red Sea line would solve these problems of reliability and security. Derby's government entered the Red Sea agreement despite the failure of the 1858 Atlantic cable, for public opinion strongly supported a secure line to India under British control. In any case the governments' role was to encourage investors by giving only a guarantee, that shareholders would receive a minimum 4.5 per cent return on their investment providing the line tested well for a month after laying. The theory was that if the line were a technical failure, there would be no call on public funds; if it worked, it should make at least some profit and the government would at worst be subsidising a cable which was of great strategic benefit to the British Empire. In fact the result was the greatest possible financial disaster for the government—and it fell upon Derby's successor as prime minister, Palmerston, and Gladstone, his Chancellor of the Exchequer. The Red Sea cable, in six sections totalling 3,500 miles and connecting Egypt with the west coast of India, was completed in February 1860. No telegram ever passed its entire length, but crucially for the guarantors each section tested successfully before failing. The government was therefore bound to pay Red Sea investors £36,000 a year for fifty years, an eventual cost to the Exchequer of £1.8 million. After this there could be no further question of direct public support of long-distance cables.

The government still believed that there was a pressing need for long-distance deep-sea cables to link the outposts of the British Empire. Its next action was arguably of much greater

value to the submarine telegraph industry than any number of financial guarantees. An inquiry into the technical aspects of long-distance telegraphy was set up, under the auspices of the Board of Trade and the Atlantic Telegraph Company. The committee was chaired by a respected Board of Trade technical expert, Captain Douglas Galton. It met during 1859 and 1860, taking evidence from every significant electrical engineer with submarine cable experience. In this new industry, some of these experts were still in their twenties: Charles Bright had been chief engineer on the 1858 expedition at the age of twenty-six, Jenkin was a year younger. Thomson, already a towering figure in the field, was not yet forty.

Galton's report, published in 1861, included detailed recommendations on cable construction, laying and operating. His committee summarised best practice and also suggested further definition and standardisation of electrical units. A number of electrical engineers, most notably Thomson and Jenkin, were already working to develop much more delicate and sensitive instruments to send and receive messages, and for cable testing. The British Association quickly formed its own committee, under the direction of Fleeming Jenkin, to deal with the matter of electrical units. The work of Galton, and of those responding to his challenges, proved decisive in the future of long-distance submarine telegraphs.

The period between Galton's report and the next attempt to lay a cable across the Atlantic, in 1865, coincides exactly with the duration of the Civil War in the United States. This is not to say that war directly delayed the project, although some of the US Navy officers who had been involved in the Atlantic cable scheme found themselves fighting on opposing sides. In fact the war strengthened the desire for a transatlantic cable. There was a clamour for news of a conflict whose effects were widely felt in Britain. The Reuter news agency even built its own telegraph line in 1863, covering the 80 miles from Cork to Crookhaven in the far south-west of Ireland, where incoming steamships from Newfoundland could be intercepted and the most urgent news from America despatched to London ahead of Reuters' rivals. The need for faster and more reliable communications was underlined by events during the war, particularly the *Trent* incident which almost drew the United Kingdom into the American conflict. Cyrus Field, an Anglophile and firm supporter of the Union, worked tirelessly to sustain the Atlantic project while the war raged around him. Appealing to meetings of American businessmen for funds, Field argued the cable's benefits to commerce while also emphasising it could improve international understanding.

The American Civil War strengthened the desire for a transatlantic cable.

Above all, it was problems attracting new funds which led to the delay after 1861. While each successive disappointment brought nearer the prospect of technical success, the public did not distinguish between degrees of failure, so that with each renewed attempt it became harder to raise money from increasingly sceptical investors. The Civil War may also have made potential backers in Britain wary of supporting an Anglo-American scheme. Some leading promotors of the 1850s cables had suffered heavy losses which made them unable or unwilling to continue, and they were replaced as directors of the Atlantic Telegraph Company by a new breed of wealthy entrepreneur.

The financial arrangements and company structures in place for the next attempt on the Atlantic, in 1865, were every bit as innovative as the technology. There was a marked change in approach from the 1850s. It had been necessary to bring in city financiers and men with experience of large-scale business, in place of the regional merchants who had dominated the earlier company. Cyrus Field, his idealism and optimism intact, retained a central role. A distinctly more cynical group gathered around him, among them Daniel Gooch,

best known for his work as engineer and manager of the Great Western Railway; Thomas Brassey, one of Britain's leading railway promoters, who invested £60,000 in the new project; and John Pender, with wealth founded in Manchester textiles and a long-standing interest in submarine telegraphs.

Even with Brassey and other substantial backers, there was a shortfall. The £700,000 required was raised partly through new fund-raising devices, made possible by a change in company laws in 1856 and 1862. The introduction of limited liability allowed a restructuring of the cable-making and laying industry. By merging the main submarine cable contractors with the company which made cable cores, Pender created the Telegraph Construction and Maintenance Company Ltd. (Telcon) in 1864. Telcon subscribed half the capital required, partly through deferred payments and also by accepting telegraph company stock in place of cash. Control of the Atlantic Telegraph Company and of Telcon had fallen to a small and close-knit group of large-scale investors.

Along with this streamlined organisation and the technical improvements—a cable manufactured with care in line with Galton's recommendations, improved instruments, more sensitive laying equipment, a profounder understanding of electricity—the 1865 expedition enjoyed another great advantage over previous attempts: there was at last a ship large enough to store the entire cable. Brunel's *Great Eastern*, the biggest ship in the world, launched in 1860 as a passenger liner, had proved a white elephant and bankrupted previous owners. She was laid up in 1863 and offered at auction. Gooch bought her for a knock-down price, stripped out the fittings, converted the holds to cable tanks, and chartered the ship to Telcon. Weighing 19,000 tons and powered by 11,500 h.p. steam engines, the *Great Eastern* offered manoeuvrability as well as size. All seemed set fair for the 1865 expedition.

But like its predecessors, the attempt, which began off the west coast of Ireland in June 1865, ended in failure. After a number of minor problems had been overcome during the early stages,

the *Great Eastern* had laid 1,200 miles of the line and was only two days away from its destination at Heart's Content, Newfoundland, when the cable again snapped. Usually it was possible to grapple for broken cables, splice them and continue, but this time the weather made retrieval impossible. The spot was marked with a buoy and the attempt abandoned.

Success had once again eluded the scheme's backers. There was frustration and disappointment, but tinged with a belief that the objective was close to being achieved. This had been a setback, not a catastrophe. The projectors immediately began to organise another attempt for the following summer. New problems had arisen. A major and sudden obstacle was the discovery that the Atlantic Telegraph Company, which had been established under an Act of Parliament in 1856, was acting outside its powers in trying to raise its capital by a further £600,000 to finance the 1866 expedition. There was no parliamentary time to amend the company's charter. To avoid another year's delay, Gooch and Pender established a new limited liability company, the Anglo-American Telegraph Company Ltd., to take over the project. Ultimately this solution led to other difficulties, for the relationship between the Anglo and Atlantic companies was troubled and ill-defined, and the arrangements led to further rifts between old and new investors. But for 1866, Gooch and Pender's actions saved the scheme. The balance of funds needed was secured through Telcon and the merchant bank of Morgan and Co., only days before a stock market crash which might have ended any hopes of laying a cable that summer.

The 1866 expedition achieved everything that had been hoped for. In July, the *Great Eastern* landed a new cable in Newfoundland only two weeks after embarking from Valentia. By the beginning of September the 1865 line had been retrieved and repaired, and two Atlantic cables were in operation. Queen Victoria again exchanged congratulations with her American counterpart, President Andrew Johnson. Gooch received a baronetcy, Thomson and others involved were knighted. The celebrations were muted in comparison with those of 1858, especially in the United States, where war had recently ended and the new Atlantic telegraph, much more than on previous expeditions, was seen as a product of British work and capital.

John Pender was vexed not to have been honoured. His contribution to the Atlantic venture, especially after 1862, had been substantial, and ultimately he risked everything he owned on the 1866 attempt. Experience with the Atlantic line had shown Pender that intercontinental cables were no longer a gamble, that technical improvements had reduced them to an acceptable risk. Moreover they could be exceptionally profitable. This encouraged him to continue promoting long-distance telegraphs, and the companies he launched during the following years laid cables to the Far East, Australasia and South America. Once a line was established, he followed a pattern of consolidating it into his parent company. Pender made another fortune, and was finally rewarded with his knighthood in 1888. The global communications empire which he had founded eventually became Cable & Wireless Ltd.

In contrast with Pender's hard-nosed pragmatism, Cyrus Field was driven by a higher vision. Yet Field was no inno-

> *Perhaps the most exciting aspect of the new cable to the general public was the novelty of fresh news from across the Atlantic.*

cent in business; he too had risked everything and then gained considerably from the Atlantic cable. His ideals were themselves business-oriented: world peace was advantageous to commerce. Whether the telegraph did improve international relations is questionable, for faster communications do not necessarily lead to better understanding. For Britain, the cable network certainly eased the task of ruling a far-flung empire. It also brought the benefits to commerce which Field had foreseen and transformed the financial markets of the world, bringing them into one global system. Not least, and perhaps the most exciting aspect of the new cable to the general public, was the novelty of fresh news from across the Atlantic, whetting an enduring appetite for more. It was here, rather than through diplomacy and politicians, that the cultures of two continents began to converge.

Although the successful cable of 1866 did not generate the same instant

elation as the short-lived effort of 1858, its impact was far-reaching. Achieving the Atlantic crossing marked a turning point in long-distance telegraphy. Deep-sea cables, no longer an heroic struggle against the elements, had become instead a mature technology and a serious business.

FOR FURTHER READING:

Gillian Cookson and Colin A. Hempstead, *A Victorian Scientist and Engineer: Fleeming Jenkin and the Birth of Electrical Engineering* (Ashgate, 2000); Hugh Barty-King, *Girdle round the Earth: the story of Cable and Wireless* (Heinemann, 1979); Charles Bright, *Submarine Cables: their history, construction and working* (Arno, New York, 1974 [1898]); B. S. Finn, *Submarine Telegraphy: the Grand Victorian Technology* (Science Museum, 1973); Daniel R. Headrick, *The Invisible Weapon: Telecommunications and International Politics, 1851–1945* (Oxford University Press, 1991); Donald Read, *The Power of News: the History of Reuters, 1849–1989* (Oxford University Press, 1999).

Dr Gillian Cookson, Editor of the Victoria County History of Durham, is based in the History Department, University of Durham. She is grateful to the Leverhulme Trust for supporting the research on which this article is based.

Father of The Computer Age

Howard H. Aiken's Mark I announced to the world the power of the computer

By I. Bernard Cohen

HOWARD H. AIKEN HOLDS AN ambiguous position in the history of the computer. Although a number of historians have declared that his first machine—the IBM ASCC (Automatic Sequence Controlled Calculator), known today mainly by the simpler name Mark I—inaugurated the computer age, many accounts of the birth of the computer either ignore his role altogether or consider him to have belonged to a pre-computer age.

Aiken was a giant of a man: in his physical stature, his force of will, his originality of mind, and his achievement. Standing erect at six feet and some inches tall, he towered over most of his students and colleagues. Graced by nature with a huge dome of a head, he had piercing eyes, crowned with huge beetling and somewhat satanic eyebrows. When he spoke to you in repose, he wore old-fashioned tortoise-rimmed pince-nez eyeglasses, attached to a black tape that went around his neck. In the course of conversation he would emphasize a point he was making by staring at you for a moment in silence; then, blinking his eyes and giving his nose a slight twitch, he would cause the glasses to fall, revealing his full face. You then knew that you had his undivided attention.

Aiken was the type of person who related to people by extremes. When he met you, almost from the very start you were placed at either the top of his scale or the bottom; there was never a middle ground. On a scale from 1 to 10, Aiken would almost at once rate you as a 0 or an 11. People reacted to him in the same way and on the same scale. His students and associates either admired him and established friendly relationships or found him "impossible." Friends and colleagues and former students on the "plus" side remained loyal and devoted for the rest of their lives, and Aiken himself cherished long-term relations. Those on the "minus" side tend to remember just those occasions when he was intransigent and difficult.

Only a person endowed with strong internal force could have survived the rigors of Aiken's adolescence and early adulthood. His life permitted no middle ground, and he judged others by his own demanding standards, inviting an equal sort of judgment from them. Only someone with a strong personality and a tough-minded aggressiveness could have forced a reluctant Harvard to become a computer center. Only a person such as Aiken could have been a trumpeter announcing the dawn of the computer age.

Was Aiken the "inventor" of the "computer," or even the "first inventor" among others? Those questions are extremely complex and raise important problems of exactly what is meant by "inventor," "computer," and "first" inventor. Partisans of various early machines are currently arguing—somewhat fruitlessly, it must be confessed—over which machine was the first computer.

Among the claimants are the Atanasoff-Berry ABC, the Colossus machines developed in England for code breaking during World War II, Konrad Zuse's Z3 in Germany, and the Eckert-Mauchly ENIAC. At the very least Aiken was certainly *an* inventor of one of the early machines from which the modern computer has developed. What is more significant in the annals of history, in the view of many of the people involved, and of historians and later computer scientists as well, is that Howard Aiken and his machine ushered in the computer age in which we live.

Standard works on computer history contain statements such as "the digital computer age began when the Automatic Sequence Controlled Calculator (Harvard Mark I) started working in 1944," and "the Harvard Mark I . . . marked the beginning of the era of the modern computer" and "the real dawn of the computer age." In 1980, in one of the first major scholarly studies on the origin of the digital computer, the historian Paul Ceruzzi concluded that "if one were to look for a date from which to mark the dawn of the computer age," one might well choose "August 7, 1944, when the existence of such machines was first made known to the world"—that is, the day the Mark I was publicly announced.

Like many pioneers, Aiken had a multifaceted career that influenced a number of different aspects of his new field. Collectively these broader innova-

From *American Heritage of Invention & Technology*, Spring 1999, pp. 56-63. © 1999 by Forbes, Inc. Reprinted by permission of *American Heritage*, a division of Forbes, Inc.

The technician Robert Hawkins, Aiken, and Richard Bloch in September 1946.

tions were so important that they actually outweigh in significances the features of any of the machines with which he was associated. The portrait of such an innovative and influential scientist is thus of double interest: as the presentation of the life and character of an extraordinary individual and as the record of an important phase in the birth of the time in which we live.

Howard Hathaway Aiken was born in Hoboken, New Jersey, on March 8, 1900, an only child. When he was just entering his teens, his family—consisting of him, his parents, and his maternal grandparents—moved to Indianapolis. Soon after, his father left home and was never seen by his family again. Young Aiken was just ready to start high school when it became his responsibility to

support his mother and grandparents. This meant quitting school to go to work. He got a job installing telephones and continued his education by means

Aiken related to people by extremes. He put them at the top of his scale or the bottom, with no middle.

of correspondence-school courses. Later in life he enjoyed telling how as an adolescent boy he had installed all the phones in the red-light district of Indianapolis.

Someone in the school system recognized Aiken's intellectual brilliance, especially in mathematics, and helped him

obtain a night job with the Indianapolis Light and Heat Company, permitting him to go back to school. Thereafter, during high school, he worked a 12-hour night shift and attended school during the day. He not only had time to do his homework but whiled away hours by learning to knit and knitting his own socks.

When Aiken graduated from high school, in 1919, the school officials once again became active in his behalf. The superintendent of public instruction wrote a letter about him to every Midwestern public utility located in a university town. As a result Aiken was offered a job with a utility company in Madison, Wisconsin, and that, he said, was why he went to the University of Wisconsin. The family moved to Madi-

Above: The Mark I, with paper-tape readers (center) and electric typewriters for output (right).

Left: Dials used to set numerical constants.

son, where he supported himself and them working as a watch engineer on the night shift of the Madison Gas and Electric Company while attending college during the day. In 1973, shortly before Aiken's death, Henry Tropp (a math professor at Humboldt University) and I conducted a three-day interview with him in which he told us of his joy in discovering that Wisconsin had adopted an 8-hour day that was "much easier" than the 12-hour shift in Indianapolis.

After his graduation in 1923 Aiken became the company's chief engineer. As he put it, "I was promoted from switchboard operator to chief engineer overnight." During the next 10 years he held a succession of better and better positions in different companies in the electric-power industry, rising in his profession. Nevertheless, despite his success, he found the managerial side of engineering unsatisfying and decided to go back to school. He spent a year in the physics department at the University

of Chicago but found it a disappointing experience. In 1933—at the age of 33 and much older and more experienced than most graduate students—he enrolled in the Ph.D. program in physics at Harvard.

Mark I was 51 feet long, weighed five tons, used 530 miles of wire, and contained 760,000 parts.

At Harvard he became part of a group interested in such matters as the thermionic emission of electrons, the physics of antennas, reflections from the upper atmosphere, and the like. His thesis topic was a study of the conductivity of vacuum tubes, specifically the theory of space-charge conduction. He began teaching while still a graduate student, and on receiving his Ph.D., in 1939, he was appointed faculty instructor, Har-

vard's equivalent of assistant professor. He rose steadily to full professor. By the time he received his Ph.D., however, his focus of interest had already shifted from electron physics to the design and use of computers.

The shift, Aiken said, came about while he was doing research for his thesis. The subject of the thesis, he explained, was space charge, "a field where one runs into [partial] differential equations in cylindrical co-ordinates . . . in nonlinear terms, of course." Before long his thesis research came to consist primarily of "solving nonlinear [differential] equations." The only methods then available for numerical solutions of problems like his made use of electromagnetic desk calculators about the size of today's cash registers, and calculations like those he needed were "extremely time-consuming." It became apparent—"at once," he said—that the labor of calculating "could be mechanized and programmed and that an individual didn't have to do this." He also realized that a computing machine would be of great use in solving pressing problems in many scientific fields, in engineering, and even in the social sciences.

By April 1937 Aiken had progressed far enough in his general thinking and design to seek support from industry in producing such a machine. In preparation he drew up a proposal stating the need for it, the principal features of its mode of operation, and its general method of solving problems. His philosophy was later expressed in an assignment he drew up for one of his Harvard classes in computer science. "The 'design' " of a "computing machine," the students were informed, "is understood to consist in the outlining of its general specifications and the carrying through of a rational determination of its functions, but does not include the actual engineering design of component units."

In this clear statement the primary concerns were the logic of the machine, its mathematical operations, and its general architecture; its actual technological specifications were secondary. To judge from all the information available, Aiken's design would not have specified what particular components or even what types of components—mechanical, electromechanical, or electronic—were to be used or how the various components would be linked. He essentially would have specified the need to perform certain types of mathematical operations and to have a means of programming them so they could be performed in a certain predetermined sequence, and he would have indicated the need for storing certain tables of numerical data. The design could apply equally well to a machine constructed of mechanical, electromechanical, or electronic components or any combination of them.

As is generally well known, Aiken's eventual machine was built by IBM and was based on electromagnetic relays rather than vacuum tubes. It may seem odd that a graduate student in the physics of vacuum tubes should have had his machine operate with relays rather than tubes. The reason was, as he explained it to us, that if the Monroe Calculating Machine

Company had undertaken to build his machine, it would have been largely mechanical; if RCA had done it, it would have been electronic; but since IBM turned out to be willing, the functioning elements were electromagnetic, of the type IBM used in its business machines.

As Aiken drew up his proposal for a new sort of calculating machine, he had to be sure that the physics department would find a place for it. The department was not at first very enthusiastic; the department chairman reported to Aiken that one of the laboratory technicians, Carmello Lanza, had asked why on earth Aiken wanted to build such a machine when there was already one in the Physics Research Laboratory and nobody had ever used it.

Aiken at once sought out Lanza, who took him into "the attic" and showed him a set of calculating wheels. These, it turned out, had been built a century earlier by Charles Babbage for use in his Difference Engine, a machine that had been designed to embody many of the features of today's computers. The set of wheels had been presented to Harvard by Babbage's son in 1886, on the 250th anniversary of Harvard's founding. Aiken went at once to Widener Library and, for the first time, came to learn of Babbage's ideas.

On April 22, 1937, Aiken made contact with his first choice for a prospective builder of his machine, the Monroe Calculating Machine Company, America's foremost manufacturer of calculating machines. Although the chief engineer was enthusiastic, his management was not interested. Aiken's next try was IBM. There his first contact was with James Wares Bryce, known affectionately within the company as "the father engineer." Bryce had been granted more than 400 patents, an average of about one per month since beginning his career in 1900. In 1936, on the centenary of the U.S. Patent Office, he was honored as one of the country's 10 greatest living inventors. Aiken's meetings with him were the first steps toward the construction of the Automatic Sequence Controlled Calculator.

As all histories of IBM make clear, no important decision was ever made at

IBM without the explicit approval of its president, Thomas J. Watson, Sr. Watson was a powerful figure, a titan in his sphere, endowed with just as forceful a personality as Howard Aiken. Anyone who has read anything at all about these two men will know that there had to be an eventual collision course and a terrible clash. It would happen after IBM built Aiken's dream machine.

In November 1937, encouraged by Bryce, Aiken submitted a formal proposal to IBM. In it he set forth the need for such a supercalculator and the kinds of problems it would solve. He then explained the mathematical functions or series of steps that the machine would have to perform and the types of mathematical operations it would be called on to execute. He stressed the need to make it able to perform its work in a series of predetermined automatic sequences, controlled by a set of specific instructions. In today's language, we would say that the machine was to be programmed. This quality was eventually embodied in its formal name, Automatic Sequence Controlled Calculator.

In those days the word *computer* meant a human being, usually a female, armed with a desk calculator and a book of tables, not a machine. Which is why most of the computer engineers, designers, and programmers in the 1940s referred to the new types of computing devices as "calculating machines."

When IBM first agreed to build Aiken's machine, it was envisaged that the company would supply the parts but much of the assembling would be done in the Harvard machine shops. This soon proved impractical, and construction was done at IBM's plant in Endicott, New York. A senior engineer, Clair D. Lake, was assigned to oversee the project. Francis E. (Frank) Hamilton was responsible for most of the practical decisions, and Benjamin M. Durfee did most of the actual wiring and assembly of the components. Beginning in 1938, Aiken spent long weekends and two whole summers in Endicott, explaining the operations the machine would have to perform and helping design the circuits that would let it execute the commands.

Over the next years he also spent many days in Endicott helping translate his requirements into machine componentry. It was soon apparent that although the IBM engineers who were assigned to the task of translating Aiken's were extremely gifted men, skilled in circuits and componentry, they knew very little mathematics. They could not really understand the kinds of problems the new machine was being designed to solve.

In April 1941 Aiken, an officer in the U.S. Naval Reserve, was called to active duty, so he could no longer pay regular visits to Endicott. He was assigned to the Naval School of Mine Warfare, in Yorktown, Virginia, and he designated Robert V. D. Campbell, a graduate student in physics at Harvard, to serve as his deputy during the final stages of construction. He was extremely fortunate in getting Campbell. Campbell had a solid background in physics and was adept at applied mathematics, and he made a number of creative decisions on his own. His already important role became even greater in February 1944, when the giant machine was disassembled and shipped from Endicott to Harvard, where it was installed in a large room in the basement of the Physics Research Laboratory. Campbell was now in full charge of the machine until Aiken was assigned to Harvard by the Navy in the spring of 1944, and he programmed and ran the first problems. He also took responsibility for working out all the initial problems of error and unreliability. His share in the final testing and operation of the ASCC/Mark I was much larger than is apparent in most histories of the computer.

The first two problems set for the new machine came from Ronald King, a physicist specializing in electromagnetic theory and the physics of radio transmission, and James D. Baker, an astronomer whose specialty was telescope and lens design. King recalls that the problem he sent Campbell was to "work out some integrals." By the time the machine computed those results, however, it had been turned over to the Navy, and its programs and outputs had at once become "classified." As a result, King, who had no Navy clearance, could

not gain access to the work the computer had done for him. He got, he told me, "a couple of pages of tables with numbers on them, and that was all." Still, they were "very useful." Baker's problem was the design for the Army Air Forces of a high-power telephoto lens in which corrections and adjustments would be made for effects such as changes in atmospheric pressure with altitude.

In April 1944 Aiken was transferred from Yorktown to Cambridge, where his new assignment was to take charge of the computer operation; in May the machine was turned over to the Navy for the duration of the war and became an official unit of the Bureau of Ships under Aiken's command. By August the Mark I was in full operation with a large staff of Navy personnel, including a number of officers, among them Grace Hopper (see "Amazing Grace," by J. M. Fenster, Fall 1998 issue), and Richard M. Bloch, who became the chief programmer.

To celebrate the completion of the machine and its successful installation at Harvard, a ceremony of dedication was planned, with many admirals, government officials, Harvard faculty, and others present, a formal luncheon, and speeches by President J. B. Conant of Harvard, Aiken, and Thomas J. Watson. When Watson arrived in Boston the day before the ceremony, he found that Harvard had issued a news release identifying Aiken as the primary inventor of the new machine and downplaying IBM'S contribution. It made him so angry that he threatened to boycott the event altogether, and Conant, Aiken, and other Harvard scientists had to rush in to calm him. In the end Harvard issued a revised news release acknowledging the importance of the IBM inventors, and IBM published a booklet about the machine stressing the company's contribution. At the ceremony Watson stole the limelight by making a gift to Harvard of $100,000 to defray the future costs of operating and maintaining the computer. At the time, a Harvard professor earned approximately $10,000 a year, so this was the equivalent of 10 professors' salaries—or about $1,000,000 in today's currency. The total cost of the machine

to IBM is usually reckoned to be around $200,000 in 1930s dollars.

This was a very large sum of money. In retrospect it is astonishing that IBM would have invested so much in a proposal by a young Harvard instructor just finishing his graduate work, especially when the engineers who were actually building the machine considered it "screwball." Who could be sure it would actually function as Aiken predicted? Furthermore, it was understood from the start that this project would not lead to a new product line at IBM; it was going to be a contribution to science and engineering and in no way a source of potential profit.

One reason IBM had embarked on such a costly adventure with no guarantee of success was that Bryce was a true believer in Aiken's proposal. He had no doubt that Aiken's dream would be made a practical reality. And Watson relied heavily on Bryce's judgment.

In 1944 and 1945 Mark I ran almost continuously, 24 hours a day and seven days a week. The wartime problems the machine was asked to solve included studies of magnetic fields associated with the protection of ships from magnetic mines and mathematical aspects of the design and use of radar. No doubt the most important wartime problem was a set of calculations for implosions brought from Los Alamos by John Von Neumann. Only a year or more later did the staff learn that these calculations had been made in connection with the design of the atomic bomb. Mark I's outstanding success and backlog of jobs led the Navy to ask Aiken in early 1945 to design and construct a second such machine. Aiken did so. It became known as Mark II.

Mark I was gigantic, an imposing sight, 8 feet high, 51 feet long, and almost 3 feet deep. A portion of it is on permanent exhibit in the main lobby of the Science Center at Harvard University; this gives only a partial notion of its original grandeur. It weighed five tons, used 530 miles of wire, and contained 760,000 parts. Relying on technology developed by IBM for statistical and accounting business machines, it used traditional IBM parts such as electromagnetic relays, counters, cam contacts, card punches, and electric typewriters but also incorporated elements of a new design, including relays and counters never before used in an IBM machine. These were smaller and faster than those in use. The input consisted of a punched tape, and the output was a series of punched cards or a printout from a standard IBM electric typewriter. The computer had 2,200 counter wheels and 3,300 relay components.

Its operation was powered by a long, horizontal, continuously rotating shaft that made a hum that has been described as being like that of a gigantic sewing machine. In later language, Mark I would be described as a parallel synchronous calculator. It had a word length of 23 decimal digits, with a twenty-fourth place reserved for an algebraic sign. Calculations were done in decimal numbers with a fixed decimal point. Its 60 registers for the input of numerical data (the constants that appear in any algebraic or differential equation) each contained 24 dial switches corresponding to 24 digits. For any problem these had to be set by hand.

The location of each of these 60 registers was assigned a number, so that the instructions could use the location to identify a number being called up in the course of a calculation. The operative portion of the machine consisted of 72 additional registers, or "accumulators." Each register was made up of 24 electromagnetic counter wheels, again providing the capacity for 23-digit numbers, with one place reserved for a sign. This second set of panels comprised both the store or storage and the processing unit.

A typical line of coding in the program would instruct the machine to take the number in a given input register (either a constant or a number in the store) and enter it in some designated register in the store. If there already was a number in that register, the new number would be added to it. The programmer had a code book, stating the designation of each location and each operation.

There were separate devices for multiplication and division and four tape readers. One was used to feed the instructions into the machine, and the

other three held tables of functions and could supply values as needed. There was also provision for the interpolation of values given on the tapes. Thus there were built-in "subroutines" (as Aiken called them) providing for a number to be converted by some built-in function (such as a sine, an exponential, a logarithm, or raising to some power) before being entered into the store.

Programs were fed into the machine by punched tape. The programmer first reduced the problem to a sequence of mathematical steps and then used the "code book" to translate each step into the necessary coding or instructions.

Aiken opened the curtain on the computer era and then filled the stage with some of its great players.

Mark I's instructions were essentially single-address instructions. Those who wrote programs for Mark I later recalled that the process was very much like programming later computers in machine language.

Although similar in many ways to later machines, Mark I incorporated one feature that today's sequenced program computers do not have: If you did not explicitly tell Mark I to go ahead and execute the next instruction, it stopped. Programmers had to enter a seven after each command to instruct the computer to proceed. If the machine didn't get that signal or some other automatic signal, it just stopped dead and waited for directions. From some points of view this was a tremendous advantage; for example, it was wonderful for debugging step by step. Mark I was the only sequenced program computer to include this feature.

The chief programmer, Dick Bloch, kept a notebook in which he wrote out pieces of code that had been checked out and were known to be correct. One of his routines computed sines for positive angles less than $\pi/4$ to 10 digits. Rather than use the slow sine unit built into the machine, Grace Hopper simply copied Bloch's routine into her own program whenever she knew it would suit

her requirements. This practice ultimately allowed the programmers to dispense with the sine, logarithm, and exponential units altogether. Both Bloch and Bob Campbell had notebooks full of such pieces of code. Years later the programmers realized that they were pioneering the art of subroutines and actually developing the possibility of building compilers.

Mark I continued to function at Harvard for 14 years after the war, producing useful work until it was finally retired in 1959. During that time, it also served generations of students at Harvard, where Aiken had established a pioneering program in what was later to be called computer science—with courses for undergraduates and graduate students leading to a master's degree or a Ph.D. Many important figures in the computer world were introduced to the subject on the Harvard Mark I.

In retrospect, Mark I's greatest significance may have lain in its dramatic public demonstration that a large-scale machine could actually perform an automatic sequence of calculations according to a program, and do so without error. Mark I did not, however, influence later computer technology as a machine since its computing elements were made of electromagnetic relays rather than of vacuum tubes, such as were used in ENIAC, and thus lay outside the path to the future of computers.

Because Mark I used relay technology, it was very slow. It produced results faster than conventional computing methods could but not nearly as fast as machines to be unveiled soon afterward, such as ENIAC. Addition or subtraction required one machine cycle, taking 0.3 seconds. Multiplication required 20 cycles, or 6 seconds, and division could take as much as 51 cycles, or more than 15 seconds. Because of this, in later models division was handled by the multiplication of reciprocals.

Although Mark I was slow, it not only was programmed, rather than being hard-wired for each problem, but was also extremely versatile. Whereas ENIAC was restricted in its original design by the mission of computing ballistic tables, Mark I could accommodate a large variety of programs.

HARVARD UNIVERSITY PHOTO LAB, CRUFT LABORATORY

A neat-looking board hides a dense undergrowth of wires as naval personnel grapple with construction of the Mark II in 1946.

Aiken built three later machines at Harvard. Mark II, like Mark I, used relays as its operating components; Mark III pioneered in using magnetic drum memory and some solid-state elements, along with vacuum tubes. Mark IV had magnetic core memory and was all electronic, using selenium solid-state devices and, later, ones made of germanium.

One of Mark III's unusual features was its automatic coding machine. This unit had a tremendous array of keys corresponding to various subroutines that were stored inside it. If a programmer needed to find the sine of a number, for example, all he or she had to do was to hit the sine key and the whole sine routine would automatically enter in the program. As Grace Hopper recalled, "In other words, Mark III had what today would be called a compiling machine. With this magnificent keyboard you essentially could punch in the program you wanted to run in a form very similar

to mathematical notation." Apparently this was the only such coding machine ever built.

Nevertheless, these machines did not set the pace for the development of computer architecture in the years after World War II. One reason was that Aiken steadfastly opposed the use of a single store for both instructions and data, which became a central feature of post–World War I computers.

What, finally, was Aiken's importance and influence? It comes down to four principal achievements. First, he demonstrated that it was possible to produce a machine to be programmed to execute a series of commands in a predetermined sequence of operations—without error. The widespread publicity that surrounded the dedication of Mark I gave notice to the world of the dawn of the computer age.

Second, Aiken's lectures all over the world on the importance of computers

and their potential uses were extremely important in gaining support for development of computers. Third, he initiated the application of computers to data processing—not just mathematical problems—including computer billing and accounting, for instance, for electric and gas companies.

Finally, he established at Harvard the world's first full-fledged graduate program in what is known today as computer science, and it served as a model for programs at other universities. The roster of Aiken's pupils is astonishing. It includes two of the chief designers of IBM's System/360 and a number of present and former chairmen of computer science departments. Among others who received their training or apprenticeship under Aiken were Grace Hopper, pioneer of the compiler and certain computer languages; An Wang, founder of the computer company that bore his name; and numerous Europeans who came to spend time working in Aiken's Harvard Computer Lab and learning the art and science of the computer.

Some historians of the computer believe that this last, the establishment of computer science as a legitimate and recognized part of university curricula and research programs, may have been more important than anything else Aiken did. He opened the curtain on the computer age, and then he filled the stage with some of its greatest players. In so doing, he built a monument more lasting than brass, of longer duration than any single machine. He was a true computer pioneer.

I. Bernard Cohen is the Victor S. Thomas Professor of the History of Science Emeritus at Harvard University. His book Howard Aiken: Portrait of a Computer Pioneer *has been published by MIT Press.*

Greetings from Mars

*The remarkably clever—and cheap—Pathfinder mission
inaugurates a new era in space exploration*

By Sharon Begley

FOR SIX AND A HALF LONG HOURS mission controllers had been sitting anxiously with their eyes fixed on a single desktop terminal, scanning the computer screen for interplanetary e-mail. Suddenly, just about the time that the towns near the Jet Propulsion Laboratory (JPL) in Pasadena, Calif., were getting ready to load their Fourth of July fireworks, the screen bloomed with fireworks of its own. As the exuberant sound of the Beatles' "Twist and Shout" rang out in the science team's room, the JPL crew got what they'd been waiting for: the first pictures of Mars since the Viking missions of 1976. It was also proof positive that the Pathfinder spacecraft would meet one of its main scientific goals: taking images of the Red Planet. Soon after, the first-ever high-resolution color images of Mars arrived. It was the ultimate Kodak moment. The photo showed gleaming black solar panels atop Pathfinder's open "petals," or sides; the little sixwheeled, microwave-oven-size dune buggy of a rover that was all set to become the first-ever mobile explorer of another planet, and the deflated air bags that had cushioned Pathfinder's pinpoint landing and now lay under the petals like crumpled beach towels. And beyond all that: Mars.

Coming down at 2,250 bits per second, the first images elicited oohs and ahs even from the mission's engineers and geologists. Those landscapes and the hundreds of other images that followed over the holiday weekend showed Pathfinder sitting on a rock-strewn plain

under a salmon sky, with hills, crater rims and plateaus in the distance. Pathfinder was in a channel in Ares Vallis—Mars Valley—which geologists believe was formed by a flood of Noachian proportions (a volume of water equal to the five Great Lakes) 1.5 billion to 3 billion years ago. The inundation carried down rocks from the surrounding highlands. One of them, a blue-gray, squarish stone much darker than its neighbors, was "the one we want to get to," said JPL's Matthew Golombek, Pathfinder's project scientist, when he saw the first photos. Unlike its neighbors, it was not covered with Martian dust but was studded with mysterious bumps. Not that anyone was suggesting Romulan Braille, but . . .

For a whole night and part of the day it looked like Golombek might not get his wish. Commands radioed up from JPL to the lander were not being forwarded to the rover, perhaps because the rover's modified Motorola radio modem had fallen out of sync with the lander's due to frequency drift. Controllers spent the night "power-cycling"—turning on and off—the lander's modem, while the rover's cycled automatically once an hour. Late the next afternoon deputy project manager Brian Muirhead barked out the news that brought a sigh of relief that could be felt clear across the JPL campus: "Flight control, we have rover data." The rover was back in the game.

With the sun blazing above Ares Vallis, the rover would slowly unfold its legs like a cat awakening from a long slumber, and reach its full height of an

imposing 12 inches. Then it would roll down a steel ramp to become the universe's first "areologist." Like the pontiff kissing the ground after stepping off the plane in a new country, the rover would lower its principal instrument to lock onto the reddish Martian soil at the landing site. For the next 10 hours the Alpha Proton X-Ray Spectrometer would barrage the soil with alpha particles (two protons and two neutrons) from its supply of radioactive curium-244. The alphas excite atoms in the soil, making them emit x-rays or protons. The number, and energy, of the emissions reveal which chemical elements go into Martian soil.

Back at JPL, 119 million miles away, rover driver (and videogame master) Brian Cooper got ready for his big moment by studying a display of the Martian landscape on his Silicon Graphics workstation. By the next day and throughout this week, he would be working the ultimate in radiocontrolled cars. Wearing special goggles that turned the image three-dimensional, Cooper would move a cursor of a rover icon to the rock that had the scientists so excited. His computer had calculated how Sojourner, named after the Civil War era abolitionist Sojourner Truth, could get there. Then it would radio up the directions. After 10 minutes the radio signal would arrive on Pathfinder, get relayed to the rover, and Sojourner would be off. Using infrared lasers, like supermarket scanners, to avoid hazards, the rover would crawl along at one inch every two seconds until it reached the

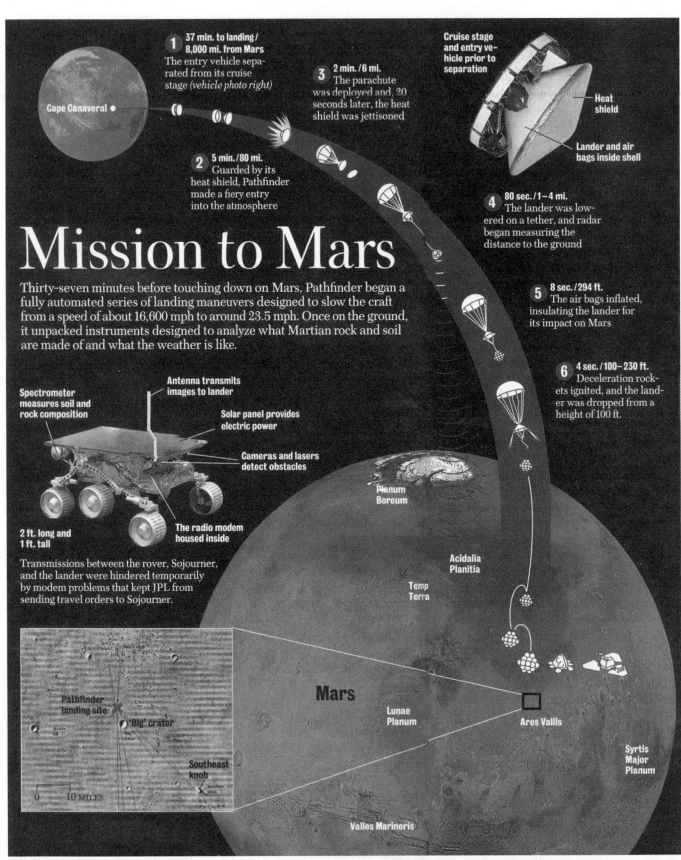

1 37 min. to landing / 8,000 mi. from Mars
The entry vehicle separated from its cruise stage *(vehicle photo right)*

3 2 min. / 6 mi.
The parachute was deployed and, 20 seconds later, the heat shield was jettisoned

Cape Canaveral

Cruise stage and entry vehicle prior to separation

Heat shield

Lander and air bags inside shell

2 5 min. / 80 mi.
Guarded by its heat shield, Pathfinder made a fiery entry into the atmosphere

4 80 sec. / 1–4 mi.
The lander was lowered on a tether, and radar began measuring the distance to the ground

Mission to Mars

Thirty-seven minutes before touching down on Mars, Pathfinder began a fully automated series of landing maneuvers designed to slow the craft from a speed of about 16,600 mph to around 23.5 mph. Once on the ground, it unpacked instruments designed to analyze what Martian rock and soil are made of and what the weather is like.

5 8 sec. / 294 ft.
The air bags inflated, insulating the lander for its impact on Mars

6 4 sec. / 100–230 ft.
Deceleration rockets ignited, and the lander was dropped from a height of 100 ft.

Spectrometer measures soil and rock composition

Antenna transmits images to lander

Solar panel provides electric power

Cameras and lasers detect obstacles

The radio modem housed inside

2 ft. long and 1 ft. tall

Transmissions between the rover, Sojourner, and the lander were hindered temporarily by modem problems that kept JPL from sending travel orders to Sojourner.

Planum Boreum

Acidalia Planitia

Temp Terra

Mars

Lunae Planum

Ares Vallis

Syrtis Major Planum

Pathfinder landing site

'Big' crater

Southeast knob

0   10 MILES

Valles Marineris

PHOTOS CLOCKWISE FROM TOP: JULIAN BAUM & DAVID ANGUS—PHOTO RESEARCHERS: NASA; JPL—NASA; JPL—NASA; JPL—NASA; JPL—NASA; NASA: ASTROGEOLOGY TEAM, U.S. GEOLOGICAL SURVEY, FLAGSTAFF, ARIZ.; JPL—NASA

SOURCES: NASA, JPL. RESEARCH BY ANNA KUCHMENT. GRAPHIC BY KARL GUDE, CHRISTOPH BLUMRICH AND STANFORD KAY—NEWSWEEK

Mars Pathfinder began its 309 million-mile journey to Mars on Dec. 4, 1996, at Cape Canaveral, Fla.

7 The lander, enveloped in four air bags, hit the survace at a speed of 23.5 mph and bounced three times

8 After the Patherfinder stopped bouncing, the air bags deflated and retracted

9 The lander's three petals unfolded, revealing the rover, IMP camera, high-gain antenna and solar panels

rock. Then it would again deploy its spectrometer, which looked like one of those eyes bobbing at the end of a spring on a fright mask, to glom onto the rock and figure out what it is made of. That promised to tell scientists whether Mars did, or does, have the right stuff to evolve life.

Despite the rover glitch, the Independence Day triumph inaugurated a bold new era of planetary exploration by proving that "better, cheaper, faster" missions, as NASA Administrator Daniel Goldin puts it, can succeed. "This is a new way of doing business," Vice President Al Gore said in a congratulatory phone call to JPL on the Fourth. "and its [validity] is being borne out by your dramatic success today." Thanks to Pathfinder, the Mars program is on track to launch two spacecraft every 26 months to the Red Planet. One will bring pieces of rock or samples of soil back to Earth by 2005. By the time the last interplanetary ferry returns with its quarry, scientists should know without any doubt whether the planet most similar to Earth ever supported life. Pathfinder may even pave the way to a human mission. In an interview the day before Pathfinder landed, Goldin told NEWSWEEK that the Johnson Space Center in Houston is close to designing a manned mission to Mars that met all his criteria: it would have to carry a price tag below $20 billion, be as safe for the astronauts as engineers can possibly make it, promise a big scientific payoff and be executed in collaboration with other countries. Said Goldin, "We could have something ready to present to the president by early in the next century."

The iconoclastic Pathfinder project shattered the conventions of planetary missions. For 30 years, spacecraft have all behaved like cautious tourists who take a breather in the hotel room before plunging into the local scene: after the cruise through space, the craft slipped into orbit around the moon or the target planet. Only after a few loops did the craft, or part of it, land. Not Pathfinder. Pushed to astonishing feats of engineering by the demand from NASA that Pathfinder be designed, built and launched in one quarter the time, and at one quarter the cost, of missions of the

1970s and '80s, JPL built a spacecraft that did what no other has done before. Pathfinder sailed to Mars and plunged directly into the atmosphere of the Red Planet without taking a single orbit to slow down.

Cruising interplanetary space at 12,000 miles per hour relative to the sun, Pathfinder was screaming across the Martian sky from northeast to southwest at a ballistic 16,600 miles per hour by the Fourth of July. (The Viking landers of 1976 cruised down at about half that speed.) Having jettisoned the "cruise stage" that had flown it through space, Pathfinder pierced the Martian atmosphere, by then on the dark side of the planet (graphic, preceding page). After 70 seconds it was feeling a deceleration force of nearly 20 g's, which made onboard accelerometers kick off an automatic landing sequence whose guts were right in keeping with the Independence Day spirit: a barrage of 41 "pyro" devices—firecrackers and mortars.

TWO MINUTES AFTER ENTRY, ONE mortar shot out a 24-foot parachute that cut Pathfinder's speed by 80 percent. Then the firecrackers started popping like a Grucci finale. In quick succession the pyros blew off the heat shield that had been protecting Pathfinder from the searing heat of entry, shot the "back shell" away and made the lander rappel like a mountaineer down a 65-foot-long braided Kevlar tether.

When the radar altimeter sensed the ground about 1,000 feet below, 11-foot-tall, six-lobed air bags, one on each of Pathfinder's four sides, inflated at supersonic speed, giving the whole contraption the look of a gigantic albino raspberry, with Pathfinder completely cocooned inside. Immediately three retrorockets fired with such huge thrust that Pathfinder actually hung motionless in the air for a split second 100 feet above the surface before free-falling, hitting the dusty red plain of Ares Vallis at 23.5 miles an hour.

And hitting, and hitting … Pathfinder landed as no mission ever has: not with the stately touchdown of an Apollo moon lander but like a wild beach ball. Pathfinder bounced crazily across the

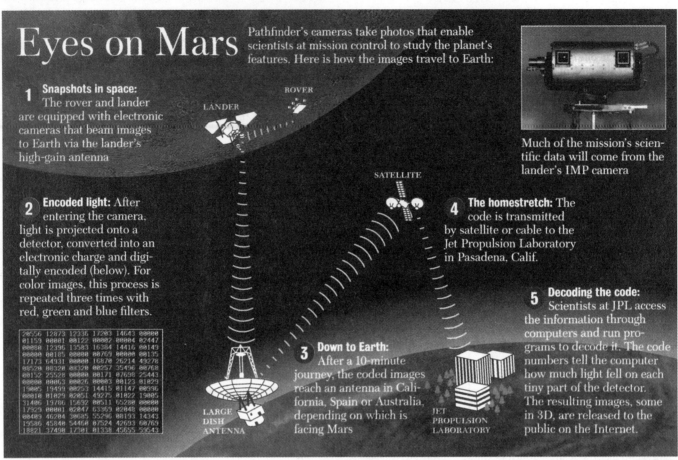

Eyes on Mars

Pathfinder's cameras take photos that enable scientists at mission control to study the planet's features. Here is how the images travel to Earth:

1 Snapshots in space: The rover and lander are equipped with electronic cameras that beam images to Earth via the lander's high-gain antenna

Much of the mission's scientific data will come from the lander's IMP camera

2 Encoded light: After entering the camera, light is projected onto a detector, converted into an electronic charge and digitally encoded (below). For color images, this process is repeated three times with red, green and blue filters.

4 The homestretch: The code is transmitted by satellite or cable to the Jet Propulsion Laboratory in Pasadena, Calif.

5 Decoding the code: Scientists at JPL access the information through computers and run programs to decode it. The code numbers tell the computer how much light fell on each tiny part of the detector. The resulting images, some in 3D, are released to the public on the Internet.

3 Down to Earth: After a 10-minute journey, the coded images reach an antenna in California, Spain or Australia, depending on which is facing Mars

LANDER, ROVER, SATELLITE, LARGE DISH ANTENNA, JET PROPULSION LABORATORY

SOURCE: JUSTIN MAKI, JET PROPULSION LABORATORY, DIAGRAM BY CHRISTOPH BLUMRICH, RESEARCH BY ANNA KUCHMENT—NEWSWEEK

valley three times, reaching heights of 47 and 23 feet. The undignified landing was forced by the mission's budget: there wasn't a line to pay for a traditional, rocket-assisted landing. When Pathfinder finally stopped, a winch automatically reeled in and deflated the air bags. Then the lander's three sidewalls came partway down like an opening lotus flower. After a journey of 309 million miles, Pathfinder, launched atop a Delta rocket from Cape Canaveral, Fla., last Dec. 4, had landed. The control room at JPL erupted in euphoric applause, hugs, backslaps and even a jig. It wasn't just any landing, either; Pathfinder landed downside down despite all the tumbling around.

Mars is a Whitman's Sampler of virtually every cool feature in the solar system. It has ancient cratered plains like the moon, and the longest (2,500 miles) and deepest (six miles) canyon—Valles Marineris—in the solar system. It boasts the highest volcano of any planet (Olympus Mons), and sinuous channels carved by long-evaporated rivers. Its mostly carbon-dioxide atmosphere exerts less than 1 percent the pressure of Earth's. But otherwise Mars is like a little sibling, half the size but with a day only 37 minutes longer and with terrestrial-like seasons (because Mars's poles, like Earth's, are tilted). In the landing area at this time of year, temperatures range from that of a winter day in North Dakota (minus 10 degrees Fahrenheit) to the coldest ever recorded on Earth (in Vostok, Antarctica)—minus 127.

Embracing the notion that 90 percent of life is just showing up, NASA has always emphasized that Pathfinder's main goal was just to make it to Mars. That alone would prove that the cut-rate approach to space actually works. But such low expectations had space scientists seeing, and even turning, red last week. Peter Smith of the University of Arizona fairly sputtered that "Pathfinder will do as much good science as supposedly pure-science missions."

Smith's own experiment, the Imager on Mars Pathfinder (IMP), was snapping away. The stereoscopic, color camera had sprung up from the lander on a jack-in-the-box mast and started shooting soon after sunrise on Ares Vallis. IMP seemed happy—holes that vent gases were arranged in a smile—and so did the scientists. IMP's 24 color filters could make out details invisible to the Viking cameras. The plain where Pathfinder landed was littered with bigger rocks than Viking ever saw, oriented in ways that promise to provide clues to the ancient flood, and made of minerals that may reveal what Mars was like billions of years ago, when scientists suspect it resembled the ancient (and life-creating) Earth. Because the rocks on Ares Vallis were presumably carried down by the flood from the highlands, Sojourner gets to sample rocks from many places without leaving its neighborhood.

KNOWING WHAT THE MARTIAN highlands are made of should solve several puzzles. First, it should nail down whether the "Mars meteorites" in Antarctica really are from

Martian highlands. If the rocks at the South Pole have the same ingredients as those on Ares Vallis, there will be no question that long before Earth sent spacecraft to Mars, Mars had sent chunks of itself (blasted out by meteor impacts) to Earth. One of those hunks is the meteorite in which scientists last August claimed to detect signs of primitive, extinct life. Second, since the highland crust is thought to be as old as 3.5 billion to 4.5 billion years, studying its rocks could reveal whether the conditions were right, at a time when life was getting started on Earth, for life to spring into being on Mars.

Another payoff from determining what Mars is made of is that "once you've identified the rock types and minerals," says Golombek, "any geologist can tell you how it formed." Did it, for instance, form at a hydrothermal spring? Because such springs get their heat from geothermal sources, they could still survive on Mars even though the rest of the liquid water is gone. Hydrothermal springs, warm and wet, would be ideal places to search for signs of lingering Martian life.

Designing and building Pathfinder and Sojourner cost $171 million, which would have been a mere rounding error in the $3 billion (in today's dollars) Viking budget. Forced to get a spacecraft to Mars on a supersaver ticket, the engineers behaved like kids trying to build a computer using only some castoff circuit boards and ingenuity. Since they couldn't do it the clunky, hidebound way, they came up with the Apple of spacecraft. "The cost cap forced the technology," says JPL's William Dias. Better software, in particular, let NASA get by with tens rather than hundreds of people on the operations team: the computers are so good that one person, albeit working 12- to 14-hour shifts, can do the work of several. "We did it in one quarter the time and at one quarter the cost of the old way," said Goldin. "If we'd gone with the old style it

would've taken another seven years to get off the ground. I told them to get creative, to think out of the box, and they did."

Although their average age was only thirtysomething and many of them hadn't even made it to high school at the time of America's last successful Mars mission, the Pathfinder team showed respect for the classics. They reproduced the heat shield and parachute design from Viking, for instance. "We hit on using the old design and then sat around scratching our heads, asking, 'What exactly was that [heat shield] formula again?' " recalls JPL's Rob Manning, the chief fight systems engineer. They actually coaxed some Viking vets out of retirement to help.

But the team also broke new ground. They tested and tested and retested their components as they went along, rather than designing the whole craft completely and then testing it. "Compared to past missions," says Manning, "Pathfinder was much more, um, empirical." In other words, the designers threw every disaster they could think of at the lander and rover. To make sure the lander's petals would open up even if it was smack up against a boulder, for instance, they made the petal motors strong enough to flip the lander—and then they executed a lander backflip at the JPL "Mars yard" test site.

The rover designers started off slowly in their tests of Sojourner's grit. At first they merely ran over the toes of a willing scientist. Then they worked up to 10-inch rocks. And the air bags, something no previous space mission has ever used, got impaled. "Days and days of simulations on a supercomputer still didn't really explain what happened when an air bag hit a spiked rock," says Manning, "so we collected lava rocks, shipped them on a train to a testing facility outside Cleveland and then dropped the air bags onto them." Having dusted each spike with colored powder, the engineers could tell whether damage

to a bag, dropped from the equivalent of 10 stories on Mars, was made by "Old Yeller" or some other spike. "Basically we ripped the hell out of the bags to know how to redesign them," says Pathfinder project manager Tony Spear.

Pathfinder, true to its name, has cut a trail for NASA's ambitious 10-year program of Mars missions. "This gives us confidence that we can build things for only a fraction of the cost of [past] missions and have them work," says JPL's Donna Shirley, manager of the Mars program. "This is the basis for the whole future of planetary exploration." And what a future. The Pathfinder lander could last months beyond its "nominal" mission length of 30 sols, or Martian days, adding to the photo album as well as making meteorological observations on Ares Vallis as the region changes with the seasons. Next March 15, the Mars Global Surveyor, launched in 1996, is scheduled to begin two years of photographing and precisely mapping Mars's surface. Among MGS's targets: the "face," a rock formation that those who regard "Men in Black" as a documentary believe was built by a Martian civilization. Then, every 26 months, when Earth and Mars are aligned so the trip is as short as possible, a lander and an orbiter will take off for the Red Planet. By 2005 some of the landers will start bringing pieces of Mars back to Earth so scientists can scrutinize them for signs of life. And if the engineers come through the way Administrator Goldin expects, it may not be long after until astronauts join in the excavation. The first crewed mission could launch as early as 2011 and take six months to arrive. If that happens, those Martian pioneers may well look back on Pathfinder as the scout that showed the way, allowing earthlings to break the bonds tethering them to their natal planet and set sail throughout the solar system, ushering in a new age of exploration for the new millennium.

With ADAM ROGERS *at JPL*

Unit 4

Unit Selections

Key Points to Consider

❖ Is there a point in industrialization at which there is no turning back?

❖ Was the Maginot Line a waste of time and money? Why did it not protect France?

❖ Why did the women of Germany accept Nazi ideology?

❖ What happened at Nanking? Is this an expected part of warfare?

❖ Does Churchill fit the "Great Man Theory" (great events produce great men)?

❖ What went wrong with DDT? Was it a case of technology run amok, as in the case of Chornobyl (see unit 5)?

DUSHKIN ONLINE Links   www.dushkin.com/online/

These sites are annotated on pages 4 and 5.

At the beginning of the twentieth century, Great Britain occupied the foremost position in world leadership. Its fleet possessed global reach and served as the world's policeman. British financial strength was unsurpassed and the British pound sterling was the money standard for world markets. Still, other nations-Germany, Japan, and the United States-were rising in prestige and strength. Japan, for example, after being forced to open its ports to Matthew Perry in 1853–1854, embarked upon a successful program of industrialization called the Meiji Restoration. By 1900, its efforts to meld Western industry with traditional culture was complete, as Richard Perren brings out in "On the Turn—Japan, 1900."

In the Russo-Japanese War, 1904–1905, Japan flexed its newly found muscle to become the first non-European power to defeat a European nation in modern warfare.

The prestige and power of the West, in addition, diminished in the twentieth century with the difficulties of World War I, the Great Depression, World War II, and the cold war. World War I left 10 million dead and a heritage of barbarism. Great Britain emerged exhausted as the great debtor nation of the world, and the Soviets began their long experiment with communism by executing Nicholas II, the last czar of Russia. Only after the fall of the USSR was it possible to identify and rebury the czar and his family, as explained by Bill Powell and Owen Matthews in "Home at Last." The rumor that Anastasia, the czar's daughter, had escaped the murder was also laid to rest.

In the 1930s the Great Depression undermined the financial strength of the West and raised a question about the stability of the capitalist economic system. Fascism fed on the economic misery and, with that in mind, Adolf Hitler began his destructive career. The Nazis attempted to form a perfect society, in part by eliminating Jews, Gypsies, and other designated undesirable people. Women in the Third Reich were assigned the role of producing children in order to man the armies of Hitler. Having been attacked by the Germans in 1870 and also in 1914, the French built a complex, concrete defensive line along the French-German border. The Maginot Line was ingenious, expensive, and useless. The line held during the German assault in 1940, but then the Germans simply went around it. At their surrender, the French turned the line over to the Germans. Winston Churchill became the war leader of Great Britain during this crisis and inspired his

nation to continue resistance to Hitler, as described in "His Finest Hour." Great Britain held on until the United States became the "arsenal for democracy."

Fighting in World War II had already begun in Asia with the Japanese invasion of China in 1937—Asian historians state that World War II really began at this time. The Japanese conquest of Nanking is noted for its brutality, which included torture, murder, and rape. This was an event that was known but not explored by historians until recently. After a 4-year struggle, the war in the Pacific came to an end with the explosion of two atomic bombs over Japan.

As Allied armies captured various portions of Germany, death camps were exposed, revealing the barbarity of Germany under Hitler. The shock of the Holocaust demanded an assertion of the rule of law over that of revenge. German leaders, not the German people, were to be held accountable. This was carried out at the Nuremberg trials, which set a precedence for war crimes trials wherever war atrocities were found. Following the surrender of Japan, the Allies also conducted war crimes trials for Japanese leaders as well.

An unexpected outcome of the war was the approval of the use of DDT to control insects that carried disease. The pesticide killed fleas, lice, and mosquitoes and, thus, saved troops and civilians from the ravages of typhus, yellow fever, and malaria. It was hailed as a miracle chemical and found its way into widespread peacetime use. Unfortunately, as discovered later, DDT did not readily deteriorate and caused long-term damage to fish and birds. It was a product of wartime that eventually brought attention to the fragile nature of the environment.

On the Turn—Japan, 1900

From isolation to Great Power status—Richard Perren explains how a mania for Westernisation primed the pump of Japan's transformation at the turn of the century.

Richard Perren

Richard Perren is Senior Lecturer in Economic History at the Department of History, University of Aberdeen and author of Japanese Studies from Earliest Times to 1990: A Bibliographic Guide *(Manchester University Press, 1992).*

Following the Meiji Restoration in 1868, when rule by the emperor replaced the government of Japan by the Tokugawa shogun, the country embarked on a process of modernisation. In the next thirty years Western experts were imported to train the Japanese at home, selected Japanese were sent abroad to learn from the West, and Japan's new leaders embarked on a programme of radical reform. By these means they aimed at transforming a country that was weak and backward into a strong modern industrial nation. This new Japan would be capable of dealing with Western powers on equal terms and of throwing off the humiliating 'unequal treaties' they had imposed between 1858 and 1869.

When the Emperor Meiji died in 1912, control was concentrated in a highly centralized state whose functions were carried out through Western-style political, administrative and judicial institutions operating in the name of the emperor. Western-style armed forces upheld the position of the Japanese state at home and abroad. A modern and efficient education system served the aims of the state. Western-style economic and business institutions were in place, and factory-based industry firmly established. Japan had already been victorious in two major wars, against China in 1894–95 and Russia in 1904–5. She had not only achieved the much desired revision of the unequal treaties, but was a world power with an alliance with Britain, and a possessor of colonies. Yet the country still retained many traditional features, and had only adopted those characteristics of the West that were absolutely necessary to achieve its desired aims.

How far had the transformation process gone by 1900, and can the decade of the 1890s be described as a 'turning point'? To answer this we need to judge when Japan passed beyond that point in time when her modernisation could not have been reversed. Because the whole process of Japanese modernisation involved a complex interaction of social, economic, and political change it is not possible to ascribe a precise date to its completion. Nevertheless, there are a number of factors to suggest that by 1900 it had reached a stage where it was unlikely to be reversed.

It was the authorities that had to provide the necessary pump-priming and make strategic decisions about which areas of Japanese life needed to be transformed. It had become a traditional habit of the Japanese to look to officialdom for example and direction in almost everything, and this habit naturally asserted itself when it became necessary to assimilate a foreign civilisation which for nearly three centuries had been an object of national repugnance. This required the education of the nation as a whole and the task of instruction was divided among foreigners of different nations. The Meiji government imported around 300 experts or *yatoi*—a Japanese term meaning 'live machines'—into the country to help upgrade its industry, infrastructure and institutions. Before the Franco-Prussian War, Frenchmen were employed in teaching strategy and tactics to the army and in revising the criminal code. The building of railways, installing telegraphs and lighthouses, and training the new navy was done by Englishmen. Americans were employed in forming a postal service, agricultural development, and in planning colonisation and an educational system. In an attempt to introduce Occidental ideas of art, Italian painters and sculptors were brought to Japan. German experts were asked to develop a system of local government, train Japanese doctors and, after the Franco-Prussian War, to educate army officers. A number of Western observers believed that such wholesale adoption of an alien civilisation was impossible and feared that it would produce a violent reaction.

Although this did not occur, many early innovations were not really necessary to modernisation but merely imitations of Western customs. At that time the distinction between the fundamental features of modern technology and mere Occidental peculiarities was by no means clear. If it was necessary to use Western weapons there might also be a virtue in wearing Western clothes or shaking hands in the Occidental manner. Moreover, Meiji Japan had good reason to adopt even the more superficial as-

From *History Today*, June 1992, pp. 26–32. © 1992 by History Today, Ltd., 20 Old Compton Street, London W1V 5PE. Reprinted by permission.

pects of Western culture. The international world of the nineteenth century was completely dominated by the Occident, and in view of the Western assumption of cultural superiority, the Japanese were probably correct in judging that they could not be regarded as even quasi-equals until they possessed not only modern technology but also many of the superficial aspects of Western culture. The resulting attempts in the 1870s and 1880s to borrow almost anything and everything Western may now seem to us to be amusingly indiscriminate, but it is perfectly understandable.

As the object of modernisation was to obtain equal treatment by the West many of the cultural innovations, besides being more than outward forms to the Japanese themselves, had an important psychological influence on Western diplomats and politicians. Under the shogun, members of the first Japanese delegation to the United States in 1860 wore traditional samurai dress with shaved pate and long side hair tied in a bun and carried swords. Under the emperor, Western-style haircuts were a major symbol of Westernisation. Soldiers and civilian functionaries wore Western-style uniforms, and politicians often adopted Western clothes and even full beards. In 1872 Western dress was prescribed for all court and official ceremonies. Meat eating, previously frowned on because of Buddhist attitudes, was encouraged, and the beef dish of *suki-yaki* was developed at this time. Western art and architecture were adopted, producing an array of official portraits of leading statesmen as well as an incongruous Victorian veneer in the commercial and government districts of the cities and some rather depressing interiors in the mansions of the wealthy.

Though the pace of change was hectic at first, and the adoption of Western forms seemed indiscriminate, it soon slowed as the Japanese became more selective about which aspects of their society they wanted to transform. Their adaptability meant the contracts of most Western experts and instructors only needed to be short-term, the average length of service being five years, and *yatoi* were less in evidence by the 1890s. The craze for Westernisation

reached its height in the 1880s, but thereafter there was a reaction against unnecessary imitations and many of its more superficial features, like ballroom dancing, were dropped. Other social innovations subsequently abandoned were the prohibition of prostitution and mixed bathing, both of which were initially enforced to placate the prejudice of Western missionaries.

In reforming the legal system, Western concepts of individual rather than family ownership of property were adopted. But for purposes of formal registration of the population the law continued to recognise the old extended family or 'house', known in Japanese as the *ie*. This consisted of a patriarch and those of his descendants and collateral relatives who had not yet established a new *ie*. Within this structure the position of women was one of obedient subservience. In the 1870s the theme of liberation of women from their traditional Confucianist bondage was taken up by a number of Japanese intellectuals, influenced by Western writers on the subject. At the same time a number of women activists publicly engaged in politics. As both movements lacked public appeal they waned in the 1880s. In 1887 the Peace Preservation Ordinance, which remained in force to 1922, banned women from political parties and meetings. Women under the Civil Code of 1898 had no independent legal status and all legal agreements were concluded on a woman's behalf by the male to whom she was subordinate— either father, husband, or son. Women had no free choice of spouse or domicile and while they could in theory protest against this situation, they could do so only in a non-political manner. Such action posed a challenge to the whole social orthodoxy on which the Japanese state was founded, so in practice few women protested.

One Western institution whose adoption would have made a very favourable impression on the West, but which made next to no headway in Japan, was Christianity. Like the women's movement it had some impact among Japanese intellectuals, but prejudices against it ran too deep. In 1889 less than a quarter of one per cent of Japanese were Christians.

The only religion that did flourish was Shinto which was one of the traditional faiths of Japan. Revived interest in it had been a key element in the intellectual trends that led to the imperial restoration. But there was little deep interest in religion among Japan's new leaders. Though the government continued to control and support the main Shinto shrines, the many cults that made up the faith lapsed into a traditional passive state forming no more than a ceremonial background to the life of the Japanese people.

There was great enthusiasm for Westernisation over the matter of constitutional reform, and this dated back to the early 1870s when Meiji rulers realised change here was necessary to gain international respect. In the next decade the major tasks for building a modern political constitution were undertaken. In 1882 the statesman Ito Hirobumi led a study mission to several European capitals to investigate the theories and practices he believed were most appropriate for Japan. Before his departure he decided not to slavishly reproduce any Western system but that whatever example was taken as a model would be adapted to Japan's special needs. Most of his time was spent in Berlin and Vienna, and after his return to Japan work on the new constitution began in the spring of 1884. A new peerage was created, in December 1885 a cabinet type government was introduced, and to support it, a modern civil service with entry by examination was established. The Meiji constitution which took effect from November 1890 was essentially a cautious, conservative document which served to reinforce the influence of the more traditionally-minded elements in Japan's ruling class. While distinctively Japanese, it compared most closely with the German model of the monarchy.

This constitution, though nominally democratic, retained power in the hands of a small ruling élite with minimal interference from or responsibility to, the majority of the population. There was to be a bicameral parliament, called, in English, the Diet. The House of Peers was mostly made up from the ranks of the new nobility and the lower house chosen by an electorate limited to adult males paying taxes of fifteen yen or more. In 1890 this was limited to 450,000 persons or 5 per cent of adult males. Even when the taxation qualification was reduced to ten yen in 1902 it only increased the electorate to 1,700,000 males. The constitution's architects hoped that the provisions for democratic government it contained would be counterbalanced by other safeguarding provisions. Most important of these was the position of the emperor, who was accorded a position of primacy in the state. The imperial family were said to rule over Japan in perpetuity, and under the constitution the emperor was the repository of absolute and inviolable sovereignty. This was underlined by making cabinet and armed forces responsible not to political party, nor to the Diet, or the Japanese people, but to the emperor alone.

The emperor as an individual had little personal influence on events, and was not strong enough to unify the various factions that vied for political power. This was only possible by reference to pre-existing traditions of Japanese culture. These were invoked to stress the duties of loyalty and obedience to the sovereign, and through him to the state. As early as October 1890 the Imperial Rescript on Education, often seen as the basic tool for inculcating the orthodox philosophy of the state, showed the strong influence of the Confucian view that the state was essentially a moral order. This edict made only passing reference to education itself, but showed the revived influence of Confucian ideology in its stress on harmony and loyalty to the throne. Its central concept of mass indoctrination through formal education was an entirely modern emphasis. Intensive drilling of Japanese children with lessons in patriotism became possible when funds were available for universal compulsory education. In 1885 only 46 per cent of children of statutory school age were in school, though by 1905 this had risen to 95 per cent.

The purpose of educational reform, at its most basic level, was to turn out efficient recruits for the army, factory, and farm. This was because political and military modernisation, as well as industrialisation, depended on new skills, new attitudes and broader knowledge. Japan's leaders realised from the 1870s that social and intellectual modernisation was a prerequisite to success in other fields. But in the social and intellectual areas, as in economics, the responsiveness of thousands of individuals was more important than the exhortations of authority.

While political and social reform and cultural change were limited in extent and selective in their nature by the end of the 1890s, the same picture emerges in economic life. Industrial modernisation took two forms—the reorganisation of traditional industries, and the transplantation of new industries from the West. Some traditional industries, like cotton-spinning, experienced radical change and the introduction of factory production, while others made slower progress. Japan was an important exporter of raw silk but that industry was not dependent upon elaborate or expensive machinery. The production of cocoons was a labour-intensive industry, already carried out as a by-employment in peasant households. Gradually small factories equipped with improved but relatively simple and inexpensive power-driven machines were introduced. The investment in this industry was thus spread thinly over a great number of producers. Where large investments of capital were absolutely necessary, as with Japan's strategic heavy industries like iron and steel, armaments, and ship-building, the initial investment was made by the government. But even here success was not immediate and these early concerns were sold off to Japanese businessmen at low prices in the 1880s. In some of the new industries success came sooner than in others. In 1897–1906, 90 per cent of railways rolling stock was built in Japan but 94 per cent of locomotives were still imported, mainly from England and Germany. It was not until after 1900 that the basis of heavy industry in Japan was firmly established.

Indeed, the whole of Japanese economic and social life in 1900 was still firmly rooted in traditional forms with quite a small modern superstructure. But for Japan the term 'traditional' needs qualification because it does not necessarily mean that pre-modern Japanese economy and society was antagonistic to change. In spite of Japan's decision to isolate itself for almost 300 years, features evolved that could be built upon once the country was forced to accept Western influence. The growing volume of research on the period before 1868, in the form of local and regional studies, has reinforced the view that Japan was a relatively advanced pre-industrial economy. For an underdeveloped country it was already well provided with a basic infrastructure by the time the process of modernisation began in earnest. Agricultural output per head of the population was quite high and premodern Japan possessed a substantial degree of commerce. In the more backward northern regions, on the island of Hokkaido, and also parts of the extreme southern island of Kyushu, medieval forms of social and economic organisation persisted until quite late. But on the more advanced regions of the main island of Hunshu, especially the Kanto Plain around Edo—the old name for Tokyo—and Osaka, there was a thriving urban-centred commercial economy. Merchants and traders supplied the wants of the towns of the region and production for exchange, and not just subsistence, was carried on in the countryside.

Much of Japan's growth after 1868 was built upon the foundations of its pre-modern economy. Partly under the protection and encouragement of government most of the capital-intensive investments went into railways, steamships, and mechanised heavy industrial plants. But just as important in promoting development at that time were a vast number of small improvements and minor capital undertakings. Before 1940 the majority of roads were of unsurfaced dirt and bridges were simple wooden structures. Agricultural construction, represented primarily by irrigation works, changed little from Tokugawa times. Only after the turn of the century did most Japanese make Western products a part of their daily lives, and they were adapted to a traditionally Japanese life-style. In Tokyo in 1910 most of the dwellings were made of wood and only about an eighth used brick, stone, or plaster. Within the houses most furniture was still the traditional kind and most of the food eaten was of a traditional type. This meant that there was still an enormous market to be supplied by peasant farmers, village entrepreneurs, small businesses and traditional craftsmen. In 1890 nearly 70 per cent of Japanese investment was in the traditional sector and it still accounted for 45 per cent, fifteen years later.

But the success of Japan's modernisation efforts needs to be judged not only by what happened within the economy itself, or by the changes within Japanese society. Reform was undertaken as a means to an end and that end was recognition as an equal by the West. This was necessary before there was any chance of removing the unequal treaties of the 1850s and 1860s and contained two major restrictions on Japanese sovereignty. Firstly, there was the provision of 'extra-territorial jurisdiction'. Under this Westerners accused of crimes were not tried by Japanese courts, but by consular courts within the foreign settlements of the seaports of Japan set out in the treaties. The other restriction was the loss of tariff autonomy. Eager for markets, the Western powers placed severe limits on Japanese import and export duties. These measures were the usual way for nineteenth-century Western powers to regulate diplomatic and commercial relations with Oriental countries, the model being the treaties imposed on China after the Opium War of the 1840s. For Japan the actual consequences of the treaties were not particularly damaging. No great market for opium was developed, and the opening of Japanese industry to competition from the West forced the pace of economic change instead of allowing inefficient industries to shelter behind protective tariffs. Foreigners resident in Japan were restricted to the treaty ports and needed official permits to travel outside so were never a great intrusion into Japanese life. And the justice dispensed in the consular courts was generally fair to both Japanese and Westerners.

Nevertheless, the fact of these treaties' existence was rightly regarded as a great humiliation as they usurped functions which are the proper preserve of a fully independent state. They came up for renewal periodically and from 1871 onwards Japan asked for their revision. In that year refusal was a foregone conclusion, as even the Japanese could see that the conditions originally necessitating extra-territorial jurisdiction had not undergone any change justifying its abolition. In later years Western nations were reluctant to allow their citizens to come under the power of a legal system that was still not fully reformed, despite the abolition of torture as an accepted legal practice in 1876 and the introduction of a Code of Criminal Procedure, framed in accordance with Western ideas, in 1882. But this was the start of what the West wanted and when negotiations were reopened in 1883, Japan included as compensation for the abolition of consular jurisdiction a promise to remove all restrictions on trade, travel, and residence for foreigners within the country. These and subsequent discussions in the 1880s reached no definite conclusion, mainly because the Japanese refused to grant foreigners living in the country the right to own freehold property. It was not until 1894 that a final settlement of the consular question became a real possibility when Britain agreed to abolish consular jurisdiction by 1899.

The five year delay was for two reasons. Before the new treaty came into force Japan had to fully implement a new legal code. The thorough recodification of the law this required was a slow and difficult task as most legal reforms were introduced piecemeal. This area is probably the strongest example of direct Western pressure being applied to change a fundamental feature of Japanese life. Drafts drawn up, largely under French influence, were submitted in 1881 and again in 1888, but a completely revised legal code only went into effect in 1896, removing the final impediment to ending extra-territorial jurisdiction in 1899. The other cause for delay was to allow Japan to renegotiate the rest of its treaties—of which there were over fifteen—with other Western powers, so that all nations were on an equal footing. This aspect was undoubtedly made possible by the successful outcome with Britain. Tariff autonomy was not finally restored to Japan until twelve years after 1899, but up to 1911 she was allowed to increase import and export duties.

The successful negotiations in 1894 were important as a turning point for the Japanese and for the West. The greatest opponents of the loss of extra-territorial jurisdiction were the few hundred foreign merchants and businessmen who lived and worked in the treaty ports. But for Japan this was a national political question that had provoked fierce debates in the Diet and in the press. The first treaties between Japan and the West were signed when the nation was still in a state of torpor from its long slumber of seclusion, and under circumstances of duress. The redemption of her judicial and fiscal authority had been, for thirty years, the dream of Japanese national aspiration, and both domestic and foreign policies had been shaped with this one end in view. For Japan's rulers, innovation after innovation, often involving sacrifices of traditional sentiments, were introduced for the purpose of assimilating the country and its institutions to the standard of Western civilisation. By 1900 Japan was still not regarded as a full equal by Western nations, but she was now accorded greater respect. In the next decade this was built upon with the Anglo-Japanese Alliance in 1902, the defeat of Russia in 1905, and the annexation of Korea in 1910. By 1912 there was no doubt that Japan had achieved 'Great Power' status.

FOR FURTHER READING

H. J. Jones, *Live Machines,* (Vancouver, 1980); J. P. Lehnann, *The Roots of Modern Japan,* (Macmillan, 1982); H. Wray and H. Conroy, eds., *Perspectives on Modern Japanese History,* (Honolulu, 1983); J. Hunter, *The Emergence of Modern Japan,* (Longman, 1989); O. Checkland, *Britain's Encounter With Meiji Japan, 1868–1912,* (Macmillan, 1989); E. O. Reischauer and A. M. Craig, *Japan: Tradition and Transformation,* (Allen & Unwin, 1989).

Home at Last

Finally, the murdered Romanovs will be laid to rest. Their deaths were the real beginning of the 20th century. Their controversial burial marks its close.

By Bill Powell and Owen Matthews

THE ROMANOVS WILL COME HOME this week, their five three-and-a-half-foot wooden coffins borne through St. Petersburg to their final resting place in a dignified, if not quite grand, procession. For six years the remains of the last tsar, Nicholas II, head of one of Europe's most storied families, were kept in a setting that hardly evoked imperial grandeur: since being exhumed in 1991, his bones, along with those of his wife, Alexandra, three of their daughters and four servants, sat most of the time in polyethylene bags on a store-room shelf in an old criminal morgue in Yekaterinburg. There lay the House of Romanov, the family that presided over imperial Russia for more than three centuries.

Vladimir Ilyich Lenin personally ordered the assassination, in 1918, of the tsar and his family. (The assassins also murdered the cook, maid, valet and family physician.) The authorities of the Soviet Union had wanted Nicholas II, Alexandra and their family out of sight and out of mind. But in that, as in so much else, they failed. Thanks in part to Russian monarchists in exile, but mainly to the mythmaking power of Hollywood, the Romanov legend (if not the reality of their grim demise) endured, both at home and abroad.

In 1991 President Boris Yeltsin invited Vladimir Kirillovich Romanov, father of Maria Romanov, the current pretender to the throne, to St. Petersburg. He was greeted by a crowd of 60,000. At the time, in the flush of the latest Russian revolution, a poll showed 18 percent of the population supported a restoration of the monarchy. Six years later the few Romanovs interested in restoration had failed to capitalize on the sentiment, and the Yeltsin government filled the vacuum. Reassured by the new polling, Yeltsin last year began serious preparations to give the country's last imperial rulers a decent burial. After four years of deliberation, a government commission concluded that the remains discovered near Yekaterinburg in the late 1970s were those of the Romanovs. Yeltsin appointed his deputy prime minister, Boris Nemtsov, to make the appropriate arrangements. And this week, 80 years to the day after their brutal murder in Ipatyev House (demolished in 1977 by an up-and-coming communist politician named Boris Yeltsin), Russia was to engage in a simple and honorable act of national healing. Five Romanovs were to be laid to rest in the Peter and Paul Cathedral next to Peter and Catherine the Great.

The ceremony will go on as scheduled, but not, as the government had hoped, in a spirit of reconciliation or healing. This is Russia, after all, and in Russia—imperial, communist or even new—nothing ever comes easily, not least an attempt to come to terms with a turbulent, haunted history. Aleksi II, the politically powerful patriarch of the Russian Orthodox Church, the institution most closely allied with the legacy of the Russian imperials, decided last month not to preside at the interment.

The church said it's still not sure the remains are authentic. That virtually no one else has similar doubts evidently doesn't matter.

Boris Yeltsin, with an eye toward his own historical legacy, had wanted to attend the Romanov burial. But once the church balked, Yeltsin decided he couldn't take the political risk of defy-

---

*A*ND THE REST IS HISTORY: *In an epochal act of murder, Tsar Nicholas II and his wife, Alexandra, were killed with their daughters, Maria, Tatiana, Olga and Anastasia and their son, Alexis. Five of the family skulls have been recovered: those of Maria and Alexis apparently were burned to ash.*

---

ing it. And though nearly 50 Romanov descendants will be there, at least three outspoken members of the family will not, saying that the relative modesty of the planned ceremony is beneath their

26. Home at Last

Family Ties: From Autocracy to Democracy

The execution of Nicholas II, his wife, Tsarina Alexandra, and their five children ended 300 years of uninterrupted Romanov rule. It did not, however, prevent descendants from laying claim to the throne. A look at the Romanovs before and after the last tsar.

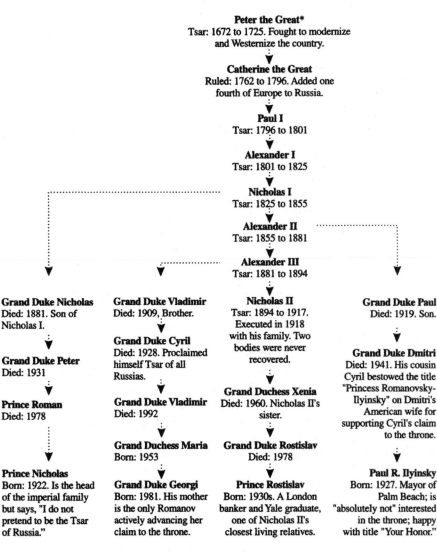

Peter the Great*
Tsar: 1672 to 1725. Fought to modernize and Westernize the country.

Catherine the Great
Ruled: 1762 to 1796. Added one fourth of Europe to Russia.

Paul I
Tsar: 1796 to 1801

Alexander I
Tsar: 1801 to 1825

Nicholas I
Tsar: 1825 to 1855

Alexander II
Tsar: 1855 to 1881

Alexander III
Tsar: 1881 to 1894

Grand Duke Nicholas
Died: 1881. Son of Nicholas I.

Grand Duke Peter
Died: 1931

Prince Roman
Died: 1978

Prince Nicholas
Born: 1922. Is the head of the imperial family but says, "I do not pretend to be the Tsar of Russia."

Grand Duke Vladimir
Died: 1909, Brother.

Grand Duke Cyril
Died: 1928. Proclaimed himself Tsar of all Russias.

Grand Duke Vladimir
Died: 1992

Grand Duchess Maria
Born: 1953

Grand Duke Georgi
Born: 1981. His mother is the only Romanov actively advancing her claim to the throne.

Nicholas II
Tsar: 1894 to 1917. Executed in 1918 with his family. Two bodies were never recovered.

Grand Duchess Xenia
Died: 1960. Nicholas II's sister.

Grand Duke Rostislav
Died: 1978

Prince Rostislav
Born: 1930s. A London banker and Yale graduate, one of Nicholas II's closest living relatives.

Grand Duke Paul
Died: 1919. Son.

Grand Duke Dmitri
Died: 1941. His cousin Cyril bestowed the title "Princess Romanovsky-Ilyinsky" on Dmitri's American wife for supporting Cyril's claim to the throne.

Paul R. Ilyinsky
Born: 1927. Mayor of Palm Beach; is "absolutely not" interested in the throne; happy with title "Your Honor."

*THOSE WHO RULED BETWEEN PETER AND CATHERINE NOT SHOWN.
RESEARCH BY ANNA KUCHMENT, GRAPHIC BY KARL GUDE—NEWSWEEK

care less about the disposition of Nicholas and Alexandra's bones. But for the political and religious establishments in Moscow, the burial was destined to be excruciatingly complicated. The abdication and subsequent assassination of Nicholas, and the revolution to which he was sacrificed, are among the 20th century's seminal events. From them flow the heinous Terror in Russia, the second world war and the cold war. Touch the Romanov bones and you touch a part of a century's central nervous system. A powerful reaction was inevitable.

The fall of the Romanovs is a study in brutality. Robert K. Massie, author of "Nicholas and Alexandra," reports that they were awakened after midnight and were sent from their bedrooms to the basement of Ipatyev House. Nicholas carried his 13-year-old-son, Alexis, who was crippled by hemophilia. Alexandra was next, followed by her daughters, Olga, 22, Tatiana, 21, Maria, 19, and Anastasia, 17. In the rear came the family physician, the cook, the maid and the valet. Two chairs were brought, and the mother and the boy sat down. The others, told that they were to be photographed, arranged themselves in two lines behind the chairs.

Suddenly, 11 men burst into the room. Each held a revolver; each had been assigned a specific victim. After the first round of bullets, the three younger sisters and the maid remained alive—thanks in part to corsets of hidden jewels that deflected the gunfire. The sisters, pressing against the walls, died in a second round. One of the executioners stepped up to the writhing boy lying on the floor and kicked him in the head. The chief executioner put the muzzle of his revolver directly into the boy's ear and fired two shots.

Only the maid was still alive. Rather than reload, the executioners took rifles from the next room and pursued her with bayonets. Running back and forth along the wall, screaming, she tried to fend off the bayonets with her hands. She fell, and her body was pierced more than 30 times. Rifle butts crushed the victims' faces to render them unrecognizable. The bleeding bodies were wrapped in bedsheets, loaded into a truck and taken into the forest. There they were

erstwhile imperial dignity. (According to 75-year-old family head Nicholas, only one Romanov—Maria Vladimirovna, granddaughter of Nicholas II's first cousin—makes any claim to the throne.)

A funeral that was to have been a step toward political maturity for a Russia emerging from 70 years of darkness has instead turned into the latest chapter of the ongoing Romanov tragedy. "The

country had a chance to obliterate a large historical blemish—the massacre of this family that they concealed and lied about for years," says Harvard University historian Richard Pipes. "Instead, it's an opportunity missed."

It may have been naive to think it could have been otherwise. Most ordinary Russians, struggling to make ends meet as their nation's transition to capitalism now flags dangerously, couldn't stripped and thrown down a mine shaft. Lenin, sitting in the Kremlin, was informed that it was over.

The nine skeletons, burned with acid and gasoline, were discovered in 1979 in a wooded, swampy spot 12 miles northwest of Yekaterinburg. Confident they had found the burial spot of the imperial family, geologist Aleksandr Avdonin and Gely Ryabov, a famous Moscow filmmaker, were nonetheless petrified as they dug. As Massie writes in "The Romanovs, The Final Chapter," Avdonin said later, "All my life I had searched for this . . . and then, as we started to lift up the planking, I thought to myself, 'let me find nothing!' "

Fearful of the repercussions of their discovery, the two a year later returned the remains they'd unearthed to the same site. Then they vowed not to utter a word about their discovery until, Avdonin would later tell Massie, "the circumstances in our country changed." The bones of the tsar and his family remained buried in the woods for an additional 13 years, until, in 1991, they were officially exhumed from their shallow grave.

For the next six years, the remains were subjected to hundreds of forensic tests. Scientists compared the DNA with samples taken from Nicholas II's brother Georgy, who died in 1891 and is buried in the Peter and Paul Fortress. Prince Philip, Duke of Edinburgh and Alexandra's grandnephew, gave blood samples to be tested against the DNA of the skeleton thought to be Alexandra's. In both cases, laboratories in Russia, the United States and Britain confirmed the genetic match. The investigators also electronically superimposed the photographs of the skulls on archive photographs of the family. They compared the skeletons' measurements with clothing known to have belonged to the tsar and his daughters. They matched the platinum dental bridgework on one skull's jaw to the empress's dental records.

Again, every test came up with exact correlations.

Only two slight mysteries remained. Two of the family's children's bodies were missing: Alexis and the second youngest daughter, Maria. Investigators concluded that they had been burned to ash by the executioners, who did not have time to destroy the rest of their victims. That notion matched the historical testimony of the chief executioner, Yakov Yurovsky, unearthed from a long-secret Moscow archive during *glasnost* in 1989.

The missing bodies have helped spawn a whole industry of Romanov rumor and myth. A variety of crackpots have turned up all over the world claiming either to be Romanovs who escaped execution or their direct descendants. In Moscow today Nikolai Dalsky parades around in an admiral's uniform convinced he's a direct descendant of Alexis, the tsarevich. Another man, Oleg Filatov, says he's also a direct descendant of the poor tsarevich—the hemophiliac who Filatov somehow believes survived several gunshot wounds.

The most powerful of the Romanov myths is, of course, Anastasia's. In 1920 a woman named Anna Anderson turned up in a Berlin hospital, claiming to be the heiress to the Romanova throne. In 1956 Hollywood got into the act with an Ingrid Bergman film. And today an animated version of "Anastasia" is attracting millions of young, impressionable viewers all over the world with an egregiously sweet story: that somehow the beautiful young princess survived to find romance and happiness. How many parents tell their children the truth? That Anastasia, after having been shot several times in the wee hours of July 17, 1918, quivered as she lay in her own blood in the dark basement. And that at some point, one of the 11 gunmen took his bayonet and stabbed that last bit of life out of her. As British historian Orlando Figes writes succinctly in his masterful

book on the revolution, "it is inconceivable that any of the Romanovs survived this ordeal."

IT IS, IN FACT, THE SAVAGERY OF THE "ordeal" that is its most important historical legacy. It presaged the Terror that was to come in Russia, the moment when, as historian Pipes has written, a government assigned itself "the power to kill its citizens not for what they had done but because their death 'was needed.' " That is a moment surely worth recognizing—and laying to rest—however belatedly. But as Yeltsin's government learned, in a country just seven years removed from Soviet communism, it is also obviously easier said than done—at least in so public a manner. One of the ironies about the controversy over the imperial interment is that Russia has actually made quiet progress in coming to terms with the revolutionary period. The more bitter irony is that it is the Russian Orthodox Church, to which the late tsar was so devoted, that has effectively tarnished what could have been a historic ceremony. The church remains a powerful but opaque institution in Russia, and its decision last month to undermine Yeltsin has triggered a fevered, but relatively uninformed, speculation that evokes Soviet-era Kremlinology.

The intrigue, circa 1998, cannot help but evoke, to some Russians, another era: "It's just like 1916," says Edvard Radzinsky, who wrote the first biography of Nicholas II using the primary materials first made available during glasnost. "A weak government, an invisible head of state, key issues blotted out by amazing, Byzantine intrigues . . . and a hypocritical church looking after its own interests instead of taking an opportunity to unite society." Amid it all, the Romanov cortege will trundle through St. Petersburg this week, finally laying the last tsar and his family to rest. At home at least, if not yet in peace.

The Maginot Line

It is known as a great military blunder, but in fact this stout network of ingenious bunkers did what it was designed to do

By Rudolph Chelminski

Rudolph Chelminski has been living and working in France for more than 30 years. He has written most recently for Smithsonian *about fine French cheeses.*

The Ossuary of Douaumont, situated on a wooden bluff overlooking the city of Verdun in northeastern France, is a huge, cruciform vault: 150 yards of white limestone surmounted by a 150-foot tower resembling an artillery shell. The monument honors the 700,000 French and German soldiers who were killed in the scarcely believable carnage of the 1916 Battle of Verdun, the pivotal engagement of World War I. The interior is an echoing, cave-like cloister punctuated by 18 alcoves standing over as many burial chambers. It is only when the visitor quits the oppressive cavern and emerges into daylight that he notices the little windows running along the outside walls. Something grayish-white catches the eye, and it requires a few seconds to realize that it is human bones: endless stacks of anonymous human bones, 500 cubic feet of them under each alcove, the remains of 130,000 unidentified men collected after the 1918 armistice. More eloquently than any speech, position paper or strategic concept, the Douaumont Ossuary explains why the French built the Maginot Line.

A network of fortifications conceived as an obstacle to any future German invasion, the Maginot Line is notorious as a universal metaphor for bungling. But in fact it was not quite the abject blunder it has been made out to be. In many ways, it was a model of ingenious en-

gineering and technological accomplishment. It was designed to do certain things and in those succeeded admirably. Its shortcomings derived not from failures of execution but from the inability of its proponents to anticipate how much warfare would change in a mere two decades.

Certainly no one could blame the French for trying. *La Der' des Der'* (The Last of the Last) they called World War I, when the nightmare finally ended. France was bled white, its finances a shambles, its northern provinces devastated. From the president of the republic to the lowliest peasant, the same appalled determination gripped the French as the nation headed into the 1920s: *plus jamais ça*. Never again. Less than two years after the armistice, a Superior Council of War directed by French president Alexander Millerand was already considering the best design for a fortified wall. Germany had invaded twice in the previous 50 years. Now, Millerand and his experts saw it coming again.

They were right, but there was something of the self-fulfilling prophecy in their mind-set. French foreign policy and the draconian strictures of the Treaty of Versailles, which Germany was obliged to sign, must share some of the blame for the rise to power of a revanchist firebrand named Adolf Hitler. It is an indication of the state of European relations in those pre-Common Market days that France's Teutonic neighbor was known as the "beast that sleeps on the other side of the Rhine."

It was not until January 1930 that appropriations for the anti-German frontier

fortress came to a vote in the Chamber of Deputies. The minister of war, a veteran who had been seriously wounded in 1914, was the session's main speaker. His name was André Maginot. "Whatever form a new war may take," he warned, "whatever part is taken in it by aviation, by gas, by the different destructive processes of modern warfare, there is one imperious necessity, and that is to prevent the violation of our territory by enemy armies. We all know the cost of invasion, with its sad procession of material ruin and moral desolation."

It was settled then: France would protect future generations behind a wall of high technology. The deputies gave Maginot a huge budget for a five-year building program. Inevitably, there were cost overruns and revisions, and it was necessary to extend the ambitious project year by year. Final touches on the Maginot Line, the so-called Great Wall of France, were still being completed in 1939 when war was declared.

Predictably, the Line turned out to be a bigger bite to chew than most of the enthusiastic legislators had anticipated. There were 471 miles to cover opposite Germany, Luxembourg and Belgium to the North Sea—not even counting the border with Switzerland or, worse, Italy, where Benito Mussolini was making bellicose noises. Army engineers faced a daunting challenge.

The plan was to defend five great swaths of territory: the Italian frontier, from the Mediterranean to Switzerland; the border along Switzerland itself; the Franco-German separation along the

Rhine, from Basel to Wissembourg, a small city at France's northeastern point north of Strasbourg; from there westward to the Ardennes Forest; and thence along Belgium's southern frontier westward to the English Channel.

Some sections were relatively simple. The border with Italy, already fortified in the 19th century, was extremely mountainous. The old forts would be updated, and modern, reinforced-concrete ones would be added. The border with Switzerland was considered safe, the country being a little porcupine of a fortress all by itself.

The long section along the Rhine looked secure to the Maginot planners because the river itself was a wonderful barrier, needing only to be reinforced with mines, barbed wire, riverbank machine-gun bunkers, infantry and, a few kilometers back, a series of small, cheap "generic" forts and bunkers, each manned by no more than 20 to 30 soldiers. French military experts calculated that their steel-domed, concrete machine-gun bunkers would withstand any light weapons, while cannon heavy enough to subdue them would breach dikes in the area and create a flood that would only make matters even tougher for the invader.

Above and west of the Rhine, two crucial areas where French soil met German soil received the most exquisite attention and the lion's share of funds: the Lauter River valley near Wissembourg and the region around the industrial city of Metz. This, in other words, was Alsace and Lorraine, that ancient Franco-German bone of contention. In these two *régions fortifiées,* French engineers poured a debauch of energy and inventiveness into some 50 *ouvrages,* or large fortifications. In the gaps between they strewed a seemingly impenetrable swarm of smaller blockhouses.

Each ouvrage lay within cannon reach of another one, allowing commanders to call on a neighbor to lay a barrage of antipersonnel fire directly on top of their fortifications if enemy troops appeared, an operation known as "delousing." The same cannon could, of course, free the smaller blockhouses of their "lice" with friendly fire. Every eventuality seemed to be covered.

The ouvrages were of an entirely new type, as revolutionary, and as hyped in the press, as such later French technical innovations as the air-suspended Citroën automobile and the Concorde supersonic plane. Buried 100 feet and more under hills and ridges, they all followed a similar design based around a long central tunnel of stone and reinforced concrete with a "life zone" at one end and fighting zone at the other, reached by secondary tunnels, stairways and elevators. The largest of the ouvrages, manned by 1,000 or more soldiers, had five miles or so of tunnels through which men, equipment and munitions were transported by trolley—dubbed the *métro*—a photogenic novelty that repeatedly adorned the front pages of prewar newspapers.

Powered entirely by electricity and equipped with everything from winestorage areas by the kitchen to a dentist's chair, jail cell and morgue, each ouvrage was a self-sufficient unit, a little underground city with its own wells, food supply and power generator, capable of up to three months of total autonomy, like a submarine underwater. The World War I obsession with gas attacks was parried by a ventilation-filtration system that created a slight overpressure within the fortifications, and as in naval warfare, the cannon crews fired blind, guided by ground-level observers telephoning to subterranean fire-control command posts.

The typical ouvrage took the shape of a gigantic tree sprawling underground. The command and living areas were the roots, from which a long trunk tunnel led to branch tunnels, which led to individual bunkers armed with cannon, mortar and machine guns—up to 17 of them in the biggest fortifications. The cannon (mostly paired sets of the venerable, but still deadly accurate, French 75s) were housed in steel "pop-up turrets" set inside circular shafts of reinforced concrete. With nothing but the easy arc of a rounded steel dome protruding aboveground, the weapon was practically invulnerable when retracted. When the orders to fire were given, the dome rose about two feet to expose the twin barrels within the rotating shaft.

Inside each cannon turret, a diorama of the surrounding countryside was drawn (and often prettified and colored by bored gunners) along the circular wall, allowing artillery crews to visualize the targets corresponding to the numbered coordinates sent up to them by fire control. And naturally, the French—being a mathematically inclined people—had previously calculated every square yard within each cannon's range and assigned its coordinate.

The ouvrage of Simserhof at Bitche, a pretty little city near the western edge of the Lauter fortified region, is nicely representative of the clever defensive ideas poured with such prodigality into the Line. One of the half-dozen Maginot ouvrages that have been tidied up and opened to the public, Simserhof's gloomy netherworld is so replete with tricks that visitors are tempted to conclude that French military engineers must have actually had fun imagining the perfect modern fortress: take that — and that!

The main entrance is reached via a retractable steel drawbridge over an antitank ditch, after which a seven-ton steel door set into the hillside gives onto nearly three miles of concrete passageways, lying at an average depth of 118 feet under Alsatian sandstone. During combat, 812 men worked three eight-hour shifts, "hot-bedding" it like submarine crews. The main entrance, a theoretical weak point despite the tank ditch and the seven-ton door, was protected by a 47-millimeter antitank gun, but in case the defenders preferred shooting men rather than panzers, they could retract the 47 by means of an overhead rail and, presto! slot a heavy machine gun into its place. Many of the Line's machine guns were mounted on cams that raised or lowered the barrels as the guns swept the terrain around them, maintaining their hail of bullets at about a foot above the ground.

Might some of the Germans infiltrate through the machine-gun fire and approach the outside walls, crawling where no one could see them? No problem: a little hand-operated launcher rather like a mail chute would deliver grenades out to the other side, *ploop-bang.*

Might the enemy somehow get past the door into the passageway? Then they would be mowed down by machine guns in a bunker—a bunker within a fortress!—set into the wall a few meters farther back.

Might they pass the bunker? If worst came to worst, the passageway was mined so the push of a button could collapse the tunnel with a single explosion.

Might they still come on, in spite of it all? Well, the men could evacuate through the secret emergency exit, a special little tunnel leading to a vertical escape shaft.

It is a jewel of ingenuity, this emergency exit, the perfect symbol for the cunning attention to detail that went into the conception of the Maginot Line. Every ouvrage had such an exit, as much as 130 feet of ladder straight up through the protective earth, ending in a well-disguised manhole at ground level. But what if the German discovered the manhole early on? They could attack down through it, couldn't they? The planners had taken that into account: if attackers lifted the cover, they would find nothing but gravel.

The trick was simple. The evacuation shaft was twice as deep as necessary, with the top half being entirely filled with gravel stoppered by a steel gate. The little exit tunnel from the ouvrage debouched at exactly that midpoint. The officer in charge activated a lever, the steel gate opened, the gravel clattered down into the bottom half of the shaft, and the men climbed out.

Two thousand laborers worked around the clock from 1929 to 1933 just to dig Simserhof. After that, endless brigades of specialists moved in to equip it.

The problem was that neither time nor budget permitted the French to protect their entire frontier with such formidable defenses. There were gaps, big ones, and the Germans knew it. For all intents and purposes, the Maginot Line ended just east of the city of Sedan, directly under the great forest of the Belgian Ardennes, a natural barrier that the French general staff calmly asserted to be as secure as the Rhine. "With special modifications, the Ardennes Forest is impenetrable," said Marshal Pétain in 1934 as he and other top French brass

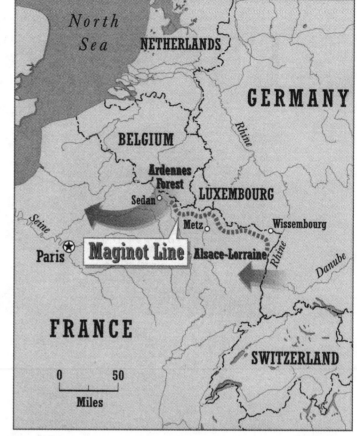

Harold Smelcer

Arrows show how the Germans went around the Maginot Line, through the Ardennes Forest and across the Rhine. The Line itself stood firm.

were overseeing the Line's construction. "Therefore, this sector is not dangerous."

Beyond the Ardennes and along the Belgian border to the English Channel, there was no serious effort at fortification. After all, the French reasoned, their ally Belgium was itself a fine barrier to the Germans, a buffer state whose resistance would offer the French an eight-day delay for organizing their defenses. That reasoning was calculated on the walking speed of foot soldiers. But by then the Germans were motorized and mechanized.

As the crises that led up to the outbreak of war followed one upon another—Germany's reoccupation of the Rhineland and annexation of Austria (the *Anschluss*), the surrendering of the Sudetenland to Hitler under the Munich Pact appeasement policy, Germany's subsequent invasion of Poland—local infantry division commanders in the exposed border regions were allowed to fortify ad hoc, more or less as they pleased, where they pleased. This long

stretch soon became decorated with thousands of mismatched little artisanal pillboxes. "*Une misère*," wrote one commentator, "*une illusion*."

Pétain's glib assurances about the Ardennes returned to haunt him in May 1940 when the tanks of Gen. Heinz Guderian, the architect of the German Army's revolutionary *Blitzkrieg* (lightning war) tactics, punched an enormous hole in Belgian and French defenses and flooded down through the Ardennes to encircle the home armies and isolate the Maginot Line. Close behind Guderian's tanks, the Germans struck through the Ardennes with 44 divisions. They simply followed the normal civilian roads down through the forest. The Belgians had never carried out the program of modifications—barriers, traps, road destruction—that Pétain had so confidently anticipated. Facing the swift-moving invaders, some 40 French divisions were immobilized within the Maginot Line or as "interval" troops protecting it from without, while an-

Before World War II, the layouts of the Line's *ouvrages,* or large underground fortifications, were a military secret. Illustrators surmised that they were compact, like battleships (left), when in fact they were elongated and spread out (below). Barracks complete with a wine cellar, a chapel, a dentist's chair and a morgue could house a thousand men. Trolleys carried troops, arms and munitions to combat bunkers through tunnels often more than five miles long.

Bowring Cartographic

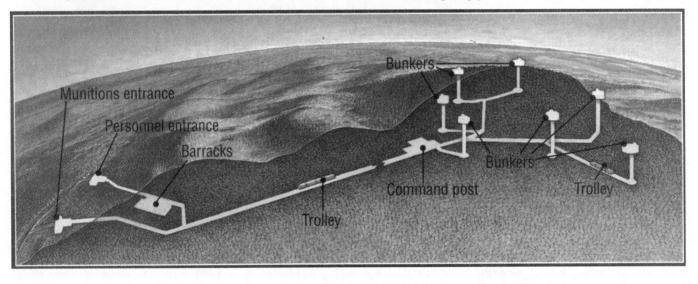

other 30 or so divisions were stretched out along the border from Montmédy, where the Line ended, to the Channel.

The Germans came with modern tanks, fighters, Stuka dive-bombers and fast-firing cannon, especially the dreaded high-velocity 88s, among the most devilishly effective weapons of World War II. The French had few antiaircraft guns, a scarcity of planes to protect their heads and only outdated tanks on the ground. Out in the open where armies clashed, it was a wipeout. Out-maneuvered, outgunned and outflanked, French field forces suffered a humiliating rout.

The myth of the natural barrier of the Rhine fell quickly. French planners, reasoning that their riverside pillboxes would be immune to attack because

heavy artillery would breach dikes in the area, had failed to take into account the flat-trajectory 88s. Small enough to pose no danger to the dikes, their shells nonetheless blasted bunkers to smithereens. The combination of the terrible 88s, Stuka dive-bombers and troops with hand-carried charges then subdued the small forts behind the river, sometimes within minutes.

German gunners developed a simple but deadly tactic for dealing with the exposed machine-gun and observation turrets of smaller fortifications. Repeatedly firing shells from their 88s at exactly the same spot, they burrowed holes, jackhammer-like, through the turrets' 12 full inches of solid steel. Eight shots were generally enough to do the trick, each

hit showing in a spectacular spray of sparks and "ringing the bell" by sending massive, head-splitting reverberations through the turrets.

The invaders had enjoyed an earlier measure of success by overpowering the small ouvrage of La Ferté, the Maginot Line's westernmost fortification, located just a few kilometers from Sedan. One lucky shot scored a direct hit into the observation slit of a turret, killing the three men inside. Under cover of an artillery barrage and smoke screen, infantrymen then shoved grenades, smoke bombs and explosive charges into the opening. Over the next 24 hours, those among La Ferté's 106-man crew who survived the initial assault asphyxiated in their spent gas masks. Smoke and

Troops from an American cavalry unit used a badly scarred Maginot fortification as a shield. Americans fired on such bunkers to see how they would hold up under heavy punishment. They were very impressed.

toxic fumes from the explosions above had filled the tunnels, but the men would not leave. The commander of the ouvrage had written earlier to his wife: "We know that our mission requires us to die on the spot."

The Germans made heavy propaganda from that victory, but La Ferté was not a true "battleship" of the Line. Built late, when time and funds were running out, it was only a glorified blockhouse, bereft of artillery. Indeed, during the early stages of the invasion, the Germans dealt with the Maginot Line mainly by avoiding it. Then, in mid-June, on the same day Wehrmacht troops entered Paris, they launched Operation Tiger, a direct offensive on the Line ordered by Hitler himself. They attacked in the area of the Sarre River, east of Metz, bringing to bear an incredible variety of weapons that included everything from 88s to an array of cannon that fired comfortably from beyond the range of the Line's short-barreled 75s. As Stukas swarmed unopposed overhead to add their 250-kilo bombs to the concert, the ouvrages underwent a hellish deluge of fire that impressively plowed the surrounding landscape and

occasionally killed lookouts when shells scored direct hits on observation turrets. But deep within their concrete carapaces, the crews went about their business as safely as the Line's early visionaries had predicted.

In other respects, too, the Maginot Line proved to be every bit as formidable as its builders had hoped. It has often been said that the Germans had an easy time taking the Line from behind because its cannon were "pointing the other way." In fact, the big guns in turrets were able to rotate 360 degrees, blasting away in every direction. "German officers told me they felt like rabbits trying to run from shotguns," said Roger Bruge, the author of several books on the Line and France's leading authority on the subject. Those 75s followed them from step to step, and if ever any vehicle was unlucky enough to get within range, it just got blasted.

It is an incontrovertible fact that the Maginot Line failed to foil a German invasion. Within the space of six weeks, France's military collapse was total. The most galling irony of all for Frenchman, though, was that the Maginot Line itself never was taken. The fierce German at-

tacks against it failed. The ouvrages held out: not a single artillery piece was neutralized. When the Line was handed over to the enemy, it was still intact.

With the signing of an armistice in June, the fighting was suspended (except for the subsequent resistance of the French underground) until the Allied invasion of Normandy four years later. Unwilling to believe it, still aching for a fight and still operational, the large ouvrages held out until July 1 when, on direct orders from the French commander in chief, the Maginot Line's forces marched out to be taken prisoner. Resisting further would have been useless vainglory. Now, goggle-eyed like rustics at a county fair, German troops could enter the legendary fortresses and wonder at all the tricks their clever enemy had prepared for them.

During the rest of the war, the Germans made occasional use of the Line for storage, training and field hospitals, and, briefly, against the Americans during the Ardennes offensives. The French Army repossessed it after the war, but modern warfare had rendered it useless. The soldiers padlocked the big steel doors and walked away with a moue of disgust.

A curious mixture of pride and embarrassment still pervades talk of the Maginot Line today in French military and government circles. No one quite knows what to do with it. It won't go away, and it is far too big and ponderously ubiquitous to get rid of. Then, too, there is an abiding fascination with it throughout the world. Today the Maginot Line is associated with France scarcely less indelibly than the Eiffel Tower.

An obvious thought springs to mind: Why not exploit that recognition for tourism? In the Alsatian city of Haguenau, 7½ miles from the German border, Claude Damm struggled with the government for years to get access to the dilapidated and unused ouvrage of Schoenenbourg, near the picture-postcard village of Hunspach. Damm is the president of the Association of Friends of the Maginot Line in Alsace.

"So you want to play soldier," grumbled the colonel in charge in Strasbourg, impervious to Damm's argument that, like it or not, the Line had become an important part of France's national heritage and as such ought to be opened to the public. In 1982 Damm finally wrested a key from the Ministry of Defense—there was something comical about undoing a padlock to enter the Maginot Line—and he and his friends and volunteers have been at work ever since, fixing elevators, replacing lights and generally making the ouvrage ready for tourists. Damm's association bred cousin groupings in several different localities throughout Alsace and Lorraine, and today at least six fortifications—Schoenenbourg, Simserhof, Four à Chaux, Hackenberg, Fermont, Marckolsheim—are open for visits under the authority of local townships, and staffed by volunteers.

The military establishment still largely acts as if the Line does not exist, and over the years the government has sold off many of the smaller forts and blockhouses or simply ceded bunkers to farmers whose fields were encumbered with cold concrete. The largest ouvrages are far too vast for civilian use, and although there have been desultory attempts at commercialization—a disco here, a mushroom farm there—such enterprises have usually lasted no more than a few months, as the inherent inadaptability of the military-specific design became apparent. There are said to be a few private houses built atop some of the 30-man blockhouses, which, if nothing else, assures the lords of these curious manors some of the best and most burglar-proof wine cellars anywhere in creation. And, yes, a number of today's happy owners of André Maginot's fortifications are German.

Women in the Third Reich

(Translated and excerpted from "Frauen im Dritten Reich," by Renate Wiggershaus in Auf, Austrian feminist quarterly, No. 33, 1982.)

As a result of the second wave of the women's movement, it is now generally accepted that women are in the best position not only to study the social situation of contemporary women, but also to explain women's roles in the more distant past. Indeed, the writing of history always contributes to the defense or criticism of the dominant order. In this way, historians' neglect has further enforced in the minds of their descendants the marginal existence of women in past centuries.

Girls who attended school after World War II certainly never heard of Lilo Herrmann in their history classes. Herrmann was a young woman and mother who, on June 20, 1938, was one of the first killed because of her brave and steadfast resistance to fascism. Nor did they hear of Hanne Martens, an actress and antifascist, whose skull was crushed by an SS man when she refused to be hanged naked. Nor of Martha Gillesen, who was shot in the head by SS officers, after she, with the rest of her resistance group, was tied up with barbed wire and given an injection in the tongue, so that she could not scream. Nor of Kaete Larsch, tortured to death, when she would not betray others in the resistance. Nor of the resistance fighter Johanna Kirschner, who was sentenced in half an hour and condemned to death in June of 1944.

We could list thousands of women's names: those who resisted and were sentenced and condemned in the so-called people's court; or who were gassed, shot, abused to death, experimented on or starved to death in concentration camps, or who died doing hard labor. Only the memories of the abuse and other horrors people endured and a thorough mourning for the terrible suffering of so many innocent people will protect later generations from similar experiences.

What did Nazi ideology have to say about women? Reading national socialist writings, what stands out most clearly is an unbelievable contempt for women. In 1921, just two years after women got the vote, the Nazi party voted unanimously in their first general meeting that "a woman can not be accepted to the party leadership!" In fact, a woman was never nominated by the NSDAP to serve in local or provincial parliaments, or in the Reichstag. Joseph Goebbels, the State Minister for People's Enlightenment and Propaganda, explained the political disenfranchisement of women in the following way during his speech at the opening of the exhibit "Woman" in Berlin:

The National Socialist movement is the only party that keeps women out of direct involvement in daily politics . . . We have not kept her out of parliamentary-democratic intrigues because of any disrespect toward women. It is not because we see in her and her mission something less worthy, but rather that we see in her and her mission something quite different from the vocation which men

have . . . Her first and foremost, and most appropriate place is in the family, and the most wonderful duty which she can take on is to give her country and her people children, children which carry on the success of the race and assure the immortality of the nation.

Another Nazi leader, party member number two and president of the Reich's Tourist Bureau Hermann Esser, instructed women in the following way: "Women belong at home in the kitchen and the bedroom, they belong at home and should be raising their children."

And Adolf Hitler, who was Fuehrer of the German nation for twelve years, announced:

What a man contributes in hero's courage on the battlefield, a woman contributes in her eternally patient sacrifice, in her eternally patient suffering. Every child that she brings into the world is a battle which she undergoes for the existence of her people.

So it is not surprising that women who had no children were seen as "duds in population politics." Families with fewer than four children had not fulfilled their "duty to the people's preservation rate," and woman who had many children received a "mother's cross."

These are the symptoms of the boundlessly controlling behavior of the Nazis toward women. Why wasn't National Socialism widely rejected by women? The German women's movement had been active for twenty years; by that time there was a tradition of collective struggle for women's rights. Since many women had lost fathers, sons, or brothers and were alone, they were forced to live very difficult, independent lives.

Of course, women were not a homogenous group that acted and thought alike. Taking a close look at the many different ways in which women acted during the Third Reich, I generally differentiate four groups. First, there were women who sooner or later resisted the Nazis and their terrible deeds. Many had to pay with their lives. They are, however, unknown—the heroines of history.

Then there were their adversaries: women who allowed themselves to be the tools of other people's torture and who for their part abused and beat people, and killed them in terrible ways. These women were most often dumb, young, arrogant and lured by the relatively good standard of living provided by the party. Since they often came from broken, authoritarian families, they often misused the power that they had over defenseless victims.

Between these two groups of women, there were the ignorant and those who just went along with things. Of course these groups were also heterogeneous. In each group there were women from every social class.

Among the ignorant women I count those who were totally apolitical (they usually remained apolitical after the war; they did not learn anything). These were the women who only thought about keeping their families alive; it didn't matter what happened to their neighbors. Even today, the "complete mastery of potatoes and their characteristics" is praised in German society "the art of gourmet potato dumplings" is admired, and pages are devoted to the potato, and thus the "triumph of survival" is celebrated. When concentration camps are mentioned, it's in a pithy aside: The Americans "posted horrible pictures of concentration camps on the walls." Even today, such ignorance sends chills up your spine.

The "fellow travellers" included the so-called leaders of Nazi women's organizations, such as the blond-haired woman, leader of the *Reichs*-women and eleven-time mother, Gertrud Scholtz-Klink, and also the women who voted for

Hitler and fit in one way or another. However, people's belief that women helped Hitler to power has no basis in fact.

In the presidential election of 1932, 51.6 percent of women voted for Hindenburg, 26.5 percent for Hitler. In the second vote, 56 percent were for Hindenburg and 33.6 percent for Hitler. In both votes the number of men's votes was about 2 percent greater than women's. Many voted conservatively, so that the misogynist Center Party got a large percentage of women's votes, but not the Nazis.

We should not forget that women had just been granted the active and passive vote, and thus were not practiced in political matters. They were not able to recognize their own interests and to represent them politically. Even for those who had started leaving the home hearth, there hadn't been enough time to overcome their dependent intellectual, social and economic status in the family or in their professions. In the first years of Nazi rule, they were driven back to their traditional domain, the family, and thus shut out of all social activities. Next the eradication of unemployment became women's burden, as many were fired from their posts and jobs. Married women who worked were denounced as "double earners."

Only a few women recognized that being shut out of the workplace and restricted to the home, with loans available only to those families where the mother didn't work, and the awarding of privileges to families with many children would serve only one purpose: the strengthening of "national manpower", in other words, the "production of human material." In 1932, there was an average of 59 births per 1,000 women, but by 1938 it was already 81 births. The slogan was: "Give the Fuehrer children."

The so-called "Fountain of Life" (Lebensborn), an organization founded in 1935 by the national leader of the SS, Heinrich Himmler, was concerned with this "strengthened propagation." There, "racially worthy" girls were at the service of SS men for the procreation of Aryan children; here antifeminism and racism were bound up in the most intricate way. The administrator of these

breeding institutions said, in all openness, that the goal was the production of human material: "Thanks to the 'Fountain of Life', we'll have 600 more regiments in thirty years."

There are reasons why so many women were blind to the dangers of the misogynist and racist ideology of the Nazis. For one thing, National Socialism was not so different from the attitude, opinion and posture of the conservatives, the German nationalists and the populists of the Weimar Republic, who were also often misogynist. For hundreds of years, the German people had been accustomed to state elitism and authoritarian behavior. This is also one of the reasons why there was no violent wave of protest from women collectively when the countless women's unions were dissolved, or forced to dissolve themselves, or when the decision that only 10% of students at the university could be female was announced, or when women were forbidden to take up influential positions, such as that of judge or administrator.

In western history, the struggle for women's equality and recognition is very young. At that moment when the women's movement could have developed on a broader level, it was destroyed. The refined strategy of strengthening and praising women in their traditionally dictated roles of caring housewife and mother had a very strong effect on the unenlightened. Never before had women been so directly addressed; never before had their reproductive function received so much recognition. Surely we should try to understand what drove the "fellow travellers" and the ignorant women to accept the degrading roles assigned to them by men.

What came out of the ignorance and willing sacrifice of these women is only a part of our history. The other part is often hidden from us.

Immediately after the war, numerous books were published by women who told how the war affected them, of their terrible suffering, but also of their bravery and the courage of antifascist women. The books quickly sold and only a few of them got a second printing. Yet these books relate the horrifying details, without which our knowledge of the very superficial. Nanda Herbermann, for example, describes in her book *The Blessed Abyss* (which has been out of print for years) what she experienced in an imprisonment that came about for no obvious reason:

> In complete darkness, I felt a stool which had been screwed into the floor. I heard the groaning and whimpering of the poor souls who were next to me, above and below, languishing in cell after cell in solitary confinement. Some of them had lost their sanity. No wonder! They raged and beat on the doors of their cells, sang crazy songs all through the night. Still others sang distorted old church songs in desperate voices, like animals, until one of the wardens came and beat them terribly—they even sometimes locked dogs in the cells, so that the trained animals could attack the victims. Among those detained were some out of whom dogs had bitten huge pieces of flesh; some had lost half an ear, others a piece of their nose, or their hand or whatever. Still others in the cell block were found covered with blood hard as ice. In this house of death, it was always bitterly cold. There I sat, barefoot in the darkness, freezing in my deepest soul.

The horror that we read in these lines should not make us turn away helplessly. Rather, the knowledge of the suppressed crimes and the unspeakable suffering should give us the conviction, the anger and courage we need in the fight against Naziism, which even now survives in our democracy and threatens us. The danger of being mere objects of political processes still exists. The scorn and mockery of pacifism, for example, has a tradition. ("To be a pacifist shows a lack of character and disposition," said Adolf Hitler in 1923.)

In a world where they make the stationing of neutron bombs appealing by saying, "they reduce the chances that these or any other weapons will ever be used;" in a world where we speak of the "balance of terror" and the "spiral of atomic retribution," women resistance fighters can be role models. With clear consciences, the women resistance fighters of the Third Reich set themselves against an ideology that did not value human life; they fought bravely and confidently for the old revolutionary goals: equality, justice and above all, humanity. For this they were tortured and for the most part murdered. But our memories of them and their courageous deeds can help us to prevent similar events—in whatever form they take—from ever being repeated in the future.

From the series Vitae, *by Angelika Kaufmann*

143

Exposing the Rape of Nanking

Exclusive excerpts from a Chinese-American author's unflinching re-examination of one of the most horrifying chapters of the second world war.

By Iris Chang

THE CHRONICLE OF humankind's cruelty is a long and sorry tale. But if it is true that even in such horror tales there are degrees of ruthlessness, then few atrocities can compare in intensity and scale to the rape of Nanking during World War II.

were mowed down by machine guns, used for bayonet practice, or soaked with gasoline and burned alive. By the end of the massacre an estimated 260,000 to 350,000 Chinese had been killed. Between 20,000 and 80,000 Chinese women were raped—and many soldiers

war (Great Britain lost 61,000 civilians, France 108,000, Belgium 101,000, and the Netherlands 242,000), the horrors of the Nanking massacre remain virtually unknown to people outside Asia. The Rape of Nanking did not penetrate the world consciousness in the same manner

---

'The killing went on nonstop, from morning until night'

The broad details of the rape are, except among the Japanese, not in dispute. In November 1937, after their successful invasion of Shanghai, the Japanese launched a massive attack on the newly established capital of the Republic of China. When the city fell on December 13, 1937, Japanese soldiers began an orgy of cruelty seldom if ever matched in world history. Tens of thousands of young men were rounded up and herded to the outer areas of the city, where they

diers went beyond rape to disembowel women, slice off their breasts, nail them alive to walls. So brutal were the Japanese in Nanking that even the Nazis in the city were shocked. John Rabe, a German businessman who led the local Nazi party, joined other foreigners in working tirelessly to save the innocent from slaughter by creating a safety zone where some 250,000 civilians found shelter.

Yet the Rape of Nanking remains an obscure incident. Although the death toll exceeds the immediate number of deaths from the atomic bombings of Hiroshima and Nagasaki (140,000 and 70,000 respectively, by the end of 1945) and even the total civilian casualties for several European countries during the entire

as the Jewish Holocaust or Hiroshima because the victims themselves remained silent. The custodian of the curtain of silence was politics. The People's Republic of China, Taiwan, and even the United States all contributed to the historical neglect of this event for reasons deeply rooted in the cold war. After the 1949 Communist revolution in China, neither the People's Republic of China nor Taiwan demanded wartime reparations from Japan (as Israel had from Germany) because the two governments were competing for Japanese trade and political recognition. And even the United States, faced with the threat of communism in the Soviet Union and mainland China, sought to ensure the friendship and loyalty of its former en-

From *Newsweek*, December 1, 1997, pp. 55-57. Adapted from *The Rape of Nanking: The Forgotten Holocaust of World War II*,
© 1997 by Iris Chang. Reprinted by permission of Basic Books, a division of HarperCollins Publishers, Inc.

emy Japan. In this manner, cold-war tensions permitted Japan to escape much of the intense critical examination that its wartime ally was forced to undergo.

In trying to understand the actions of the Japanese, we must begin with a little history. To prepare for what it viewed as an inevitable war with China, Japan had spent decades training its men. The molding of young men to serve in the Japanese military began early: In the 1930s, toy shops became virtual shrines to war, selling arsenals of toy soldiers, tanks, rifles, antiaircraft guns, bugles, and howitzers. Japanese schools operated like miniature military units. Indeed, some of the teachers were military officers, who lectured students on their duty to help Japan fulfill its divine destiny of conquering Asia and being able to stand up to the world's nations as a people second to none. They taught young boys how to handle wooden models of guns, and older boys how to handle

they could search for the soldier. When the Chinese commander refused, the Japanese shelled the fort. The confrontation escalated, and by August the Japanese had invaded Shanghai. Conquering China proved to be a more difficult task than the Japanese anticipated. In Shanghai alone Chinese forces outnumbered the Japanese marines ten to one, and Chiang Kai-shek, leader of the Nationalist government, had reserved his best troops for the battle. For months the Chinese defended the metropolis with extraordinary valor. To the chagrin of the Japanese, the battle of Shanghai proceeded slowly, street by street, barricade by barricade.

LITTLE WAS SPARED ON THE PATH to Nanking. Japanese veterans remember raiding tiny farm communities, where they clubbed or bayoneted everyone in sight. Small villages were not the only casualties; entire

cember 13, 1937, the Japanese 66th Battalion received the following command:

"All prisoners of war are to be executed. Method of execution: divide the prisoners into groups of a dozen. Shoot to kill separately. Our intentions are absolutely not to be detected by the prisoners."

There was a ruthless logic to the order: the captives could not be fed, so they had to be destroyed. Killing them would not only eliminate the food problem but diminish the possibility of retaliation. Moreover, dead enemies could not form up into guerrilla forces.

But executing the order was another matter. When the Japanese troops smashed through Nanking's walls in the early predawn hours of December 13, they entered a city in which they were vastly outnumbered. Historians later estimated that more than half a million civilians and ninety thousand Chinese troops were trapped in Nanking, com-

---

'It would be disastrous if they were to make any trouble'

---

real ones. Textbooks became vehicles for military propaganda. Teachers also instilled in boys hatred and contempt for the Chinese people, preparing them psychologically for a future invasion of the Chinese mainland. One historian tells the story of a squeamish Japanese schoolboy in the 1930s who burst into tears when told to dissect a frog. His teacher slammed his knuckles against the boy's head and yelled, "Why are you crying about one lousy frog? When you grow up you'll have to kill one hundred, two hundred chinks!"

In the summer of 1937 Japan finally seized the opportunity to provoke a full-scale war with China. One night in July several shots were fired at members of a Japanese regiment, garrisoned by treaty in the Chinese city of Tientsin, and a Japanese soldier failed to appear during roll call after the maneuvers. Japanese troops advanced upon the nearby Chinese fort of Wanping and demanded that its gates be opened so that

cities were razed to the ground. Consider the example of Suchow, a city on the east bank of the Tai Hu Lake. One of the oldest cities of China, it was prized for its delicate silk embroidery, palaces, and temples. Its canals and ancient bridges had earned the city its Western nickname as "the Venice of China." On November 19, on a morning of pouring rain, a Japanese advance guard marched through the gates of Suchow, wearing hoods that prevented Chinese sentries from recognizing them. Once inside, the Japanese murdered and plundered the city for days, burning ancient landmarks, and abducting thousands of Chinese women for sexual slavery. The invasion, according to the China Weekly Review, caused the population of the city to drop from 250,000 to less than 500. By the time Japanese troops entered Nanking, an order to eliminate all Chinese captives had been not only committed to paper but distributed to lower-echelon officers. On De-

pared with the fifty thousand Japanese soldiers who assaulted the city. General Kesago Nakajima knew that killing tens of thousands of Chinese captives was a formidable task: "To deal with crowds of a thousand, five thousand, or ten thousand, it is tremendously difficult even just to disarm them. . . . It would be disastrous if they were to make any trouble."

Because of their limited manpower, the Japanese relied heavily on deception. The strategy for mass butchery involved several steps: promising the Chinese fair treatment in return for an end to resistance, coaxing them into surrendering themselves to their Japanese conquerors, dividing them into groups of one to two hundred men, and then luring them to different areas near Nanking to be killed. Nakajima hoped that faced with the impossibility of further resistance, most of the captives would lose heart and comply with whatever directions the Japanese gave them.

All this was easier to achieve than the Japanese had anticipated. Resistance was sporadic; indeed, it was practically nonexistent. Having thrown away their arms when attempting to flee the city as the Japanese closed in, many Chinese soldiers simply turned themselves in, hoping for better treatment. Once the men surrendered and permitted their hands to be bound, the rest was easy.

After the soldiers surrendered en masse, there was virtually no one left to protect the citizens of the city. Knowing this, the Japanese poured into Nanking, occupying government buildings, banks, and warehouses, shooting people randomly in the streets, many of them in

way. The next day, tired of killing in this fashion, they set up machine guns. Two of them raked a cross-fire at the lined-up prisoners. Rat-tat-tat-tat. Triggers were pulled. The prisoners fled into the water, but no one was able to make it to the other shore."

Next, the Japanese turned their attention to the women. The rape of Nanking is considered the worst mass rape of world history with the sole exception of the treatment of Bengali women by Pakistani soldiers in 1971. Kozo Takokoro, a former soldier in the 114th Division of the Japanese army in Nanking, recalled, "No matter how young or old, they all could not escape the fate of be-

One of the most bizarre consequences of the wholesale rape that took place at Nanking was the response of the Japanese government. The Japanese high command made plans to create a giant underground system of military prostitution—one that would draw into its web hundreds of thousands of women across Asia. The plan was straightforward. By luring, purchasing, or kidnapping between eighty thousand and two hundred thousand women—most of them from the Japanese colony of Korea but many also from China, Taiwan, the Philippines, and Indonesia—the Japanese military hoped to reduce the incidence of random rape of local

Even war correspondents recoiled at the violence

the back as they ran away. As victims toppled to the ground, moaning and screaming, the streets, alleys, and ditches of the fallen capital ran rivers of blood. During the last ten days of December, Japanese motorcycle brigades patrolled Nanking while Japanese soldiers shouldering loaded rifles guarded the entrances to all the streets, avenues, and alleys. Troops went from door to door, demanding that they be opened to welcome the victorious armies. The moment the shopkeepers complied, the Japanese opened fire on them. The imperial army massacred thousands of people in this manner and then systematically looted the stores and burned whatever they had no use for.

These atrocities shocked many of the Japanese correspondents who had followed the troops to Nanking. Even seasoned war correspondents recoiled at the orgy of violence, and their exclamations found their way into print. From the Japanese military correspondent Yukio Omata, who saw Chinese prisoners brought to Hsiakwan and lined up along the river: "Those in the first row were beheaded, those in the second row were forced to dump the severed bodies into the river before they themselves were beheaded. The killing went on nonstop, from morning until night, but they were only able to kill 2,000 persons in this

ing raped. We sent out coal trucks from Hsiakwan to the city streets and villages to seize a lot of women. And then each of them was allocated to 15 to 20 soldiers for sexual intercourse and abuse."

Surviving Japanese veterans claim that the army had officially outlawed the rape of enemy women. But rape remained so deeply embedded in Japanese military culture and superstition that no one took the rule seriously. Many believed that raping virgins would make them more powerful in battle. Soldiers were even known to wear amulets made from the pubic hair of such victims, believing that they possessed magical powers against injury.

THE MILITARY POLICY forbidding rape only encouraged soldiers to kill their victims afterwards. Kozo Takokoro was blunt about this. "After raping, we would also kill them," he recalled. "Those women would start to flee once we let them go. Then we would bang! shoot them in the back to finish them up." According to surviving veterans, many of the soldiers felt remarkably little guilt about this. "Perhaps when we were raping her, we looked at her as a woman," Shiro Azuma, a former soldier in Nanking, wrote, "but when we killed her, we just thought of her as something like a pig."

women (thereby diminishing the opportunity for international criticism), to contain sexually transmitted diseases through the use of condoms, and to reward soldiers for fighting on the battlefront for long stretches of time. Later, of course, when the world learned of this plan, the Japanese government refused to acknowledge responsibility, insisting for decades afterwards that private entrepreneurs, not the imperial government, ran the wartime military brothels. But in 1991 Yoshiaki Yoshimi unearthed from the Japanese Defense Agency's archives a document entitled "Regarding the Recruitment of Women for Military Brothels." The document bore the personal stamps of leaders from the Japanese high command and contained orders for the immediate construction of "facilities of sexual comfort" to stop troops from raping women in regions they controlled in China.

The first official comfort house opened near Nanking in 1938. To use the word *comfort* in regard to either the women or the "houses" in which they lived is ludicrous, for it conjures up spa images of beautiful geisha girls strumming lutes, washing men, and giving them shiatsu massages. In reality, the conditions of these brothels were sordid beyond the imagination of most civilized people. Untold numbers of these women (whom the Japanese called "public toilets") took their own lives when they learned their destiny; others died from disease or murder. Those who survived suffered a lifetime of shame and isolation, sterility, or ruined health.

In interview after interview, Japanese veterans from the Nanking massacre reported honestly that they experienced a complete lack of remorse or sense of wrongdoing, even when torturing helpless civilians. Hakudo Nagatomi spoke candidly about his emotions in the fallen capital: "I remember being driven in a truck along a path that had been cleared through piles of thousands and thousands of slaughtered bodies. Wild dogs were gnawing at the dead flesh as we stopped and pulled a group of Chinese

prisoners out of the back. Then the Japanese officer proposed a test of my courage. He unsheathed his sword, spat on it, and with a sudden mighty swing he brought it down on the neck of a Chinese boy cowering before us. The head was cut clean off and tumbled away on the group as the body slumped forward, blood spurting in two great gushing fountains from the neck. The officer suggested I take the head home as a souvenir. I remember smiling proudly as I took his sword and began killing people."

After almost sixty years of soul-searching, Nagatomi is a changed man. A doctor in Japan, he has built a shrine of remorse in his waiting room. Patients can watch videotapes of his trial in

Nanking and a full confession of his crimes. The gentle and hospitable demeanor of the doctor belies the horror of his past, making it almost impossible for one to imagine that he had once been a ruthless murderer. "Few know that soldiers impaled babies on bayonets and tossed them still alive into pots of boiling water," Nagatomi said. "They gang-raped women from the ages of twelve to eighty and then killed them when they could no longer satisfy sexual requirements. I beheaded people, starved them to death, burned them, and buried them alive, over two hundred in all. It is terrible that I could turn into an animal and do these things. There are really no words to explain what I was doing. I was truly a devil."

His Finest Hour

*With courage and sheer will, Churchill rallied a nation
and turned back Hitler's tyranny*

By John Keegan

Sixty years ago this month, in May 1940, Western civilization was threatened with defeat. Liberty, the principle on which it rests, was menaced by a man who despised freedom. Adolf Hitler, the dictator of Nazi Germany, had conquered Western Europe. He challenged Britain, the last outpost of resistance, to submit. He believed Britain would, and with good reason. Its Army was beaten, its Navy and Air Force were under attack by the all-conquering German Luftwaffe. He believed no one would oppose his demands.

He was wrong. One man would and did. Winston Churchill, recently appointed prime minister, defied Hitler. He rejected surrender. He insisted that Britain could fight on. In a series of magnificent speeches, appealing to his people's courage and historic greatness, he carried Britain with him. The country rallied to his call, held steady under a concentrated air bombardment, manned the beaches Hitler planned to invade, and took strength in the struggle of "the Few," Britain's fighter pilots, in their eventually victorious battle against Hitler's air power. By the end of the year, by the narrowest of margins, Britain had survived. Hitler's war plan was flawed, never to recover, and the Western world lived to fight another day. Western civilization had found a new hero in crisis, whose example would lead it to eventual triumph.

Most of the 20th century's men of power were the antithesis of Churchill. They ruled by standards the opposite of those to which Churchill held. Churchill believed in liberty, the rule of law, and the rights of the individual. They rejected such standards. Lenin, Stalin, Hitler, Mao Zedong elevated power itself into a value in its own right. Truth, for Lenin, was a bourgeois concept, to be manipulated for revolutionary ends. Stalin despised truth, taking pleasure in forcing revolutionary idealists to deny their beliefs and confess to crimes of which they were not guilty. Hitler went further. He propagated the idea of the big lie that, if large enough, became undeniable. Mao encouraged a Cultural Revolution that vilified his civilization's historic culture and encouraged the ignorant to humiliate the learned and wise. In Bolshevik Russia, Nazi Germany, and Maoist China, civilization itself was threatened with death.

Two titans. Indeed, civilization might well have gone under in the years of the great dictators. That it did not was because of its defenders, men of principle who were also men of courage. Foremost among them were two titans of the Anglo-Saxon world, Franklin Delano Roosevelt and Winston Churchill. That they were Anglo-Saxons was no coincidence. Both derived their moral purpose from the Anglo-Saxon tradition of respect for the rule of law and freedom of the individual. Each could champion that tradition because the sea protected his country from the land-bound enemies of liberty. Roosevelt's America was protected by the vast expanse of the Atlantic Ocean, Churchill's

England by the English Channel. The channel is a puny bastion by comparison with the Atlantic. It was Churchill's will, buttressed by the power of the Royal Navy and Royal Air Force, that made the channel an insurmountable obstacle to Hitler's attack on liberty.

In terms of moral stature, there is little to choose between the two men. Roosevelt was a great American, consistently true to the principles on which the great republic was founded. Churchill was a great Englishman, committed with an equivalent passion to the Anglo-Saxon idea of liberty that had inspired America's founding fathers. There was this difference. The challenge of dictatorship came later to the United States than to Britain. It also came as an indirect threat. Hitler could never have invaded America. He might, following his military triumph in northwest Europe in the summer of 1940, all too easily have invaded Britain. A weaker man than Churchill might have capitulated to the threat. His refusal to contemplate surrender elevates him to a status unique among champions of freedom. Churchill was the Western world's last great hero.

Who was Churchill? The son of a prominent parliamentarian, Lord Randolph Churchill, and his beautiful American wife, Jennie Jerome, daughter of the proprietor of the *New York Times,* Winston was born into the purple of British society. His grandfather was Duke of Marlborough, a title conferred on his great ancestor, victor of the 18th-century War of the Spanish Succession—Queen Anne's War to Americans—and the place of his birth, in 1874, was Blenheim Palace, given to the first duke by a grateful nation as a trophy of generalship.

The young Winston wanted for nothing by way of privilege and connections. Unfortunately, he wanted for money. His father, a younger son, was profligate with the wealth he inherited. Jennie was extravagant with her American income. After Lord Randolph's early death, Winston was left to make his way in the world. He yearned to follow his father into politics. Without money, however, a political career was closed to him.

He had, moreover, been a failure at school. Headstrong and wayward, careers with prospects—business, the law—were thus closed to him. He took the only option open to a penniless youth of his class. He joined the Army.

Not without difficulty. Even the comparatively simple Army exams defeated Winston at his first two attempts. He passed into the Royal Military College only on his third try, which would have been his last attempt. His grades qualified him only for the cavalry, which did not look for brains. In 1895, he joined the 4th Hussars. In 1896 he went with his regiment to India.

Soldiering may have been a career of last resort. Winston embraced it enthusiastically. He was deeply conscious of his descent from Queen Anne's great general. He also had a passionate and adventurous nature. While a junior lieutenant he used his leave to visit the fighting in Cuba between Spain and the rebels. In India he used his connections to go as a war correspondent to the Northwest Frontier; in 1898 he again went as a correspondent to the Sudan, which Britain was recapturing from the Mahdi, an inspirational Islamic leader; and in 1899 he went, again as a correspondent, to the Boer War in South Africa.

Along the way, Churchill discovered a talent. He could write. The gift did not come without effort. In his hot Indian barracks he had spent his afternoons reading the English classics—Gibbon, Macaulay—and imitating their style. It was an unusual occupation for a young cavalry officer, particularly one who enjoyed the practice of his profession.

Churchill was bored by routine but loved action. He was physically fearless and had no hesitation in killing Queen Victoria's enemies. On the Northwest Frontier, he had clashed at close quarters with rival tribesmen. In the Sudan he had ridden in the British Army's last great cavalry charge. In South Africa he had fought in several battles and made a daring escape from Boer captivity.

But bravery in action did not, he early recognized, win cash returns. Vivid journalism did. By his 25th year he had made himself not only one of the most successful war correspondents of his age but also a bestselling author. His books on Indian tribal warfare, the recapture of the Sudan, and the Boer War sold in thousands, both in Britain and America, and he added to his literary income by well-paid lecturing. In 1900, with the money accumulated by writing, he was independent enough to stand for a parliamentary seat and win.

His literary success had not made him popular. Senior soldiers resented the way he had used family influence to escape from regimental duty. In the political world he was thought bumptious and self-promoting. Churchill did not care. He knew he was brave. Having proved that fact to his own satisfaction, he felt liberated to pursue his fundamental ambition, which was to achieve in politics the position he believed his father had been denied. Churchill adulated his father. The admiration was not returned. Lord Randolph regarded his son as a disappointment and often told him so. Despite the rebuffs suffered at his father's hands, Churchill took up Lord Randolph's pet cause—"Tory Democracy," which sought to align the Conservative Party of property owners with the interests of the working man. At the outset of his parliamentary career, Churchill spoke of "taking up the banner he had found lying on a stricken field," and, as an act of piety, he later wrote his father's biography. But the banner of Tory Democracy found so few followers that Churchill soon despaired of his father's party. In 1904 he left the Conservatives and joined the Liberals. "Crossing the floor" was a foolhardy act for a young parliamentarian. He thereby made himself the enemy of all of his former colleagues without any certainty of finding new friends on the other side.

The reformer. Such were his gifts of oratory, however, that Churchill escaped the floor crosser's common lot. In 1905 he was promoted to ministerial rank, only an under secretaryship but at the Colonial Office, whose work interested him. In that office he returned self-government to the Boers, whom he greatly admired. In 1908 he made a real leap, joining the cabinet as president of the Board of Trade. His responsibilities included social policy, and he was able to introduce a series of measures that benefited the working man, including unemployment pay and the creation of a job placement service. By 1910, when he became home secretary (a cabinet-level position similar to minister of the interior), he made a reputation as a radical social reformer, doing in the Liberal Party what he had hoped to achieve as a Tory Democrat.

Had he been kept in the social ministries, he would have built on the reputation. In 1911, however, he was made first lord of the admiralty at the height of Britain's competition with Germany in a costly naval race. Churchill loved the Royal Navy and fought successfully to win it the funds it needed. When the crisis came in July 1914, the fleet greatly outnumbered Germany's and was ready for war. Churchill sought every chance to bring it into action, actually leading a division of sailors turned soldiers in the defense of Antwerp during the German advance into Belgium. Soon afterward came the opportunity to use the Navy's battleships in the sort of decisive campaign he craved to direct. With the war in France stalemated, Churchill successfully argued that a diversionary effort should be made against Turkey, Germany's ally, by seizing the Dardanelles, the sea route from the Mediterranean to the Black Sea.

The campaign proved a failure from the start. The fleet was repulsed in March 1915, when it tried to bombard its way through the Dardanelles. When troops were landed the following month, they were quickly confined to shallow footholds on the Gallipoli Peninsula. By the year's end, casualties had risen to hundreds of thousands, and no progress had been made. In January 1916 Gallipoli was evacuated. By then Churchill was a discredited man. He had resigned political office and rejoined the Army in a junior rank, commanding a battalion in the trenches.

The reactionary. He was the only politician of his stature to serve in the trenches, and the gesture—which put him often in great danger—restored something of his reputation. In 1917 he became minister of munitions, in 1919 war minister. In the war's aftermath his responsibilities involved him in the Allied intervention against Russian Bolsheviks and in the negotiations of Irish independence. In none of his posts could he show himself at his best, however, and his political career in the 1920s took a downward path. In 1924 he fell out with the Liberal leadership over economic policy and returned to the Conservatives. As chancellor of the exchequer in 1925 he helped to precipitate the general strike of 1926 against the resulting financial stringency. He was henceforth regarded as a social reactionary by the working man he had championed when a young Liberal. He soon after acquired a reactionary name in imperial policy also. The freedom he had been eager to grant the Boers he thought inapplicable in India, and over that issue he left the Conservatives' upper ranks. By 1932 he was a lonely man. Hated by the Liberals and the new Labor Party, isolated in his own Conservative Party, he sat on the back benches of the House of Commons, frustrated and increasingly embittered.

He had consolations. His wife, the former Clementine Hozier, was one. She was a woman of strong character whom Churchill had married in 1908. Clemmie never lost faith in him. Their children also brought much pleasure. Writing, above all, filled the gap left by the collapse of his political career. Ever short of money, Churchill worked hard as a journalist to cover the costs of his ample way of life. He also found time out of office to complete his most substantial literary work, a life of his great ancestor, the first Duke of Marlborough.

Even as he brooded on the back benches, however, Churchill was identifying a new cause. He had thus far had

four lives, as a soldier, as an author, as a social reformer, and as a minister at the center of events. He now embarked on a fifth, as a Cassandra of Britain's present danger. Russian Communism had outraged his libertarian beliefs in the early Bolshevik years. In Hitler, whose rise to power began in 1933, he recognized a new enemy of liberty and one whose policies directly menaced his own country. The foreign policy of the government from which he stood aloof was one of appeasement. Anxious to protect Britain's fragile economy in the aftermath of the Great Depression, it preferred to palliate Hitler's demands rather than spend money on the rearmament that would have allowed it to oppose them. Year after year, between 1933 and 1938, Churchill warned of Germany's growing military might. He found support among experts in government who surreptitiously supplied him with the facts to authenticate his warnings. Official government persisted in denying their truth.

War is declared. Then, in 1938, the facts could no longer be denied. Hitler browbeat Czechoslovakia into surrendering much of its territory. He peremptorily incorporated Austria into Greater Germany. Neville Chamberlain's administration accepted that rearmament must now take precedence over sound economic management. France, too, bit the bullet of preparation for war, if war should come. When Hitler's aggressive diplomacy was directed against Poland, Britain and France issued guarantees to protect its integrity. Hitler chose to disbelieve their worth. He deluded himself. Two days after the Wehrmacht invaded Polish territory on Sept. 1, 1939, Britain and France declared hostilities against Germany. The Second World War had begun.

The Second World War was to be the consummation of Churchill's lifelong preparation for heroic leadership. He had proved his abilities as a soldier, as an administrator, as a publicist, as a statesman, as a master of the written and spoken word, and as a philosopher of democracy. In the circumstances of climactic conflict between the principles of good and evil, all the difficulties of his eventful life were to be overlaid by a

magnificent display of command in national crisis.

Hitler almost won the Second World War. By July 1940 he had conquered Poland, Belgium, the Netherlands, and France, beaten their armies, and expelled the British Army from the Continent. He stood poised to conquer Britain also. On his strategic agenda, once Britain was invaded, stood the conquest of the Balkans and then the Soviet Union. He looked forward to being the master of Europe, perhaps of the world.

So certain was Hitler of victory that, during September 1940, he delayed the invasion of Britain in the expectation of Churchill's suing for peace. His expectation was false. There had been a moment, in late May, when Churchill was tempted to negotiate. Once it became clear that the Royal Navy could rescue the Army from Dunkirk he put that temptation behind him. Britain would fight. Its Army might be in ruins, but its Navy was intact, and so was its Air Force. To invade Britain, Hitler must first destroy the Royal Air Force so that he could sink the Royal Navy. Only then could his invasion fleet cross the English Channel. Churchill convinced himself that his Air Force would defeat the Germans in a Battle of Britain. In midsummer 1940 he set out to convince the British people also.

As war leader, Churchill was to display vital qualities: courage, boldness, intellect, cunning, and charisma all founded on deep moral purpose. His courage, and the charisma his courage created, were shown first in the series of great speeches he made to Parliament and the people in the invasion summer of 1940. On May 19, just over a week after Chamberlain resigned, Churchill broadcast to the nation: "I speak to you for the first time as prime minister," he began. He went on to describe how the Allied front was collapsing before the German attack, calling the moment "a solemn hour for the life of our country, of our empire, of our Allies, and, above all, of the cause of freedom." Further details of the crisis followed. He concluded, "We have differed and quarreled in the past, but now one bond unites us all—to wage war until victory is won, and never to surrender ourselves to servitude and shame, whatever the cost and agony may be. . . . Conquer we must—conquer we shall."

On May 13 he had already told the House of Commons that he could offer only "blood, toil, tears, and sweat" but went on, "You ask: What is our aim? I can answer in one word: Victory. It is victory. Victory at all costs. Victory in spite of all terror, victory, however long and hard the road may be." On June 4 he made to the Commons the same declaration in words that were to become the most famous he ever uttered.

"We shall not flag or fail," he said. "We shall go on to the end. . . . We shall defend our island, whatever the cost may be. We shall fight on the landing-grounds; we shall fight in the fields and in the streets. . . . We shall never surrender." The effect was electrifying. A taut and anxious House put aside its fears and rose to cheer him to the rafters. His words, soon transmitted to the people, also electrified them. They caught a mood of popular disbelief that so great a nation should stand in such sudden danger and transformed it into one of dogged defiance. It was from this moment that began what philosopher Isaiah Berlin identified as the imposition of Churchill's "will and imagination on his countrymen" so that they "approached his ideals, and began to see themselves as he saw them."

There had always been a strong element of the populist in Churchill. From his father he had inherited the watchword "Trust the people," and it was because of his democratic ideals that he had, as a young statesman, thrown himself so enthusiastically into legislating for the welfare of the working man. In his later posts it was the welfare of his country as a whole that had come to concern him, and his fellow politicians' laxity of purpose in defending its interests that had dispirited him and alienated him from government. Now, in the supreme crisis of his country's life, he found the voice once more to speak to his people's hearts, to encourage and to inspire. In another great speech to the Commons on June 18, the day of the French capitulation to Hitler, he appealed directly to their sense of greatness. "If we can stand up to Hitler, all

Europe may be free, and the life of the world may move forward into broad, sunlit uplands. But if we fail, then the whole world, including the United States, including all that we have known and cared for, will sink into the abyss of a new Dark Age. Let us therefore brace ourselves to our duties and so bear ourselves that if Britain and its Commonwealth last for a thousand years, many will say, 'This was their finest hour.' "

Britain's year of 1940 would have been the finest hour of any nation. The British, under the threat of invasion and starvation by the U-boats too, heavily bombed in their cities, without allies, without any prospect of salvation at all, wholly exemplified how a finest hour should be lived. They dug the dead and the living from the rubble, manned their beaches, tightened their belts, and watched spellbound the aerobatics overhead of Fighter Command's fighting—and eventually winning—the Battle of Britain. Above all, they lent their ears to Churchill's great oratory. Speech by speech, they were taught by him to shrug off danger, glory in "standing alone," and determine to wait out isolation until the turn of events brought hope of better days.

Churchill's courage, and the charisma he won by it, was matched by his extraordinary boldness in adversity. A lesser man would have husbanded every resource to defend his homeland under the threat of invasion. Under such threat, Churchill nevertheless sought means to strike back. Identifying Hitler's ally, the Italian dictator, Benito Mussolini, as a weak link in the Axis system, Churchill stripped the home islands of troops to reinforce Britain's Army in the Middle East, where, in December 1940, it inflicted a humiliating defeat on the garrison of Italy's overseas empire. The setback caused Hitler to send Field Marshal Erwin Rommel to Mussolini's aid and, when Churchill next detached troops to aid Greece as well, to complicate his plans for the invasion of Russia by launching an offensive into the Balkans. Hitler's Russian timetable never recovered.

Churchill's boldness, based on the weakest of capabilities, thus won huge advantages. His real strategic priority,

throughout the months of "standing alone," had, however, been to bring the United States into the war against Hitler on Britain's side. America was indeed Britain's last best hope. In June 1941, Hitler attacked the Soviet Union but, in a few weeks, Stalin's lot was even worse than Churchill's. German troops stood deep inside Russian territory, and the Red Army was falling to pieces. Churchill had offered Stalin a British alliance, but it was aid from the weak to the weak. Only America could reverse the balance for either.

Churchill's intellect had told him so from the inception of the disaster of 1940. A master of strategic analysis, he saw that Britain's numerical and economic inferiority to Hitler's Fortress Europe could only be offset by massive American assistance. He was also aware that an America at peace, barely recovering from the depths of the Great Depression, could be brought to intervene only step by step. It was there his cunning showed. Half American as he was, and long intimate with his mother's homeland, he recognized the strength of American suspicions of Britain's imperial position. He understood that President Roosevelt's profession of commitment to common democratic ideals and repugnance of European dictatorship was balanced by calculations of national interest and domestic policy. Where a less subtle man might have blustered and demanded, Churchill cajoled and flattered. All his efforts at establishing a "special relationship" were made by indirect appeal, through artistry and symbolism.

Five pledges. At Argentia Bay in August 1941, where Roosevelt arrived on the USS Augusta and Churchill on the HMS Prince of Wales—to be sunk five months later off Malaya by the Japanese—the prime minister extracted from the president five pledges: to give "massive aid" to Russia; to enlarge American convoys to Britain; to strengthen convoy escorts; to send American bombers to join the Royal Air Force; and to patrol the western Atlantic against U-boats. The two statesmen also agreed on a commitment to world democracy later to be known as the Atlantic Charter. It was a heartening encounter, of which

Churchill made the most at home. The results still fell short of what Britain needed: a full-blooded American alliance.

That was brought him in the weeks after Dec. 7, 1941, when the Japanese Combined Fleet attacked Pearl Harbor. "So we have won after all," Churchill confided to himself that evening. His hopes ran ahead of events. Pearl Harbor merely opened a Japanese-American war. It was Hitler's megalomaniacal decision on December 11 to declare war on the United States that made America Britain's ally. Even then Churchill had much careful diplomacy to complete before he could be sure that the weight of the American war effort would be concentrated in Europe rather than in the Pacific. In the opening months of 1942 the American people's ire was directed against Japan, not Germany. Even though Roosevelt shared Churchill's judgment that Germany was the more dangerous enemy, America's generals and admirals had to be convinced of the correctness of "Germany first" as a strategy. The admirals never fully accepted it. The generals were brought to do so only by reasoned argument. Then, paradoxically, they had to be restrained. George Marshall, Roosevelt's great chief of staff, and Dwight Eisenhower, future supreme Allied commander and president, pushed in mid-1942 for an attack on Hitler's Fortress Europe at the earliest possible moment. Their impetuosity aroused Churchill's caution. Strong though his gambling instinct was, his memory of the Dardanelles disaster, the greatest setback of his career, remained with him. He was terrified by the prospect of a beaten Allied army falling back into the sea. His relief at Marshall's and Eisenhower's recognition of the prematurity of their plans was evident to all.

His caution would persist throughout 1943. It is from that year that the waning of his powers of leadership dates. He was approaching his 70th year and failing in health. He suffered a mild heart attack and other illnesses. He was confronted by a vote of confidence in the Commons, where sufficient of his old enemies remained to reproach him for the military disasters at Singapore and Tobruk. Roosevelt stood by him. "What can we do to help?" the president had asked after the fall of Tobruk in June 1942. Other Americans were less patient. They pressed for action from which Churchill increasingly appeared to shrink. The Russians were even more exigent.

Left out. Stalin took to deriding British halfheartedness, eventually to mocking Churchill to his face. At the three-power Tehran conference of November 1943, Stalin taunted Churchill to declare a final date for the invasion of Europe. Roosevelt lent Churchill no support. It was the beginning of a new, Russo-American special relationship, from which Churchill felt excluded. He was becoming an old man. His glory days were over.

There was to be a recovery. On May 8, 1945, the day of Germany's surrender, he made a speech to the London crowds in which he found his old voice and repaid the people for all he had asked of them in the dark days of 1940. "God bless you all," he trumpeted. "This is your victory. Everyone, man or woman, has done their best. Neither the long years nor the dangers, nor the fierce attacks of the enemy, have in any way weakened the independent resolve of the British nation. God bless you all." He, however, was not to be repaid for his lionlike wartime courage. His reputation as a young social reformer was long forgotten. The reputation given him by his Liberal and Labor opponents as a reactionary was not. In July 1945 the electorate voted against the Conservatives by a landslide. Churchill ceased to be prime minister, not to return to office for six years.

When he did resume the premiership in 1951, his powers had left him and his administration of government was an embarrassment. His resignation, forced by illness in 1955, was greeted with relief even by his closest friends and family. Yet the years since 1945 had not been without achievement. He had written a great history of the Second World War, which won him the Nobel Prize for Literature. He had become a European statesman, welcomed and honored in all the European countries that, in 1940, he had promised to liberate from Nazi tyranny and lived to see free again. He had become a hero in the United States, his mother's homeland, where he remains today the object of a cult status he does not enjoy in his own country. He had, above all, become the standard-bearer of a new crusade against a new tyranny, that of Stalinism. At Fulton, Mo., on March 5, 1946, he had warned against the descent of an "Iron Curtain" cutting off Eastern and Central Europe from the free world. The development reminded him, he said, of the appeasement years of the '30s, and he urged America and his own country not to become "divided and falter in their duty" lest "catastrophe overwhelm us all."

The Fulton speech, now so celebrated, aroused strong hostility at the time, both in America and Britain. It nevertheless laid the basis for the West's democratic resistance to the spread of communist dictatorship that, culminating in the fall of the Berlin Wall in 1989, at last restored the world to the condition of freedom that had been Churchill's central ideal and for which he had struggled all his life. "I asked," he answered his critics after the Fulton speech, "for fraternal association—free, voluntary. I have no doubt it will come to pass, as surely as the sun will rise tomorrow."

Churchill's sun, at the beginning of the third millennium, has risen and, if it should seem to shine fitfully at times and places, is nevertheless the light of the world. No other citizen of the last century of the second millennium, the worst in history, deserved better to be recognized as a hero to mankind.

Sir John Keegan, defense editor of the Daily Telegraph *and a contributing editor of* U.S. News, *is author of 20 books of military history. He is at work on a biography of Churchill for Viking Press.*

Judgment at Nuremberg

*Fifty years ago the trial of Nazi war criminals ended: the world had witnessed
the rule of law invoked to punish unspeakable atrocities*

Robert Shnayerson

The author, formerly editor of Harper's,
*has written extensively on the U.S. Su-
preme Court and on legal matters.*

In the war-shattered city of Nuremberg, 51 years ago, an eloquent American prosecutor named Robert H.
Jackson opened what he called "the first
trial in history for crimes against the
peace of the world." The setting was the
once lovely Bavarian city's hastily refurbished Palace of Justice, an SS prison
only eight months before. In the dock
were 21 captured Nazi leaders, notably
the fat, cunning drug addict Hermann
Göring.

Their alleged crimes, the ultimate in
20th-century depravity, included the
mass murders of some six million Jews
and millions of other human beings
deemed "undesirable" by Adolf Hitler.
"The wrongs which we seek to condemn
and punish," said Robert Jackson, "have
been so calculated, so malignant and so
devastating, that civilization cannot tolerate their being ignored because it cannot survive their being repeated."

Here were satanic men like Ernst
Kaltenbrunner, the scar-faced function-
ary second only to Heinrich Himmler in
overseeing the death camps and the Nazi
police apparatus; Alfred Rosenberg, co-
founder of the Nazi Party and chief
theorist of anti-Semitism; and Hans
Frank, the vicious and venal Nazi pro-
consul in Poland. At the time, many
asked why such messengers of evil were
to be allowed even one day in court,
much less the 403 sessions they were

about to undergo. It was a question that
Jackson, on leave from his job as a Justice of the U.S. Supreme Court to prose-
cute this case, quickly addressed in his
opening statement.

With the kind of moral clarity that
marked American idealism at the time,
Jackson declared, "That four great nations, flushed with victory and stung
with injury stay the hand of vengeance
and voluntarily submit their captive enemies to the judgment of the law is one
of the most significant tributes that
Power ever has paid to Reason. . . . The
real complaining party at your bar is
Civilization. . . . [It] asks whether law is
so laggard as to be utterly helpless to
deal with crimes of this magnitude."

So began, in November 1945, the
century's most heroic attempt to achieve
justice without vengeance—heroic because the victors of World War II had
every reason to destroy the vanquished
without pity. Heroic because they ultimately resisted the temptation to impose
on the Germans what the Nazis had imposed on their victims—collective guilt.
Instead, they granted their captives a
presumption of innocence and conducted a ten-month trial to determine
their personal responsibility.

Locked up in solitary cells each
night, constantly guarded by American
M.P.'s mindful of recent suicides among
high-ranking Nazis, the defendants
spent their days in a giant courtroom
built for 400 spectators, listening to evidence drawn from 300,000 affidavits
and meticulous German documents so

voluminous they filled six freight cars.
Nearly all were ready to acknowledge
the horrific facts while cravenly assign-
ing blame to others. (Göring, who died
unrepentant, was the exception.) When
it was all over in October 1946, and ten
defendants had been hanged messily in
the Palace of Justice's gymnasium, this
first Nuremberg trial stood as the judicial Everest of those who hoped, as
Jackson did, that the rule of law could
punish, if not prevent, the atrocities of
war.

The exercise of justice at Nuremberg
reverberates across this century. And
next month, on November 13 and 14,
scholars will ponder the lessons of history at an international conference on
the trials, sponsored by the Library of
Congress and the U.S. Holocaust Memorial Museum.

How this trial, and the 12 that followed, came to be held is a story in itself. In April 1944, two Jews who
escaped the Auschwitz death camp described its horrors to the world. They
detailed Germany's technology of genocide, such as the camp's four new gas-
and-burn machines, each designed to
kill 2,000 prisoners at a time. They pin-
pointed a huge slave-labor operation at
nearby Birkenau, run by Germany's fine
old industrial names (I. G. Farben and
Siemens among others), where Allied
prisoners and kidnapped foreign laborers were fed so little and worked so hard
that as many as one-third died every
week. Their testimony paved the way to
Nuremberg.

From *Smithsonian* magazine, October 1996, pp. 124–141. © 1996 by Robert Shnayerson. Reprinted by permission of the author.

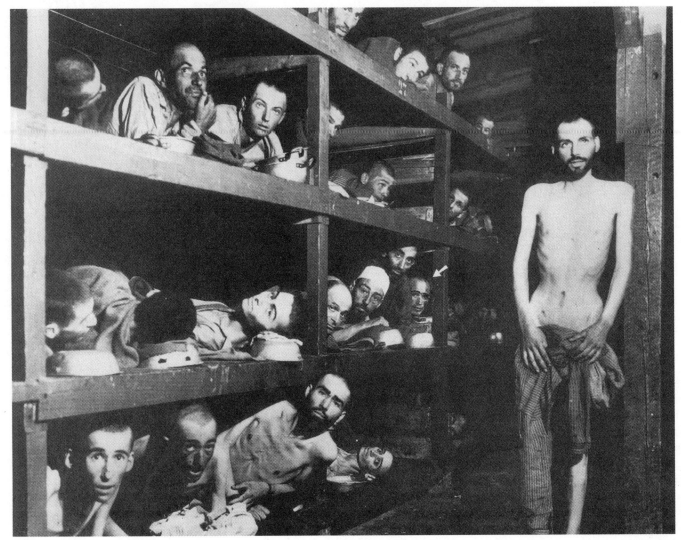

Death camp images, such as this one from Buchenwald, helped convict Ernst Kaltenbrunner, Himmler's deputy. Elie Wiesel, future chronicler of the Holocaust, is indicated by the arrow.

The Allied leaders had little trouble agreeing that German war crimes must be punished. But punished how? Treasury Secretary Henry Morgenthau Jr. urged that all captured Nazi leaders be shot immediately, without trial, and that Germany be reduced to the status of an agricultural backwater. Secretary of War Henry Stimson thought dooming all Germans to a kind of national execution would not do. It violated the Allied (if not Soviet) belief in the rule of law. It would deny postwar Germany a working economy and perhaps, ultimately, breed another war.

Roosevelt, who wanted to bring G.I.'s (and their votes) home promptly, sought a compromise between Morgenthau and Stimson. The man asked to find it was Murray Bernays, a 51-year-old lawyer turned wartime Army colonel in the Pentagon.

Immediately, a basic but legally complex question rose to the fore—what is a war crime, anyway? At the end of the 19th century, the increased killing power of modern weapons led to the various Hague and Geneva conventions, binding most great powers to treat civilians humanely, shun the killing of unarmed prisoners and avoid ultimate weapons, such as germ warfare, "calculated to cause unnecessary suffering." Such "laws of war" are quite frequently applied. They have saved thousands of lives. In combat the basic distinction between legitimate warfare and atrocities occurs when acts of violence exceed "military necessity."

Before Nuremberg, jurisdiction over war crimes was limited to each country's military courts. After World War I, when the victors accused 896 Germans of serious war crimes, demanding their surrender to Allied military courts, the Germans insisted on trying them and accepted a mere 12 cases. Three defendants never showed up; charges against three others were dropped; the remaining six got trivial sentences.

Bernays envisioned a different scenario: an international court that held individuals liable for crimes the world deemed crimes, even if their nation had approved or required those actions. The accused could not plead obedience to superiors. They would be held personally responsible.

Other big questions remained. One was how an international court trying war crimes could legally deal with crimes committed by the Nazis before the war. Another involved the sheer volume of guilt. The dreaded Schutzstaffel, or SS (in charge of intelligence, security and the extermination of undesirables), and other large Nazi organizations included hundreds of thousands of alleged war criminals. How could they possibly be tried individually? Bernays suggested putting Nazism and the entire Hitler era on trial as a giant criminal conspiracy. In a single stroke, this would create a kind of unified field theory of Nazi depravity, eliminating time constraints, allowing prosecution of war crimes and prewar crimes as well. He also suggested picking a handful of top Nazi defendants as representatives of key Nazi organizations like the SS. If the leaders were convicted, members of their organizations would automatically be deemed guilty. Result: few trials, many convictions and a devastating exposé of Nazi crimes.

Roosevelt promptly endorsed the plan, with one addition. The Nazis would be charged with the crime of waging "aggressive" war, or what the eventual indictments called "crimes against peace"—the first such charge in legal history.

Nobody was more enthusiastic about the strategy than Robert Jackson. Then 53, Jackson was a small-town lawyer from western New York with a gift for language. He had served in various posts in New Deal Washington before Roosevelt elevated him to the Supreme Court in 1941. By July 21, 1945, barely two months after Germany surrendered, Jackson had won President Truman's approval for a four-power International Military Tribunal and had persuaded the Allies to conduct it in Nuremberg.

A master list of 122 war criminals was put together, headed by Hermann Göring, the ranking Nazi survivor. (Hitler, Himmler and Goebbels were dead by their own hand. Martin Bormann, Hitler's secretary, had vanished, never to be found.) Reichsmarschall Göring, a daring World War I ace, had not allowed defeat to tarnish his reputation for candor, cunning and gluttony.

He had turned himself in at a weight of 264 pounds (he was 5 feet 6 inches tall). His entourage included a nurse, four aides, two chauffeurs and five cooks. His fingernails and toenails were painted bright red. His 16 monogrammed suitcases contained rare jewels, a red hatbox, frilly nightclothes and 20,000 paracodeine pills, a painkiller he had taken at the rate of about 40 pills a day. He managed to charm some of his captors to the point of almost forgetting his diabolism.

On August 8, 1945, the Charter of the International Military Tribunal (IMT, unveiled by the victorious Allies in London, declared aggressive war and international crime. The IMT charter was grounded in the idea that Nazism was a 26-year-long criminal conspiracy. Its aim: to build a war machine, satisfy Hitler's psychopathic hatred of Jews and turn Europe into a German empire. Judges representing the four powers (the United States, Great Britain, France and the Soviet Union), plus four alternates, were named. They were to take jurisdiction over high-ranking Nazis deemed personally guilty of war crimes, conspiracy to commit war crimes, crimes against peace and crimes against humanity.

The 24 men named in the original indictment represented a wide spectrum of Germany's political-military-industrial complex. With Martin Bormann (tried in absentia), the list of those actually presented for trial was further reduced by two surprise events. Robert Ley, the alcoholic, Jew-baiting boss of the German Labor Front, which had governed the lives of 30 million German workers, hanged himself in his cell on the night of October 25. And, at the last moment, the prosecutors realized their key industrial defendant, the weapons maker Alfried Krupp, had not personally run his family's slave-labor factories until after the war began, giving him an easy defense against the prewar conspiracy charge. (Krupp was later sentenced to 12 years for war crimes, but he was released from prison in 1951.)

The trial of the remaining defendants began on the morning of November 20, 1945. In the refurbished courtroom, floodlights warmed the new green curtains and crimson chairs, illuminating the two rows of once fearsome Nazis sitting in the dock guarded by young American soldiers. Göring had shed 60 pounds during his six months of confinement, acquiring what novelist John Dos Passos, reporting for *Life*, called "that wizened look of a leaky balloon of a fat man who has lost a great deal of weight." Next to him in the front row were the ghostly Rudolf Hess, feigning amnesia; Joachim von Ribbentrop, Hitler's foreign minister; and Field Marshal Wilhelm Keitel, the Führer's Wehrmacht chief. Next in order of indictment came Ernst Kaltenbrunner (ill and absent for the first three weeks), Alfred Rosenberg and Hans Frank, who somehow thought his captors would spare his life when he handed over one of the trial's most damning documents—his 38-volume journal. (He would be sentenced to hang.)

Throughout that first day, as black-robed American, British and French judges and their two uniformed Soviet colleagues peered somberly from the bench, listening via earphones to translations in four languages, the prosecutors droned an almost boring litany of sickening crimes—shooting, torture, starvation, hanging—to which, in descending tones of indignation, from Göring downward, the accused each pleaded not guilty.

The next morning, Robert Jackson opened the prosecution case on Count One, conspiracy to commit war crimes. "This war did not just happen," Jackson told the judges. The defendants' seizure of the German state, he continued, "their subjugation of the German people, their terrorism and extermination of dissident elements, their planning and waging of war . . . , their deliberate and planned criminality toward conquered peoples—all these are ends for which they acted in concert."

"We will not ask you to convict these men on the testimony of their foes," Jackson told the court. There was no need. Allied agents had found 47 crates of Alfred Rosenberg's files hidden in a 16th-century castle, 485 tons of diplomatic papers secreted in the Harz Mountains, and Göring's art loot and

Luftwaffe records stashed in a salt mine in Obersalzberg.

One especially incriminating find—indispensable to the conspiracy theory—was the notes of Hitler aide Col. Friedrich Hossbach from a meeting between Hitler, Göring and other Nazis in Berlin on November 5, 1937. Hossbach quoted Hitler insisting that, as Europe's racially "purest" stock, the Germans were entitled to "more living space" in neighboring countries, which he planned to seize, he said, "no later than 1943–45."

During the opening weeks, the pace of the trial was slow. Most of the American prosecution team neither read nor understood German. What with translation gaffes, repetitions and monotone readings, the documentary evidence—reams of it—at times had judges yawning and the defendants themselves dozing off.

Of course, the banality of overdocumented evil did not soften the prosecution's gruesome narrative. And a month into the recitation of Hitler's prewar aggressions from the Rhineland to Austria to Czechoslovakia, the Americans suddenly animated the documents by showing films of Nazi horrors. One German soldier's home movie depicted his comrades in Warsaw, clubbing and kicking naked Jews. In one scene, an officer helped a battered young woman to her feet so that she could be knocked down again.

An American movie documented the liberation of concentration camps at Bergen-Belson, Dachau and Buchenwald, filling the darkened courtroom with ghastly images of skeletal survivors, stacked cadavers and bulldozers shoveling victims into mass graves. In his cell that night, Hans Frank burst out: "To think we lived like kings and believed in that beast!" Göring was merely rueful. "It was such a good afternoon, too—" he said, "and then they showed that awful film, and it just spoiled everything."

Even when badly translated, Jackson's documents made a mesmerizing record of Hitler's appalling acts on the road to Armageddon. They revisited his rise to power as the people's choice in the depression year 1932. Billing him-self as Germany's economic savior, the Führer immediately began spending so much on weapons that in six years, the treasury was almost empty. A diversion was called for.

Thrilling his admirers—millions of still worshipful Germans—Hitler bullied British and French leaders into selling out Czechoslovakia at the pusillanimous Munich conference in 1938 (SMITHSONIAN, October 1988). Next, Nazi thugs were unleashed on *Kristallnacht*, the "Night of Broken Glass" (November 9)—a nationwide campaign of anti-Semitic violence. Huge chunks of Jewish wealth wound up in Nazi pockets. Göring, the biggest thief, further demeaned his victims by ordering German Jews to pay the regime a "fine" of one billion marks ($400 million). As he explained it, "The Jew being ejected from the economy transfers his property to the state."

Hjalmar Schacht, then head of the Reichsbank, warned Hitler in January 1939 that his arms race was fueling runaway inflation. Hitler immediately fired Schacht and ordered new currency, largely backed by stolen Jewish property. Schacht, long a Hitler apologist, then began working secretly for U.S. intelligence and wound up at Dachau. Now, to his disgust, he sat in the Nuremberg dock.

According to trial documents, Hitler's profligacy helped propel his aggressions. By 1941, Hitler had made his suicidal decision to renege on the nonaggression pact signed with Stalin in 1939 and invade the Soviet Union. "What one does not have, but needs," he said, "one must conquer."

It began well, on June 22, 1941, and ended badly. By late 1942, with German casualties soaring at Stalingrad, Hitler had lost so many soldiers in Russia that he had to keep drafting German workers into the army, replacing them with foreign laborers, mainly French and Russian prisoners. In early 1943, with more than five million industrial slaves already toiling in Germany, the surrender at Stalingrad forced Hitler's manpower boss, Nuremberg defendant Fritz Sauckel, to kidnap 10,000 Russian civilians per day for work in Germany. Few survived longer than 18 months—a powerful incentive for Russians still at home to flee the kidnappers and join Soviet guerrillas in killing German troops.

Hitler's campaign to "Aryanize" Germany began before the war with the deliberate poisoning of incurably sick people and retarded children—labeled "garbage children." The regime's contempt for non-Aryan life conditioned millions of Germans to turn a blind eye to more and more epidemic evils—the death camps, the ghastly medical experiments, the relentless massacres of those Hitler called "Jews, Poles, and similar trash."

Listening to the facts, the almost incomprehensible facts, even the defendants longed for some answer to the overpowering question—why? Why did one of the world's most advanced nations descend to such acts so easily? So swiftly? The trial provided few answers. Hitler's truly diabolic achievement, French prosecutor François de Menthon observed, was to revive "all the instincts of barbarism, repressed by centuries of civilization, but always present in men's innermost nature."

For weeks, the prosecution cited such acts as the use of Jewish prisoners as guinea pigs in military medical experiments to determine the limits of high-altitude flying by locking them in pressure chambers, slowly rupturing their lungs and skulls. How long downed German pilots could last in the ocean was determined by submerging prisoners in icy water until they died. To develop a blood-clotting chemical, the doctors shot and dismembered live prisoners to simulate battlefield injuries. Death did not end this abuse. A Czech doctor who spent four years imprisoned at Dachau, where he performed some 12,000 autopsies, told investigators that he was ordered to strip the skin off bodies. "It was cut into various sizes for use as saddles, riding breeches, gloves, house slippers, and ladies handbags. Tattooed skin was especially valued by SS men."

The scale of Hitler's madness was almost beyond imagination. The documents showed that after conquering Poland in 1939, he ordered the expulsion of nearly nine million Poles and

Jews from Polish areas he annexed for his promised Nordic empire. The incoming colonists were "racially pure" ethnic Germans imported from places like the Italian Tirol. The SS duly began herding the exiles from their homes toward ethnic quarantine in a 39,000-square-mile cul-de-sac near Warsaw. Opposition grew; progress slowed. In righteous rage, the SS unleashed hundreds of *Einsatzgruppen*—killer packs assigned to spread terror by looting, shooting and slaughtering without restraint. Thereafter, the SS action groups murdered and plundered behind the German Army as it advanced eastward.

By January 1946, prosecutor Jackson was at last animating his documents with live witnesses. The first was a stunner. Otto Ohlendorf, blond and short, looked like the choirboy next door. In fact he was 38, a fanatic anti-Semite and the former commander of Einsatzgruppe D, the scourge of southern Russia. He testified with icy candor and not an iota of remorse.

How many persons were killed under your direction? asked Jackson. From June 1941 to June 1942, Ohlendorf flatly replied, "90,000 people."

Q. "Did that include men, women, and children?" A. "Yes."

Rather proudly, Ohlendorf asserted that his 500-man unit killed civilians "in a military manner by firing squads under command." Asked if he had "scruples" about these murders, he said, "Yes, of course."

Q. "And how is it they were carried out regardless of these scruples?"

A. "Because to me it is inconceivable that a subordinate leader should not carry out orders given by the leaders of the state."

The prosecution rested after three months, capped off by another movie distilling still more Nazi horror, and displays of macabre human-skin lampshades and shrunken Jewish heads submitted as evidence.

German defense lawyers then spent five months trying to cope with major handicaps. Most had grown to abhor their clients. All were unfamiliar with adversarial cross-examinations used in the United States and Britain, to

say nothing of key documents that the Americans tended to withhold before springing them in court.

They managed to outflank the court's ban on tu quoque evidence (meaning, "If I am guilty, you are, too")—a stricture aimed at keeping Allied excesses, notably the mass bombing of German cities, out of the trial. In the dock was Adm. Karl Dönitz, accused of ordering U-boats to sink merchantmen without warning and let the crews drown whenever a rescue attempt might jeopardize the Germans. Dönitz never denied the charge. Instead, his lawyer produced an affidavit from Adm. Chester Nimitz, commander of the wartime U.S. Pacific fleet, stating that American submariners had followed the same policy against Japanese ships. (In the end, he was sentenced to ten years; upon release in 1956, he lived 24 more years, to age 88.)

The prosecution had depicted a vast conspiracy to wage war and commit atrocities. But in choosing representative Nazis as defendants, it wound up with 21 men who, though all pleaded ignorance or powerlessness, were otherwise so different that many hated one another. Each tried to save himself by accusing others. As a result, the defense naturally failed to muster a united front, and the prosecution's conspiracy theory steadily unraveled.

The trial's highlight was the star turn of its one wholly unabashed defendant, Hermann Göring. In three days of direct examination, Göring sailed through an insider's history of Nazism, defending Germany's right to rearm and reoccupy territory lost by the Versailles treaty. He laughed off the notion that his fellow defendants were ever close enough to Hitler to be called conspirators. "At best," he said, "only the Führer and I could have conspired."

Jackson's cross-examination was a disaster. Göring understood English well; while questions were translated into German, he had time to improvise his answers. At one point, Jackson prodded Göring to admit that the Nazis' plan to occupy the Rhineland, enacted without warning in 1936, was a Nazi secret, hidden from other countries. Göring smoothly answered, "I do not believe I can recall reading beforehand the publi-

cation of the mobilization preparations of the United States."

Jackson conducted a bizarre cross-examination of Albert Speer, Hitler's personal architect of gigantic edifices and stage manager of the Nuremberg rallies. Smart, suave, handsome, not yet 40, the wellborn Speer ranked high among Hitler's few confidants and was chief of all Nazi war production for the regime's last three years. He oversaw 14 million workers; he could hardly claim ignorance of their condition or how they were recruited. In the spring of 1944, for example, he ordered 100,000 Jewish slave workers from Hungary as casually as if they were bags of cement.

On the witness stand, Speer said he had become totally disillusioned with Hitler when the Führer responded to Germany's inevitable defeat by ordering a nationwide scorched-earth policy: the total destruction of everything in the path of the Allied armies. Rejecting Hitler's monomania, which he called a betrayal of ordinary Germans, Speer told the court, "It is my unquestionable duty to assume my share of responsibility for the disaster of the German people." And he revealed—offering no proof—that in February 1945 he had set out to assassinate Hitler by dropping poison gas through an air shaft in the Führer's bunker, only to find the shaft sealed off.

Speer, the most attractive defendant at Nuremberg, had been debriefed by interrogators avid for his special knowledge of how German war factories managed to keep humming despite immense Allied bombing. Some saw him as just the kind of man needed to rehabilitate postwar Germany. Under cross-examination, he got mostly easy questions, typically prefaced by Jackson's disclaimer, "I am not attempting to say that you were personally responsible for these conditions."

That Speer actually received a 20-year sentence seems remarkable, given his adroit performance. That his equally (or perhaps less) culpable colleague, Fritz Sauckel—brutal, lowborn, ill spoken—was sentenced to death, seems as legally unfair as it was morally deserved.

After Robert Jackson's powerful summation of the trial's "mad and melancholy record," the case went to the trial judges, from whom no appeal was permitted. The great unspoken issue at Nuremberg was the question of collective guilt, and hindsight clarifies the extraordinary dilemma those eight judges faced 50 years ago. Collective guilt had tainted the Versailles treaty and helped ignite the Holocaust. It is the fuel of human barbarism, currently on display from Rwanda to Serbia. And though the Nuremberg judges were given every reason to savage the Nazi tyranny, they came to believe that justice could be served only by asserting the principle of individual responsibility. Justice required, in fact, a virtual rejection of the United States' whole grand conspiracy concept.

The Nazi Party founders had been charged with conspiring for 26 years (1919–45) to launch World War II and related atrocities. All 22 defendants (including Bormann) stood accused of planning aggressive war; 18 were charged with wartime crimes and crimes against humanity, such as genocide. If the court approved, seven Nazi organizations would also be convicted, rendering all their thousands of members guilty without trial.

The problem was that conspiracy is a crime of joint participation. Conviction required proof that two or more people knowingly agreed at a specific time and place to use criminal means to achieve criminal ends. But the distinguished French judge, Donnedieu de Vabres, urged his colleagues to observe that the defendants had seemed to act less in cahoots with, than in bondage to, a megalomaniac. Jackson's documents showed the "Führer Principle" in practice—the madness of Hitler's erratic orders, executed by lackeys too blind, venal or terrified to disobey. The evidence seemingly proved chaos, not organized conspiracy.

The judges, risking a backlash from Europe's Nazi victims by sharply limiting their verdicts to the hard evidence, ruled that the war conspiracy began not in 1919 but on November 5, 1937, at the "Hossbach conference" in which Hitler's aides heard his schemes for conquering Germany's neighbors.

The conspiracy charge (Count One) was restricted to eight defendants (led by Göring) who knowingly carried out Hitler's war plans from 1938 onward. In effect, the defendants were liable only for actual wartime crimes beginning September 1, 1939—a dizzying number of crimes but one that eliminated perhaps a third of the prosecution's evidence and produced three acquittals, including that of Schacht.

Under such an approach, guilt for simply belonging to the Nazi organizations was impossible. The court held that only the SS, the Gestapo-SD and the top Nazi leadership had been proved "criminal," meaning that their members had voluntarily joined in committing war crimes after 1939. That left several million potential defendants for lower courts to handle. But since the Nuremberg judges ruled them all innocent until proven guilty, relatively few were ever tried—the prosecutorial job was too formidable.

The trial removed 11 of the most despicable Nazis from life itself. In the early morning hours of Wednesday, October 16, 1946, ten men died in the courthouse gymnasium in a botched hanging that left several strangling to death for as long as 25 minutes. Ribbentrop departed with dignity, saying, "God protect Germany." Göring had cheated the hangman 2½ hours earlier. He killed himself in his cell, using a cyanide capsule he had managed to hide until then. In one of four suicide notes, he wrote, "I would have consented anytime to be shot. But the Reichsmarschall of Germany cannot be hanged."

The Nuremberg trial never remotely enabled the world to outlaw war. By 1991, the wars of the 20th century had killed more than 107 million people. And given Nuremberg's uniqueness—winners in total control of losers—the court of 1945 may seem irrelevant to the wars of the 1990s, in which ethnic killers, such as Gen. Ratko Mladic, the Bosnian Serb implicated in the mass murder of unarmed prisoners, manage to avoid justice.

Yet the United Nations' seven "Nuremberg Principles" hold that no accused war criminal in any place or position is above the law. What the Nuremberg judges really achieved, in fact, has never been more relevant. By rejecting group guilt and mass purges, the 1945 judges defied hatred and struck a blow for peace that may yet, half a century later, help temper the madness of war.

The Short-Lived Miracle of DDT

DDT was a savior in the 1940s and a curse by the 1960s. Its story shows how a technology that does enormous good can also do enormous harm.

By Darwin H. Stapleton

EARLIER THIS YEAR A GROUP OF journalists assembled by New York University voted *Silent Spring* (1962), by the ecologist Rachel Carson, the second most influential piece of American journalism of the twentieth century. Drawing on a wide range of scientific studies, Carson demonstrated to the public that DDT, the miracle chemical of World War II and the keystone of the World Health Organization's global antimalaria program in the 1950s, was less a benefit to humanity than a danger to the global ecosystem. Within a decade Carson's book and the movement it spawned led to the banning of DDT in the United States and in most other industrial countries. The meteoric rise and precipitous decline of DDT is at once an epic of human achievement in war, a dramatic chapter in the long struggle against malaria, and a cautionary story about the outcome of unbridled enthusiasm for new technology.

If not for the frantic search for an effective insecticide early in World War II, there might have been no story to tell. When the United States entered the war, scientists in the Office of Scientific Research and Development (OSRD) knew that one of the greatest threats to troops in wartime has always been disease, especially insect-transmitted diseases that thrive when thousands of people are thrown together in close quarters and new environments. Brig. Gen. Nathanael Greene learned that hard lesson in 1776,

when one-third of his Continental Army was stricken with louse-borne typhus during the Long Island campaign. Typhus was also an important factor in the defeat of Napoleon's Grand Army when it invaded Russia in 1812.

Typhus was an even greater problem in World War I. Millions of soldiers on the Eastern Front were infected, with large numbers dying from the disease. Even after the war, typhus devastated refugees and returnees throughout Eastern Europe. Mosquito-borne malaria was another serious problem in World War I. During the Salonika campaign the British had 162,000 soldiers unfit for combat because of malaria, compared with 28,000 killed or injured in battle. The French army at Salonika at one time had less than 20 percent of its troops ready for combat because of the same disease.

By the close of the War to End All Wars, it was unmistakably clear that insect-carried disease could be disastrous for armies. Yet two decades later none of the combatants entering the next world war had significantly improved their abilities to cope with insects. It was therefore no surprise to any informed observer when, in the first year after the United States entered World War II, the entire 1st Marine Division had to be withdrawn from the Pacific front because more than half its men had contracted malaria. This serious defeat, which occurred without enemy action, came in the summer of 1942, soon after

the OSRD had begun collaborating with the Agriculture Department's Bureau of Entomology and Plant Quarantine to find a way to control or eliminate battle-zone insects. The bureau's laboratory in Orlando, Florida, became the center for a program to test every known insecticide and insect repellent.

In 1942 the laboratory tried thousands of commercial and noncommercial chemicals and preparations, focusing mainly on lice, which seemed likely to be the greatest enemy. A few lice and a promising chemical would be put on a civilian volunteer's arm, in a sleeve firmly taped at each end. After 24 hours the sleeve was opened. If the lice had died, new ones were inserted, but no more insecticide was added. This process was repeated until the lice survived. Through most of 1942 only one product liked lice for as long as eight days: pyrethrum, a natural insecticide derived from tropical plants that is widely used today in spray insecticides. Unfortunately, the major sources of pyrethrum were found primarily in war-threatened areas of equatorial Africa and in other tropical areas occupied by enemy troops, such as Indonesia. Moreover, pyrethrum often irritated skin when it was applied directly.

The laboratory at Orlando kept trying every new concoction that came to its notice. Late in 1942 a new insecticide called Gesarol arrived from J. R. Geigy, a chemical dye com-

From *American Heritage of Invention & Technology,* Winter 2000, pp. 34–41. © 2000 by Forbes, Inc. Reprinted by permission of *American Heritage,* a division of Forbes, Inc.

pany in neutral Switzerland. Its active ingredient was dichlorodiphenyltrichloroethane—DDT, for short. The OSRD laboratory tagged the sample and tested it the same way it did everything else.

If the laboratory had known DDT's recent history, or if it had not already been jaded by the extravagant claims of some other commercial products, it might have pounced on DDT immediately. Geigy, a long-established firm in the city of Basel, had entered the insecticide field in 1935, when it assigned a team of chemists headed by Paul Hermann Müller to find a product for mothproofing woolens. After testing a wide variety of chemicals on household flies, Müller and his team hit upon DDT, which had first been synthesized by a German doctoral student nearly 80 years earlier but had gone unnoticed until it was rediscovered by Müller's chemists. They found that although DDT was not immediately lethal, it killed everything in a test box within 24 hours. Most distinctive of its properties was its uncanny persistence: It remained effective for days, even weeks, without reapplication.

In the late 1930s Müller and his team tried DDT on cockroaches, mosquitoes, and many agricultural pests. They found that it combined an excellent "knockdown" characteristic (the ability to kill insects on contact) with a superior residual effect (the ability to continue killing insects that landed on surfaces sprayed with the chemical). In 1940 Geigy began selling its new product, Gesarol (DDT at 5 percent strength), as a pesticide. The next year a dust with just a 1 percent concentration proved extremely effective in stopping an infestation of potato beetles in Switzerland. By 1942 a preparation named Neocid was being marketed as a louse killer. It was used with excellent results at Italian refugee camps on the Swiss border.

Because of Switzerland's neutrality, information on DDT was freely available to all the combatants in World War II. The German army made some use of DDT, spraying it in Greece and Yugoslavia to control mosquito larvae in an attempt to reduce the incidence of malaria. However, it was the Americans who most effectively exploited the new insecticide. In August 1942 about 100

DDT had an excellent "knockdown" characteristic (the ability to kill insects on contact) and a superior residual effect (the ability to continue killing).

kilograms of Gesarol (half of it 5 percent DDT spray and half of 3 percent DDT dust) had been exported from Switzerland to Geigy's subsidiary in New York via a neutral freighter from Portugal. Copies of some of the scientific reports soon followed.

Victor Froehlicher, the head of the Geigy office in New York, laboriously translated the reports into English. They described effects so far beyond those of any existing insecticide that he found them hard to believe. On October 16, 1942, he delivered his translation and a small quantity of Gesarol to an official at the Department of Agriculture in Washington. Following government policy on insecticide research, information about DDT was thereafter treated as a secret in the United States.

Gesarol passed the sleeve test with flying colors, killing lice for nearly three weeks without renewal. Better yet, it did not seem to irritate the skin, and it had no odor. Next DDT was tried in the Orlando countryside. In one remarkable instance the natural conditions of two neighboring ponds were surveyed, and then one pond was sprayed with DDT to kill mosquito larvae. A week later the scientists were puzzled to find that not only were the larvae in the first pond dead or dying, but those in the second pond were too. They realized that even the small quantity of DDT carried from one pond to the other by ducks and other waterfowl was enough to kill the insects.

The scientists now knew that they were dealing with an exceptionally powerful formula, and the OSRD gave the

development of DDT-laden insecticides a high priority. A range of concentrations were tested for the manufacture of louse powder, and a variety of solvents were tried for sprays, because by this time it was clear that the war in the Pacific would demand a massive malaria-control effort. One American general called malaria "an enemy more dangerous than the Japanese." At first DDT had to be imported from Switzerland, but as early as May 1943 a Geigy affiliate, the Cincinnati Chemical Works, started up a pilot plant. The chemical process for synthesis of DDT was not complicated, requiring the reaction of monochlorobenzene (C_6H_5Cl) and chloral hydrate ($CCl_3CH(OH)_2$) to form DDT ($CCl_3CH(C_6H_4Cl)_2$) and water, with sulfuric acid as a catalyst. Production was limited mostly by wartime bottlenecks in the availability of the basic ingredients.

The OSRD decided to experiment with widespread field tests before beginning regular military distribution. It turned to a nonmilitary organization, the Rockefeller Foundation, to carry out much of the fieldwork. Since its creation in 1913 by John D. Rockefeller, with an endowment that eventually reached $183 million, the foundation had become a global leader in public health work, particularly with regard to parasitic and insect-borne diseases. The foundation's public health program continued one that had been initiated by the Rockefeller Sanitary Commission (1909–12) and the International Health Board (1913–28). The program had first attacked hookworm infestation, an insidious "disease of laziness" that predominantly affected the poor in the rural Southern United States and workers on plantations and industrial settlements throughout the world.

In the 1920s and 1930s the foundation expanded its public health program to include yellow fever and malaria. One of its greatest efforts came in Brazil, where in the late 1930s foundation officers eradicated *Anopheles gambiae*, a yellow-fever-carrying mosquito species that had inadvertently been introduced from Africa. Soon after the beginning of World War II, but before

Pearl Harbor, the foundation created the Rockefeller Foundation Health Commission, composed of foundation staff who had substantial field experience. The commission formed a team that could be deployed in war-damaged regions threatened with epidemics or other public health problems.

When the United States entered World War II, the OSRD asked the Rockefeller Foundation to establish a laboratory to study lice. This louse lab was set up in New York City using staff from the Rockefeller Institute for Medical Research (now Rockefeller University). The laboratory started its work with a few lice scraped from a patient at Bellevue Hospital. It then began detailed studies of the insects' biology. In the fall of 1942, after breeding a few generations of the lice and ascertaining that they carried no diseases, samples were taken to New Hampshire to infect volunteers at a conscientious objectors' camp. The lab then sent a series of promising concoctions to the camp. Where they were tested both for their effectiveness in killing the lice and for any problems they might cause by coming in contact with skin. Testing there and in Mexico reinforced the finding that pyrethrum was an effective lousicide. Early tests of DDT in the summer of 1943 suggested that it was even more potent. But with Geigy's Cincinnati plant still working out its kinks, supplies remained limited. In any case, DDT's field effectiveness was yet to be proved.

After testing pyrethrum powder in two Egyptian villages in the spring of 1943, the commission moved its North African operations to newly liberated Algeria and Tunisia, where it worked with a branch of the Pasteur Institute in Tunis that had studied epidemic disease in the region since 1893. The scientific leader of this Rockefeller Commission unit was Dr. Fred Soper, an energetic, outspoken veteran of past Rockefeller public health campaigns. He was famous among malariologists for leading the foundation's successful antimosquito campaigns in Brazil a few years earlier. Among the strategies Soper employed there was the widespread and repeated distribution on water surfaces of Paris green, a salt containing copper and arsenic, to kill mosquito larvae. But Paris green is poisonous to humans and is only briefly effective. When Soper began to use DDT, he immediately recognized its superiority over other insecticides. For the next twenty years he energetically pushed DDT as an answer to malaria. But his first mission was to demonstrate the chemical's effect on lice, a program he drove forward relentlessly and with disdain for anyone who did not see the future as clearly as he did.

In June 1943 Soper and his commission and Pasteur Institute colleagues received their first supplies of DDT. They held their initial tests at the Maison Carrée prison in Algiers, where inmates were dusted with DDT and other insecticides currently used by the Allied forces. That fall DDT was given field tests in an Algerian town with a mixed Arab and European population and at a nearby prisoner-of-war camp. Among other factors, the studies aimed to find out whether DDT powder could be effective against lice when it was dusted into clothing through neck, arm, and leg openings. The commissioners thought this would be faster than requiring each person to disrobe, and they also recognized that in most cultures civilians would be reluctant to strip naked in front of strangers.

The lessons learned from these trials were put to dramatic use in December 1943, when the allied military command in Italy asked the commission to stop an incipient typhus epidemic in Naples. The American 5th Army had captured the city on October 1 and found public health conditions deplorable; by one estimate, 90 percent of the citizens had body lice. In the next month 25 cases of typhus were identified; 42 were found in November, and 60 in the first half of December. The Associated Press reported the crisis in the United States a few days later and said that a quarter of the cases had resulted in death. Although the troops had not suffered any typhus casualties, humanitarian concerns made it imperative for the Allies to act quickly.

When the Rockefeller Foundation Health Commission was called in, a large quantity of the current production of DDT was earmarked for Naples, with 60 tons dispatched immediately. Commission officers set up five delousing stations in the city, and on New Year's Day 5,000 civilians were dusted using a hand-operated blower that had been developed and modified in the North Africa trials. By the end of the month 1.3 million residents of Naples and the surrounding region had received insecticidal baths with DDT and pyrethrum. Typhus continued to fester in January, began to decline in February, and in March decreased abruptly to a few cases a day. The epidemic was over.

Nothing like this result had ever been seen before. From then on the British and American armies decreed that "DDT marches with the troops." It also proved vitally important in liberated German concentration camps, where by the spring of 1945 typhus had become rampant.

Important as these triumphs were, the fight against lice and typhus may ultimately have been less significant than the fight against mosquitoes and malaria. After the Allies liberated Rome and central Italy in June 1944, the Rockefeller Foundation Health Commission was asked to develop a malaria-control program, in part because the retreating German army had destroyed so much of the water-control system that drained low-lying and marshy areas. Some of the Rockefeller officers had experience with a pre-war Rockefeller Foundation antimalaria program in Italy and knew the terrain and the mosquito habitat quite well.

The commission decided that the most likely areas to suffer from malaria, and thus to impede the war effort in Italy, were the delta of the Tiber River (which included the post of Ostia, a major landing point for supplies for the Allied armies) and the Pontine marshes, which had historically been the source of malaria infestations for nearby Rome. In both areas the commission carried out massive DDT campaigns, hand-spraying the inside of houses and farm buildings and then moving on to swamps and bodies of water. This effort was the first time that DDT (mixed with kerosene or fuel oil) was sprayed from the air to distribute it quickly and widely. Some malaria developed, but there was no epidemic. As the European campaign continued, DDT was also used with effect in battle areas, first by spraying inside barracks and other military structures and then with aerial spraying of mosquito breeding zones near bases.

Now DDT, which had done much to secure victory for the Allies in Europe, had its turn in the Pacific. At first it was used in areas behind the lines, dispensed by hand sprayers. Soon, though, it was laid down in advance of landing forces, sprayed from airplanes over coastal zones so that the invading American forces would not have to worry about insects. With American production of DDT reaching two million pounds per month by the end of 1944 (it was now being manufactured by the giant Du Pont chemical company, among others), malaria was a minor problem in the last months of the war. Other diseases spread by insects were significantly affected by DDT as well. On Saipan, for example, an epidemic of dengue fever broke out soon after American troops landed in the late summer of 1944. It ended after a C–47 sprayed 9,000 gallons of a kerosene solution of DDT over the island.

With all these successes DDT came to public notice as one of the most important tools in the Allied arsenal after the official secrecy about it ended in July 1944, when Victor Froehlicher of Geigy's New York office published a thorough article about it in a chemical-industry magazine. A month later Britain, where DDT had been received, investigated, and manufactured at about the same pace as in the United States (but in smaller quantities), released a statement about its military uses. Many British civilians first heard of DDT from Winston Churchill on September 28, 1944, when, in one of his frequent radio messages, he rhapsodized about "the excellent DDT powder, which has been fully experimented with and found to yield astonishing results."

In the context of World War II's devastation, Churchill's enthusiastic assessment made perfect sense. Yet even in the glow of impending Allied victory, dis-

In wartime conditions, DDT's effectiveness made it indispensable. Yet even in the glow of impending Allied victory, disturbing evidence began to crop up.

turbing evidence had begun to crop up. In 1944 a government installation on a New Jersey island had been sprayed with DDT to rid it of annoying flies. This had worked, but along with the flies, the fish population had been drastically reduced. After the war, when spraying stopped on one Pacific island, mosquitoes returned in greater numbers than before because DDT had wiped out their natural predators. And worse news was on the way.

In 1946 reports from DDT-soaked Italy said that flies and mosquitoes were demonstrating resistance to the pesticide. By 1950 enough was known about DDT's possible ill effects on humans for the U.S. Food and Drug Administration to state that it was "extremely likely that the potential hazard of DDT has been underestimated." The FDA had studied DDT and found that it tended to accumulate in the fatty tissues of all animals, including humans. When used on dairy farms for fly control, it quickly showed up in cows' milk. The FDA also found that massive doses of DDT caused nerve damage, but it was impossible to determine the long-term effects of the low-level exposure most citizens would have.

These early hints of trouble scarcely affected the postwar juggernaut of pesticide production and distribution. In August 1945, just before the Japanese surrender, restraints on civilian sales of DDT ended in the United States, and it quickly spread to household and agriculture uses. Most people chalked up DDT's occasional problems to experience and figured that adjusting the con-

centration or the method of application would solve any problems. And even if a few animals might die, the improvements in the quality of human life far outweighed any small costs that might arise.

In the first flush of postwar giddiness, DDT, just like atomic energy and other wartime inventions, seemed a miracle. It was employed against the beetles that carried Dutch elm disease, and in a few years public health authorities were using it in mosquito-control programs throughout the country. Throughout the 1950s the use of DDT for malaria control expanded globally. First the Rockefeller Foundation led an experimental attempt to eradicate mosquitoes from Sardinia, and then the Pan-American Health Organization (led by the insecticide warhorse Fred Soper) and later the World Health Organization entered the fray. Early results were dramatic, as malaria infection rates fell sharply. The age-old scourge was virtually eliminated from the Southern United States; worldwide, reliable estimates suggest that DDT had prevented five million malaria deaths by 1950. In 1948 Müller was awarded a Nobel Prize for his work in discovering the wonder chemical.

As early as the mid-1950s, though, it became increasingly clear that DDT would not be the only answer to the problem of insect-carried disease. Mosquitoes were not being completely eradicated; in spite of four years of saturation spraying in Sardinia, they survived there. Moreover, insects of all types were developing resistance to DDT. While the common housefly was one of the most resilient, by 1960 some 137 species of insect pests were known to have some level of resistance. The World Health Organization stated in the 1960s that "resistance is at present the most important problem" in its insect-control programs.

But resistance was actually only part of the problem—the lesser part, as it turned out. More frightening was the steady accumulation of evidence that DDT was wreaking environmental damage on a large scale. Early fish kills following spraying raised concern, but it took some time for scientists to understand why the fish had died: some by

By 1960 some 137 insect species were known to have developed resistance to DDT. But resistance was only part of the problem—the lesser part, it turned out.

direct poisoning, but more because the DDT had killed off their food supply. Rachel Carson wrote about a massive DDT campaign to control a spruce budworm infestation in the watershed in the Canadian province of New Brunswick. Virtually all the young salmon were killed in a few days, largely because the insects in the water, on which they fed, were as susceptible to DDT as the winged insects it was aimed at.

Over the years, environmental testing revealed that DDT use had an even more insidious hazard, one that resulted from the very quality that made it so effective: its persistence. Because it deteriorated very slowly, DDT was not just killing insects but was spreading far up the food chain. By the time *Silent Spring* appeared, in 1962, there were signs that some birds of prey, particularly fish eaters, were seriously affected by environmental DDT. Bald eagles and ospreys—large, beautiful, soaring birds whose nests were familiar landmarks in coastal waters and inland lakes—had been driven close to extinction.

As early as 1947 observers found these birds producing few or no young in areas where a few years before each nest had regularly yielded one or two fledglings. Eventually scientists found evidence that DDT accumulation had interfered with the egg-making process. In some cases none at all were laid; in others, eggs were produced but were so fragile that sitting adults crushed them. Public outcry about the endangerment of the bald

eagle, a national symbol, was a major reason DDT was banned in the United States in 1972. (By then, of course, epidemics of insect-borne disease were mostly a thing of the past in this country.) Since the ban, ospreys and other birds of prey threatened with extinction have managed to restore their numbers.

In other parts of the world, DDT is still a primary insecticide, and eliminating it is less simple. In fighting the scourge of malaria, which has been resurgent in the last quarter-century, DDT is far more affordable and effective than anything else available. About two dozen developing nations (including China, India, and Mexico), which together account for nearly half the world's population, still use DDT for house-spraying campaigns. A United Nations organization has been moving to get DDT banned worldwide within the next decade, but the Malaria Foundation International, an organization of more than 350 doctors and scientists, vehemently opposes such a quick cutoff.

The foundation argues that since malaria kills 2.7 million people a year, the price in human life of such a ban would be too high, especially since the amounts of DDT being used today are much lower than in the past. (Spraying all the high-risk houses in a nation the size of Guyana, for example, requires no more DDT in a year than would once have been used on a thousand-acre cotton field.) So there may be unavoidable public health reasons to continue using DDT for nonagricultural purposes for at least a while longer.

The pesticide story is not just a matter of DDT use, however. One billion pounds of pesticides and herbicides will be used by American farmers in 1999, and against all the benefits that they bring must be balanced the serious environmental damage they will cause. Approximately 67 million wells in the United States are contaminated by pesticides in some degree. Worldwide, after a half-century of heavy use of DDT and its successors, at least 535 insects have demonstrated resistance to insecticides.

Alternatives to artificial pesticides are being examined seriously and ap-

plied extensively in agriculture, though the situation in disease control is less promising. The use of predatory insects to control pest species has grown rapidly, and scientists are researching naturally occurring pesticides. In March 1999, for example, a newspaper reported that the federal government's Agricultural Research Service had found that "the natural oil that gives peaches their perfume also kills fungus and other pests in the soil."

None of these alternatives is likely to be a safe, all-purpose magic bullet, any more than DDT was. Insect immunity will continue to crop up, and for many applications the simplicity and killing power of artificial pesticides will make them hard to resist. As choices proliferate, however, and scientists, farmers, and the general public gain an ever-deeper understanding of the intricate web of life that makes up the global ecosystem, we can hope that ways will be found to keep damage to nontarget species to a minimum and to ensure that there is no cost in human life.

In early 1999 motorists heading east near Orlando on I-4 could see a row of tall power-line towers, each fitted with a platform at the top to encourage osprey nesting. There were a dozen or more platforms, and on almost every one was a pair of osprey, newly arrived from their Caribbean wintering grounds. Their presence creates at least a partial closing of the circle. In the place where DDT was first introduced into the American environment, one of the species believed to be most seriously threatened by it has made a strong comeback. The Jekyll-and-Hyde chemical that saved soldiers, sailors, marines, and civilians in World War II and served as a potent weapon against malaria, is now fading from the global ecosystem that found it to be an unprecedentedly serious intrusion.

Darwin H. Stapleton is the director of the Rockefeller Archive Center in Sleepy Hollow, New York.

Unit 5

Key Points to Consider

❖ To what extent was the Marshall Plan an altruistic act by the United States?

❖ What did the Korean War accomplish? Was it worth it?

❖ Who has the right to control Tibet—China or Tibet?

❖ The "Powell Doctrine" allows for fighting only over a vital national interest. Was there a vital national interest in Korea? Vietnam?

❖ When should the United States interfere in the sovereignty of others?

❖ At the time, some people thought that Francis Gary Powers should have blown up the U-2 and killed himself. Should he have done that?

❖ Is there any solution to the problem of Jerusalem, in your opinion? Explain.

❖ What happened at Chornobyl? Why is it remembered? Compare the disaster at Chornobyl with that of DDT (see "The Short-Lived Miracle of DDT," unit 4).

❖ How did the cold war end? Why did the cold war never become a "hot" war between the superpowers?

DUSHKIN ONLINE Links   www.dushkin.com/online/

These sites are annotated on pages 4 and 5.

Following World War II, it became apparent to leaders of the West that they would have trouble with the Soviet Union. In 1946, Winston Churchill, the wartime prime minister of Great Britain, warned about the descent of an "iron curtain" across central Europe and the spread of communism. American leaders calculated that the economic distress of war-torn Europe provided fertile ground for communism and persuaded the Congress and Secretary of State George Marshall to sponsor an aid program to provide a means for the countries of Europe to restore their economies. The plan, the Marshall Plan, worked and is considered an unprecedented act of generosity, as explained in "The Plan and the Man."

Although the major struggle of the cold war involves the competition between two superpowers, the United States and the Soviet Union, there were other troublesome events in the world. In 1951, the Chinese annexed Tibet and began to assimilate its culture into that of China. The world grumbled, but no one opposed the move. "Tibet Through Chinese Eyes" explains that this struggle over culture continues in Tibet. Also, the United Nations created Israel in 1947 as a refuge for the world's Jewish peoples. This enraged the Muslims of the region and continues to be a major problem today. There have been a series of Arab-Israeli wars and various schemes to divide Jerusalem, the heart of the trouble. The city is sacred to both religions and no division plan has been accepted.

In the struggle between the United States and the Soviet Union, the competition never came to a direct confrontation that escalated into warfare. With the cold war in the background, however, the United States fought in Korea and Vietnam while the Soviet Union fought in Afghanistan. In Korea the attempt by the North to subdue the South was blocked by a United Nations army consisting mainly of United States troops. For the United States, which prided itself on never having lost a war, the conflict ended where it began, along the 38th parallel line. It was a limited war with an unstable conclusion, as described in "Korea: Echoes of a War" by Steven Butler.

The U.S. defeat in Vietnam was also bitter, but the military leaders learned some lessons about the prosecution of warfare in the contemporary world. "Vietnam's Forgotten Lessons" traces the changes in military thinking that led to a spectacular success against Iraq. These lessons have been neglected, however, in other places of U.S. intrusion such as Somalia and Kosovo. The United States was also embarrassed when the Soviet Union managed to shoot down a U-2 spy plane over Soviet territory. "The Day We Shot Down the U-2" describes the event through the eyes of the son of the Soviet leader, Nikita Khrushchev. The event delayed a U.S–USSR rapprochement.

Meanwhile, although it made spectacular achievements in space exploration and in building a nuclear arsenal, a long-running war in Afghanistan drained the energy of the Soviet Union. In 1986, its nuclear power plant at Chornobyl blew up, spreading radioactive pollution in Eastern Europe. "Ten Years of the Chornobyl Era" describes the lasting effects of this accident. The cold war, however, came to an end in the late 1980s to early 1990s with a change of attitude in the Soviet Union, as Vladimir Batyuk notes in "The End of the Cold War: A Russian View." The Berlin Wall came down in 1989 and the Soviet Union fell to pieces in 1991.

The Era of the Cold War, 1950–1990

The Plan and the Man

*High vision and low politics: how George Marshall and a few good
men led America to an extraordinary act of strategic generosity.*

By Evan Thomas

DURING THE WINTER OF 1946–47, the worst in memory, Europe seemed on the verge of collapse. For the victors in World War II, there were no spoils. In London, coal shortages left only enough fuel to heat and light homes for a few hours a day. In Berlin, the vanquished were freezing and starving to death. On the walls of the bombed-out Reichstag, someone scrawled "Blessed are the dead, for their hands do not freeze." European cities were seas of rubble—500 million cubic yards of it in Germany alone. Bridges were broken, canals were choked, rails were twisted. Across the Continent, darkness was rising.

Americans, for the most part, were not paying much attention. Having won World War II, "most Americans just wanted to go to the movies and drink Coca-Cola," said Averell Harriman, who had been FDR's special envoy to London and Moscow during the second world war. But in Washington and New York, a small group of men feared the worst. Most of them were, like Harriman, Wall Street bankers and diplomats with close ties to Europe and a long view of America's role in the world. They suspected that in the Kremlin, Soviet dictator Joseph Stalin was waiting like a vulture. Only the United States, they believed, could save Europe from chaos and communism.

With sureness of purpose, some luck and not a little finagling, these men persuaded Congress to help rescue Europe with $13.3 billion in economic assistance over three years. That sum—more than $100 billion in today's dollars, or about six times what America now spends annually on foreign aid—seems unthinkable today. Announced 50 years ago next week, the European Recovery Program, better known as the Marshall Plan, was an extraordinary act of strategic generosity. How a few policymakers persuaded their countrymen to pony up for the sake of others is a tale of low politics and high vision.

Yet their achievement is recalled by many scholars as a historical blip, a moment of virtue before the cold war really locked in. A truer, if more grandiloquent, assessment was made by Winston Churchill. The Marshall Plan, and England's war leader from his retirement, was "the most unsordid act in history."

It was, at the time, a very hard sell. The men who wanted to save Europe—Harriman, Under Secretary of State Dean Acheson, diplomats like George Kennan—were unelected and for the most part unknown. They needed a hero, a brand name respected by ordinary Americans. They turned to George C. Marshall.

His name would bring blank stares from schoolchildren today, but Marshall, the army's highest-ranking general in World War II, was widely regarded then as the Organizer of Victory. "He is the great one of the age," said President Harry Truman, who made Marshall secretary of state in January 1947. Upright, cool to the point of asperity ("I have no feelings," he said, "except those I reserve for Mrs. Marshall"), Marshall made worshipers of his followers. Dean Acheson described his boss walking into a room: "Everyone felt his presence. It was a striking and communicated force. His figure conveyed intensity, which his voice, low, staccato and incisive, reinforced. It compelled respect. It spread a sense of authority and calm." Though self-effacing and not prone to speechifying, Marshall used a few basic maxims. One was "Don't fight the problem. Decide it."

Without hesitation, Marshall gave his name and authority to the plan to rescue Europe. His only advice to the policymakers: "Avoid trivia." The unveiling came in a commencement speech at Harvard on June 5, 1947. Wearing a plain business suit amid the colorful academic robes, Marshall was typically plain-spoken and direct: "Our policy," he said, "is not directed against any country or doctrine, but against hunger, poverty, desperation and chaos."

THE RESPONSE IN THE AMERICAN press was tepid, but the leaders of Europe were electrified. Listening to the address on the BBC, British Foreign Minister Ernest Bevin regarded Marshall's speech as a "lifeline to a sinking man." Bevin immediately headed for Paris to urge the French to join him in grabbing the rope.

Marshall did not want Washington to appear to be dictating to its allies. "The initiative, I think, must come from Europe," he had said at Harvard. But the Europeans fell to squabbling. The French, in particular, were wary of reviving Germany. "The Plan? There is no plan," grumbled George Kennan, the diplomat sent to Paris that summer of 1947 to monitor the talks. The Europeans were able to write shopping lists, but nothing resembling an overall program. In a cable to Marshall, Kennan predicted that the United States would listen, "but in the end, we would not *ask* them, we would just *tell* them what they would get."

First, however, Marshall's men had to persuade Congress to provide the money. In October, President Truman tried to appeal to America's sense of sacrifice, urging Americans to eat less chicken and fewer eggs so there would be food for starving Europeans. Urged to "waste not," some schoolchildren formed "clean-plate clubs," but that was about as far as the sacrificial zeal went. Members of Congress were profoundly wary. Bob Lovett, another Wall Streeter who replaced Acheson in the summer of 1947 as under secretary, managed to win over Senate Foreign Relations Committee chairman Arthur Vandenberg, mostly by feeding him top-secret cables over martinis at cocktails every night. But many lawmakers regarded foreign aid as "Operation Rathole," and viewed the rescue plan slowly taking shape at the State Department as a "socialist blueprint." Said Charles Halleck, the Republican leader in the House: "I've been out on the hustings, and I know, the people don't like it."

Clearly appealing to good will was not going to suffice. It was necessary, then, to scare the voters and their elected representatives. As it happened, Russia growled at just the right moment. In the winter of 1948, Moscow cracked down on its new satellite state of Czechoslovakia. Jan Masaryk, the pro-Western foreign minister, fell—or was pushed—to his death from his office window in Prague. At the Pentagon, the generals worried that Soviet tanks could begin to roll into Western Europe at any moment. The atmosphere in Washington, wrote Joseph and Stewart Alsop, the hawkish establishment columnists, was no longer "post-war." It was now "pre-war."

In fact, the fears of Soviet invasion were exaggerated. We now know that after World War II the Red Army began tearing up railroad tracks in Eastern Europe because Stalin feared an attack by the West against the Soviet Union. Exhausted by a war that cost the lives of 20 million Russians, the Kremlin was not ready to wage another. Because of poor intelligence, Washington did not fully appreciate Russia's weakness. Top

policymakers were aware, however, that the hysteria was exaggerated, that war was unlikely. Even so, they were not above using scare tactics in a good cause—like winning congressional approval of the Marshall Plan. Sometimes, said Acheson, "it is necessary to make things clearer than the truth."

Frightened by the talk of war, urged to recall that isolationism after World War I succeeded only in producing World War II, Congress waved through the European Recovery Plan that spring. In April the SS John H. Quick sailed from Galveston, Texas, with 19,000 tons of wheat. Before long, there were 150 ships every day carrying food and fuel to Europe. There were new nets for the fishermen of Norway, wheat for French bakers, tractors for Belgian farmers, a thousand baby chicks for the children of Vienna from 4-H Club members in America.

Politics, needless to say, sometimes interfered with altruism. Some congressmen tried to turn the Marshall Plan into a giant pork barrel, voting to send Europeans the fruits of their districts, needed or not. From Kentucky and North Carolina poured millions of cigarettes; from the Midwest arrived thousands of pounds of canned spaghetti, delivered to gagging Italians. In London drawing rooms, there was some resentment of the heavy American hand. "Our Uncle, who art in America, Sam be thy name/Thy Navy come, they will be done," went one ditty. In Paris, fearful for the purity of the culture (and the sale of wine), the French National Assembly banned the sale, manufacture and import of Coca-Cola.

A MERICAN AID HAD A DARKER side. The Marshall Plan provided the CIA with a handy slush fund. To keep communists from taking over Italy (a genuine threat in 1948), the CIA began handing out money to Italian politicians. At first, the agency had so little money that America's gentlemen spooks had to pass the hat in New York men's clubs to raise cash for bribes. But with the Marshall Plan, there was suddenly plenty of "candy," as CIA official E. Howard Hunt called it, to tempt European politicians and labor leaders.

The CIA's meddling looks sinister in retrospect (though it seemed essential in 1948, when policymakers feared Stalin could start a revolution in Italy and France "just by picking up the phone"). The actual impact of the aid is also a source of dispute. Some economists have argued that the plan played only a superficial role in Europe's recovery. They point to Europe's pent-up innovation and restorative will. But the fact is that from 1938 to 1947 the standard of living in Europe had been declining by about 8 percent a year. After the arrival of the first Marshall aid, the arrows all turned up. Europe's per capita GNP rose by a third between 1948 and 1951. American technicians brought know-how to Europe and reaped enormous good will.

Perhaps America's best export was hope. The Marshall Plan arrived at a time of despondency as well as hardship. Forced to work together, Europeans overcame some historic enmities while America shed its tradition of peacetime isolationism. Ties strengthened by the Marshall Plan evolved into the Western Alliance that stood fast until communism crumbled of its own weight in the Soviet Union. Some of the men who made the Marshall Plan possible saw the romantic and epic quality of their task. It was "one of the greatest and most honorable adventures in history," wrote Dean Acheson. His friend and successor at State, Bob Lovett, had a more practical view: the Marshall Plan was that rare government program that came in on budget, accomplished its goal—and then ended.

The men who made the Marshall Plan were practical, and their motivations can be regarded coldly as a matter of economics and power. But they also wanted to act because they believed that saving Europe was the right and only thing to do. They achieved that rarity among nations—a bold act by one that benefited all.

NEWSWEEK *Assistant Managing Editor Evan Thomas is coauthor of "The Wise Men," a history of six friends who shaped postwar American foreign policy.*

Korea: echoes of a war

After 50 years, is it time for real peace?

By Steven Butler

Big anniversaries rarely coincide with genuinely important events. Yet this week, the leaders of North and South Korea will meet for the first time ever, 50 years to the month after North Korean troops opened a massive artillery barrage and then stormed across the 38th parallel in a drive that nearly obliterated South Korea. The meeting is more than symbolic. For decades, North Korea refused to talk directly to South Korea because the Seoul government never signed the armistice that halted fighting between belligerents—United Nations forces led by the United States on one side, North Korean and Chinese forces on the other. When North Korean leader Kim Jong Il meets as an equal with South Korean President Kim Dae Jung, it will be an admission of sorts that war is finally over and that South Korea is a reality that can't be wished away.

Even so, 50 years of combat and military stalemate have left unsolved the main issue of the Korean War: how to restore unity to an ancient nation that was divided as a tragic afterthought at the end of World War II. As Japan prepared to surrender in August 1945, two American Army colonels, Dean Rusk (later President Kennedy's secretary of state) and Charles H. Bonesteel, were ordered to find a place to divide the Korean Peninsula. Within 30 minutes, they chose the 38th parallel as the spot where Soviet troops, coming south to accept the surrender of Japanese troops, would meet the American troops moving north. No one imagined it would become a permanent border. The Soviets helped establish a Stalinist-style dictatorship in Pyongyang under the leadership of Kim Il Sung.

Meanwhile, America struggled with only partial success to establish a democracy under Syngman Rhee in half a nation whose civil infrastructure and society were torn apart by 35 years of harsh Japanese colonial rule. In fact, America gave up the job as hopeless. America withdrew its occupation troops in 1949, and public and private statements by Secretary of State Acheson and military leaders suggested that the United States had resigned itself to watching all of Korea fall under Soviet influence. Who would have dreamed that a civil war launched by North Korea to reunify its homeland would have brought a massive response involving at its peak almost a quarter of a million U.S. troops and contributions from 19 other United Nations members? Certainly not Kim Il Sung nor Soviet dictator Joseph Stalin, who hesitantly gave the nod to Kim's war plans.

Collision course. America assumed—erroneously, historians say—that the invasion launched on June 25, 1950, was part of a communist master plan involving eventual expansion of communist China and a Soviet move into Western Europe. As a result, with little consideration for the consequences, President Truman ordered the 7th Fleet into the Taiwan Strait. That thwarted plans by Chinese communists to end the Chinese civil war by launching an amphibious assault against Taiwan, where remnants of Chiang Kai-shek's Nationalist Army had taken refuge. And it put China and America on a collision course from which they have yet to veer.

Of course, Truman also ordered U.S. troops into Korea, with approval from the U.N. Security Council after the So-

VIEW FROM MOSCOW

Why Stalin thought the U.S. would stay out

The Korean War might never have happened—or might have turned out quite differently—if the Soviet Union and the West had accurately gauged each other's intentions.

President Truman and his advisers reacted to the North Korean invasion on June 25, 1950, as a direct challenge to the United States by Joseph Stalin. But in the post-Soviet 1990s, archives revealed that the push actually came from North Korean President Kim Il Sung, who pestered Stalin with 48 telegrams seeking approval for an attack. Stalin refused many times, then finally gave his assent in January 1950.

But why did he change his mind? Since the Soviet dictator didn't have to explain himself to anyone, historians could only guess. Now they know for sure: Stalin, who wanted anything but a head-on confrontation with Washington, believed the United States would not respond. "According to information coming from the United States, it is really so," he told Kim, during an April 1950 meeting in Moscow, where the plan took shape. "The prevailing mood is not to interfere." The U.S. mood was reinforced, Stalin said, by the Soviet Union's successful A-bomb test the previous August. One can only imagine what might have happened if Washington had warned in advance it would resist a thrust into South Korea, says historian Kathryn Weathersby, who has studied the new evidence for the Woodrow Wilson Center's Cold War International History Project.

Miscalculation. The summary of the critical Stalin-Kim talks, contained in documents from Moscow's tightly guarded Presidential Archive, may refuel an old controversy. Secretary of State Dean Acheson notably excluded South Korea from the U.S. "defense perimeter" in a National Press Club speech on Jan. 12, 1950. Redbaiters later accused him of helping precipitate the invasion. But Acheson was merely citing Truman's policy. And the "information" Stalin alluded to was apparently the U.S. Asia policy document itself, NSC 48. Moscow would have known about it thanks to British spy Donald Maclean. Stalin cited another reason why Korea could be unified by force: the Chinese Communists' victory over the Nationalists. It was a sign of Western weakness and freed Mao's revolutionaries to help in Korea if need be.

Stalin made another major blunder. The original war plan called for an advance on the Ongjin Peninsula, which would bring a response from the South. Claiming it had been attacked first, the North would then launch the full invasion. "The war should be quick.... Southerners and Americans should not have time to come to their senses," Stalin told Kim. The U.S.S.R. would not participate directly, he said. But on June 21, four days before the war was to start, Stalin received a telegram from his ambassador in Pyongyang, warning that the South had learned of the plan. Stalin replied the same day, agreeing to Kim's proposal for an all-out attack across the 38th parallel. The World War II-style blitzkrieg virtually ensured that the West would respond, Weathersby says. Respond it did. While that's history, it may hold a lesson for dealing with tomorrow's dictators.

—Warren P. Strobel

viet delegate foolishly boycotted the proceedings. Inexperienced soldiers on soft duty in Japan were airlifted to Pusan, from where they formed Task Force Smith and raced north to block the southern advance of North Korean troops. They failed to halt the unexpectedly disciplined and well-equipped North Korean Army, and were forced into a chaotic retreat, sometimes dropping equipment on the run.

Yet Task Force Smith slowed the enemy's advance, giving America crucial extra days to move supplies and men through the port of Pusan. A wide defensive perimeter around the city held against repeated assaults from North Korean troops. Full relief came on September 15, when Gen. Douglas MacArthur launched a risky but technically brilliant assault at the port of Inchon, near Seoul, where tides as high as 30 feet seemed to make a big amphibious landing impossible. Military historians still debate whether the Inchon landing was actually necessary from a military standpoint or whether it was instead another example of MacArthurian showboating. But American troops succeeded in cutting supply and retreat lines of the overextended North Korean Army and broke the back of the invasion.

It was MacArthur's last triumph. The overconfident general sent U.S. troops north of the 38th parallel toward the Chinese border, despite warnings from China that it would enter the war on the North's side. And he blundered tactically by allowing his forces to become separated by the mountain range running down the spine of Korea. Chinese "volunteers" began infiltrating the border in late October and moved down the center of the peninsula before launching a massive counterattack in November, forcing U.S. troops into yet another disorderly retreat at a huge cost of men and equipment. It was the longest U.S. military retreat in history.

"American Caesar." In less than six months, the city of Seoul had changed hands no less than three times. U.N. forces regrouped and charged north again, but on reaching the 38th parallel, few were willing to risk going farther north again. Few, that is, except MacArthur, who threatened China with attack in public defiance of Truman's policies. Truman fired MacArthur for insubordination, causing a political uproar at home, where MacArthur was revered as a World War II hero, an "American Caesar," as biographer William Manchester called him. The war ground on—World War I style—with huge, bloody battles from entrenched positions over relatively small tactical objectives, places dubbed Heartbreak Ridge and Pork Chop Hill.

Failure to bring the war to an early close may have cost the Democrats the presidential election in 1952, and President-elect Eisenhower made good his pledge to visit Korea. Eisenhower hinted he might expand the war, perhaps even using atomic weapons. Then Stalin died, and negotiators at last settled the final issue that had held up armistice for several years: whether prisoners of war could choose repatriation or not. A committee from neutral nations screened POWs, with 23 Americans and 14,704 Chinese choosing not to go home.

Americans were anxious to forget the war and to enjoy the long economic boom of the 1950s. Yet the war changed the world, and America, in ways that few people appreciate today. For one, it was America's first taste of military defeat, and its first experience of limited warfare, where outright victory was deemed too costly an objective. The wartime demand helped restore Japan's economy, devastated by its defeat in World War II, and made the former enemy into a strategic partner in Asia. It was the first of many military interventions under the United Nations flag. It also was the event that first turned the Cold War hot, swiftly reversing the cuts in U.S. military spending that had left U.S. forces unprepared to fight. An enormous military buildup followed: Military spending nearly quadrupled in three years, and the ranks of the armed forces more than doubled from 1.5 million to 3.5 million.

And yet, the war really settled nothing—36,516 Americans and millions of Koreans and Chinese dead just to agree on an existing demarcation line. North Korea survives as perhaps the most repressive government in the world, a lone Stalinist state that embraces central planning, threatening the world with long-range missiles while its own people starve in a horrendous famine. South Korea evolved tortuously into a proud and prosperous democracy. And Korea is still divided, with over a million heavily armed men on both sides of the 38th parallel. Taiwan, too, remains dangerously estranged from China. This week's Korean summit could prove a modest step to resolving a Cold War that has ended almost everywhere else in a victory for democracy and free-market capitalism.

Tibet
Through Chinese Eyes

Many Chinese working in Tibet regard themselves as idealistic missionaries of progress, rejecting the Western idea of them as agents of cultural imperialism. In truth, they are inescapably both

by Peter Hessler

Political views on Tibet tend to be as unambiguous as the hard blue dome of sky that stretches above its mountains. In Western opinion, the "Tibet question" is settled: Tibet should not be part of China; before being forcibly annexed, in 1951, it was an independent country. The Chinese are cruel occupiers who are seeking to destroy the traditional culture of Tibet. The Dalai Lama, the traditional spiritual leader of Tibet, who fled to India in 1959, should be allowed to return and resume his rule over either an independent or at least a culturally autonomous Tibet. In short, in Western eyes there is only one answer to the Tibet question: Free Tibet.

For Han—ethnic Chinese—who live in Tibet, the one answer is exactly the same and yet completely different. They serve what the Chinese call "Liberated Tibet." Mei Zhiyuan is Han, and in 1997 he was sent by the Chinese government to act as a "Volunteer Aiding Tibet" at a Tibetan middle school, where he works as a teacher. His roommate, Tashi, is a Tibetan who as a college student

was sent in the opposite direction, to Sichuan province, where he received his teacher training. Both men are twenty-four years old. They are good friends who live near Heroes Road, which is named after the Chinese and Tibetans who contributed to the "peaceful liberation" of Tibet in the 1950s. This is how Mei Zhiyuan sees Tibet—as a harmonious region that benefits from Chinese support. When I asked him why he had volunteered to work there, he said, "Because all of us know that Tibet is a less developed place that needs skilled people."

I went to Tibet to explore this second viewpoint, hoping to catch a glimpse of the Tibet question through Chinese eyes. Before coming to Tibet, I had spent two years as a volunteer English teacher at a small college in Sichuan, which made me particularly interested in meeting volunteer teachers like Mei Zhiyuan. I also talked with other young government-sent workers and entrepreneurs who had come to seek their fortunes, and for four weeks that was my focus,

as I spent time in Lhasa and other places where there are large numbers of Han settlers.

Of all the pieces that compose the Tibet question, this is by far the most explosive: the Dalai Lama has targeted Han migration as one of the greatest threats to Tibetan culture, and the sensitivity of the issue is evident in some statistics. According to Beijing, Han make up only three percent of the population of the Tibet Autonomous Region, whereas some Tibetan exiles claim that the figure is in fact over 50 percent and growing. Tibetans see the influx of Han as yet another attempt to destroy their culture; Chinese see the issue as Deng Xiaoping did in 1987, when he said, "Tibet is sparsely populated. The two million Tibetans are not enough to handle the task of developing such a huge region. There is no harm in sending Han into Tibet to help. . . . The key issues are what is best for Tibetans and how can Tibet develop at a fast pace, and move ahead in the four modernizations in China."

Regardless of the accuracy of the official Chinese view, many of the government-sent Han workers in Tibet clearly see their role in terms of service. They are perhaps the most important historical actors in terms of the Tibet question, and yet they are also the most-often overlooked. Why did they come to Tibet? What do they think of the place, how are they changing it, and what do they see as their role?

Gao Ming, a twenty-two-year-old English teacher, told me, "One aspect was that I knew we should be willing to go to the border regions, to the minority areas, to places that are *jianku*—difficult. These are the parts of China that need help. If I could have gone to Xinjiang, I would have, but I knew that Tibet was also a place that needed teachers. That was the main reason. Another aspect was that Tibet is a natural place—there's no pollution here, and almost no people; much of it is untouched. So I wanted to see what it was like."

Shi Mingzhi, a twenty-four-year-old physics teacher, said, "First, I'd say it's the same reason that you came here to travel—because it's an interesting place. But I also wanted to come help build the country. You know that all of the volunteers in this district are Party members, and if you're a Party member, you should be willing to go to a *jianku* place to work. So you could say that all of us had patriotic reasons for coming—perhaps that's the biggest reason. But I also came because it was a good opportunity, and the salary is higher than in the interior of China."

Talking with these young men was in many ways similar to talking with an idealistic volunteer in any part of the world. Apart from the financial incentive to work in Tibet, many of the motivations were the same—the sense of adventure, the desire to see something new, the commitment to service. And government propaganda emphasizes this sense of service, through figures like Kong Fansen, a cadre from eastern China who worked in Tibet and became famous as a worker-martyr after his death in an auto accident. Han workers are exhorted to study the "old Tibet spirit" of Kong and other cadres as they

serve a region that in the Chinese view desperately needs their talents.

Central to their task is the concept of *jianku*. I heard this term repeatedly when the Chinese described conditions in Tibet, and life is especially *jianku* for Volunteers Aiding Tibet, who commit in advance to serving eight-year terms. Most government-sent Han workers fall into the category of Cadres Aiding Tibet—teachers, doctors, administrators, and others who serve for two or three years. Having graduated from a lower-level college, Mei Zhiyuan could not qualify for such a position, and as a result was forced to make an eight-year commitment. The sacrifice is particularly impressive considering that he assumed it would have serious repercussions on his health. Many Chinese believe that living at a high altitude for long periods of time does significant damage to the lungs, and a number of workers told me that this was the greatest drawback to living in Tibet. "It's bad for you," Mei Zhiyuan explained, "because when you live in a place this high, your lungs enlarge, and eventually that affects your heart. It shortens your life." During my stay in Tibet I heard several variations on this theory (one from an earnest young teacher who was smoking a cigarette), but generally it involved the lungs expanding and putting pressure on the heart. There is no medical evidence to support such a belief; indeed, in a heavily polluted country like China, where one of every four deaths is attributed to lung disease, the high, clean air of Tibet is probably tonic. Nevertheless, this perception adds to the sense of sacrifice, and it is encouraged by the government pay structure, which links salary to altitude: the higher you work, the higher your pay.

The roughly 1,000 yuan ($120) a month that Mei Zhiyuan earns is half what the local cadre teachers make. Even so, his salary is two to three times what he would make as a teacher in rural Sichuan, and he is able to send half his earnings home to his parents, who are peasants. It's good money by Chinese standards but seems hardly a sufficient incentive for a young man to be willing to shorten his life. Leaving before his eight years are up would incur

a heavy fine of up to 20,000 yuan— $2,400, nearly two years' salary, or, for a peasant family like Mei Zhiyuan's, approximately twenty tons of rice.

THE DREAM OF A UNIFIED MOTHERLAND

FROM the Chinese perspective, Tibet has always been a part of China. This is, of course, a simplistic and inaccurate view, but Tibetan history is so muddled that one can see in it what one wishes. The Chinese can ignore some periods and point to others; they can cite the year 1792, when the Qing Emperor sent a Chinese army to help the Tibetans drive out the invading Nepalese, or explain that from 1728 to 1912 there were Qing *ambans*, imperial administrators, stationed in Lhasa. In fact the authority of these *ambans* steadily decreased over time, and Tibet enjoyed de facto independence from 1913

The Chinese investment of both human and financial capital in Tibet complicates the Tibet question in ways few outsiders realize.

to 1951. An unbiased arbiter would find Tibetan arguments for independence more compelling than the Chinese version of history—but also, perhaps, would find that the Chinese have a stronger historical claim to Tibet than the United States does to much of the American West.

Most important, China's reasons for wanting Tibet changed greatly over the years. For the Qing Dynasty, Tibet was important strictly as a buffer state; *ambans* and armies were sent to ensure that the region remained peaceful, but they made relatively few administrative changes, and there was no effort to force the Tibetans to adopt the Chinese language or Chinese customs. In the Qing view, Tibet was a part of China but at the same time it was something different; the monasteries and the Dalai Lamas were allowed to maintain authority over most internal affairs.

In the early twentieth century, as the Qing collapsed and China struggled to overcome the imperialism of foreign powers, Tibet became important for new reasons of nationalism. Intellectuals and political leaders, including Sun Yat-sen, believed that China's historical right to Tibet had been infringed by Western powers, particularly Britain, which invaded Tibet in 1904 to force the thirteenth Dalai Lama to open relations. As Tibet slipped further from Chinese control, a steady stream of nationalistic rhetoric put the loss of Tibet into a familiar pattern—the humiliation by foreign powers in the nineteenth and early twentieth centuries, as Hong Kong went to the British, Manchuria and Shandong to the Japanese, Taiwan to the U.S.-funded Kuomintang. By the time Mao Zedong founded the People's Republic of China, in 1949, Tibet had figured into the nation's pre-eminent task: the reunification of the once-powerful motherland.

Tibet thus changed from buffer state to a central piece in Communist China's vision of itself as independent and free from imperialist influence. Orville Schell, a longtime observer of China, says that even today this perception is held by most Chinese. "I don't think there's any more sensitive issue," he says, "with the possible exception of Taiwan, because it grows out of the dream of a unified motherland—a dream that historically speaking has been the goal of almost every Chinese leader. This issue touches on sovereignty, it touches on the unity of Chinese territory, and especially it touches on the issue of the West as predator, the violator of Chinese sovereignty."

The irony is that China, like an abused child who grows up to revisit his suffering on the next generation, has committed similar sins in Tibet: the overthrow of the monasteries and the violent redistribution of land, the mayhem of the Cultural Revolution, and the restriction of intellectual and religious freedom that continues to this day. And

as in any form of imperialism, much of the damage has been done in the name of duty. When the Chinese speak of pre-1951 Tibet, they emphasize the shortcomings of the region's feudal-theocratic government: life expectancy was thirty-six years; 95 percent of Tibetans were illiterate; 95 percent of the population was hereditary serfs and slaves owned by monasteries and nobles. The sense is that the Tibetans suffered under a bad system, and the Chinese had a moral obligation to liberate them. Before traveling to Tibet, I asked my Chinese friends about the region. Most responded like Sai Xinghao, a forty-eight-year-old photographer: "It was a slave society, you know, and they were very cruel—they'd cut off the heads of their slaves and enemies. I've seen movies about it. If you were a slave, everything was controlled by the master. So, of course, after Liberation the rich lords opposed the changes [instituted by the Chinese]. It's like your America's history, when Washington liberated the black slaves. Afterward the blacks supported him, but of course the wealthy class did not. In history it's always that way—it was the same when Napoleon overthrew King Louis, and all of the lords opposed Napoleon because he supported the poor."

My friend is not an educated man, but many Chinese intellectuals make the same comparison. President Jiang Zemin made a similar remark during his 1997 visit to the United States (although he correctly identified Lincoln as the Great Liberator). The statistics about Tibetan illiteracy and life expectancy are accurate. Although the Chinese exaggerate the ills of the feudal system, mid-century Tibet was badly in need of reform—but naturally the Tibetans would have much preferred to reform it themselves.

Another aspect of the Chinese duty in Tibet is the sense that rapid modernization is needed, and should take precedence over cultural considerations. For Westerners, this is a difficult perspective to understand. Tibet is appealing to us precisely because it's not modern, and we have idealized its culture and anti-materialism to the point where it has become, as Orville Schell says, "a

figurative place of spiritual enlightenment in the Western imagination—where people don't make Buicks, they make good karma."

But to the Chinese, for whom modernization is coming late, Buicks look awfully good. I noticed this during my first year as a teacher in China, when my writing class spent time considering the American West. We discussed western expansion, and I presented the students with a problem of the late nineteenth century: the Plains Indians, their culture in jeopardy, were being pressed by white settlers. I asked my class to imagine that they were American citizens proposing a solution, and nearly all responded much the way this student did: "The world is changing and developing. We should make the Indians suit our modern life. The Indians are used to living all over the plains and moving frequently, without a fixed home, but it is very impractical in our modern life. . . . We need our country to be a powerful country; we must make the Indians adapt to our modern life and keep pace with the society. Only in this way can we strengthen the country."

Virtually all my students were from peasant backgrounds, and like most Chinese, the majority of them were but one generation removed from deep poverty. What I saw as freedom and culture, they saw as misery and ignorance. In my second year I repeated the lesson with a different class, asking if China had any indigenous people analogous to the Plains Indians. All responded that the Tibetans were similar. I asked about China's obligation in Tibet. The answers suggested that my students had learned more from American history than I had intended to teach. One student replied, "First, I will use my friendship to help [the Tibetans]. But if they refuse my friendship, I will use war to develop them, like the Americans did with the Indians."

THE TWO SIDES OF SUPPORT

REGARDLESS of China's motivations, and regardless of its failures in Tibet, the drive to de-

Outsiders—many of them Sichuanese—dominate Tibet's economy. Of the sixteen restaurants at the entrance to the Lhasa airport, only one was Tibetan.

velop the region has been expensive. According to Beijing, more than 200,000 Han workers have served in Tibet since the 1950s. Taxes in Tibet are virtually nonexistent; Tibetan farmers, unlike those in the interior, receive tax-free leases of land, and a preferential tax code has been established to encourage business. Low-interest loans are available, and business imports from Nepal are duty-free. Despite the dearth of local revenues, government investment is steadily developing a modern infrastructure. From 1952 to 1994 the central government invested $4.2 billion in the region, and in 1994 Beijing initiated sixty-two major infrastructure projects for which the eventual investment is expected to be more than $480 million. It is estimated that more than 90 percent of Tibet's government revenue comes from outside the region.

This investment of both human and financial capital complicates the issue of Tibet in ways that few outsiders realize. Foreign reports often refer to the exploitation of Tibetan resources as a classic colonial situation, which is misleading. Although Beijing is certainly doing what it can with Tibet's timber and mineral reserves, China spends an enormous amount of money in the region, and if self-sufficiency ever comes, it will not come soon. Tibet does have significant military value: the Chinese do not want to see it under the influence of a foreign power such as India, but not even this would seem to merit the enormous investment. In 1996 China spent some $600 million in Tibet. One foreign observer who has studied the region puts this in perspective: "For that same year

the United States gave a total of eight hundred million dollars in aid to all of Africa. That's all of Africa—we're talking about hundreds of millions of people. In Tibet there are only two and a half million. So if they become independent, who's going to be giving them that kind of money?"

"Unless you're a complete Luddite," Orville Schell says, "and don't believe in roads, telephones, hospitals, and things like that, then I think China must be credited with a substantial contribution to the modern infrastructure of Tibet. In this sense Tibet needs China. But that's not to diminish the hideous savageness with which China has treated Tibet."

Almost every aspect of Chinese support has two sides, and education illustrates the point well. I met a number of young Han teachers like Mei Zhiyuan, who were imbued with a sense of service: they were conscientious, well-trained teachers, and they were working in places with a real need for instructors. One volunteer was teaching English at a middle school where the shortage was so acute that many students had to delay the start of their English studies until the following year, when additional Han teachers were expected to arrive. I visited one district in which out of 230 secondary-school teachers, sixty were Han, and many of the Tibetan instructors had been trained in the interior at the Chinese government's expense. Such links with the interior seem inevitable, given that the Chinese have built Tibet's public education system from scratch. Before they arrived, in 1951, there were no public schools in Tibet, whereas now there are more than 4,000.

Likewise the schools I saw were impressive facilities with low student fees. In one town I toured the three local middle schools; two of them were newly built, with far better campuses than I was accustomed to seeing in China. The third school, whose grounds featured massive construction cranes fluttering with prayer flags, was being refurbished with the help of a $720,000 investment from the interior. Unlike students at most Chinese schools, those at the local No. 1 Middle School paid no tuition, and even high school students, who gen-

erally pay substantial amounts in China, had paid at most $70 a semester, including board. Everything possible was being done to encourage students to stay in school: a student's tuition and boarding charge were cut in half if only one parent worked, and transportation to and from the remote nomad areas was often free.

In a poor country such policies are impressively generous; essentially, Tibetan schools are better funded than Chinese schools. And this funding is sorely needed: the adult illiteracy rate in Tibet is still 52 percent. Only 78 percent of the children start elementary school, and of those only 35 percent enter middle school. But Chinese assistance must be considered in the context of what's being taught in the schools—a critical issue for Tibetans.

One morning I visited an elementary school on a spacious, beautiful campus, with new buildings and a grass playground that stretched westward under the shadow of a 14,000-foot mountain. Most of the school's 900 students were Tibetan. I paused at the central information board, where announcements were written in Chinese.

The board detailed a $487,800 investment that had been made by a provincial government in the interior, and displayed a short biography of Zu Chongzhi, a fifth-century Chinese mathematician. Next to this was a notice telling students to "remember the great goals." They were urged to work on doubling China's GNP from its 1980 level, and they were reminded that by 2050 China needed to achieve a GNP and a per capita income ranking in the middle of developed countries. Beside these goals was a long political section that read, in part,

> We must achieve the goal of modern socialist construction, and we must persevere in building the economy. We must carry out domestic reform and the policy of opening to the outside world.... We must oppose the freedom of the capitalist class, and we must be vigilant against the conspiracy to make a peaceful evolution toward imperialism.

It was heavy stuff for elementary school students (and indeed, if I were a

Chinese propagandist, I would think twice before exhorting Tibetan children to resist imperialism), and it indicates how politicized the climate of a Chinese school is. Despite all the recent economic changes in China, the education system is still tied to the past. This conservatism imbues every aspect of education, starting with language. Two of the schools I visited were mixed Han and Tibetan, and classes were segregated by ethnicity. The reasons here are linguistic: most Tibetan children don't start learning Mandarin until elementary school, and even many Tibetan high school students, as the Han teachers complained, don't understand Chinese well. This segregation leads to different curricula—for example, Tibetan students have daily Tibetan-language classes, whereas Han students use that time for extra English instruction. To the Chinese, this system seems fair, especially since Tibetan students have the right to join the Han classes.

But Tibetans feel that there is an overemphasis on Chinese, especially at the higher levels, which threatens their language and culture. All the classes taught by Han teachers are in Chinese or English, and most of the Tibetan teachers in the middle and high schools are supposed to use Mandarin (although the ones I spoke with said they often used Tibetan, because otherwise their students wouldn't understand). In any case, important qualifying exams emphasize Chinese, and this reflects a society in which fluency is critical to success, especially when it comes to any sort of government job. Another, more basic issue is that Tibetan students are overwhelmed. One Han teacher told me that his students came primarily from nomad areas, where their families lived in tents; yet during the course of an average day they might have classes in Tibetan, Chinese, and English, three languages with almost nothing in common.

Political and religious issues are paramount. In Lhasa I met a twenty-one-year-old Tibet University student who was angered by his school's anti-religious stance, which is standard for schools in Tibet. "They tell us we can't believe in religion," he said, "because we're supposed to be building socialism,

and you can't believe in both socialism and religion. But of course most of the students still believe in religion—I'd say that eighty to ninety percent of us are devout." One of his classmates, a member of the Communist Party, complained about the history courses. "The history we study is all Chinese history [of Tibet]," he said. "Most of it I don't believe." These students also adamantly opposed existing programs that send exceptional Tibetan middle and high school students to study in the interior, where there is nothing to offset the Chinese view of Tibet.

Such complaints reflect the results of recent education reforms. A series of them made in 1994, characteristically, represent both the good and the bad aspects of Chinese support. On the one hand, the government stepped up its campaign against illiteracy, and on the other, it resolved to control the political content of education more carefully, in hopes of pacifying the region. There has certainly been some success with this approach: I met a number of educated Tibetans who identified closely with China. Tashi, Mei Zhiyuan's roommate, seemed completely comfortable being both Tibetan and Chinese: he had studied in Sichuan, he had a good job, and he had the government's support to thank. When I asked him what was the biggest problem in Tibet, he mentioned language—but not in the way many Tibetans did. "So many [Tibetan] students can't speak Chinese," he said, "and if you can't speak Chinese, it's hard to find a good job. They need to study harder."

Most Tibetans seemed less likely to accept Chinese support at face value. But it was clear that politically they were being pulled in a number of directions at once, and my conversations with educated young Tibetans were dizzying experiences. Their questions ranged from odd ("Which do you think is going to win, capitalism or socialism?") to bizarre ("Is it true that in America when you go to your brother's or sister's house for dinner, they charge you money?"), and the surroundings were often equally unsettling. One Monday morning I watched the flag-raising ceremony at a middle school, where students

and staff members lined up to listen to the national anthem, after which, in unison, they pledged allegiance to the Communist Party, love for the motherland, and dedication to studying and working hard. With the Tibetan mountains towering above, it was a surreal scene—and it became all the more so when the school's political adviser, a Tibetan in his early thirties with silver teeth, walked over and asked me where I was from. After I told him, he said, "Here in Tibet we already have a lot of influence from your Western countries—like Pepsi, Coke, movies, things like that. My opinion is that there are good and bad things coming from the West. For example, things regarding sex. In America, if you're married and you decide that you want another lover, what do you do? You get a divorce, regardless of how it affects your wife and child. But the people here are very religious, and we don't like those kinds of ideas."

I heard a number of comments like this, and undoubtedly the education system included a great deal of anti-America propaganda. I felt that here the Chinese were almost doing the Tibetans a service; nothing depressed me more than my conversations with less-educated Tibetans, who invariably had great faith in American support and believed that President Clinton, who was then in China on last year's state visit, had come in order to save Tibet. Considering that China's interest in Tibet is largely a reaction to foreign imperialism, it's no surprise that nothing makes the Chinese angrier and more stubborn than the sight of the Dalai Lama and other exiled leaders seeking—and winning—support in America and elsewhere. And yet Tibetan

More than 90 percent of Tibet's government revenue is generated outside the region. If self-sufficiency comes to Tibet, it will not come soon.

faith in America seems naive given America's treatment of its own indigenous people, and because historically U.S. policy in Tibet has been hypocritical and counterproductive. For example, the CIA trained and armed Tibetan guerrillas in the 1950s, during a critical period of mostly peaceful (if tenuous) cooperation between the Dalai Lama and the Chinese. The peace ended when Tibetan uprisings, in which these guerrillas played a part, resulted in brutal Chinese repression and the Dalai Lama's flight to India.

America also represents modernity, and a further complication, beyond the Chinese political agenda, is that the long-isolated Tibetan society must come to grips with the modern world. One college student said, "The more money we Tibetans have, the higher our living standard is, the more we forget our own culture. And with or without the Chinese, I think that would be happening."

SICHUANESE ON THE FRONTIER

PERHAPS the most hopeful moment in recent Han-Tibetan relations came shortly after 1980, when the Chinese Party Secretary, Hu Yaobang, went on a fact-finding mission to Tibet and returned with severe criticisms of Chinese policies. He advocated a two-pronged solution: Chinese investment was needed to spur economic growth in Tibet, but at the same time the Han should be more respectful of Tibetan culture. Cadres needed to learn Tibetan; the language should be used in government offices serving the public; and religion should be allowed more freedom.

There's no question that such respect is sorely needed, especially with regard to language. I never met a single government-sent Han worker who was learning Tibetan—not even the volunteers who would be there for eight years. And in Lhasa at the Xinhua bookstore, the largest in the city, I found not one textbook for Chinese students of Tibetan—books for foreign students, yes, but nothing for the Chinese.

Some of the 1980 reforms were implemented, but they were cut short by a series of riots in Lhasa that started in 1987. To Beijing hardliners, the riots indicated that too much freedom is a bad thing, and in 1987 Hu Yaobang was purged, partly for his recommendations regarding Tibet. By the spring of 1989 martial law had been declared in Tibet, and the Chinese concluded that relaxing restrictions on Tibetan culture and religion was tantamount to encouraging unrest. The two-pronged solution was quickly cut in half: Beijing would simply develop the economy, hoping that rising standards of living would defuse political tensions while building closer economic ties with the interior. This policy has been accelerated by the enormous investments of the 1990s.

Development, however, often comes at the cost of culture. Traditional sections of Lhasa are being razed in favor of faceless modern buildings, and the economic boom is attracting hordes of Han and Hui (an Islamic minority) migrants to Tibet.

Outsiders dominate Tibet's economy—indeed, they've essentially built it, inspiring enormous resentment among the Tibetan population. I met some Tibetans who didn't mind that cadres were sent from the interior, but I never met one who wasn't opposed to the influx of migrant workers, especially the huge numbers of Han from nearby Sichuan. Longtime Han residents, too, felt this was a serious problem.

The phenomenon of *liudong renkou*, or "floating population," is affecting urban areas all across China, with some 100 million people seeking work away from home. In the west and south there are particularly large numbers of Sichuanese in the floating population, and during my travels I often heard the same prejudices: the Sichuanese migrants are uncultured, their women loose, their men *jiaohua*, sly. And worst of all, people complained, they keep coming.

Having spent two years in Sichuan, I understand why the Sichuanese so often leave. Their province, roughly the size of France, contains 120 million people, and the economy is so shaky that recent factory closings have led to

worker uprisings in some cities. Mostly the Sichuanese leave because they aren't afraid to; they have been toughened by tough conditions, and all across China that is another thing they are famous for: their ability to *chiku*—eat bitter. They work and they survive, and like successful migrants anywhere else in the world, they are resented for their success.

In Tibet the Sichuanese have helped themselves to a large chunk of the economy. This was clear from the moment I arrived at the Lhasa airport, where thirteen of the sixteen restaurants bordering the entrance advertised Sichuan food. One was Tibetan. Virtually all small business in Lhasa follows this pattern; everywhere I saw Sichuan restaurants and shops. Locals told me that 80 percent of Lhasa's Han were Sichuanese, and this may not be much of an exaggeration.

This influx is far more significant and disruptive than the importing of Han cadres, and it's also harder to monitor. One common misperception in Western reports is that these people are sent by the government: the image is of a tremendous Han civilian army arriving to overwhelm Tibetan culture. The truth is that the government has little control over the situation. "How do you cut off the people moving out there?" asked one American who had spent much time in Tibet. "What mechanism are you going to have to prevent that? They don't have any restrictions on internal travel—and we always beat them over the head about not having those, because to institute them would be a human-rights issue."

Far from arriving with an ethnic agenda, the independent migrants are for the most part completely apolitical. In Lhasa I often ate at a small Sichuan restaurant run by Fei Xiaoyun, a thirty-one-year-old native of Chengdu who, along with her husband, had been laid off in 1996 by a bankrupt state-owned natural-gas plant. Each of them had been given a two-year severance allowance of $30 a month, and when that was gone, they took their savings and bought plane tickets to Lhasa. They had left their five-year-old son with his grandmother—a common choice for migrants, including cadres. This is partly out of fear of the effects on health of living in Tibet, and also because Tibetan schools are considered worse than those in the interior and children who are registered outside their districts have to pay extra fees.

Fei Xiaoyun never spoke of the growth of the GNP, and she had no interest in developing the motherland. Once, I asked her about Prime Minister Zhu Rongji, whose economic reforms are closing factories like hers, and she didn't even recognize his name. "All of the country's big affairs I don't understand," she said with a shrug. She was simply a poor woman with her back against the wall, and like the rest of the Sichuanese who had made their way to Tibet, she was trying desperately to make a living.

But such migrants have a political effect, as Tibetans watch outsiders develop an economy from which they feel increasingly removed. This also presents a question: If the rules are the same for everybody, why are the Han entrepreneurs so much more successful than the Tibetans? The most common response is that the rules aren't the same: the Chinese have easier access to government *guanxi*, or connections. But even on a level playing field the Han would have more capital and better contacts with sources in the interior. And their migrant communities have a tendency to support recent arrivals. This is especially true of the Sichuanese—one will arrive, and then a few relatives, and before long an extended family is dominating a factory or a block of shops. In front of the Jokhang, the holiest temple in Tibet, rows of stalls sell *khataks*, ceremonial scarves that pilgrims use as offerings. It's a job one would expect to see filled by Tibetans—as one would expect those selling rosaries in front of St. Peter's to be Catholic. But one saleswoman explained that all the stalls were run by Sichuanese from three small cities west of Chengdu. There were more than 200 of them—relatives, friends of relatives, relatives of friends—and they had completely filled that niche.

One day I walked past the *khatak* sellers with a Tibetan friend, and he shook his head. "Those people know how to do business," he said. "We Tibetans don't know how to do it—we're too straight. If something's supposed to

be five yuan, we say it's five yuan. But a Sichuanese will say ten." I felt there was some truth to this—the Han are successful in Tibet for some of the same reasons that they are successful in so many places, from Southeast Asia to the United States. They have a stronger business tradition than the Tibetans, and virtually all independent Han settlers in Tibet have failed somewhere else, giving them a single-minded drive to succeed.

Consequently, Tibet feels like a classic frontier region, with typically peculiar demographics. There are disproportionately few Han children, and almost nobody comes to stay: the intention is invariably to return to the interior. The majority of the Han are men, including the government-sent workers. Of the Han women I saw in Tibet, more than a few were prostitutes; locals told me that they had come in a wave in 1994 and 1995, after the investments in the sixty-two major projects. One Han volunteer I spoke with had arrived in a group of thirteen men; one woman had applied but was rejected because the authorities felt that Tibet was no place for a young woman. The young man was resigned to finding a wife during his three paid trips home. "During vacation I'll be able to look for a girlfriend," he said. "I'll have six months. You can meet one then, and after that you can write and all when you come back here."

There were moments when everything—the ethnic tension, the rugged individualism, the hard, bright sun and the high, bare mountains—seemed more like a Jack London story than a real society. One day some American friends and I hired a driver, a twenty-five-year-old Sichuanese named Wei, who was nursing a defeated 1991 Volkswagen Santana. He had a two-year-old son at home, and he hoped to earn enough money by carrying passengers— though he wasn't registered to do so—to buy a new car in six months. We agreed to pay him $36 if he drove us to Damxung, five hours north of Lhasa. Drive he did—past the police checkpoint, where he faked his credentials ("It's simpler that way," he explained), and past a Land Rover full of foreigners driven by a Tibetan, who, realizing our driver wasn't

registered, swore he'd turn him in at Damxung. "It's because I'm Han," Wei said grimly. "And at Damxung the police will be Tibetan." He drove faster and faster, racing ahead of the Land Rover, until finally he hit a bump and ruptured the fuel line.

The car eased to a stop in the middle of nowhere. To the west rose the snow-topped Nyenchen Tanglha Mountains. The Tibetan driver cruised past, glaring. Wei cut a spare hose and patched the leak, and then he addressed the problem of injecting fuel back into the carburetor. He unhooked the fuel line and sucked out a mouthful of gas. Holding it in his mouth, he plugged the line back in. Then he walked around the front of the car and spit the fuel into the carburetor.

The car started. I could see Wei working the taste of gasoline around his mouth, and then, a few minutes later, he took out a cigarette. Everybody in the car held his breath—everybody but Wei, who lit the cigarette and sucked deeply. He did not explode. He stared ahead at the vast emptiness that stood between him and $36, and he kept driving.

That was the way a Sichuanese did things in Tibet. Gasoline was bitter but he ate it, the same way he ate the altitude and the weather and the resentment of the locals. None of that mattered. All that mattered was the work he did, the money he made, and the promise that if he was successful, he'd go home rich.

A HOUSE WITHOUT PILLARS?

TIBET gave rise to exciting stories, but it was indeed *jianku*, and the social problems made a hard place even harder. Near the end of my trip I ate dumplings at Fei Xiaoyun's restaurant, and as I ate, she complained about her situation. Business was bad, and her life was boring; she worked fifteen-hour days and she had no friends in Lhasa. She missed her son, back in Chengdu, and she probably wouldn't see him until the following year. She asked me how long it had been since I'd been home, and I said I hadn't left China in more than two years.

"We're the same," she said. "Both of us are a long way from home." I agreed, and she asked if I missed my family. "Of course I miss them," I said. "But I'll see them next month, when I go home."

It was the wrong thing to say. Her eyes went empty and then filled with tears. We sat alone in the restaurant. It was unusual for a Chinese to show emotion in public, and I didn't know what to say. Silently I ate my dumplings while she cried, the late-afternoon sun stirring the Lhasa flies that were thick about the table.

Tibet had started to depress me, and I was looking forward to leaving. Strangely, it almost seemed worse for not being as bad as I had always heard. There were definite benefits of Chinese support, and I was impressed by the idealism and dedication of some of the young Han teachers I had met. But at the same time, most efforts to develop the region were badly planned, and it was frustrating to see so much money and work invested in a poor country and so much unhappiness returned. And often I felt that the common people, who knew little of Tibet's complicated historical and cultural issues, were being manipulated by the government in ways

they didn't understand. But although I was certain that nobody was truly happy (most of the Han didn't like being there, and most of the Tibetans certainly weren't happy to have them), I wasn't sure who was pulling the strings. One could go straight to the top and probably find the same helplessness, the same strings. It was mostly the irrevocable mistakes of history, but it was also money—simple economic pressure that drove a mother away from her son to a place where the people did not want her.

This was not the first time I'd seen somebody cry in Lhasa. Five days earlier I'd spent the evening in front of the Jokhang temple, where I talked with two Tibetans. The first was a doctor who had done time in prison for writing an article warning Tibetans to protect their culture, and the second was a fifty-three-year-old who described himself as a common worker. Both men were eager to speak with an American, and they had a great deal of faith in America's ability to help solve the Tibet question. That saddened me as well. I wanted to tell them that in America there are many FREE TIBET bumper stickers, but they sit next to license plates that often bear the names of forgotten tribes who succumbed to the same forces of expansion and mod-

ernization now threatening Tibet. And the Chinese solution to the Tibet question—throwing money at the problem—also seemed very American. But I held my peace and listened.

"Look at this pillar," the worker said. He was standing next to the temple entrance, and he rested his hand on the worn red wood. "If a house doesn't have pillars, or if the pillars aren't straight, what will happen? It will fall down. It's the same thing here—our pillars are our history and our politics. If we don't have those, our society will collapse, and all of it will be lost—all of our culture."

It was dark, and I could barely make out his face, but I could see there were tears in his eyes. There was no more politically sensitive place in Tibet; virtually every major protest had happened in front of the Jokhang, and I knew it was unwise to speak so openly here. He glanced over his shoulder and continued.

"You need to tell the people of America what it's like here," he said. "You need to tell them what needs to be done." I nodded and shook his hand, but I realized I had no idea what I would recommend, or what the people of America could do. Perhaps we could build casinos.

The Day We Shot Down the U-2

*Nikita Khrushchev's son remembers a great turning point of the Cold War,
as seen from behind the Iron Curtain*

By Sergei Khrushchev

ON MAY 1, 1960, A SOVIET V-750 surface-to-air missile (known in America as the SA-Z "Guideline") shot down a U-2, one of the "invulnerable" American spy planes. The plane was a phantom—of all the secret projects of those years, perhaps the most secret. Even now, when it seems there are no secrets left, not everything connected with the U-2's last mission can be explained from the standpoint of normal human logic.

In the 1950s, years of deep freeze in the Cold War, politicians and ordinary people on both sides were gripped by the same fear: that the opposing side, whether Moscow or Washington, would seize the opportunity to deal the first, and possibly last, nuclear strike. At the 1955 Geneva meeting of the four powers—the U.S.S.R., the United States, Great Britain, and France—President Eisenhower presented his Open Skies proposal, which called for planes of the opposing blocs to fly over the territories of probable adversaries in order to monitor their nuclear arms.

Father, by then the dominant figure in the Soviet leadership, immediately rejected the idea. This made his negotiating partners intensely suspicious. They reasoned that the Soviet Union must be hiding something very dangerous. In fact, Father had the opposite motivation. The Soviets' secret was that they had nothing to hide. Father feared that the West might be tempted to launch a nuclear strike if it learned how weak its opponent really was.

Father brought home an attractive yellow brochure advertising Open Skies, which Eisenhower had given him in Geneva. Handing it to me to look over, he praised the achievements of modern technology. The photographs were indeed impressive. Taken from an altitude of six miles, the first showed the overall plan of a city; in the next you could distinguish houses, and in the next, cars. Finally in the last you could make out the murky figure of a man reclining on a lounge chair in the courtyard of his home reading a newspaper. The capabilities of American photo technology

firmly convinced Father that we must not allow American planes in our skies.

His rejection had little effect on plans in Washington. The U-2, the most advanced and high-level spy plane, which flew high enough to render it well nigh invulnerable to other aircraft, anti-aircraft guns, and surface-to-air missiles, was waiting for the go-ahead to make its first flight over Soviet territory.

The U-2 was a masterpiece of aviation technology, the pride of the Lockheed Company, and it brought deserved worldwide fame to Kelly Johnson, its designer. Its first mission was to be a prolonged flight over western regions of Soviet territory. If the Soviets ventured something similar with respect to the United States, it would be considered an attack, Eisenhower realized. Yet he approved the flight, for CIA officials had insisted that it could not yet cause a confrontation, because the plane would pass almost invisibly over Soviet territory, like a phantom. They believed the Russians weren't capable of making a breakthrough in radar and at best could only slightly improve on the American and British units they'd been supplied with during the war, which couldn't detect targets higher than nine miles. In addition, the plane would fly so high that Soviet missiles and fighter planes couldn't reach it.

The CIA timed the U-2's inaugural flight to coincide with America's national holiday, July 4, 1956. Charles Bohlen, the American ambassador in Moscow, had some general knowledge of the project, but he didn't suspect that the first flight would happen right when Khrushchev, as the embassy's guest at a holiday reception, was proposing a toast to the health of President Dwight Eisenhower.

The plane had actually crossed the Soviet border early in the morning. Father was immediately informed but didn't hurry to do anything. First we had to investigate, to consider the consequences before taking any action. He, like Bohlen, revealed nothing at the reception and joked and chatted, even though he was fuming inside.

After the first U-2 flight, Father felt the Americans must be chortling over our impotence.

The Geneva conference had appeared to give hope for a gradual (Father didn't nourish any illusions) transition from armed confrontation to, if not co-operation, at least peaceful coexistence. Therefore, such a demonstrative violation of international rules of propriety stunned Father. And the U-2 flights, especially that first one, produced more than just shock in the Soviet leadership; they profoundly influenced the policies of subsequent years.

What I remember most vividly in connection with that U-2 flight and the ones that followed later in the week was Father's reluctance to complain to the U.S. government. He felt the Americans must be chortling over our impotence and that diplomatic protest would only

add to their pleasure. Nevertheless, a protest note was sent to Washington, to show that the U-2 had failed to be invisible. Eisenhower, concerned, summoned the CIA's director, Allen Dulles, and forbade further flights over Soviet territory without the President's personal permission. Still, Eisenhower did not rule them out altogether.

Meanwhile Father summoned everybody who might be able to do something: Artyom Mikoyan, Pyotr Grushin, Andrey Tupolev, Pavel Sukhoi, and other designers of interceptors and anti-aircraft missiles. What most worried Father was the possibility that the intruder could carry an atomic bomb. The specialists categorically rejected the idea. Tupolev explained that we could be certain we were dealing with a structure built at the very edge of what was possible. In such a case, weight was calculated in grams, and the plane could not carry any substantial payload. In technology everything is interrelated and there are no miracles, so the American plane must resemble a dragonfly: a very narrow fuselage and long, thin wings. The maximum weight it could lift would be a camera, and not a big one at that. When we saw a real U-2 four years later, it turned out to be exactly like the picture drawn by the great designer.

The entire Soviet air defense system was geared to shooting down mass-produced bombers flying at about the speed of sound and at an altitude of six to eight miles. But Mikoyan and Sukhoi, both designers of interceptors, were optimistic that the new challenge could be met. Still, it would take time: three or four years of intensive work.

That didn't satisfy Father; he asked for a faster solution. Several weeks later Mikoyan came back proposing an acrobatic trick: Planes would fly to their top speeds and then use their accumulated energy to launch themselves upward. This maneuver was called, in Russian, "exit onto a dynamic ceiling" and was not considered especially difficult, but no one had ever tried it in combat. Luck would be more important than skill, since a fighter plane is almost uncontrollable in the stratosphere. Two grains of sand would have to meet in the infinite skies.

Father grasped at this straw, and the best pilots began to train. They tried the maneuver several times, but the U-2 pilots apparently never even noticed, although the method did set altitude records that were widely publicized in hopes of frightening off the Americans.

U-2s flew over the Soviet Union in 1957, 1958, and 1959—not often, but they flew. In 1959 anti-aircraft defense units began to receive new fighter planes—Sukhoi Su-9 interceptors—and missile defense forces were given new V-750 anti-aircraft missiles. Spy flights became dangerous for American pilots, but the CIA insisted they be continued.

At Camp David during Father's 1959 visit, the President expected him to bring up the subject of the U-2 flights and protest them. But Father didn't want to give his hosts the satisfaction of hearing him beg them not to peer into his bedroom.

The President may have interpreted Father's silence as a sign that he had made his peace with the situation. At any rate we will probably never understand why Eisenhower gave permission for the U-2 flight on the threshold of a crucial four-power meeting that was to be held in Paris the next May—a meeting that would be important to him, to his place in history, and to the cause of peace.

The first flight in that fatal series occurred on April 9. The plane came in from the direction of Pakistan. It was detected at 4:47 A.M., when it was 150 miles from the Afghan border and already deep inside Soviet territory. It flew unhindered to Semipalatinsk, where it photographed a nuclear testing ground, and then went toward Lake Balkhash to investigate an air defense missile site. Strenuous efforts were made to intercept it—one of which cost Capt. Vladimir Karachevsky his life when his MiG-19 lost altitude and crashed into a forest—but the target escaped, and the Soviet side said nothing.

The next flight was planned for May 1, one of the most important holidays in the Soviet Union. It would be the twenty-fourth U-2 spy mission over Soviet territory and follow a route already tested in May of 1957. From Peshawar, Francis Gary Powers would head toward

Tyura-Tam and then on to Sverdlovsk or, more precisely, to Chelyabinsk-40, a center of nuclear industry, photographing military airfields along the way. Then he was to proceed to Plesetsk, where launch sites for intercontinental missiles were being built. From Plesetsk it would be a stone's throw to Norway and the airfield at Bodo.

That morning Father appeared in the dining room right after eight o'clock. He looked gloomy, obviously not in a holiday mood. He sat at the table in silence. There was only the sound of his spoon clinking against the sides of his glass of tea, which he drank hurriedly, anxious to leave for the Kremlin, where the other members of the Central Committee Presidium were already gathered. Apparently something serious had happened.

I got up to accompany him to the car. Music could be heard beyond the high stone fence of the residence. Loudspeakers on Vorobyovskoye Highway were turned on full blast. Father usually drove us all to the Kremlin on holidays, but this time we had to get there on our own.

At the gate he finally shared the news. "They flew over again. The same place."

"How many?" I asked.

"As before, just one. It's flying at a very high altitude. This time it was detected while it was still on the other side of the border. [Defense Minister] Malinovsky called me at dawn, around six o'clock."

That was all Father knew.

I reached Red Square at about nine-thirty and began searching the VIP stands for Ivan Dmitriyevich Serbin, head of the Central Committee's Defense Industry Department. He told me the following: The intruder had reached Tyura-Tam without interference, maneuvered to obtain the best camera angles to shoot the ICBM test site there, and then flown on to the north. He was apparently heading toward Sverdlovsk.

"But why wasn't he shot down over Tyura-Tam?" I asked.

Serbin just waved his hand. "Something always happens in our Air Defense Command. Now they'll write explanations. The holiday . . ."

"So he might escape," I lamented.

"Yes, he might," responded Ivan Dmitriyevich.

"But how will we know?"

"Biryuzov is at his command center. After Sverdlovsk he'll come and let us know what has happened."

The country's Air Defense command center, located near the Kremlin, had been tracking the intruder from the border. Sergei Biryuzov, the Air Defense commander, sat behind a large table, facing a map of the whole country. The plane was being moved across the map in short hops by a sergeant sitting behind the screen. Every few minutes he was given new data on the intruder's coordinates, speed, and altitude.

To the left of the commander in chief sat Marshal Yevgeny Savitsky, Air Defense aviation commander. To Biryuzov's right was Col.-Gen. Pavel Kuleshov, in charge of anti-aircraft artillery and missiles. Staff officers milled around behind them.

The plane drew away from Tyura-Tam and turned north and slightly west. Anti-aircraft missile batteries around Sverdlovsk were alerted to wait for their target, but aircraft would initiate the operation.

Savitsky had not managed to find out from his subordinates what was going on with those aircraft. He knew that MiG-19s flown from Perm were being quickly refueled, but Su-9 pilots had not yet been found. Finally he was told that one of the Su-9 pilots, Capt. Igor Mentyukov, had been caught at the last moment at a Perm bus stop. He had been brought to headquarters on the double and was stunned to receive an order to take off at once. The adversary's plane was approaching at a high altitude, and their only hope rested on the Su-9 and on him.

Mentyukov tried to explain that the plane was not armed, that he was not ready to fly, and that the target would pass the city before he was suited up. The general reported this to Moscow. A categorical order came back from Savitsky: Take off immediately in whatever you're wearing and ram the intruder.

This meant certain death. "Take care of my wife and mother!" Mentyukov exclaimed. His wife was expecting a baby.

"Don't worry, we'll take care of everything," someone said.

Mentyukov flung himself toward the plane.

The American was already in the intercept zone. Mentyukov, following orders from ground control, began to maneuver, reaching the same altitude as the U-2 and approaching it from the rear.

The pilot engaged his radar, but there was so much interference on the screen that he couldn't see the target. The interceptor was racing forward on its afterburner at 1,200 miles an hour when a shout came from ground control: "The target is ahead! Look! Look!" But how can you spot a target when it is approaching at nearly a third of a mile a second? And when you can see it, how can you have time to maneuver and ram it? The Su-9 overflew the U-2, and neither pilot even saw the other. Mentyukov must have sighed with relief. He didn't have enough fuel for a second attack. He was ordered to turn off the afterburner and come home.

Radar operators saw on their screens that the Su-9 interceptor had disappeared and the target was again alone but still out of range. The missile battalion's chief of staff, Maj. Mikhail Voronov, counted off the seconds to himself: "Just a little farther and the intruder will be within firing range."

Powers, with no inkling of the drama unfolding around him, turned toward Kyshtym. He still had to photograph Chelyabinsk-40.

"The target is moving away," reported the operator.

As if he had known where the missiles were based, the U-2 pilot was avoiding dangerous places. Kuleshov suggested that perhaps he was equipped with a special receiver that reacted to

A Few Words in Defense of Francis Gary Powers

Setting the record straight about my father. By Francis Gary Powers, Jr.

On MAY 1, 1960, MY FATHER WAS SHOT DOWN while flying a U-2 over the Soviet Union. After the SAM-2 missile exploded near the fragile tail section of his aircraft, everything appeared to be in order until the plane nosed down and didn't respond to the controls. A few seconds passed before my father realized that the plane had been severely damaged and he was at the mercy of the Lord. He thought about activating the destruct mechanism but first had to prepare himself to use the ejection seat.

However, when my dad was ready to eject, he realized he had been thrown forward in his seat in such a way that if he used the ejection mechanism, both his legs would be severed. He decided to release the canopy enclosing the cockpit and attempt to crawl out. When the canopy was clear, he undid his seat belt and was immediately propelled up over the front of the cockpit. Before he could reach the destruct mechanism, he was thrown clear of the plane.

I've read numerous accounts of what "allegedly" happened to my father. Some say that he landed the plane and was seen drinking Russian vodka in a bar near the airport. Still others indicate sabotage. The most recent account indicates that a Russian fighter pilot brought down the U-2. All these stories have been proved false.

When my father returned home in February 1962, he was extensively debriefed and appeared in an open hearing before the Senate Armed Services Committee. The committee exonerated him of any wrongdoing, but the CIA wouldn't permit him to write his account of the incident until many years later. There were many gaps between what the government knew and what it told the public.

Some Americans questioned my father's conduct and loyalty. They especially criticized him for not "following orders" and killing himself. In fact, there had never been any such orders. To the contrary, the CIA's instructions on capture were as follows: "If capture appears imminent, pilots should surrender without resistance and adopt a cooperative attitude toward their captors."

Others claimed he had given out vital information concerning the aircraft. The opposite was true. My father gave no vital information, nor did he ever reveal the names of any pilots. Again, the CIA instructions were, and I quote: "Pilots are perfectly free to tell the full truth about their mission with the exception of certain specifications about the aircraft."

Despite the Senate committee's clearance, despite the fact that he was awarded the CIA's highest honor—its Intelligence Star for valor—and the Air Force's Distinguished Flying Cross, my father, to borrow from John Le Carré, was still a spy left out in the cold, until May 1, 2000. On that day he was posthumously awarded the POW Medal, the National Defense Service Medal, and the CIA's Director's Medal for "extraordinary fidelity and essential service." These were presented to the Powers family during a formal U.S. Air Force and CIA ceremony. Which just goes to show that it is never too late to set the record straight.

signals from the Air Defense radar detection system. The situation was becoming catastrophic. They couldn't even dream of sending up another Su-9. Savitsky ordered a formation of four MiG-19s to take off. Biryuzov didn't believe the interceptors could catch the U-2, but he had to do something.

At that moment Voronov was informed that the target was returning and would be within range in a few seconds. Regulations called for two missiles to be fired, but it was decided to launch three, just to be on the safe side. Everything proceeded automatically, as if it were a training exercise. But after the button had been pushed, only one missile fired. The other two didn't move.

Voronov felt a chill; fate really seemed to be protecting Powers. The lone missile approaching the target was now the only hope.

A fiery point blossomed in the sky. Several seconds later came the faint sound of an explosion. It was 8:53 A.M., Moscow time.

The target disappeared from the radar screens, replaced by greenish flakes of "snow." This was what would show if a plane had ejected chaff to confuse radar operators—or it if was breaking into pieces. Neither Voronov in the battalion nor people in the regiment could believe they had been so lucky. Meanwhile, Voronov's neighboring battery, under the command of Capt. Nikolai Sheludko, fired its three missiles at the disintegrating plane.

As explained later by experts, Voronov's missile did not hit the U-2 but exploded a little behind it. Powers's plane shook. Its long wings folded, tore off, and fluttered slowly down to earth. Of course, the pilot could not see that. He saw only the sky, the boundless sky, revolving before his eyes. He also felt that he had been shoved forward from the g forces. It was impossible for him to eject without the metal canopy rails above him severing his legs. He realized he could climb out, so he threw himself awkwardly over the side of the fuselage. After he disentangled himself from his oxygen hoses, his parachute worked perfectly.

On the ground, they still couldn't believe that the target was destroyed. They reported to Moscow that military actions were continuing. Missile radar operators, scouring the sky, kept finding and then losing the target. Sometimes there even seemed to be several targets, but no one asked himself where the others had come from. Everyone was gripped in nervous and feverish activity.

Now the MiG-19s took off. The first to rise was piloted by Capt. Boris Ayvazyan, followed by Sr. Lt. Sergei Safronov, ready to perform Mikoyan's acrobatic attack. Once in the air, the pilots couldn't locate the intruder. Ayvazyan and Safronov were alone at an altitude of eight miles.

Voronov was the first in the missile units to realize what was happening. The radar screen lit up as fragments of the U-2 floated down from the sky. What other proof did they need? But the generals in Sverdlovsk insisted on continuing the search. At that point, the radars of the neighboring battery detected two objects. At first the commander there, a Major Shugayev, was doubtful: "Why two? And at a low altitude?" He called staff headquarters. Air Defense Commander General F. K. Solodovnikov snapped: "None of our planes are in the air."

There was no time to think. Ayvazyan's plane disappeared from the radar screen—the pilot, low on fuel, had put it into a steep dive toward the airfield—but the missiles found Safronov. Another parachute opened up in the air, this time ours.

When Voronov first saw the American parachute, he ordered one of his officers, named Captain Kazantsev, to take his men and race to the spot where the pilot landed. The meeting between two civilizations was surprisingly calm and pedestrian. It was only after the fact that newspapers wrote about the anger and indignation of Soviet citizens. What actually happened was that the driver of a car taking friends to a neighboring village for the holiday heard an explosion somewhere high above. They stopped, got out, looked up, and saw some glittering dots, with a parachute visible among them. A few minutes later the friends were helping the pilot to his feet and disentangling him from the parachute's shroud lines. They had no idea who he was, but they marveled at his equipment. They were totally confused when they asked the pilot how he felt and he remained mute.

"Are you Bulgarian?" asked the car's owner. The whole district knew that pilots from Warsaw Pact countries trained at the neighboring airfield. The parachutist shook his head. His rescuers were baffled. They clapped him on the shoulder, confiscated his pistol, and pointed to the front seat of the Moskvich. Then one of the smarter ones, noticing the stamp on Powers's pistol, wrote "USA" in the dust on the car's dashboard. Powers nodded. They decided to take the captured spy—they had no doubt that was what he was—to the office of a nearby state farm. There Powers was received quite calmly. His captors searched his flight suit, sat him down at a table, and barely refrained from offering him a glass of vodka in

honor of the holiday. This was the affable scene that greeted the group sent by Major Voronov and the local KGB men who appeared on their heels. Powers was taken away to Sverdkovsk.

The MiG-19 fell near the village of Degtyarka, west of Sverdlovsk. Local inhabitants noticed Safronov's parachute. When they ran up to him, the pilot had stopped breathing, and blood was flowing from a deep wound in his side. The missile forces initially reported to Marshal Biryuzov that the intruder plane had been shot down. Sergei Semyonovich was relieved. But then came new information. The local fighter aircraft commander, Major General Vovk, from Sverdlovsk: "One pilot has been captured and we are looking for the second. . ." Biryuzov decided to wait for confirmation of the second spy's capture before reporting to Father personally.

Amazed and baffled, the Russians helped him from the parachute. One asked, "Are you Bulgarian?"

The marshal was debating whether to go home to change his clothes or go straight to Red Square when another call came from Sverdlovsk on the special phone. The general haltingly reported that the second parachutist had been found and that unfortunately he was one of ours, Senior Lieutenant Safronov.

"What do you mean, one of ours?" The marshal barely kept from shouting. "How many planes did you shoot down? Can't you tell the difference between ours and theirs?"

"His transponder wasn't working," lied the general. That lie was repeated many times later, until Igor Mentyukov cleared up the matter: The transponders were operating, but on the code for April, not May. In the preholiday flurry of activities, service personnel had not yet changed it. So not surprisingly, the radars perceived friendly as foe.

"How many missiles did you fire?" asked Biryuzov, gradually calming down.

"One, three, and then two more." The general in Sverdkovsk began counting. "Fourteen in all," he said, sounding depressed.

"And which one brought down the plane?"

"The first."

"Why the hell. . . ." The usually calm Biryuzov emitted nothing but unprintable expressions for the next few minutes and then slammed down the phone. The joy of victory had evaporated in a moment. "Find out which plane they shot down, an Su-9 or a MiG," he ordered Savitsky.

Savitsky called Sverdlovsk again. "A MiG-19," he reported succinctly after a few minutes of animated conversation. "First I sent up the Su-9 and ordered it to ram, but the pilot missed and flew above the target. Then they sent up MiG-19s, since the target seemed to be at a lower altitude."

"Good." Biryuzov stopped listening. He was impressed by the fact that the interceptor had flown over the high-altitude spy plane. That was an achievement in itself. But how should he report it? He had an idea.

The marshal summoned his deputies. "This is what happened," he began in a calm and confident voice. "The intruder only brushed the edge of the missile range. We expected that and sent an Su-9 to intercept it. No, better—a pair of Su-9s. There were two planes available. They had already reached the target when it entered missile range. At the extreme limit. It was decided to launch. The interceptors were ordered to leave the firing area, but one pilot only shouted in reply: 'I am attacking.' Two missiles were launched, as called for. The planes were so close together that they could not be distinguished from the ground. The radar images merged. One missile therefore hit the spy plane, while the other went after our plane. Unfortunately, it also hit its target. What was the lieutenant's name?"

"Senior Lieutenant Safronov," replied Savitsky.

"Yes, the lieutenant died a hero. And that's the end of the story! There were

But on the Other Hand . . .

The view from the American side. By T. A. Heppenheimer

SERGEI KHRUSHCHEV REPEATEDLY INSISTS THAT SOVIET LEADERS were stunned and scandalized by America's behavior, from the first U-2 flight in 1956 to Eisenhower's lack of apology or conciliation in 1960. However, *U*-2 is pronounced "you too," and such a riposte is appropriate.

Within the United States, Soviet espionage predated World War II. Stalin began by setting up a trading organization, Amtorg, that acted as a front for theft of industrial secrets. During the war, Soviet agents penetrated the heart of the Manhattan Project and made off with some 10,000 pages of technical material, all of which reached Moscow safely. Igor Kurchatov, who headed the Soviet atomic-bomb effort, made good use of these secrets. His first nuclear reactor closely followed an American design, except for being larger to compensate for the lesser purity of his uranium. The first Soviet atomic bomb, detonated in 1949, amounted to a copy of the Fat Man plutonium bomb dropped on Nagasaki four years earlier.

The U-2 was not the first American spy plane to overfly the Soviet Union. Gen. Curtis LeMay, head of the Strategic Air Command, had started by using B-45 and B-47 bombers. He later recalled a time when "we flew all of the reconnaissance aircraft that SAC possessed over Vladivostok at high noon." This was Moscow's principal Pacific naval base. However, those bombers were vulnerable; the U-2 flew much higher, which is why it took years before the Russians could knock it out of the sky.

Following an initial flurry of U-2 flights, during July 1956, Soviet diplomatic protests forced a stand-down. The next four years brought fewer than twenty subsequent overflights, each requiring personal authorization from President Eisenhower. Even so, their photography proved highly significant.

In 1956 there was considerable concern over a "bomber gap," with which Moscow might take the lead in producing long-range jet aircraft. One of the first U-2 missions produced photos that showed far fewer heavy bombers than expected. The "bomber gap" vanished.

The 1960 U-2 incident brought an end to overflights of the Soviet heartland, but from the outset the CIA had regarded the U-2 merely as an interim craft, ultimately to be superseded by spacecraft. The Soviets had similar thoughts. They never built high-flying aircraft to rival the U-2, but they actively pursued reconnaissance satellites.

The standard Soviet spacecraft of this type was Zenit ("zenith"). A variant, Vostok ("east"), carried the first cosmonauts into space, in 1961. The CIA's Discoverer spacecraft, supplanting its U-2s, also entered operational service during 1960.

Through the subsequent decades of the Cold War, both superpowers continued to build and fly reconnaissance satellites. Significantly, although they might have deployed anti-satellite weapons, they declined to do this. In both Moscow and Washington national leaders decided that they had more to gain from free mutual observation, avoiding destabilizing surprises. In this fashion, without formal diplomatic agreement, both superpowers accepted Eisenhower's Open Skies proposal as a basis for their ongoing rivalry.

T. A. Heppenheimer's books include Countdown: A History of Space Flight (*Wiley 1997*).

---

never any other missiles." The marshal looked searchingly at his deputies. He read agreement in their faces. This version suited everyone, especially Central Command.

The marshal's version was the one reported to Father. What really happened when Powers was shot down was completely "forgotten" by the participants for a long time. It was only with the coming of Mikhail Gorbachev's glasnost that those who have retired and who were in lower ranks—Voronov, Ayvazyan, and a few others—began to reveal the truth.

In Red Square the columns of troops had already marched through, and the civilian parade was in progress. The appearance of Marshal Biryuzov striding purposefully from the edge of the grandstand toward the mausoleum did not go unnoticed. Foreigners wondered what was up. Officials in the know immediately drew the right conclusion: They

shot it down! The marshal's field uniform made the right impression; everyone remembers it. Biryuzov mounted the mausoleum, leaned down toward Father's ear, whispered the news of the victory, accepted the well-deserved congratulations, and joined the military officers on the right side of the tribunal.

A few minutes later the news traveled from the mausoleum down to the stands. Grushin and Aleksandr Alekseyevich Raspletin, the designers of the V-750 missile, broke out in smiles and were besieged by people wanting to shake their hands.

Father was elated when he returned home after the celebration. I found out from him that the pilot was alive and being interrogated and that he was talking freely about everything. I remember Father repeating with relish Powers's account of how American specialists had assured him that it was impossible to shoot down the U-2. He said the espio-

nage equipment had been captured almost intact and that film found in the camera was now being developed.

Father told me right away of his plan. He would not report the pilot's capture immediately but would wait until the Americans concocted a story, and only then would he pay them back for all those years of humiliation. Sure enough, NASA's report, subsequently added to and elaborated on by the State Department, stated that "a NASA U-2 research airplane, being flown in Turkey on a joint NASA-USAF Air Weather Service mission, apparently went down in the Lake Van, Turkey, area at about 9:00 a.m. (3:00 a.m. e.d.t.) Sunday, May 1. During the flight in southeast Turkey, the pilot reported over the emergency frequency that he was experiencing oxygen difficulties. . . ." Some details followed.

Enjoying the game, Father waited to see what would happen next, but fate soon took the matter out of his hands. When, at a reception, the Swedish ambassador, Rolf Sulman, casually asked our deputy foreign minister, Jacob Malik, under which article of the U.N. charter the Soviets would raise the incident, Malik (possibly having had too much cognac) replied artlessly: "I don't know exactly. The pilot's still being questioned." The American ambassador overheard this and hurried to his embassy to inform Washington.

An hour later the chairman of the KGB called Father and reported the content of the conversation between the two diplomats. Father was angry and upset. The next day the unfortunate official was summoned to the Central Committee, given a dressing down, sacked as deputy foreign minister, and even expelled from the party (but a few days later he was forgiven).

There was no longer any point in keeping Powers's capture secret. At a session of the U.S.S.R. Supreme Soviet, Father gave a detailed account of the American version of the U-2's flight and then disproved it point by point. He read excerpts from Powers's interrogations, described the plane's route, and enumerated with relish all the espionage equipment found in the wreckage. His report culminated in a display of what he said was the developed film, which showed airfields, nuclear storage sites, and factories. He triumphantly presented the packet of photographs to the session chairman. Father brought copies of the pictures to the dacha too, and I looked at them closely. They were of outstanding quality. You could see fighter planes spread in a line along a landing strip, with fuel tanks and headquarters buildings visible.

Revelations were all very well, but some kind of mutual accommodation would have to be found before the start of the four-power conference in Paris. There were only a few days left, and Father's plans definitely did not call for disrupting the conference. He had to establish contact with Eisenhower and look for a fitting escape from that trap.

He tried to clarify the situation by making extraordinarily conciliatory remarks at a reception in the Czechoslovak Embassy on that country's May 9

national holiday. He emphasized that the door remained open despite the U-2 incident and that he was prepared to search together for a way out of the situation that had been created. He appealed directly to Americans and to the President of the United States, stating, "Today I say again that we want to live not only in peace but also in friendship with the American people. . . . I regard the U.S. Ambassador with respect, and I am sure that he had nothing to do with this encroachment. . . . I am convinced of the moral qualities of this man. . . . I believe that he is incapable of such a deed."

Unfortunately, in Washington the State Department had already admitted that Eisenhower had personally approved the program. In that, the fifth American statement issued on the U-2 incident, the State Department had implied that the United States reserved the right to fly over Soviet territory until such time as the U.S.S.R. opened its borders to inspection. After reading this pronouncement, Father flew into a rage. If its authors' purpose was to infuriate him, they succeeded.

Father decided to wait until the Americans concocted a story and then repay the humilation.

Two days later, on May 11, Father and I went to visit the wreckage of the plane, which Father had ordered to be exhibited in Gorky Park, at the same place where captured German military equipment had been displayed during the war. Foreign correspondents milled around Father at this unusual show. Upon leaving the pavilion that held the exhibit, he answered their questions willingly and delivered a lively speech, making the point that from now on anyone who violated our borders would be dealt with in similar fashion. The Americans should take note, unless they wanted to start a world war. But even now the door to reconciliation didn't slam shut. Of course, the situation had

become more complicated, yet if both parties wished it, there was still the chance to accomplish something.

Eisenhower didn't rule out such a possibility either. In the Oval Office he told Secretary of State Christian Herter that it would make sense to meet with Khrushchev in Paris before the sessions began and try to clear the air. Herter objected, saying that Khrushchev might take that as "a gesture of weakness," and Father never received this invitation. (These details from the American side come from the book *Mayday* by Michael R. Beschloss.)

Nevertheless, Father left for Paris early in hopes of meeting ahead of schedule with the President. I remember a conversation I had with him just before he left. We were taking our evening stroll at the dacha, and he suddenly started talking about Eisenhower's farm and said it would be a good idea to invite him to the dacha, to show him the crops and take a boat ride on the Moskva River. Their personal meeting in Paris failed to happen, and Father changed his tune.

"On the first day of the conference," he later recalled, "I read a declaration. There was some confusion. Especially after the phrase which stated that we were withdrawing our invitation if there were no apology on the part of the United States of America, that the President could not be our guest after what he had allowed with respect to our country. . . . Our declaration was like a bomb that swept everything away. . . . The round table, which should have united us, was shattered." Father had burned his last bridge.

The U-2 flight caused much harm and spoiled a great deal. Most important, it cast doubt on any hope for early and effective negotiations over disarmament and gravely undermined Russia's incipient trust in America as a partner. The deception by his "friend" General Eisenhower, who had gone on walks with him at Camp David and agreed that nothing was more terrible than war, struck Father to the heart. He forgave neither Eisenhower the President nor Eisenhower the man for the U-2 incident. He had learned the English words *my friend* at Camp David, and that was how he had addressed Eisenhower. Now Father bitterly told an aide, "I don't need such a friend."

In August 1960, the American Discoverer spy satellites, equipped with space photo equipment developed in the supersecret CORONA project, began to fly. The need for the U-2 disappeared; Powers's was the last flight over Soviet territory.

Still, Father decided to take political revenge for both the U-2 and Paris. He invited the heads of the world's governments to discuss the problem of decolonization at the next session of the United Nations, in September and October 1960 in the United States, and he went

to the United States without an invitation and took guests with him. At the U.N. session Father did not leave a single "machination of the imperialists" unanswered.

In response to a speech by one of the Philippine delegates, an "American lackey," that exasperated him, he even allowed himself to bang on his desk—not with his fist, as he had done numerous times before, but with a shoe. That incident, unfortunately, became famous.

The U-2's pilot, Francis Gary Powers, was tried in Moscow and sentenced to three years in prison and another seven years in a corrective labor colony. In 1962 he was exchanged for a Soviet

spy, Col. Rudolf Abel (a pseudonym; his real name was William Fischer). That was how, 40 years ago, one of the most dangerous—and fascinating—episodes of the Cold War came to an end.

Sergei Khrushchev is a senior fellow at the Thomas J. Watson Institute for International Studies, at Brown University. These and many other episodes in the Cold War are described as they appeared from the Kremlin in his new book Nikita Khrushchev and the Creation of a Superpower, *being published this year by Penn State Press.*

Vietnam's forgotten lessons

Twenty-five years after the end of the war, does the Pentagon remember the causes of America's defeat?

By Richard J. Newman

Lyndon Johnson once boasted that during the Vietnam War, "I had more control over the generals than any other civilian President in history." But President Clinton had one advantage Johnson didn't: "POTUS slides." During the war against Yugoslavia last year, intelligence analysts produced viewgraphs exclusively for the President of the United States—POTUS, in administration speak. Each contained detailed information on targets NATO commanders wanted to bomb. There was a picture of the target and data on what kind of bomb would be used. Better yet, the slides estimated how much damage would be done to nearby buildings, and how many civilians and enemy troops would be killed. If the numbers looked good, Clinton gave a thumbs-up, and bombs would fly. Key European capitals had to agree, of course, but in the end many targets were deemed too risky and relegated to the "no-strike" list.

HUGH VAN ES—UPI/CORBIS BETTMAN

Saigon, 1975.

A week into the war, Gen. Wesley Clark, NATO's top commander, was bristling. Politicians in Washington and Europe were refusing to attack targets in Belgrade, the Yugoslav capital. Command bunkers and other critical targets were ruled off-limits. Serb forces, meanwhile, were marauding through Kosovo. "Clark said, 'This is impossible,' " ac-cording to a NATO official involved in the process. "We need blanket [target] approval." The NATO chief implored his political bosses to approve more targets. He even launched warplanes toward unapproved targets, hoping to get an OK once he explained that the jets were already airborne. The ploy didn't work—not once. Only after about a month of bombing did the restrictions ease significantly, as the Serbs proved far tougher than expected.

Futility. That's no way to fight a war—at least according to the lessons the American military learned in Southeast Asia a quarter century ago. The fall of Saigon and the communist victory in Vietnam brought to a close one of the most painful—but instructive—epochs in the nation's history. The image of defeat is indelible: a Marine Corps chopper plucking desperate Americans from a Saigon rooftop while North Vietnamese troops swarm through the city. It epitomized the futility of Vietnam, a conflict fought valiantly on the ground but lost by the bullheaded decisions of those in high office. Twenty-five years later, the denunciations of the war are muted—but still accurate: 58,219 Americans died in Vietnam because shortsighted political leaders misused the nation's military.

From all the waste, however, something valuable did emerge: a military that learned how *not* to fight an enemy. "It was a very frustrating war for a lot of us," recalls Gen. Mike Ryan, the Air Force chief of staff, who flew 100 missions over North Vietnam in an F-4 fighter-bomber. On many of those flights, would engage U.S. jets, flying from air bases American pilots were forbidden to bomb. It was that kind of insanity that taught Ryan and others of his generation how to fight to win: Establish clear objectives. Give military leaders broad authority. Don't micromanage the war from Washington. And "if you're going to use American might," says Ryan, "use it in a way so we don't prolong the war." The showcase for those lessons was the 1991 Persian Gulf war, a furious, 43-day onslaught in which the U.S.-led coalition pulverized Saddam Hussein's Air Force, crippled his infrastructure, and routed 300,000 of his troops. "By God," declared President George Bush at the end of the war, "we've kicked the Vietnam syndrome once and for all."

Nearly a decade later, however, the U.S. military is beset by an identity crisis. Many of the lessons of Vietnam have been lost, forgotten, or cast aside,

ETTORE MALANCA—SIPA

PICKING THE TARGETS
A passenger train destroyed in a NATO airstrike near Belgrade during the Kosovo war last year

● *"We had the exact same things . . . as Vietnam."*

deemed inconvenient or irrelevant. Few members of the Vietnam generation remain in uniform. Only 1,379 of the Army's 475,000 soldiers, for instance, served in Vietnam. Many generals still remember Vietnam vividly, but the war has virtually vanished from the cultural memory of the rank and file. "Vietnam is history, and it's been forgotten, especially for the younger soldiers," says Command Sgt. Maj. Robert Seiler of the Division of Engineers, 4th Infantry Division at Fort Hood, Texas, who spent 27 months on the ground in Vietnam. Clothing stores at Fort Hood don't even carry Vietnam-era ribbons for soldiers' dress uniforms; they have to be specially ordered.

At a higher level, Pentagon brass have increasingly blessed practices denounced after Vietnam: gradual increases in military pressure, bombing to signal American resolve, indefinite involvement in overseas disputes. "In Kosovo," says a retired general who flew combat missions over North

Vietnam, "we had the exact same things happening as in the Vietnam War—picking targets at the White House, micromanaging the conflict in ways reminiscent of [Defense Secretary Robert] McNamara and LBJ."

Other parallels haunt. In the Persian Gulf, U.S. warplanes drop bombs on Iraq weekly, in attacks reminiscent of the limited responses to enemy aggression ordered by Lyndon Johnson. In Bosnia, Kosovo, and Colombia, the indefinite deployment of American ground troops represents the kind of "stumbling forward" strategy that prevailed in Vietnam, according to another retired four-star general.

Surprises. The difference today, of course, is that few Americans are dying in overseas missions. And a debacle on the scale of the Vietnam War seems inconceivable. But military experts worry that trends similar to those during the Vietnam years could produce ugly surprises for the Pentagon.

"There's the illusion that we can rely on technology before we have to go bloody somebody," says Marine Corps Gen. John Sheehan, who led an infantry company through the Vietnamese jungle. "But at some point, you're going to run across the Chechens. I can see 30, 40, or 50 killed because they're not going to be ready, or there won't be enough of the right guys." Retired Army Col. Rich Dunn, who led a company of engineers in Vietnam, argues that "because of the passing of the Vietnam generation, we're forgetting the lessons of Vietnam. We're starting to see things reappear that broke the Army in the 1970s."

The U.S. military—and the Army in particular—was reeling by the end of the Vietnam War. "The American Army emerged from Vietnam cloaked in anguish," wrote Maj. Gen. Robert Scales, who is now commandant of the Army War College, in *Certain Victory,* a 1993 account of how the Army evolved into the force that prevailed in Operation Desert Storm. The military draft, with its tolerance for felons and its escape hatches for privileged youth, produced a dysfunctional force. In the Army, 41 percent of soldiers scored in the lowest of four categories on mental aptitude tests. Drug use and discipline problems became rampant. Many career noncommissioned officers—the experienced sergeants who make units hum—quit when faced with a second or third tour in Vietnam. Dunn's battalion in Vietnam in 1971 suffered just one combat death—but 18 deaths from drug overdoses. As a young Marine commander dealing with discipline problems, says Gen. James Jones, now the commandant of the Marine Corps, "I had many Marines standing before me saying, 'Well, I'm here because the judge said either I go to the Marines or I go to jail for grand theft auto.' It was exhausting."

After the war, military leaders began recasting the services to avoid the kinds of problems they saw in Vietnam. The Army and Marine Corps gave commanders broader authority to give troublemakers the boot. Command assignments were lengthened so battalion commanders would get to know

their units, instead of blithely rotating through every six months to punch another ticket as they moved up the career ladder—the common practice during the war.

At the same time, the military was adapting to the end of the draft in 1973 and the start of the all-volunteer force. That move—bitterly opposed by the brass beforehand and almost universally applauded today—eventually helped the Pentagon recruit more qualified troops. By 1990, more than 95 percent of new Army recruits were high school graduates, compared with about 60 percent 20 years earlier. To test the new force, the services established some of the toughest training programs and facilities in the world, including the Air Force's Red Flag exercises and the Army's National Training Center in the California desert. In exercises, units faced an "opposition force" meant to simulate the best the Soviet Union might throw at them; often, they got clobbered—but they learned how to fight and fight smart.

Powell's way. But the biggest advances were in strategy, most notably, the so-called Powell Doctrine, named after Gen. Colin Powell, the chairman of the Joint Chiefs of Staff from 1989 to 1993. The Powell Doctrine, which actually derived from a speech Defense Secretary Caspar Weinberger gave in 1984, held that U.S. forces should be sent to war only when a "vital national interest" is at stake, when there is a clear intention of winning, and when the American public and Congress support a specific operation. Once determined to go to war, the United States should use overwhelming force to defeat the enemy as quickly as possible. In short, Powell's principles addressed virtually all the mistakes he had observed during two tours on the ground in Vietnam.

The Powell Doctrine was the ethos that inspired the Pentagon plan to repel the Iraqi troops that invaded Kuwait. Around the clock, from Day 1, hundreds of U.S. and coalition warplanes hammered targets throughout Iraq, including sensitive sites like command bunkers and power grids. "We made an absolute commitment," says retired Air Force Col. John Warden, a key architect of the

plan, "that when we decide to risk the lives of our own people, we ought to be certain we are doing so as decisively as we can."

That conviction no longer prevails. The Kosovo war, for instance, was designed from the start to be a "phased" operation, with NATO gradually increasing the pressure until Serbian leader Slobodan Milosevic caved. Air Force commanders and the Joint Chiefs of Staff lobbied vigorously for a more aggressive campaign. But the U.S. and European civilians they were appealing to recalled not the lessons of Vietnam but the lessons of Bosnia. When NATO finally intervened in that war in 1995, it took less than two weeks of bombing to halt the Bosnian Serb military campaign and ultimately compel them to sign a peace agreement. But the NATO bombing coincided with a ground campaign by the Serbs' opponents that left the Serbs vulnerable to air attacks, an advantage NATO air forces didn't have in Kosovo. "We walked into incrementalism [in Kosovo] because of NATO's experience in the past, and there was no way to move them off that as a starting point," says a senior Pentagon official. "Did we want to get into this in an incremental way? Absolutely not. But it was incrementalism or don't go."

Whose rules? This is a modus operandi military officials may have to get used to, even though it challenges one of the principal lessons military officers took away from Vietnam: that once a president has decided to go to war, he should turn the conduct of the campaign over to military professionals. "It's the wrong lesson," says Tom McNaugher of Rand, a government-supported think tank. "I don't know any way around incrementalism. Massing forces is nice, if you can get it. But if you can't get that kind of freedom of action, are you going to stand by and do nothing? That's like saying we'll only fight the wars where we get to play by our rules."

Eventually, during the Kosovo war, NATO and U.S. authorities granted permission to strike the targets military leaders wanted to hit at the outset: Power plants, TV and radio transmitters, political headquarters in Belgrade. Since NATO ultimately won—with zero combat deaths—Defense Secretary William Cohen and others have argued that incremental bombing worked. But there was a cost: The war probably went on much longer than it had to. "There were probably 30 or 40 good targets in Belgrade," says Warden, the Desert Storm strategist. "The whole war could reasonably have been done in less than 10 days—with fewer sorties, fewer attacks, fewer targets. The refugee flow never would have happened. There is a feeling that the humane way to conduct military operations is gradually, but you end up with the opposite effects. You end up killing more people."

An eerier echo of Vietnam may be the "containment" of Iraq. The plan, implemented in 1992, relies on U.S. and British jets flying patrols over northern and southern Iraq. In December 1998, Washington and London approved an intensive four-day bombing campaign against Iraq. Since then, American and British pilots have been fired at regularly by Iraqi air-defense guns and missiles. When such attacks occur, U.S. commanders choose from a number of "response options" deemed appropriate to the level of provocation. The result has been hundreds of U.S. attacks on Iraqi air defense sites, including seven so far this month.

That kind of tit-for-tat reminds many Vietnam experts of the "retaliatory" strikes against North Vietnam during the 1960s. The missions were meant not to win the war, but to signal America's resolve against North Vietnamese aggression. After North Vietnamese attacks on a U.S. installation in Pleiku in February of 1965 that killed eight and wounded more than 100, for instance, an outraged Lyndon Johnson ordered the bombing of several North Vietnamese barracks and staging areas. But he stressed that the response was "carefully limited to military areas" and was "appropriate and fitting . . . . We seek no wider war," Johnson assured the North Vietnamese.

Is the United States committing the same mistake again in Iraq? "There's no way you can plausibly argue that the bombing of Iraq will lead to the overthrow of Saddam or any kind of political outcome," says Andrew Bacevich, a retired Army colonel, Vietnam veteran, and professor of international relations at Boston University. "It's using force for signal sending and demonstrating our determination. That was completely—completely—discredited after Vietnam." Military commanders accede to the policy, Bacevich says, because "they need to demonstrate their relevance," in order to justify continued funding from Congress.

Are there no better solutions for the military challenges the United States faces today? "We have a lot of angst about [Iraq]," admits one senior Pentagon official. "But if containment in the long run works, it will be declared a victory." Even Warden, a strong advocate of overwhelming force, agrees that "in the scheme of things, [containment of Iraq] has been pretty cheap. We have exercised control at a pretty low price."

The need for soldiers to do things other than fight and win wars is forcing the Pentagon's top officers to question whether the lessons they learned in Vietnam still apply. "The debate should be more sophisticated than to say we have a military just to use in case of fire," says Jones, the Marine Corps commandant. "For the United States to remain in a position of leadership, we're going to have to engage [in foreign countries]. In my opinion, we do windows."

Mogadishu moment. The willingness to mop up messes that don't directly affect the United States might have surfaced earlier if not for the deaths of 18 soldiers in Somalia in October 1993. A force of more than 25,000 U.S. troops that entered the African nation to help end a famine caused by tribal warfare had dwindled to just 4,000. But then the mission changed. The new objective? Hunting down warlords. When the Battle of Mogadishu erupted on Oct. 3, 1993, the U.S. force lacked the armor to extract soldiers trapped in alleys by armed and angry Somali clansmen. Only after the battle did the U.S. ramp up the force again. "It was the Powell Doctrine again after 3 October," says retired Maj. Gen. Carl Ernst, who commanded the U.S. relief force. "Then it got real quiet."

Those lessons of Mogadishu have colored every American ground mission since. U.S. troops entered Bosnia in 1996—after four years of debate over whether they should even get involved there—with enough tanks and artillery to defeat the entire army of most nations. Unlike their European counterparts, U.S. troops in Bosnia and Kosovo must wear flak jackets and Kevlar helmets virtually everywhere they go. While it's hard to argue against the value of protecting soldiers, some analysts believe the Powell Doctrine has become so rigid that it makes the military ineffective. "The Army is hung up on the Powell doctrine, and it's going to make them irrelevant," says one veteran of Vietnam who works as a consultant for the Army. "You ask for 24 helicopters and they give you 5,200 guys," he moans, referring to the two months it took the Army to deploy 24 Apache attack helicopters to Albania last year and prepare them for the Kosovo War. The Apaches and their crews were deemed fully ready to fight just days before the war ended. They were never used.

Others see pernicious effects in the Pentagon's seeming obsession with avoiding casualties, a corollary of the Powell Doctrine. In a paper published in December, three West Point instructors argued that such airtight "force protection" is eroding the military principle of self-sacrifice. The result, they claim, is "a major breakdown in . . . the professional military ethic within the United States Army."

Slowly, the Pentagon is shifting away from the Powell Doctrine, even as it continues to oppose broader roles for its troops, like taking on routine police functions in Kosovo and Bosnia. Army Chief of Staff Gen. Eric Shinseki has vowed to transform heavy Army units that take weeks to get to overseas conflicts into fast-deploying shock troops that can be fighting within days. Last week, an independent panel reviewing national security policy, led by former Sens. Gary Hart and Warren Rudman, issued a report urging the Pentagon to prepare more of its force for "constabulary" missions around the world—the very sort of operation General Powell opposed as chairman of the Joint Chiefs.

Echoes. Other changes are transforming the military Powell left behind. The Army is losing captains—field-grade officers with four to 10 years of experience—at a record rate. Few experienced NCOs stay in the Army past the 20-year point at which they are eligible for retirement benefits. A recent survey of hundreds of Army majors at the Command and General Staff College at Fort Leavenworth, Kan., revealed that young officers question the value of many Army missions and are losing respect for their leaders. "Senior leaders are devoted to micromanagement and their own career advancement—they spend most of their time avoiding mistakes instead of explaining to soldiers why they are on a deployment and what impact they are making," reads one summary of the survey.

Those complaints sound hauntingly familiar to some old-timers. A groundbreaking Army study from 1970, which sought to explain the disarray wrought by Vietnam, found that "the existing climate includes . . . selfish behavior that places personal success ahead of the good of the Service; looking upward to please superiors instead of looking downward to fulfill the legitimate needs of subordinates; [and] preoccupation with the attainment of trivial short-term objectives."

There's no doubt that today's Army is far better trained and staffed than it was 30 years ago, but there *are* some signs of trouble. "There're lots of data showing that morale throughout the armed forces is the lowest it's been in a long time," says retired Lt. Gen. Walt Ulmer, who conducted the 1970 Army study and helped lead a recent survey of 12,000 service members. The Army has formed two "blue-ribbon" panels to study the problem. But if it doesn't manage to stop the current "hemorrhaging of talent," says Ulmer, "we won't have any good people left in three or four years—and we might not know until we lose the next war."

Ten Years
of the Chornobyl Era

*The environmental and health effects of nuclear power's
greatest calamity will last for generations*

by Yuri M. Shcherbak

"It seemed as if the world was coming to an end ... I could not believe my eyes; I saw the reactor ruined by the explosion. I was the first man in the world to see this. As a nuclear engineer I realized all the consequences of what had happened. It was a nuclear hell. I was gripped by fear."

These words were written to me in 1986 by the head of the shift operating the reactor that exploded at the Chornobyl nuclear power plant in northern Ukraine. The explosion and a resulting fire showered radioactive debris over much of eastern Europe. The author of the words above, along with several others, was later jailed for his role in the disaster, although he never admitted guilt.

Subsequent official investigations have shown, however, that responsibility for this extraordinary tragedy reaches far beyond just those on duty at the plant on the night of April 25 and early morning of April 26, 1986. The consequences, likewise, have spread far beyond the nuclear energy industry and raise fundamental questions for a technological civilization. Before the explosion, Chornobyl was a small city hardly known to the outside world. Since then, the name—often known by its Russian spelling, Chernobyl has entered the chronicle of the 20th century as the worst technogenic environmental disas-

ter in history. It is an internationally known metaphor for catastrophe as potent as "Stalingrad" or "Bhopal." Indeed, it is now clear that the political repercussions from Chornobyl accelerated the collapse of the Soviet empire.

Because of the importance of this calamity for all of humanity, it is vital that the world understands both the reasons it happened and the consequences. The events that led up to the explosion are well known. Reactor number four, a 1,000-megawatt RBMK-1000 design, produced steam that drove generators to make electricity. On the night of the accident, operators were conducting a test to see how long the generators would run without power. For this purpose, they greatly reduced the power being produced in the reactor and blocked the flow of steam to the generators.

Unfortunately, the RBMK-1000 has a design flaw that makes its operation at low power unstable. In this mode of operation, any spurious increase in the production of steam can boost the rate of energy production in the reactor. If that extra energy generates still more steam, the result can be a runaway power surge. In addition, the operators had disabled safety systems that could have averted the reactor's destruction, because the systems might have interfered with the results of the test.

At 1:23 and 40 seconds on the morning of April 26, realizing belatedly that

the situation had become hazardous, an operator pressed a button to activate the automatic protection system. The action was intended to shut the reactor down, but by this time it was too late. What actually happened can be likened to a driver who presses the brake pedal to slow down a car but finds instead that it accelerates tremendously.

Within three seconds, power production in the reactor's core surged to 100 times the normal maximum level, and there was a drastic increase in temperature. The result was two explosions that blew off the 2,000-metric-ton metal plate that sealed the top of the reactor, destroying the building housing it. The nuclear genie had been liberated.

Despite heroic attempts to quell the ensuing fire, hundreds of tons of graphite that had served as a moderator in the reactor burned for 10 days. Rising hot gases carried into the environment aerosolized fuel as well as fission products, isotopes that are created when uranium atoms split apart. The fuel consisted principally of uranium; mixed in with it was some plutonium created as a by-product of normal operation. Plutonium is the most toxic element known, and some of the fission products were far more radioactive than uranium or plutonium. Among the most dangerous were iodine 131, strontium 90 and cesium 137.

From *Scientific American,* April 1996, pp. 44-49. Reproduced with permission. © 1996 by Scientific American, Inc. All rights reserved.

A plume containing these radioisotopes moved with prevailing winds to the north and west, raining radioactive particles on areas thousands of miles away. Regions affected included not only Ukraine itself but also Belarus, Russia, Georgia, Poland, Sweden, Germany, Turkey and others. Even such distant lands as the U.S. and Japan received measurable amounts of radiation. In Poland, Germany, Austria and Hungary as well as Ukraine, crops and milk were so contaminated they had to be destroyed. In Finland, Sweden and Norway, carcasses of reindeer that had grazed on contaminated vegetation had to be dumped.

WIDESPREAD EFFECTS

The total amount of radioactivity released will never be known, but the official Soviet figure of 90 million curies represents a minimum. Other estimates suggest that the total might have been several times higher. It is fair to say that in terms of the amount of radioactive fallout—though not, of course, the heat and blast effects—the accident was comparable to a medium-size nuclear strike. In the immediate aftermath of the explosion and fire, 187 people fell ill from acute radiation sickness; 31 of these died. Most of these early casualties were firefighters who combated the blaze.

The destroyed reactor liberated hundreds of times more radiation than was produced by the atomic bombings of Hiroshima and Nagasaki. The intensity of gamma radiation on the site of the power plant reached more than 100 roentgens an hour. This level produces in an hour doses hundreds of times the maximum dose the International Commission on Radiological Protection recommends for members of the public a *year*. On the roof of the destroyed reactor building, radiation levels reached a frightening 100,000 roentgens an hour.

The human dimensions of the tragedy are vast and heartbreaking. At the time of the accident, I was working as a medical researcher at the Institute of Epidemiology and Infectious Diseases in Kiev, some 60 miles from the Chor-

nobyl plant. Sometime on April 26 a friend told me that people had been arriving at hospitals for treatment of burns sustained in an accident at the plant, but we had no idea of its seriousness. There was little official news during the next few days, and what there was suggested the danger was not great. The authorities jammed most foreign broadcasts, although we could listen as Swedish radio reported the detection of high levels of radioactivity in that country and elsewhere. I and some other physicians decided to drive toward the accident site to investigate and help as we could.

We set off cheerfully enough, but as we got closer we started to see signs of mass panic. People with connections to officialdom had used their influence to send children away by air and rail. Others without special connections were waiting in long lines for tickets or occasionally storming trains to try to escape. Families had become split up. The only comparable social upheaval I had seen was during a cholera epidemic. Already many workers from the plant had been hospitalized.

The distribution of the fallout was extremely patchy. One corner of a field might be highly dangerous, while just a few yards away levels seemed low. Nevertheless, huge areas were affected. Although iodine 131 has a half-life of only eight days, it caused large radiation exposures during the weeks immediately following the accident. Strontium 90 and cesium 137, on the other hand, are more persistent. Scientists believe it is the cesium that will account for the largest radiation doses in the long run.

All told, well over 260,000 square kilometers of territory in Ukraine, Russia and Belarus still have more than one curie per square kilometer of contamination with cesium 137. At this level, annual health checks for radiation effects are advised for residents. In my own country of Ukraine, the total area with this level of contamination exceeds 35,000 square kilometers—more than 5 percent of the nation's total area. Most of this, 26,000 square kilometers, is arable land. In the worst affected areas there are restrictions on the use of crops, but less contaminated districts are still under cultivation.

The heavily contaminated parts of Ukraine constitute 13 administrative regions (oblasts). In these oblasts are 1,300 towns and villages with a total population of 2.6 million, including 700,000 children. Within about 10 days of the accident, 135,000 people living in the worst-affected areas had left their homes; by now the total has reached 167,000. Yet it is clear that the authorities' attempts to keep the scale of the disaster quiet actually made things worse than they need have been. If more inhabitants in the region had been evacuated promptly during those crucial first few days, radiation doses for many people might have been lower.

The region within 30 kilometers of the Chornobyl plant is now largely uninhabited; 60 settlements outside this zone have also been moved. Formerly busy communities are ghost towns. The government has responded to this unprecedented disruption by enacting laws giving special legal status to contaminated areas and granting protections to those who suffered the most. Yet the repercussions will last for generations.

MULTIPLE ILLNESSES

The medical consequences are, of course, the most serious. Some 30,000 people have fallen ill among the 400,000 workers who toiled as "liquidators," burying the most dangerous wastes and constructing a special building around the ruined reactor that is universally referred to as "the sarcophagus." Of these sick people, about 5,000 are now too ill to work.

It is hard to know, even approximately, how many people have already died as a result of the accident. Populations have been greatly disrupted, and children have been sent away from some areas. By comparing mortality rates before and after the accident, the environmental organization Greenpeace Ukraine has estimated a total of 32,000 deaths. There are other estimates that are higher, and some that are lower, but I believe a figure in this range is defensible. Some, perhaps many, of these deaths may be the result of the immense psychological stress experienced by those living in the contaminated region.

One medical survey of a large group of liquidators, carried out by researchers in Kiev led by Sergei Komissarenko, has found that most of the sample were suffering from a constellation of symptoms that together seem to define a new medical syndrome. The symptoms include fatigue, apathy and a decreased number of "natural killer" cells in the blood.

Natural killer cells, a type of white blood cell, can kill the cells of tumors and virus-infected cells. A reduction in their number, therefore, suppresses the immune system. Some have dubbed this syndrome "Chornobyl AIDS." Besides having increased rates of leukemia and malignant tumors, people with this syndrome are susceptible to more severe forms of cardiac conditions as well as common infections such as bronchitis, tonsillitis and pneumonia.

As a consequence of inhaling aerosols containing iodine 131 immediately after the accident, 13,000 children in the region experienced radiation doses to the thyroid of more than 200 roentgen equivalents. (This means they received at least twice the maximum recommended dose for nuclear industry workers for an entire year.) Up to 4,000 of these children had doses as high as 2,000 roentgen equivalents. Because iodine collects in the thyroid gland, these children have developed chronic inflammation of the thyroid. Although the inflammation itself produces no symptoms, it has started to give rise to a wave of cases of thyroid cancer.

The numbers speak for themselves. Data gathered by the Kiev researcher Mykola D. Tronko and his colleagues indicate that between 1981 and 1985—before the accident—the number of thyroid cancer cases in Ukraine was about five a year. Within five years of the disaster the number had grown to 22 cases a year, and from 1992 to 1995 it reached an average of 43 cases a year. From 1986 to the end of 1995, 589 cases of thyroid cancer were recorded in children and adolescents. (In Belarus the number is even higher.) Ukraine's overall rate of thyroid cancer among children has increased about 10-fold from preaccident levels and is now more than four cases per million. Cancer of the thyroid metastasizes readily, although if caught early enough it can be treated by removing the thyroid gland. Patients must then receive lifelong treatment with supplemental thyroid hormones.

Other research by Ukrainian and Israeli scientists has found that one in every three liquidators—primarily men in their thirties—has been plagued by sexual or reproductive disorders. The problems include impotence and sperm abnormalities. Reductions in the fertilizing capacity of the sperm have also been noted. The number of pregnancies with complications has been growing among women living in the affected areas, and many youngsters fall prey to a debilitating fear of radiation.

The optimists who predicted no long-term medical consequences from the explosion have thus been proved egregiously wrong. These authorities were principally medical officials of the former Soviet Union who were following a script written by the political bureau of the Communist Party's Central Committee. They also include some Western nuclear energy specialists and military experts.

It is also true that the forecasts of "catastrophists"—some of whom predicted well over 100,000 cancer cases—have not come to pass. Still, previous experience with the long-term effects of radiation—much of it derived from studies at Hiroshima and Nagasaki—suggests that the toll will continue to rise. Cancers caused by radiation can take many years before they become detectable, so the prospects for the long-term health of children in the high-radiation regions are, sadly, poor.

The hushing up of the danger from radiation in Soviet propaganda has produced quite the opposite effects from those intended. People live under constant stress, fearful about their health and, especially, that of their children. This mental trauma has given rise to a psychological syndrome comparable to that suffered by veterans of wars in Vietnam and Afghanistan. Among children evacuated from the reactor zone, there has been a 10- to 15-fold increase in the incidence of neuropsychiatric disorders.

The catastrophe and the resulting resettlement of large populations have also caused irreparable harm to the rich ethnic diversity of the contaminated areas, particularly to the so-called *drevlyany,* woodland people, and *polishchuks,* inhabitants of the Polissya region. Unique architectural features and other artifacts of their spiritual and material culture have been effectively lost as abandoned towns and villages have fallen into disrepair. Much of the beautiful landscape is now unsafe for humans.

The Ukrainian government, which is in a severe economic crisis, is today obliged to spend more than 5 percent of its budget dealing with the aftermath of Chornobyl. The money provides benefits such as free housing to about three million people who have been officially recognized as having suffered from the catastrophe, including 356,000 liquidators and 870,000 children. Ukraine has introduced a special income tax corresponding to 12 percent of earnings to raise the necessary revenue, but it is unclear how long the government can maintain benefits at current levels.

Today the Chornobyl zone is one of the most dangerously radioactive places in the world. In the debris of the ruined reactor are tens of thousands of metric tons of nuclear fuel with a total radioactivity level of some 20 million curies. The radiation level in the reactor itself, at several thousand roentgens per hour, is lethal for any form of life. But the danger is spread far and wide. In the 30-kilometer zone surrounding the reactor are about 800 hastily created burial sites where highly radioactive waste, including trees that absorbed radioisotopes from the atmosphere, has been simply dumped into clay-lined pits.

These dumps may account for the substantial contamination of the sediments of the Dnieper River and its tributary the Pripyat, which supply water for 30 million people. Sediments of the Pripyat adjacent to Chornobyl contain an estimated 10,000 curies of strontium 90, 12,000 curies of cesium 137 and 2,000 curies of plutonium. In order to prevent soluble compounds from further contaminating water sources, the wastes must be removed to properly designed and equipped storage facilities—facilities that do not yet exist.

COST OF CLEANUP

The two reactors that are still in operation at the Chornobyl plant also pose a major problem (a fire put a third out of action in 1992). These generate up to 5 percent of Ukraine's power; the nuclear energy sector altogether produces 40 percent of the country's electricity. Even so, Ukraine and the Group of Seven industrial nations last December signed a formal agreement on a cooperative plan to shut down the whole Chornobyl plant by the year 2000. The agreement establishes that the European Union and the U.S. will help Ukraine devise plans to mitigate the effects of the shutdown on local populations. It also sets up mechanisms to allow donor countries to expedite safety improvements at one of the reactors still in use. In addition, the agreement provides for international cooperation on decommissioning the plant, as well as on the biggest problem of all: an ecologically sound, long-term replacement for the sarcophagus that was built around the ruin of reactor number four.

The 10-story sarcophagus, which is built largely of concrete and large slabs of metal and has walls over six meters thick, was designed for a lifetime of 30 years. But it was constructed in a great hurry under conditions of high radiation. As a result, the quality of the work was poor, and today the structure is in need of immediate repair. Metal used in the edifice has rusted, and more than 1,000 square meters of concrete have become seriously cracked. Rain and snow can get inside. If the sarcophagus were to collapse—which could happen if there were an earthquake—the rubble would very likely release large amounts of radioactive dust.

In 1993 an international competition was held to find the best long-term solution. Six prospective projects were chosen for further evaluation (out of 94 proposals), and the next year a winner was selected—Alliance, a consortium led by Campenon Bernard of France. The consortium's proposal, which entails the construction of a "supersarcophagus" around the existing one, unites firms from France, Germany, Britain, Russia and Ukraine. The group has already conducted feasibility studies. If the project goes forward, design work will cost $20 million to $30 million, and construction—which would take five years—upwards of $300 million. Final disposal of the waste from the accident will take 30 years. One possibility being explored is that the waste might be encased in a special glass.

Chornobyl was not simply another disaster of the sort that humankind has experienced throughout history, like a fire or an earthquake or a flood. It is a global environmental event of a new kind. It is characterized by the presence of thousands of environmental refugees; long-term contamination of land, water and air; and possibly irreparable damage to ecosystems. Chornobyl demonstrates the ever growing threat of technology run amok.

The designers of the plant, which did not conform to international safety requirements, are surely culpable at least as much as the operators. The RBMK-1000 is an adaptation of a military reactor originally designed to produce material for nuclear weapons. There was no reinforced containment structure around the reactor to limit the effects of an accident. That RBMK reactors are still in operation in Ukraine, Lithuania and Russia should be cause for alarm.

The disaster illustrates the great responsibility that falls on the shoulders of scientific and other experts who give advice to politicians on technical matters. Moreover, I would argue that the former Soviet Union's communist leadership must share the blame. Despite then President Mikhail S. Gorbachev's professed support for glasnost, or openness, the regime hypocritically closed ranks in the aftermath of the tragedy in a futile and ultimately harmful attempt to gloss over the enormity of what had occurred.

The event offers a vivid demonstration of the failures of the monopolistic Soviet political and scientific system. The emphasis under that regime was on secrecy and on simplifying safety features in order to make construction as cheap as possible. International experience with reactor safety was simply disregarded. The calamity underscores, further, the danger that nuclear power plants could pose in regions where wars are being fought. Of course, all such plants are potentially vulnerable to terrorist attack.

Chornobyl has taught the nations of the world a dreadful lesson about the necessity for preparedness if we are to rely on nuclear technology. Humankind lost a sort of innocence on April 26, 1986. We have embarked on a new, post-Chornobyl era, and we have yet to comprehend all the consequences.

FURTHER READING

CHERNOBYL: A DOCUMENTARY STORY. Iurii Shcherbak. Translated by Ian Press. St. Martin's Press, 1989.

CHORNOBYL: LIVING WITH THE MONSTER. Mike Edwards in *National Geographic*, Vol. 186, No. 2, pages 100–115; August 1994.

RADIATION AND HUMAN IMMUNITY [in Russian]. Sergei Komissarenko. Naukova Dumka, Kiev, 1994.

CARING FOR SURVIVORS OF THE CHERNOBYL DISASTER: WHAT THE CLINICIAN SHOULD KNOW. Armin D. Weinberg et al. in *Journal of the American Medical Association*, Vol. 274, No. 5, pages 408–412; August 2, 1995.

YURI M. SHCHERBAK is ambassador of Ukraine to the U.S. He graduated from Kiev Medical College in 1958 and has advanced degrees in epidemiology. Besides having published extensively in epidemiology and virology, he is the author of 20 books of poetry, plays and essays. In 1988 Shcherbak founded and became leader of the Ukranian Green Movement, now the Green Party. In 1989 he won a seat in the Supreme Soviet of the U.S.S.R., where as an opposition leader he initiated the first parliamentary investigation of the Chornobyl accident.

The End of the Cold War

A Russian View

Vladimir Batyuk *describes how the Gorbachev reforms, and the collapse of the Warsaw Pact and Soviet Union, changed Moscow's view of the world.*

WHILE THE GEOPOLITICAL DIF-ferences between Russia and the West should not be un-derestimated, the Cold War was funda-mentally about ideology not geopolitics. By contrast, the British-Russian Great Game of the nineteenth century never led to anything like the Cold War, since the ideological differences between the Russian and the British empires at that time were insignificant.

Russia and the other great European powers then belonged to the same privi-leged club, ruled by a like-minded European aristocracy. The Russian Revo-lution, a product of the First World War, was both a symptom of, and a contribu-tion to, the decay of that cosmopolitan aristocracy and of the ideological unity of Europe that it epitomised. The Rus-sian form of Communism thus became an attempt to create an alternative, non-Western way of life. In this sense, ideo-logically the Cold War began as early as 1917. After 1945, with the Soviet Un-ion ascending to the status of super-power, the Cold War was transferred also to the sphere of geopolitics. At the end of the 1980s, however, it became obvious that the Communist experiment had failed miserably. The Soviet way of life, characterised by such ugly features as economic hardships, technological standstill and moral degradation, lost its appeal even for the Soviet people them-selves. In the 1920s and 1930s, the West had been scared by Soviet Communist propaganda. In the 1980s, on the other hand, the Soviet authorities had to jam Western broadcasts in order to maintain control over its population.

No wonder that the Communist ide-ology, which had stimulated the Cold War on the Soviet side, deteriorated gradually. By the 1940s the slogan of 'World Proletarian Revolution' had al-ready disappeared from Soviet propa-ganda. After 1970, the Soviet leaders preferred not to mention such words as 'Communism' or 'class struggle'. And Mikhail Gorbachev, who proclaimed the primacy of 'values common to all man-kind' over the 'class struggle', was merely following in the footsteps of his predecessors, who had gradually rid themselves of the revolutionary features of Communist ideology. The weakening of that revolutionary appeal had led to the deep transformation of Soviet for-eign policy, thus paving the way for the end of the Cold War.

It is no wonder that arms control and confidence-building measures stood at the heart of the rapprochement between the Soviet Union and the West at the end of the 1980s and the beginning of the 1990s. During that time, dozens of bilateral and multilateral arms-control treaties were concluded between the two, including such breakthrough agree-ments as the treaty on the Elimination of Intermediate-Range and Shorter-Range Missiles (the INF Treaty); the treaty on Dangerous Military Activities; the Vienna Document of 1990 (on trans-parency in military forces and activities, and verification); the treaty on Conven-tional Armed Forces in Europe (the CFE

Ideologically, the Cold War began in 1917. After 1945 it was transferred to the sphere of geopolitics.

Treaty); the treaty on the Reduction and Liquidation of Strategic Offensive Arms (START I); the treaty on Open Skies; the treaty between the United States and Russia on the Reduction and Liquida-tion of Strategic Offensive Arms (START II); the Chemical Weapons Ban Convention and the Complete Nuclear Test Ban Convention.

The titles of these agreements and treaties look impressive. More signifi-cantly,they highlighted the dramatic change in Moscow's approach to the whole question of arms control. For the first time, the principle of equal security for both parties was safeguarded by treaty. Mechanisms of on-site inspections, moni-toring and challenge inspections were in-

This article first appeared in *History Today*, April 1999, pp. 28-33. © 1999 by History Today, Ltd. Reprinted by permission.

cluded in a number of these documents—the START 1 treaty alone included sixteen different verification and control mechanisms. Contacts, information exchange and cooperation between Russian and Western military all increased dramatically. Also, nuclear risk reduction centres were created.

For the first time since the Cold War began, these treaties led to a reduction of arms, not just to a more sophisticated arms race (as was the case during the détente period). An entire class of nuclear arms—intermediate and shorter-range nuclear missiles—was liquidated, thus eliminating a whole stratum of the pyramid of nuclear weapons. The reduction of the most dangerous destructive weapons—offensive strategic arms—began under the START 1 treaty, signed on July 31st, 1991. Even though the ambiguity of some its provisions made impossible the two-fold reduction of the Russian and American strategic arsenals as envisaged by Moscow and Washington, the treaty did make it possible to reduce these arsenals by a third, amounting to 8,000 strategic nuclear warheads. The realisation of the CFE treaty also made possible an unprecedented reduction in conventional arms: by the mid-1990s, about 49,000 tanks, armoured personnel carriers, heavy guns, aircraft and helicopters had been destroyed under the provisions of this treaty by the European nations, US and Canada. Moreover, the implementation of the Treaty made a massive surprise attack and large-scale offensive operations impossible for the first time in the history of Cold War Europe. And the break-through in transparency at the end of the 1980s made it possible to conclude the Chemical Weapons Ban Convention and the Complete Nuclear Test Ban Convention.

None of these changes in attitudes to arms control in the Soviet Union would have been possible without *perestroika* and *glasnost*. Gorbachev's 'new political thinking' changed Moscow's attitude to the West: the latter was no longer seen as an irreconcilable enemy; rather, Gorbachev and his supporters looked to the West as a partner to the solution of such international problems as arms control, proliferation, environmental protection

and so on. Of special importance was Moscow's co-operation with the West in local crisis management. The memoirs of the former US Secretary of State, James Baker, show that for Washington there was no problem in recognising military parity with the Soviet Union on lower levels: all the US-Soviet arms control debates at the end of the 1980s and beginning of the 1990s were about technical details, not about philosophy.

After Gorbachev won the Nobel Prize for Peace, the people grumbled, 'Better for him to have won the Prize for Economics'.

For the leaders of the West, the Soviet willingness to renounce the Brezhnev Doctrine (the assertion following the invasion of Czechoslovakia in 1968 that the states under the Warsaw Pact would intervene in the internal affairs of any of its members which exposed the rest of them to the danger of anti-socialist activity) and to give up the 'anti-imperialist struggle' in the Third World, was evidence that *perestroika* was for real. The strongest argument the Western leaders used to their Soviet counterparts was that, if openness and freedom of choice were good for the Soviet people, they might also be good for the peoples of Eastern Europe, Angola, Afghanistan, Cambodia and Nicaragua.

At the end of the 1980s and beginning of the 1990s, US-Soviet cooperation contributed greatly to the peaceful settlement of a number of local crises. The withdrawal of Soviet troops from Afghanistan was completed in April 1989, as a result of the Geneva accords, to which the Soviet Union and the United States were signatories. In Nicaragua free elections in February 1990 contributed to national and regional reconciliation, something which would probably have been impossible if Moscow and Washington had not agreed to cancel the flow of arms to their respective allies, the Sandinistas and Contras. In Angola and Namibia the Soviet Un-

ion and the United States sponsored the peace process, the withdrawal of Cuban and South African troops, proclamation of independence in Namibia (in March 1989) and national reconciliation in Angola. Finally, in Cambodia the combined efforts of Vietnam, China, the USSR and the United States culminated in the 1991 Paris Peace Agreement, by which the Vietnamese troops withdrew from Cambodia, and free elections were held.

All these regional conflicts were intensively debated by Moscow and Washington at ministerial level. The respective situations there were discussed regularly by heads of corresponding departments in the US Department of State and the Soviet Ministry of Foreign Affairs.

Moscow's willingness to recognise the results of the velvet revolutions in Eastern and Central Europe in 1989 became the real turning point in the history of the Cold War. Neither the Soviets nor the West were ready for such rapid developments in the region that year. In May, the Hungarian government dismantled for the first time a part of the Iron Curtain, namely, a barbed-wire fence along the Austrian border; in the same month, Solidarity won a decisive victory in the first free Polish parliamentary elections; during the summer, the flow of refugees from East Germany through the unprotected Austrian-Hungarian border increased constantly; in October, the local Communist parties in the GDR and Czechoslovakia lost control of the situation, and hundreds of thousands of demonstrators demanded free elections and human rights; on November 9th, the infamous Berlin Wall was pulled down by tens of thousands of East Germans; in December, the Czechoslovakian Communist government resigned in the face of mass demonstrations; on December 22nd, the Ceaucescu regime in Romania was overthrown by armed rebellion supported by the people. In June 1991, the Communist government in Albania fell, and by the end of the year, the Soviet Union itself followed.

Such a quick, virtually painless collapse of the so-called 'socialist camp' would have been impossible without the dramatic changes in international relations caused by the end of the Cold War. To cite just one example: on December 24th, 1989, J. Matlock, the US Ambassador to the USSR, informed the Soviet deputy Foreign Minister, I. Aboimov, that Washington would not object if Moscow interfered militarily in Romanian affairs to support anti-Ceaucescu forces. This Washington-sponsored version of the Brezhnev Doctrine 'the other way round' became a symbol of change in the US-Soviet dialogue over Eastern Europe.

However, the American historians Michael Beschloss and Strobe Talbott have rightly stated that 'if there was a single point at which the Cold War ended, it was probably . . . the moment when Gorbachev acceded to German unification within NATO.' The decision of the NATO Defence Planning Committee to review NATO military strategy made on May 23rd, 1990, together with Helmut Kohl's pledge to reduce the numerical strength of the unified German army, furthered Gorbachev's decision to accede to Western pressure on that issue.

After Gorbachev won the Nobel Prize for Peace in 1990, the common people in the Soviet Union, tired of the economic mess at home, grumbled, 'Better for him to have won the Nobel prize for Economics'. By 1990, it became clear that what remained of the Soviet economy could not survive without outside help. Massive Western aid to the USSR was first debated during Gorbachev's visit to the United States in May–June 1990. Dennis Ross, Director of the Policy Planning Staff in the State Department under James Baker, asked Gorbachev's adviser Yevgeny Primakov, 'How much do you really need?' Primakov replied, 'About $20 billion a year for three years'.

By the time of the G-7 summit in London in 1991, Primakov and the economist Grigory Yavlinsky had prepared a plan of radical economic reforms, which were to be supported by massive Western aid. Though Gorbachev apparently approved the plan, he could not inspire enthusiasm for it in London. The Western leaders did not feel that it presented any real changes in Soviet economic policy.

During his very first meeting with Gorbachev, in March 1989, Secretary Baker had told him that, in his experience, it was better to move sooner rather than later on issues such as price reform. 'We were twenty years late on price reform, so two or three more years won't hurt', Gorbachev had replied. But he was wrong. The delay in genuine economic reform ultimately ruined his career and the Soviet Union's integrity. Three years later, in January 1992, Baker was to meet another Kremlin leader, the Russian president Boris Yeltsin.

For the leaders of the new democratic Russia, the West seemed a natural ally while the Cold War was a tragic aberration of history, caused by Communist ideology. The first Russian Foreign Minister Kozyrev strikingly declared:

> We are coming from the premise that no single developed democratic civil society, based on rational principles, can threaten us. . . . The developed nations of the West are Russia's natural allies. It is high time to proclaim firmly, at last, that we are neither enemies, nor junior poor brothers, following the instructions of the rich and malevolent West.

Moreover, Yeltsin's government even took concrete steps towards forging a strategic alliance between Russia and the West, in particular between Russia and the US. On December 20th, 1991, Yeltsin raised the question of Russia's admission to NATO. A month later, on the eve of his first official visit to the United States, he proposed joint co-operation in development of a ballistic missile defence programme. Undoubtedly, Western financial help for economic reforms, initiated by Russian deputy prime minister Egor Gaidar at the beginning of 1992, was of special importance to the Russian leadership. In an interview to CNN on January 30th, Kozyrev expressed his confidence that a new Marshall Plan for Russia and other new independent states would be approved.

This new liberal ideology was enthusiastically taken up by a broad spectrum of Russian intelligentsia, because it corresponded to the deeply ingrained pro-Western feelings of the Russian intellectual elite. They sincerely believed

that Russia could easily return to the Western, free and prosperous world, out of which she had been forced by the Bolshevik revolution in 1917. In the atmosphere of enthusiasm that prevailed among Russian liberals at the beginning

> *'We were twenty years late on price reform, so two or three more years won't hurt,' said Gorbachev. But he was wrong.*

of 1992, such a return was viewed as an eminently possible and practical solution to the majority of the country's foreign and national security problems.

However, this new liberal strand within Russian foreign policy soon had to face harsh reality. Firstly, the West never expressed much enthusiasm for the integration of Russia into Western security structures such as NATO. Secondly, NATO's eastward expansion and more particularly, the prospect that the former Soviet Republics might also be permitted to join, caused serious concern to the Russian elite. Thirdly, the United States had adopted a reserved position over the proposed US-Russian co-operation in strategic defence and the idea died out. Fourthly, American activity in the sphere of defence against ballistic missiles caused troubles in the Russian foreign policy community.

Finally, post–Cold War competition in the sphere of arms trade aggravated US-Russian rivalry, especially in such regions and countries as Eastern Europe, Latin America, Iran, China and India. Washington expressed its concern over Russian dual-technology sales in Iran and India, which presumably violated the non-proliferation agreements. Moscow, in turn, rejected such allegations as manifestations of American double standards and hypocrisy and suspected the US of attempting to oust Russia from her traditional arms markets such as Eastern Europe.

After the collapse of Communism, it was non-Marxist ideologies that prevailed in the interrelationships between the two sides, and this is why Moscow and her Western partners have, so far, been able to find acceptable solutions to these problems in their relationship.

After *perestroika* had emancipated the Soviet citizens from the fear of 'aggression of American imperialism', the geopolitical rationale for the USSR's existence had also disappeared in the minds of the Soviet people. On being asked about the reasons for the collapse of the Soviet Union, one former member of the Gorbachev government replied: 'Can you imagine a state that included both Denmark and Iran?' The USSR encompassed a vastly divergent number of nations. For example, if Estonia, one of the former Soviet Baltic Republics, was ethnically and culturally akin to Finland, the Central Asian Republic of Tadjikistan, with its Farsi-speaking and Muslim population, was similarly close to neighbouring Iran.

Only the Communist ideology had cemented the Soviet empire, uniting such different ethnic groups after 1917 (in similar vein, monarchist and Orthodox ideology had cemented the Russian empire before 1917). Thus the meltdown of Communist ideology undermined both the Soviet system of alliances and, eventually, the USSR itself.

Another reason for collapse was the disintegration of the centralised Soviet economic system. This system had been based on the unequal distribution of national income between members of the Soviet Federation, with some of the Soviet republics, such as the Caucasus republics, Byelorussia, Ukraine and Moldavia receiving a disproportionately high share of resources, while Russia and the republics of Central Asia were donors.

The beginning of the dismemberment of the Soviet empire posed a difficult dilemma for the Russian ruling elite: whether to concentrate all the scarce Russian resources on the consolidation of the fast-disintegrating Soviet Union, or to attempt to invest these resources in the domestic development of Russia. Yeltsin and his entourage chose the second path, and so far the Russian Federation has preferred to focus on domestic development in preference to the restoration of empire.

This policy faces fierce resistance on the part of Russian traditionalists who claim that it was a deliberate decision on the part of 'democrats' to destroy 'our Soviet Motherland' in order to obtain power. They also proclaim that Russia cannot be a typical nation state, like France or Great Britain: the Russians are imperial people, and thus, Russia's fate, they say, is to be an empire. Besides this, they argue, while Russia stopped her Cold War against the West, the latter failed to follow suit, continuing its cunning and predatory anti-Russian policies, aimed at the total destruction of Russia.

So far, however, the traditionalists, have failed to produce any new holy creed which would cement the new empire. Besides which, Russia will not face any serious threat from abroad in the foreseeable future, and therefore, the most serious threats to her national security come from within. No new empire, regardless of its ideological background, would save Russia either from economic collapse or disintegration. Moscow now cannot afford to allocate scarce resources on anything other than halting the consequences of economic and financial crisis.

The country's rulers thus face an uneasy dilemma: either to safeguard Russia's real national interests, abandoning nostalgia for the glorious imperial past, or to put forward the idea of a new Russian empire. The difficulties that the ratification process of the Russian–Ukrainian Friendship Treaty faced in the Russian Parliament demonstrated that Moscow is still unable to find an acceptable solution to that dilemma.

FOR FURTHER READING

Mikhail Gorbachev, *Perestroika and New Thinking for our Country and for the Whole World* (Moscow, Politizdat, 1987); James A. Baker, *The Politics of Diplomacy. Revolution, War, and Peace, 1989–1992* (G.R Putnam's Sons, New York 1995); M. Beschloss and S. Talbott *At the High Levels: The Inside Story of the End of the Cold War* (Little, Brown, and Company, Boston, 1993); A. Kozyrev, 'Transformed Russia in the New World'.

Vladimir Batyuk is Senior Researcher at the Institute for American and Canadian Studies in Moscow.

Unit 6

Key Points to Consider

❖ How can people be stopped from manufacturing (and using) weapons of mass destruction? Which weapons are likely to be used by terrorists?

❖ Is the rise in population a real problem? How so?

❖ Is global warming a problem? Is there any historical precedence that is informative?

❖ Is there anything useful about warfare? Is it sometimes necessary?

❖ Why should anyone be concerned about African orphans? What will be the impact of these orphans and AIDS on human history?

❖ If someone from India asked you why the United States was a success, what would you say?

❖ Compare the different views about the end of the cold war found in Michael Barone's article "The American Century" with those of Vladimir Batyuk in "The End of the Cold War: A Russian View" (unit 5).

DUSHKIN ONLINE Links   www.dushkin.com/online/

These sites are annotated on pages 4 and 5.

The cold war and its aftermath left unresolved problems for the contemporary world, a world in which every nation is linked to the welfare of others. The Soviet landscape was left in an environmental shambles with polluted air, food, and water. The new nations of the former USSR are too poor to repair the damage and their recovery will take decades. There also has been a proliferation of knowledge about methods of mass destruction, not only with atomic weapons, but also with poison gases and infectious diseases. Almost any determined nation can manufacture these items, and recent scares from Iraq and North Korea confirm the possibility. The article "Bombs, Gas and Microbes: The Desperate Efforts to Block the Road to Doomsday" outlines the problem, but the solution is elusive. It may be that the era of the cold war, when two superpowers controlled most of the weaponry, will seem a simple world indeed.

In the background of contemporary concerns is the increasing world population that will shortly reach 6.5 billion. Can the planet sustain the projected population of 9 billion in 2050? The population of democratic India will pass communist China in the near future mainly because China enforces a one-child-per-family policy. Are the Communists right about this one? No one knows the capacity of the planet, but it would seem likely that there will be shortages in many areas as the population grows. "Like Herrings in a Barrel" summarizes the growth of the world population. The peoples of the world, moreover, are moving to the cities and into manufacturing. Air pollution has resulted from such movement and there is a

consensus among scientists that the air is becoming warmer. Again, it is difficult to predict consequences, but the article, "The Weather Turns Wild," provides some answers.

Some groups are still at each other's throats, such as in the Sudan, where a civil war has raged for 18 years. In the Near East, terrorism keeps the flames of hatred going between the Israelis and Palestinians. In Central Africa, Uganda and Rwanda fell into warfare after a disagreement about which faction to support in the Congo Republic. The result, as explained in "Congo's Hidden War," was 1.7 million deaths. Such warfare destroys property and creates refugees. The difficulties in Africa, moreover, are compounded by disease, particularly AIDS, which has created an "orphan crisis," according to the article, "10 Million Orphans." This is unlike anything that has ever happened to humanity in the past.

In contrast to the troubles in Russia, the Near East, and Africa, the United States is a stunning success. It is the superpower at the top of a pyramid of nations, and is a place that people risk their lives in open boats and hidden containers to reach. Michael Barone, in "The American Century," compares the United States of 1900 to that of 2000. The increase in such areas as education, wealth, government spending, and life expectancy is startling. Barone gives an overview of American history during the twentieth century and credits the hard work of the American people for their achievement at home and in the world. This is a self-congratulatory article, but the accomplishments of the United States in the twentieth century cannot be denied.

Global Problems, Global Interdependence

Like herrings in a barrel

In 1,000 years, the human race has multiplied 20-fold. Today's 6 billion people may be 9 billion by 2050. Yet the increase has slowed; rich nations breed less

The power of population is so superior to the power of the earth to produce subsistence for man that premature death must in some shape or other visit the human race. The vices of mankind are active and able ministers of depopulation . . . but should they fail in this war of extermination, sickly seasons, epidemic, pestilence and plague advance in terrific array, and sweep off their thousands and ten thousands. Should success be still incomplete, gigantic, inevitable famine stalks in the rear, and with one mighty blow levels the population with the food of the world.

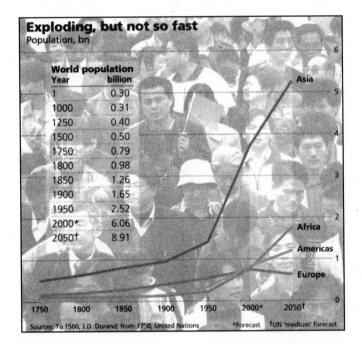

Exploding, but not so fast
Population, bn

World population	
Year	billion
1	0.30
1000	0.31
1250	0.40
1500	0.50
1750	0.79
1800	0.98
1850	1.26
1900	1.65
1950	2.52
2000*	6.06
2050†	8.91

Sources: To 1500, J.D. Durand; from 1750, United Nations   *Forecast †UN 'medium' forecast

WHEN Thomas Malthus, an English economist, in 1798 published his "Essay on the Principle of Population", quoted above, he caused a sensation. At the time the world's population was close to 1 billion, having risen slowly and erratically from maybe 300m at the start of the millennium; which in turn was probably not much, if at all, more than it had been in 1AD. And today? Give or take the odd 100m of us, 6 billion.

When Malthus wrote, there was no widespread sense that numbers were running out of control. The general mood was upbeat. Indeed, most thinkers considered a growing population a good thing: more people, more hands at work, more output.

A century earlier, a pioneer statistician, Gregory King, had predicted that the human race would double from its then total of around 650m in about 600 years' time, and ventured boldly:

If the world should continue to [16052AD], it might then have 6,500m.

In fact it will do so in about 2006.

By Malthus's time, a few prophets of doom had begun to give forth. Giammaria Ortes, an Italian economist, wrote

in 1790 that no one wanted to see humanity grow

not only beyond the number of persons that could breathe on the earth, but to such a number as could not be contained on all its surface, from lowest valley to highest mountain, crammed together like dried herrings in a barrel.

But Malthus's message was much more urgent than that. Some—probably unrepresentative—American figures gathered by Benjamin Franklin had persuaded him that, unless checked, most populations were likely to double every 25 years, increasing at a geometric rate (1,2,4,8,16 and so on), while food supplies would grow at only an arithmetic rate (1,2,3,4,5 and so on). Sooner or later the food was bound to run out.

Mankind had a choice: either let matters take their course, thus inviting "positive" checks—wars, plagues and famines—to reduce numbers to sustainable levels; or adopt "preventative" checks to ensure fewer children, for example by bridling passion and delaying marriage. Malthus was not optimistic that enough people would choose restraint. He himself tried to set an example by not marrying until he was 38 (and then had three children in quick succession).

Malthus was wrong in expecting populations to double every 25 years. But not far wrong: in the 200 years since he wrote, the time it takes mankind to double has shrunk from several centuries to 40 years. And he was clearly right to note that the earth's resources are finite, though he vastly underestimated man's ingenuity in utilising them more efficiently, and at making new inventions. Technology and innovation, speeded up by the industrial revolution, allowed food supplies to increase at a faster-than-arithmetical rate. Even during Malthus's lifetime, crop land was being expanded rapidly as forests were felled, and innovations such as crop rotation and selective breeding brought large increases in yields. These continue, through the "green revolution" of the 1950s to today's high-yielding, if unloved, genetically engineered crops.

What Malthus could not have predicted, since nothing like it had ever happened before and it was barely under way by his day, was something known now as the "demographic transition": the way societies alter as they get richer. First comes a decline in mortality, leading to a short population explosion; then, after an interval of variable length, a steep decline in the birth rate, which slows, halts or may even reverse the rise in numbers.

For most of human history, people had lots of children, of whom many died in infancy. If things were going well,

and there were no serious wars, epidemics or famines, more would be born, more would survive longer, and populations would rise. From about 1000 to 1300, Europe enjoyed a spurt of economic growth. A lot of new land was taken into cultivation, and the number of cities multiplied. The population doubled or trebled.

Enter, in 1347, via the Mediterranean, the Black Death. Within a few years this plague had traversed the continent. By 1400 Europe's population had shrunk by maybe 25m, about one-third. Plague reappeared periodically over the next three centuries, the last big wave rolling over north-western Europe in the later 17th century, soon after the Thirty Years War, which had already slashed Germany's population. In the New World, smallpox brought by Spanish *conquistadors* and European settlers in the 16th century killed maybe 10m–20m of the native populations. Not even the 20th century has escaped such scourges: the worldwide flu of 1918–19 is thought to have caused 25m–40m deaths, far more than the first world war; and since 1980 AIDS has killed some 12m people, so far.

In pre-industrial Europe, frequent food crises also served as periodic population checks. When bad harvests pushed up the cost of grain, more people died and, while the trouble lasted, couples had fewer children. Figures from Tuscany (not alone) in the 16th–18th centuries show grain prices and mortality closely correlated. But by the 19th century the days of famine in Europe were largely over, except in Ireland, where the potato blight of 1846–47 and its side-effects may have killed a sixth of the 8m-odd people.

THE TRANSITION BEGINS

By the mid-19th century most of Europe was in the first stage of the demographic transition. Mortality had lessened, as wars, famines and epidemics had; local food shortages were rarer, thanks to better economic organisation and transport; public health, medical care (notably, midwifery) and the control of infectious diseases such as cholera and smallpox had improved. The population spurted,

as Malthus had predicted. Between 1800 and 1900 Europe's population doubled, to over 400m, whereas that of Asia, further behind in the demographic transition, increased by less than 50%, to about 950m.

Europe by now was crowded, and most worthwhile land already under the plough. But there was space elsewhere. Thanks to a steady trickle of migration over the previous three centuries, North and South America by 1800 each held about 4m people of European extraction. From around 1850 that trickle became a flood. Over the next 100 years or so, some 50m Europeans quit their continent, most going to North America, others to South America and the Antipodes. At the peak of this wave of emigration, Europe was exporting about a third of the natural increase in its population.

But something else was happening there that would have taken Malthus by surprise: as people came to expect to live longer, and better, they started to have fewer children. They realised they no longer needed several babies just to ensure that two or three would survive. And as they moved from country to town, they also found that children were no longer an economic asset that could be set to work at an early age, but a liability to be fed, housed and (some of them) educated, for years. Worse, with too many children, a mother would find it hard to take and keep a job, to add to the family income. Nor were offspring any longer a guarantee against a destitute old age: in the new industrial society, they were likelier to go their own way.

Thanks to Europe's new-found restraint, in the past 100 years or so its population has risen only 80%, to 730m, and most countries' birth rate is now so low that numbers are static or falling. But their composition is very different from the past: better living standards, health and health care are multiplying old heads, even as the number of young ones shrinks.

In contrast, Asia's population over the same time has nearly quadrupled, to more than 3.6 billion. North America's too has grown almost as fast, but largely thanks to immigration. Africa's has multiplied 5½ times, and Latin America's nearly sevenfold.

Why these differences? From around 1950, mortality in developing countries also began to fall, and much faster than it ever had in Europe. The know-how needed to avoid premature death, especially of small children, travelled so readily that life expectancy in many poor countries is now not far behind the rich world's. But the attitudes and values that persuade people to have fewer children are taking longer to adjust.

Yet adjust they do. In China, the world's most populous country, with over 1.2 billion people, and still relatively poor, the demographic transition is already almost complete; not only has mortality come down faster than in other countries with similar income levels, but in recent decades a sometimes brutal population policy (now being relaxed a little) has restricted couples to one or two children. India's population rushed ahead for longer, and has just reached 1 billion, despite attempts to slow it, including a period in the 1970s when the government promoted large-scale sterilisation. The UN's "medium-variant" forecast is that by 2050 India's headcount may be over 1.5 billion, slightly ahead of China's. Yet in India too fertility has fallen fast. Only in Africa is population growth still rampant, though slowed by AIDS, which in some countries is killing a large proportion of the young adults.

DOES MORE MEAN WORSE?

Demographers like to dramatise this recent population growth by asking a spooky question. Of all the people who have ever lived, how many are alive today? The answer requires a lot of guesswork, except for the very recent past; but a fair estimate for the number of people born throughout human history is 80 billion–100 billion. With mankind now numbering 6 billion, the astonishing answer must be: 6–7%. The figures are even more spectacular if you count man-

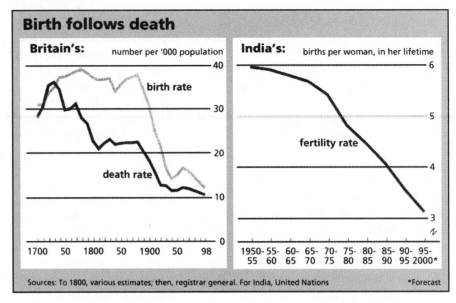

years lived rather than people, because life for early man was usually short: at birth, he could expect 20 years of it in 10000BC, only 27 as late as 1750AD, and 58 today. On that reckoning, those alive today account for one-sixth of the time that humans collectively have spent on earth.

Is all this rise in numbers necessarily a bad thing? Economists have disputed endlessly: does it promote economic growth, by expanding the workforce, or, if it happens too quickly, choke growth off? Their answers seem to boil down to an unhelpful "It all depends." But then governments' population policies are not guided solely by economics. Prussia's Frederick the Great made a sharp political point when he observed in the 18th century that "a country's wealth is the number of its men." Two centuries later, Mao Zedong insisted that "China's vast population should be viewed as a positive asset."

Of course, numbers are not the only measure. The United States, with its 275m people, has less than 5% of the planet's population, yet it dominates the other 95%. Still, in many rich countries the birth rate has now fallen so low that the population is actually shrinking; and in some their governments see this as a problem. Their main fear may be that soon there will be too few young workers around to pay for older ones' pen-

sions. But at the back of their minds there may also be the thought that, say, a Japan of 105m people in 2050 (the UNC's medium forecast) might carry less clout than today's Japan of 125m.

Many say the globe is already overcrowded, risking environmental disasters such as global warming and pervasive pollution. Nonsense, say others: with careful management it could carry plenty more, say 10 billion. A few optimists, if that's the word, muse that, with a bit of squeezing and the astute use of technology, the figure might be several times that, maybe even 100 billion.

One thing is sure: even if from tomorrow every couple on earth practised Malthusian restraint and stopped at two children, the momentum built up by the huge population growth in developing countries since 1950 will keep numbers rising fast for decades to come; the UNC's medium forecast for 2050 is 8.9 billion people. But, fingers crossed, soon thereafter even the poorest countries may have lost their enthusiasm for large families, while couples in some richer countries may—may—have rediscovered that two children are, and have, more fun than one. A century or so from now, if mankind survives that long, its number may have reached a new (and surely better) steady state.

The Weather Turns Wild

Global warming could cause droughts, disease, and political upheaval

By Nancy Shute

The people of Atlanta can be forgiven for not worrying about global warming as they shivered in the dark last January, their city crippled by a monster ice storm that hit just before the Super Bowl. So can the 15 families in Hilo, Hawaii, whose houses were washed away by the 27 inches of rain that fell in 24 hours last November. And the FBI agents who searched for evidence blown out of their downtown Fort Worth office building, which was destroyed by a tornado last March. Not to mention the baffled residents of Barrow, Alaska, who flooded the local weather office with calls on June 19, as rumbling black clouds descended—a rare Arctic thunderstorm.

But such bizarre weather could soon become more common, and the consequences far more dire, according to a United Nations scientific panel. Last week, the Intergovernmental Panel on Climate Change met in Shanghai and officially released the most definitive—and scary—report yet, declaring that global warming is not only real but man-made. The decade of the '90s was the warmest on record, and most of the rise was likely caused by the burning of

oil, coal, and other fuels that release carbon dioxide, as well as other so-called greenhouse gases. What's more, future changes will be twice as severe as predicted just five years ago, the group says. Over the next 100 years, temperatures are projected to rise by 2.5 to 10.4 degrees worldwide, enough to spark floods, epidemics, and millions of "environmental refugees."

By midcentury, the chic Art Deco hotels that now line Miami's South Beach could stand waterlogged and abandoned. Malaria could be a public health threat in Vermont. Nebraska farmers could abandon their fields for lack of water. Outside the United States, the impact would be much more severe. Rising sea levels could contaminate the aquifers that supply drinking water for Caribbean islands, while entire Pacific island nations could simply disappear under the sea. Perhaps the hardest-hit country would be Bangladesh, where thousands of people already die from floods each year. Increased snowmelt in the Himalayas could combine with rising seas to make at least 10 percent of the country uninhabitable. The water level of most of Africa's largest rivers, including the

Nile, could plunge, triggering widespread crop failure and idling hydroelectric plants. Higher temperatures and lower rainfall could stunt food production in Mexico and other parts of Latin America.

No more words. "The debate is over," says Peter Gleick, president of the Pacific Institute for Studies in Development, Environment, and Security, in Oakland, Calif. "No matter what we do to reduce greenhouse-gas emissions, we will not be able to avoid some impacts of climate change."

This newest global-warming forecast is backed by data from myriad satellites, weather balloons, ships at sea, and weather stations, and by immense computer models of the global climate system. As scientists have moved toward consensus on warming's inevitability, there has been growing movement to come up with realistic adaptations to blunt the expected effects. Instead of casting blame at polluting SUV drivers, environmentalists and businesses alike are working to create feasible solutions. These range from measures as complex as global carbon-dioxide-emissions taxes to ones as simple as caulking leaks in

The travails of a warmer world

Average worldwide temperatures (in Fahrenheit)

Global climate change may drastically affect human society, directly and indirectly. Scientists forecast a potential 2.5-to-10.4-degree spike in global temperature by the year 2100. The steep rise could set off a cascade of nasty effects, from pestilence and famine to wars and refugee movement.

high 68.2°
66°
64°
62°
low 60.3°
60°
58°
56.5° Projection
56°
1860 1925 1990 2100

Sources: Phil Jones, University of East Anglia; Intergovernmental Panel on Climate Change

Heat wave: Deaths from heatstroke worldwide may double by 2020.

Crops: Drought and high temperatures could cause crop failure and malnutrition.

Pollution: Sunlight breaks pollution into noxious substances, causing more respiratory problems.

Disease: Warmer, wetter conditions may amplify insect-borne diseases, such as malaria; flooding could spawn more water-borne illness.

Water wars: Droughts may bring on conflicts over scarce water resources, pitting upstream nations against downstream neighbors.

Coral bleaching: Warmer water could bleach coral reefs, leading to their destruction. This may deplete fisheries, disrupting food supplies and tourism.

Refugees: Floods displaced 230 million people in China in the 1998 La Niña rains. Future floods could do similar damage by submerging homes and contaminating water.

Fires: Drier summers and higher temperatures create ideal conditions for wildfires. In 1997, some 40,000 people were treated for smoke inhalation in Southeast Asia.

Floods: Sea levels will rise in the next century, leaving people more vulnerable to storm surges. Earlier melting snow could cause rivers to overflow.

U.S. East Coast: West Nile virus has already spread from New Hampshire to North Carolina.

Mexico: Rising temperatures could cut maize crops by 20 percent to 60 percent.

Brazil: Models project that populous northeastern Brazil could suffer some of the most severe crop setbacks because of drought.

NORTH AMERICA

SOUTH AMERICA

(Graphic continued on next page)

Russian and Chinese natural gas pipelines. The take-home message: Change is difficult but not impossible, and the sooner we start, the easier it will be. Civilization has adjusted to drastic weather changes in the past (see box, "Weathering the storms") and is well positioned to do so again. Indeed, while governments squabble over what is to be done, major corporations such as BP Amoco and DuPont are retooling operations to reduce greenhouse gases. "I am very, very optimistic," says Robert Wat-

son, an atmospheric scientist, World Bank official, and leader of the IPCC panel that created the report.

Concern about greenhouse gases is hardly new; as early as the 1700s, scientists were wondering whether atmospheric gases could transmit light but trap heat, much like glass in a greenhouse. By 1860, Irish physicist John Tyndall (the first man to explain why the sky is blue) suggested that ice ages follow a decrease in carbon dioxide. In 1957, Roger Revelle, a researcher at the

Scripps Institution of Oceanography in California, declared that human alteration of the climate amounted to a "large-scale geophysical experiment" with potentially vast consequences.

Such dire predictions had been made before and not come true, and this environmental hysteria emboldened skeptics. But by 1988, the evidence was hard to rebut; when NASA atmospheric scientist James Hansen told a congressional hearing that global warming had arrived, climate change became a hot political

(Graphic continued from
previous page)

Marshall Islands, Tuvalu, Kiribati: Swelling oceans could cover these islands, forcing residents to evacuate.

Nigeria: A 3-foot rise in sea level could displace almost 4 million people and leave parts of the capital city, Lagos, underwater.

Bangladesh: Faster melting snowpacks in the Himalayas, rising sea levels, and cholera outbreaks could force millions from their homes.

South Africa: Malaria may surge in areas previously too cold for mosquitoes to inhabit.

Zimbabwe: River flow along the Zambezi could fall steeply, disrupting crop production and possibly producing refugees.

Australia: The Great Barrier Reef could be ruined as a tourist attraction if the water temperature increases by a mere 3.6 degrees.

ROD LITTLE, ROB CADY, AND STEPHEN ROUNTREE—USN&WR

Reporting by Rachel K. Sobel and Kevin Whitelaw
Sources: National Center for Atmospheric Research, University of Virginia, Worldwatch Institute, National Climatic Data Center, World Meteorological Organization, and staff reports

topic. At the 1992 Rio de Janeiro Earth Summit, 155 nations, including the United States, signed a treaty to control greenhouse emissions, which also include other gases such as methane. That accord led to the 1997 Kyoto protocol calling for reducing emissions of developed nations below 1990 levels but placing no emissions restrictions on China and other developing nations. In November, talks over the treaty broke down over the issue of how to measure nations' progress in reducing emissions.

They are set to resume by midyear, after the Bush administration has formulated its position.

Doubters remain. Some argue that climate is too chaotic and complex to trust to any computerized prediction, or that Earth's climate is too stable to be greatly upset by a little more CO_2. "I don't see how the IPCC can say it's going to warm for sure," says Craig Idso, a climatologist and vice president of the Center for the Study of Carbon Dioxide and Global Change in Tempe, Ariz. He

calls predictions of drastic warming "a sheer guess" and says that extra carbon dioxide "is going to be nothing but a boon for the biosphere. Plants will grow like gangbusters."

But these skeptics appear to be losing ground. "There are fewer and fewer of them every year," says William Kellogg, former president of the American Meteorological Society and a retired senior scientist at the National Center for Atmospheric Research. "There are very few people in the serious meteorological community who doubt that the warming is taking place."

If the majority view holds up and temperatures keep rising, over the next century global weather patterns will shift enough to affect everyday life on every continent. The effects would vary wildly from one place to the next; what might be good news for one region (warmer winters in Fairbanks, Alaska) would be bad news for another (more avalanches in the Alps). Weather would become more unpredictable and violent, with thunderstorms sparking increased tornadoes and lightning, a major cause of fires. The effects of El Niño, the atmospheric oscillation that causes flooding and mudslides in California and the tropics, would become more severe. Natural disasters already cost plenty; in the 1990s the tab was $608 billion, more than the four previous decades combined, according to Worldwatch Institute. The IPCC will release its tally of anticipated effects on climate and societies on February 19 in Geneva. Key climate scientists say that major points include:

Death and pestilence. Cities in the Northern Hemisphere would very likely become hotter, prompting more deaths from heatstroke in cities such as Chicago and Shanghai. Deaths would also increase from natural disasters, and warmer weather would affect transmission of insect-borne diseases such as malaria and West Nile virus, which made a surprise arrival in the United States in 1999. "We don't know exactly how West Nile was introduced to the U.S., but we do know that drought, warm winter, and heat waves are the conditions that help amplify it," says Paul Epstein, a researcher at Harvard's School of Public Health (see box, "Mercury Rising").

Wildfires. Rising temperatures and declining rainfall would dry out vegetation, making wildfires like last summer's—which burned nearly 7 million acres in the West and cost $1.65 billion—more common, especially in California, New Mexico, and Florida.

Rain and flooding. Rain would become more frequent and intense in the Northern Hemisphere. Snow would melt faster and earlier in the Rockies and the

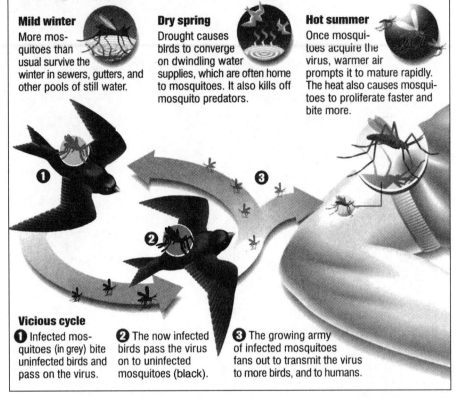

Mercury rising: droughts and fevers

Cycles of extreme weather, likely caused by global warming, may have helped fuel the spread of West Nile virus in North America by boosting the mosquito population.

Mild winter
More mosquitoes than usual survive the winter in sewers, gutters, and other pools of still water.

Dry spring
Drought causes birds to converge on dwindling water supplies, which are often home to mosquitoes. It also kills off mosquito predators.

Hot summer
Once mosquitoes acquire the virus, warmer air prompts it to mature rapidly. The heat also causes mosquitoes to proliferate faster and bite more.

Vicious cycle
❶ Infected mosquitoes (in grey) bite uninfected birds and pass on the virus.
❷ The now infected birds pass the virus on to uninfected mosquitoes (black).
❸ The growing army of infected mosquitoes fans out to transmit the virus to more birds, and to humans.

Source: *Scientific American*

ROBERT KEMP—*USN&WR*

Himalayas, exacerbating spring flooding and leaving summers drier. "This is the opposite of what we want," says Gleick. "We want to be able to save that water for dry periods."

Rising sea levels. Sea level worldwide has risen 9 inches in the last century, and 46 million people live at risk of flooding due to storm surges. That figure would double if oceans rise 20 inches. The IPCC predicts that seas will rise anywhere from 3.5 inches to 34.6 inches by 2010, largely because of "thermal expansion" (warmer water takes up more space), but also because of melting glaciers and ice caps. A 3-foot rise, at the top range of the forecast, would swamp parts of major cities and islands, including the Marshall Islands in the South Pacific and the Florida Keys.

Water wars. Drought—and an accompanying lack of water—would be the most obvious consequence of warmer temperatures. By 2015, 3 billion people will be living in areas without enough water. The already water-starved Middle East could become the center of conflicts, even war, over water access. Turkey has already diverted water from the Tigris and Euphrates rivers with dams and irrigation systems, leaving downstream countries like Iraq and Syria complaining about low river levels. By 2050, such downstream nations could be left without enough water for drinking and irrigation.

Refugees. The United States is the single largest generator of greenhouse gases, contributing one quarter of the global total. But it, and other higher-latitude countries, would be affected less by climate change than would more tropical nations. The developing world will be hit hardest—and least able to cope. "Bangladesh has no prayer," says Stephen Schneider, a climatologist at Stanford University, noting that flooding there, and in Southeast Asia and China, could dislocate millions of people. "The

HISTORY LESSONS
Weathering the storms

It was a pretty good run as societies go: over a millennium with all the material wealth, political organization, and advanced arts and learning that the word *society* implies. Then, at the dawn of the 10th century A.D., the Classic Maya civilization abruptly imploded, leaving deserted cities, trade routes, and pyramids throughout the southern Yucatán.

Three hundred years later, a very different story unfolded on California's Channel Islands. The Chumash people there rapidly transformed themselves from scattered populations of hunter-gatherers into a sophisticated trading culture with clear political leadership and an areawide monopoly on the production of trading beads. The connection? Both groups, climate reconstructions show, were confronted with sudden, dramatic, and long-lasting climate change.

It may be our fault this time around, but climate swings have always affected human societies. Writing in the current issue of the journal *Science,* Yale archaeologist Harvey Weiss cites more than a dozen examples of ancient cultures collapsing in the face of rapidly altered weather. Bad news for a society facing massive global change. But perhaps we can learn something from the Chumash, who, says University of California–Los Angeles archaeologist Jeanne Arnold, "came up with creative political and economic responses to their changing environment." Prospective survivors of climate upheaval, in other words, should be flexible and must be wary of leaders who are overly occupied with building monuments, getting re-elected, and other such trivialities.

Choices. "Different cultures have different philosophies about things like making changes," says Brian Fagan, a University of California–Santa Barbara archaeologist. In his forthcoming book, *The Little Ice Age,* Fagan details how various European nations dealt with that unusually cool period, which stretched from 1300 to 1850. The French endured famine, disease, and general wretchedness when cold, wet weather spoiled their traditional cereal crops year after year. The Dutch suffered the same miserable weather but were quicker to adopt new crops and intensive farming methods, perhaps, suggests Fagan, sparking the development of mature market economies.

Confronting massive climate change is never easy—excavations show evidence of dislocation and violence during the Chumash restructuring. But the record at least suggests that climate is not necessarily destiny. Fast-forward to 2001. Scientists tell us we have the technology to adapt, and unlike the Akkadians of Mesopotamia (done in by drought, circa 2290 B.C.) or the Peruvian Moche civilization (drought backed by floods some three millenniums later), we have advance notice that trouble's coming. All we need then is the flexibility of the Dutch and the political will of the Chumash. Will we find them? That's one for the historians in a couple of hundred years. If there are any of them left.
—Thomas Hayden

rich will get richer, and the poor will get poorer. That's not a stable situation for the world."

Those daunted by this roster of afflictions will be cheered, a bit, by the United Nations group's report on how to fend off these perils, which will be released March 5 in Ghana. Not only is humanity not helpless in the face of global warming, but we may not even have to give up all the trappings of a First World lifestyle in order to survive—and prosper.

The first question is whether it's possible to slow, or even halt, the rise in greenhouse gases in the atmosphere. Scientists and energy policy experts say yes, unequivocally. Much of the needed technology either has already been developed or is in the works. The first step is so simple it's known to every third grader: Conserve energy. Over the past few decades, innovations from higher gas mileage to more efficient refrigerators to compact fluorescent lights have saved billions of kilowatts of energy. The second step is to use less oil and coal, which produce greenhouse gases, and rely more on cleaner energy sources such as natural gas and wind, and later on, solar and hydrogen. In Denmark, 13 percent of electricity now comes from wind power, probably the most economical alternative source. In Britain, a company called Wavegen recently activated the first commercial ocean-wave-energy generator, making enough electricity to power about 400 homes.

Taxing ideas. But despite such promising experiments, fossil fuels remain far cheaper than the alternatives. To reduce this cost advantage, most Western European countries, including Sweden, Norway, the Netherlands, Austria, and Italy, have levied taxes on carbon emissions or fossil fuels. The taxes also are intended to nudge utilities toward technologies, like coal gasification, that burn fossil fuels more cleanly. In Germany, where "eco-taxes" are being phased in on most fossil fuels, a new carbon levy will add almost 11 cents to the price of a gallon of gasoline.

But the United States has always shunned a carbon tax. John Holdren, a professor of environmental policy at Harvard's Kennedy School of Government, says such a tax could stimulate economic growth and help position the United States as a leader in energy technology. "The energy technology sector is worth $300 billion a year, and it'll be $500 to $600 billion by 2010," Holdren says. "The companies and countries that get the biggest chunk of that will be the ones that deliver efficient, clean, inexpensive energy."

A growing number of companies have already figured that out. One of the most advanced large corporations is chemical giant DuPont, which first acknowledged the problem of climate change in 1991. Throughout the past decade, the company worked to cut its carbon dioxide emissions 45 percent from 1990 levels. Last year, it pledged to find at least 10 percent of its energy from renewable sources.

Even more surprising was the dramatic announcement by oil giant BP in 1997 agreeing that climate change was indeed occurring. Even with other oil firms protesting that the evidence was too thin, BP pledged to reduce its greenhouse-gas emissions by 10 percent from 1990 levels by 2010. At the same time, BP Amoco is pouring money into natural gas exploration and investing in renewable energy like solar power and hydrogen.

Even America's largest coal-burning utility company is experimenting. American Electric Power of Columbus, Ohio, is testing "carbon capture," which would separate out carbon dioxide emissions and dispose of them in deep underground saline aquifers, effectively creating carbon-emission-free coal power. Application is at least a decade away. "If we're able to find creative solutions, they're going to place us at a competitive advantage in our industry," says Dale Heydlauff, AEP's senior vice president for environmental affairs.

In automobile manufacturing, there is already a race on for alternatives to fossil fuels. Several automakers like Ford, DaimlerChrysler, and Volkswagen have developed prototypes of cars run by hydrogen fuel cells rather than gasoline. The performance is very similar to that of today's cars, but the cost remains, for now, prohibitive. Fuel-cell vehicles are unlikely to be mass-produced until after 2010, and even then, people will need a push to make the switch. "Climate change is too diffuse to focus people's attention," says C. E. Thomas, a vice president at Directed Technologies, an Arlington, Va., engineering firm working on fuel cells. "But if we have another war in the Middle East or gasoline lines, that will get their attention."

Even with these efforts, and many more, climatologists point out that turning the atmosphere around is much harder than turning a supertanker. Indeed, atmospheric changes already underway may take hundreds of years to change. As a result, some vulnerable countries are already taking preventive, if costly, measures. More than half of the Netherlands lies below sea level and would be threatened by increased storm surges. Last December, the Dutch government outlined an ambitious plan to bolster the sea defenses. Over the next decade, the Netherlands will spend more than $1 billion to build new dikes, bolster the natural sand dunes, and widen and deepen rivers enough to protect the country against a 3-foot rise in ocean levels.

Some of the most successful adaptations to climate change probably won't involve high-tech gizmos or global taxes. They'll be as simple as the strips of cloth distributed to women in Bangladesh, which they use to screen cholera-causing microbes from water. Villages where women strained water have reduced cholera cases by 50 percent.

"Society is more robust than we give it credit for," says Michael Glantz, a political scientist at the National Center for Atmospheric Research. Like farmers who gradually change to new crops as wells grow dry, people may learn to live comfortably in a new, warmer world.

With reporting by Thomas Hayden, Charles W. Petit, Rachel K. Sobel, Kevin Whitelaw, and David Whitman

Bombs, Gas and Microbes

The desperate efforts to block the road to doomsday

India and Pakistan have reawakened the world to the dangers of nuclear weapons. Chemical and biological ones may be just as hard to control

IT DID not need the nuclear tests conducted last month by India and Pakistan to show that the nuclear age, which has dominated the second half of this century, is destined for a longer half-life than many had begun to hope. Indeed, almost a decade since the cold war ended and the threat of nuclear Armageddon that had hung over the world for more than 40 years was supposedly lifted, fears about the spread of weapons of mass destruction—nuclear, chemical and biological weapons and the missiles to deliver them—have, if anything, intensified.

Such fears are not irrational. The collapse of the otherwise unlamented Soviet Union brought with it the danger that ex-Soviet weapons scientists might start to hawk their skills abroad—as some have. In any event, the secrets of building nuclear and chemical weapons are now decades old and increasingly hard to keep. Moreover, regional rivalries that used to be bottled up by America and the Soviet Union lest they led to a superpower confrontation are bottled up no longer. The rivalry between India and Pakistan had long driven a slow-motion arms race, in both missile and nuclear technology, before last month's tit-for-tat testing of bombs. Other potential flashpoints include the Korean peninsula and the Middle East, where tensions between Israel and its Arab neighbours are rising as hopes for peace collapse.

As India and Pakistan have proved, such regional pressures to proliferate should not be underestimated. Yet so far only a few countries have actually crossed the threshold to build weapons of mass destruction. One reason is general abhorrence of their use. The destruction visited on Hiroshima and Nagasaki in 1945 ensured that nuclear weapons were from then on held in reserve as a deterrent, rather than used as weapons for waging war. Similarly, most countries have ruled out the use of chemical weapons as too nasty for the battlefield (though Iraq has already proved one exception, both in its war with Iran and in its determination to suppress its own Kurdish population). Biological weapons—less useful in the heat of the battle, as their awful effects may take several days to appear—have likewise been stigmatised.

Restraint, however, has not rested entirely on moral injunctions. As important in halting the spread of the horrible new weapons have been arms-control regimes. These work by raising the technical barriers and the costs to would-be proliferators. The question raised by the decisions of India and Pakistan to step across the nuclear threshold, however, is whether such regimes can really work.

The most intensive efforts have gone into controlling nuclear weapons. The Nuclear Non-Proliferation Treaty (NPT), which came into force in 1970 and was extended indefinitely in 1995, divides the world into two groups: the five nuclear haves (America, Russia, China, Britain and France, which had tested a nuclear weapon before January 1st 1967) and the rest. The haves promise to work towards nuclear disarmament, as part of an effort towards general and complete disarmament, and the have-nots promise not to acquire nuclear weapons of their own, in return for help with their civilian nuclear industry.

Is it a fair bargain? It is certainly one freely entered into by the 186 states that have signed the treaty: only India, Pakistan, Israel, Brazil and Cuba still sit outside.

In its near-universality, the NPT is one of the most successful arms-control regimes on record. Its system of obligations and checks has persuaded many countries that could have built nuclear weapons not to do so. In the 1980s Argentina and Brazil used the monitoring help and methods of the International Atomic Energy Agency (IAEA), the NPT's watchdog, when they decided to roll back their competing nuclear-weapons programmes. In 1993 South Africa announced that it had built, then dismantled, six nuclear devices before it

Reprinted with permission from *The Economist*, June 6, 1998, pp 23-25. © 1998 by The Economist, Ltd. Distributed by The New York Times Special Features.

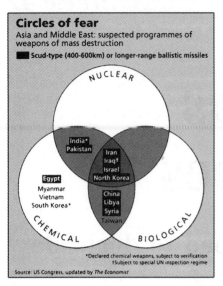

Circles of fear
Asia and Middle East: suspected programmes of weapons of mass destruction

■ Scud-type (400-600km) or longer-range ballistic missiles

NUCLEAR

India*
Pakistan

Iran
Iraq†
Israel
North Korea

Egypt
Myanmar
Vietnam
South Korea*

China
Libya
Syria
Taiwan

CHEMICAL   BIOLOGICAL

*Declared chemical weapons, subject to verification
†Subject to special UN inspection regime

Source: US Congress, updated by The Economist

joined the NPT in 1991—and then invited the IAEA in to check its nuclear records.

Yet the NPT regime at one point nearly collapsed under the burden of its own complacency. After the Gulf war ended in 1991, it emerged that Iraq, which had signed the treaty, had secretly come within a year or two of building itself a bomb, despite regular IAEA inspections. Since the hardest part of building a bomb is getting hold of the highly enriched uranium or plutonium for its explosive core, the inspectors had been spending most of their time—at the behest of member governments— simply accounting for the nuclear material that was known to exist (because countries had declared they had made it). After Iraq had shown up the flaws in that cosy system of checking, and IAEA inspectors had caught North Korea telling lies about exactly how much plutonium it had produced, the agency was asked to devise a new, far more intrusive inspection system that would do more to deter cheats.

Under the new rules, inspectors have to be given much more information about nuclear activities and facilities in a country—and not just those where nuclear fuel is present; countries are also required to pass on more information about their trade in sensitive nuclear materials; and inspectors can use much more sophisticated equipment and sampling, including environmental monitoring, to ensure that no secret nuclear activity is taking place. The new proto-

col to the NPT incorporating the extra powers required came into force in 1997. It is not binding on a country unless that country has explicitly accepted it, and so far only a handful have.

Alongside the NPT and the work of the IAEA, there are two groups that seek to prohibit or control trade in sensitive 'is made up of 33 nuclear-exporting countries and provides a list to the IAEA of items which, if exported to an NPT member, should trigger the application of IAEA safeguards; the group also exchanges confidential information on exports to countries that are outside the treaty. The Nuclear Suppliers' Group has a slightly larger membership and operates a code that goes beyond strict NPT obligations, laying down rules about trade in nuclear exports, including any that could be used for either civilian or military purposes.

However, most recent efforts to control nuclear proliferation have concentrated on bringing into force the Comprehensive Test-Ban Treaty that was opened for signature in 1996, and on negotiating a new treaty to cut off the production of fissile material for bomb making. Both treaties are seen as crucial if support for the NPT among the non-nuclear states is not to waver. Yet neither will be easy to achieve.

Although 149 countries have put their signatures to a ban on tests, only 13 have fully ratified the treaty. Yet, to ensure that a test ban is truly comprehensive, the treaty cannot come fully into force until ratified at least by all 44 countries that have nuclear reactors on their territory. These include both India and Pakistan, neither of which has signed the test ban, but also other countries, such as Israel (which has signed but not ratified it) and North Korea (which shows no sign of doing either). Assuming the treaty is still in limbo, its members will meet next year to decide how to proceed. One possibility would be to try to bring the proposed monitoring and information-gathering system into effect, as a confidence-building step, before the treaty itself comes legally into force.

Neither a test ban nor a fissile-materials cut-off treaty (which has a lot of support but has been caught up in bick-

ering at the United Nations Conference on Disarmament in Geneva) would actually oblige countries that have nuclear weapons to abandon them. However, each in its own way would help to cap the ability of those with nuclear weapons to keep building more such weapons and testing ever more sophisticated designs.

CONFOUNDED CHEMICALS

The guardians of the Chemical Weapons Convention (CWC), which came into force just over a year ago, have in many ways an even harder task. Whereas it takes a lot of deliberate and nowadays increasingly noticeable effort to build up a nuclear-weapons capability, many countries have sizeable chemicals industries. Moreover, many chemicals with humdrum civilian uses can be combined to make deadly weapons.

For many years, it was against international law to use chemical weapons, but not to manufacture or stockpile them. The CWC, by contrast, outlaws all chemical weapons and requires the destruction of all stockpiles. It also bans trade in some chemicals and restricts it in others (non-signatories will find it increasingly difficult to buy chemicals from CWC members). Within 30 days of signing the convention, governments must give an account of the chemicals industry on their territory, with declarations subject to inspection, including 'And, unlike the NPT's rules, the CWC's apply equally to all.

Already the convention has had its successes. Among the handful of countries that declared a chemical-weapons stockpile, which must now be destroyed under the supervision of the Organisation for the Prohibition of Chemical Weapons (OPCW), were India and South Korea, neither of which had previously admitted to having a chemical-weapons programme. France and China, which had both previously had chemical-weapons programmes, said they destroyed their weapons shortly before signing the convention (those claims are subject to verification by OPCW inspectors). America and Russia, with the world's biggest stockpiles of chemical weapons (33,000 tonnes and 40,000 tonnes of them respectively), are destroying theirs, although Russia, which has only just started, is desperately short of funds for the job.

In their first year the OPCW's inspectors set a furious pace, with over 200 inspections in 25 countries, checking both on the destruction of weapons stocks and on the accuracy of industrial declarations. The danger, to some of the convention's critics, is that all this could prove ineffectively costly—with inspectors spending too much time on official declarations and too little ferreting out illicit activity.

The convention's chief deterrent power against cheats is the right to carry out short-notice challenge inspections, but none has yet been tried. That is in part because many countries are still in "technical non-compliance", taking an age to pass the national legislation and work through the bureaucratic procedures necessary to collect the industrial information that the convention demands. Governments with these problems are reluctant to challenge information supplied by others, however dubious it looks (Pakistan, Iran and some countries in the Balkans were thought to have chemical-weapons programmes but have not declared any), until they have their own house in order. But challenge inspections have to be shown to be possible if they are to have their intended deterrent effect. The real strength of the convention has therefore yet to be shown.

Other problems loom: barely noticed in the recent furore over the Indian and Pakistani nuclear testing, the American Senate last month attached amendments to enabling legislation that, if allowed to stand, would give the president the right to refuse challenge inspections. Many countries are uneasy about such inspections, which they fear might enable others to walk off with their commercial secrets. But for America to give itself the right to block them, contrary to the convention it has already ratified, sets a bad precedent that others might seek to exploit for sinister purposes.

Another big problem is the number of hold-outs. So far a gratifying 168 countries have signed and 110 have rati-

fied the convention. But the CWC's most obvious bald spot, the Middle East, is also a region of serious concern about proliferation: though Israel and Jordan have signed the convention, they are still to ratify it, and so are not yet bound by the reporting and inspection regime. Meanwhile, most other Arab states, led by Egypt, have refused to sign, citing Israel's refusal to sign the NPT.

DEVILISH BREW

If searching out hidden chemical weapons is like looking for a needle in a haystack, trying to track a hidden biological-weapons programme is like looking for the eye of a needle in a haystack. In theory it takes only a tiny amount of a biological agent, such as botulinum, anthrax or plague, to spread destruction on a vast scale (making biological weapons closer to nuclear weapons in their potential effects). Luckily, turning biological agents into usable weapons is not always easy.

So far more than 130 countries have ratified the 1972 Biological and Toxins Weapons Convention (BWC), which prohibits development and production of such weapons (their use has been outlawed since 1925). But as yet the convention has no built-in checks. Groups of experts have been trying for several years to devise a new verification protocol, but it is difficult to strike a balance between useful checks and the need for bio-tech companies to preserve their legitimate commercial secrets. Even more so than chemical inspections, biological ones would need to rely heavily on the right to carry out sudden searches to investigate suspicious activity or unusual outbreaks of disease.

But if the biological-weapons convention has survived this long without such weapons being used, why worry? One reason is that, like any other arms-control regime, unless it is seen to be enforced it will fall into disrepute. What is more, as other proliferation loopholes are plugged, biological weapons, which are easier to make than nuclear weapons and more destructive than chemical ones, may become the weapon of choice for rogue governments or terrorist groups.

In 1992 Russia, one of the sponsoring governments for the convention, admitted that in the past it had illegally built biological weapons. Although it now claims to have abandoned the programme, not everyone is convinced. Aum Shinrikyo, the Japanese sect that released a nerve gas, sarin, on the Tokyo metro in 1995, killing a dozen people, is now known to have experimented with biological agents too, which it attempted to spray from rooftops and trucks both in central Tokyo and near American military bases in Japan. None of the experiments appears to have worked.

But it was Iraq's industrial-sized biological-weapons programme, uncovered by UN inspectors after the Gulf war, that injected the new urgency into efforts to bolster the BWC. After repeated denials, Iraq eventually confessed to producing biological weapons. Some biological agents had even been loaded into missile warheads and artillery shells ready for use against American and allied troops. Although inspectors have since uncovered many of the details of the programme, Iraq has still failed to account for several tonnes of the medium used for growing microbes and other specialised materials. The fear is that Iraq could restart production of anthrax and other substances within weeks unless the inspectors are allowed to complete their job.

Iraq and other countries suspected of trying to develop biological weapons often got their start in the business by ordering toxic microbes from western germ banks, ostensibly for the development of vaccines and suchlike. This has added to calls for much tighter controls. At the moment trade in such substances is monitored only by the Australia Group, an informal body of more than 20 supplier countries formed in 1985 to harmonise export controls on chemicals that could be used to produce either chemical or biological weapons.

RANGE OF POSSIBILITIES

But even if a verification protocol is eventually bolted on to the BWC, some governments are getting nervous about the threat from biological weapons, which can be distributed by anything from crop-spraying aircraft to aerosol canister. America is considering the stockpiling of vaccines for use in the event of a biological threat against civilians (vaccines are already available for American troops).

Usually, however, the quickest way to deliver a bomb, and the one that is hardest to defend against, is by missile. The Missile Technology Control Regime (MTCR) was set up in 1987 in an attempt to restrict the sales of equipment and technology for missiles with a range (300 kilometres, or 190 miles) and payload (500kg, or 1,100lb) that would enable them to carry nuclear warheads. Export guidelines were later extended to cover missiles capable of carrying any type of weapon of mass destruction. The MTCR now has some 30 members.

But the controls are far from perfect. Russia is a member of the MTCR, but Russian companies have long been accused of supplying technology and know-how to anyone who will pay for it, most recently Iran, which is thought to be trying to build a new missile with a range of up to 1,300km, capable of striking Israel, Saudi Arabia and Turkey. China, a major exporter of missile technology in the past, has said it will keep to the basic guidelines of the MTCR, but refuses to join it. It has been repeatedly criticised by America for providing missiles and know-how to others, including Pakistan. Other hard cases include Iraq (which is banned by UN rules from building missiles of more than 150km range but has been caught trying to circumvent the restrictions), Libya, Syria and North Korea. Both Iran and Pakistan are thought to have benefited from North Korea's missile programme to develop longer-range missiles.

The spread of weapons technologies seems inexorable. The best protection is to persuade countries to forgo particularly dangerous technologies in their own interests. Both India and Pakistan may find that, once the euphoria over their demonstrated nuclear prowess has faded, their security is not improved, indeed may even be worsened, by having—and facing—powerful new weapons loaded on missiles that bring a hair-trigger instability to any future crisis.

In the end, getting at the roots of regional disputes is the only sure way to reduce the danger of a hideously lethal exchange. Arms-control regimes can help by building confidence that obligations not to build or to deploy certain deadly weapons are being kept. Yet such regimes are only as strong as the will of those whose task it is to enforce them. It is the hard cases that will test the world's resolve to prevent the further spread of nuclear, chemical or biological weapons. India and Pakistan are the latest of these. They will not be the last.

Congo's hidden war

Uganda and Rwanda used to be friends. For nearly two years now, they have been fighting each other in Congo—with devastating consequences

KIGALI AND KAMPALA

THEY could not agree who had started the war in Kisangani, nor who ended it. For six days last week, Rwandan and Ugandan soldiers, on foreign soil and more than 500 kilometres (310 miles) from home, rained shells and mortar fire on each other, killing up to 250 civilians in this sprawling riverside town in central Congo, and wounding over 1,000. Much of central Kisangani, including the imposing cathedral at the river's edge, was destroyed. It was the third, and by far the most brutal, time the two armies have battled for control of the town since they began fighting each other there nearly a year ago.

It is dispiriting enough that Rwanda's president, Paul Kagame, and Uganda's president, Yoweri Museveni, old friends once considered part of a "new generation" of African leaders, should be at war. It is doubly so that the wider consequences should be so grave: their struggle, waged deep inside Congo, is a serious setback for efforts by the United Nations and others to help Africa solve its wars.

The UN had agreed to send 5,500 troops to Congo to monitor a peace deal signed a year ago by the country's government and the five countries with soldiers on its territory: Zimbabwe, Angola, Namibia, Rwanda and Uganda. But repeated breaches of the ceasefire have delayed the UN deployment. Now the whole operation is in doubt. On June

13th, a furious Kofi Annan, the UN's secretary-general, called on the Security Council to use sanctions and other punitive measures to force Uganda and Rwanda to pull their troops out.

The latest battle for Kisangani ended on June 11th, when Rwanda announced

a unilateral withdrawal of its troops, citing concern about "unnecessary fighting and the loss of innocent lives" in the city, but boasting of a tactical victory. For their part, the Ugandans denied defeat, saying their forces too had unilaterally withdrawn to avoid further

casualties. Both sides said they would withdraw to 100km from the city, though that would still leave their armies deep inside Congo. Whether they do even that, and then stay put, depends on the powers of persuasion of the UN on the ground. So far, the UN has only 21 unarmed observers in Kisangani, and no peacekeepers at all.

What has this fighting been about? The two countries first invaded the country in 1996 to drive Mobutu Sese Seko from power and install Laurent Kabila as president. When, once in office, President Kabila did not do as they ordered, the two invading presidents tried to oust him, but they failed and then fell out over their aims in Congo. Each accused the other of using the war against Mr Kabila for his own ends. In August 1998, Rwanda sent thousands of soldiers to help its proxy, the rebel Congolese Rally for Democracy (RCD). Though the Ugandans then joined in, Rwanda accused them of failing to fight the same war, of pursuing short-term commercial interests and of losing sight of the real enemy. When the RCD split in two, Rwanda and Uganda backed different factions and Uganda sponsored a third.

Uganda does not micro-manage the rebels it supports in Congo as Rwanda does. It has argued throughout that its aim has been to "empower" them. President Museveni accuses Rwanda of trying to destroy Congo, and says that Rwanda manipulates and gags its rebels, and does not understand how to build support among the people. Rwandans repeatedly single out Mr Museveni's chief of staff, Brigadier James Kazini, as the man who plunged Kisangani into war: he dispatched his men to the town when it was already occupied by Rwandans and their rebel friends.

But other motives are mixed in. One is the control of mineral wealth: the diamond trade thrives in and around Kisangani, and some Ugandans close to Mr Museveni have grown rich exporting gold and other commodities from the country's north-east. The Rwandans also argue that they are acting to protect their national security; many of their countrymen are still under threat, they say, from

Congo-based exiles who took part in the 1994 Rwandan genocide.

The battle for Kisangani has become part of a wider rivalry for regional supremacy. To that end, Rwanda has gained territory for its proxy army from the past week's fighting. It has consolidated its control of the town's two airports, while the Ugandans have withdrawn across the nearby river Tshopo. Between the two of them, Rwanda and Uganda now hold sway over more than half of the entire country.

The former friendship between the two presidents now looks irreparably damaged. When Mr Kagame, once a top officer in Mr Museveni's guerrilla army, was sworn in as president of Rwanda in April, Mr Museveni was notably absent. Mr Kagame now talks angrily of Rwandans "growing tired of being told what to do". They have become disillusioned with the Ugandan president over the past 18 months. "The man is now our main problem," says a senior Rwandan official. "He lies at summit meetings, he passes the buck to his commanders, he uses the media to attack us."

For their part, Ugandans feel betrayed by Mr Kagame, whom they say they helped to seize power. They were outraged by the news that he had recently met his sworn enemy, President Kabila. Now they accuse Mr Kagame of cutting a secret deal with him.

As relief agencies began this week to fly food into Kisangani, there were the first signs for months that normal life might resume. Tens of thousands of refugees ventured back from surrounding hiding places. The UN monitors also moved back in. But they are ill-equipped to do much to stop further warfare. The two foreign armies have been fighting each other, on and off, in Kisangani since May, despite ceasefire promises to the UN.

Even if the latest ceasefire holds, huge damage has already been done. A recent study for the International Rescue Committee, a refugee agency based in New York, suggests that a staggering 1.7m of the deaths in eastern Congo since August 1998 can be attributed, directly or indirectly, to the fighting.

SIERRA LEONE
STAYING ON

BRITISH marines were being carried by helicopter to a naval ship off Freetown this week. But, as Britain withdrew its frontline forces from Sierra Leone as scheduled, its involvement in the country and the region seemed to be deepening, not diminishing.

One reason is that the United Nations force in Sierra Leone is a shambles. An unpublished report, drawn up by a UN team that visited the country after the seizure of some 500 UN peacekeepers by rebels last month, is described by officials as a "bombshell". It reveals that some units disobey orders, many are under-equipped and badly trained, and some have fled at the rumour of rebel attack. The UN operation is badly managed, with little co-ordination between the UN's special representative, Oluyemi Adeniji, a Nigerian, and its military chief, Major-General Vijay Kumar Jetley, an Indian. This has widened resentment between African and non-African peacekeepers.

Britain, which promises to "go the distance" with Sierra Leone, has agreed to second officers and special forces to help its army and the UN with such matters as military intelligence, tactical advice and logistics. It will also supply Sierra Leone's army with ammunition and train 1,000 new recruits.

The immediate strategy is for the motley bands that make up the "pro-government" forces to advance on the rebel Revolutionary United Front (RUF) and, directed by British advice, drive it north and east. The UN force will follow behind, securing liberated areas. Last year's peace deal has been shelved, and there is broad agreement that Foday Sankoh, the RUF leader, now languishing in a Freetown prison, cannot be trusted as someone to negotiate with. The RUF, it is hoped, may collapse under attack.

The main objective is to take the diamond fields in the east, which finance the rebels' war chest. This will be the toughest military task the government forces have undertaken, because the rebels will cling on to control of the diamonds. It is also possible that the government forces will disintegrate as they reach the diamond areas, even before they have to fight. During the nine years of civil war, many soldiers, including some from a West African peace-keeping force and foreign mercenaries, have settled in and dug for diamonds, making territorial deals with the rebels or even joining them.

From the diamond fields, the threads of the conflict lead over the border. The RUF smuggles diamonds into neighbouring Liberia, where President Charles Taylor, who helped launch the RUF, is, according to the British, swapping them for weapons and ammunition. Mr Taylor denies this. But, as the British point out, the closer government forces get to the diamond areas, the more active he has become in supporting the RUF.

Britain wants to put a stop to this, and has called for an international ban on diamonds from Liberia as well as from Sierra Leone. But it has no embassy or influence in Liberia. This week John Prescott, Britain's deputy prime minister, was dispatched to the regional superpower, Nigeria, to try to persuade President Olusegun Obasanjo to put pressure on Mr Taylor. And Britain managed to persuade the European Union to suspend 50m euro ($48m) of aid to Liberia.

Yet, when Britain turned to America, the country with the most influence in Liberia, it was rebuffed. Liberia was founded in 1821 by American slaves seeking freedom, and retains close links with the United States. But Madeleine Albright, America's secretary of state, recently told Britain bluntly that America could do nothing to help and would not back a ban on Liberian diamonds. Liberia is regarded in Washington as the preserve of the black American lobby, and Bill Clinton's officials will not invade it—particularly since Jesse Jackson, a prominent black American, is Mr Clinton's special envoy to Africa. Mr Jackson is also a close friend of Mr Taylor.

Dismayed by the lack of American co-operation, British officials admit privately that they intend to seek help from an unlikely quarter: Libya's Muammar Qaddafi. Colonel Qaddafi once nurtured both Mr Taylor and Mr Sankoh, among

other African radicals, but has recently shown himself willing to behave a bit more helpfully. Britain now wants to put that to the test. It is finding that "going the distance" in Sierra Leone is taking it down some strange paths.

SOUTH AFRICA
HALF TRUTH

JOHANNESBURG

SICELO DLOMO was a teenager when he was shot dead in a black township 12 years ago. Until South Africa's Truth and Reconciliation Commission delved into the case, Dlomo's parents believed that their son, a student anti-apartheid activist, had been murdered by the security police. But, last year, four of his friends admitted that they had killed him because they suspected he was an informer. In February this year, the commission granted the four amnesty, and recommended reparations for Dlomo's family. Since then, the family has heard nothing, and got nothing.

The commission was set up in 1995, in order to uncover the truth about the ghastly crimes of the apartheid period and to promote national reconciliation. It was given the power to grant amnesty to those who confessed fully, provided that their crimes were politically motivated, and that the violence used had been "proportional" to their objectives. Most of its work was completed in 1998, but decisions are still dribbling out of the overloaded amnesty committee. The reparations team has barely got going.

The commission has recommended that about 20,000 victims should be paid between 17,000 and 23,000 rand ($2,400–3,300) a year for up to six years. This would cost about 3 billion rand. But the government has stumped up only a tenth of this, and only a tenth of the money set aside for reparations has been paid out. Roughly 10,000 of the beneficiaries have at least received initial payments, but of as little as 2,000 rand.

Meanwhile, apartheid killers continue to be let off. Most notorious is Craig Williamson, a spy chief who sent

the letter bomb that killed Ruth First, an anti-apartheid campaigner and academic who was married to Joe Slovo, the late Communist leader, and another bomb that killed a woman and her six-year-old daughter. He was granted amnesty on June 1st. So, the next day, was Johan van der Merwe, a former police chief, for the killing of three ANC guerrillas in 1986. Wouter Basson, known as "Dr Death" for his role in devising gruesome ways of killing people, is currently up for amnesty.

Without the lure of amnesty, however, few would have confessed—let alone relinquished power—and much of the truth would have remained buried. The confessions of those seeking amnesty may be the more reliable part of the commission's contribution to history. Accounts by the victims, a collection of which were released on compact disc in April, were rarely subjected to cross-examination, often uncorroborated, and sometimes contradicted. In short, a people's history, part truth, patchy justice.

ISRAEL
WOBBLING

JERUSALEM

EHUD BARAK'S "peace coalition" is in danger of imploding. On June 13th, the largest partner in his Labour-led government, the ultra-Orthodox Shas party, said it would pull out, after a long row over money for its religious schools. This would deprive the prime minister of a parliamentary majority. Mr Barak says he can cobble together another coalition. But, even if he does, it will be even more unwieldy than the current one—and would probably not last long.

Mr Barak insists that, if he can make a new coalition stick together long enough to let him negotiate a peace deal with the Palestinians, he could then put that to the people, at a referendum or general election, and still emerge triumphant. Talks with the Palestinians resumed near Washington this week, vigorously prodded along by President Bill Clinton's team.

A pitiful score for South African cricket

JOHANNESBURG

WHEN an amiable man named Banjo started hanging around the locker rooms used by the South African cricket team, no one suspected foul play. When Banjo handed out bags of biltong (beef jerky), the team hungrily accepted. But when he allegedly gave Hansie Cronje, the South African captain, a bag stuffed with $10,000, it became clear what he was up to. "Banjo the Biltong Man", or Mahomed Cassim, was allegedly out to bribe players to perform badly. Some, it now seems, agreed.

Cricket's biggest international scandal unfolded in April, when the Indian police said they had taped evidence of Mr Cronje doing deals with bookmakers. Astounded South Africans defended their hero, pooh-poohing the allegations and casting doubt on the competence of the Indian police. Then, however, Mr Cronje confessed to accepting money from bookies to "forecast" results. He resigned and went to pray with his pastor, Ray McCauley, a former Mr Universe finalist. The nation mourned. Mr Cronje, it was said, was a symbol of a country that no longer knew the difference between right and wrong. But worse was to come.

On June 15th, Mr Cronje admitted to a commission of inquiry that the bookies had wanted more than forecasts. With bribes and death threats, he said, they persuaded him to try to rig matches. Sev-

eral times, he offered his team-mates money to play badly. Most refused, but two succumbed. Herschelle Gibbs, a young batsman from a poor family, confessed that he had agreed to score fewer than 20 runs in a one-day match against India this year, for $15,000. He was not paid, however, because he went on to score 74. Henry Williams, a fast bowler, accepted a similar offer to bowl feebly, but was injured and had to leave the field. Ali Bacher, the head of the United Cricket Board of South Africa, claimed this week that an umpire was bribed during a test match with England.

Vast fortunes are bet on cricket, so unscrupulous bookies will pay handsomely to influence scores. Cricket stars, though nicely off, earn far less than first-class footballers or golfers.

Cricket fans have long suspected that one-day internationals can be dodgy. But it is the scale of the corruption, the force of the evidence, and the fact that even test matches, the five-day struggles that constitute the game's most sacred institution, may also have been sullied, that has caused such shock. Mr Cronje says he will retire from cricket. Mr Gibbs and Mr Williams could each face a life ban. None is likely to go to jail: South Africa has offered each one immunity from criminal prosecution in return for full disclosure.

been the quest for peace, with all else subordinated to that. Ideological disputes among his coalition members should have been kept firmly in abeyance. Instead, Mr Barak appointed the leader of the fiercely secularist party, Meretz, to the sensitive post of education minister, thereby ensuring endless squabbling with Shas over its fast-growing network of schools. A more astute or experienced politician might have stepped in early, perhaps shuffling the cabinet to wrest education back from Meretz. But Mr Barak may have left it too late. Towards the end of the week, he was suggesting that the Shas schools should be removed from the education ministry, drawing angry threats from Meretz.

Shas's Council of Torah Sages has instructed its ministers to resign at the next cabinet meeting, scheduled for June 18th. By not withdrawing them immediately, the rabbis have deliberately left the door open for further negotiations with the prime minister. But Mr Barak is already reaching out to other small parties with a view to forming a minority government if he has to. This would be supported in parliament by the ten members representing Arab parties, which Mr Barak is not ready to accept as fully fledged coalition partners.

Alternatively, if the peace talks with the Palestinians fail to produce a deal that he can take to the people, Mr Barak might be tempted to turn to the rightist Likud, to try to set up a unity government. Ariel Sharon, the Likud leader, claims he would spurn any such offer. But seasoned pundits say the grizzly old general is feeling the hot breath of younger bloods anxious to dislodge him from the party leadership. He may yet be persuaded to consider a couple of years of comfortable cohabitation with his former army subordinate, Mr Barak.

But Mr Barak's optimism is not as infectious as it was a year ago, when, campaigning on a land-for-peace platform, he trounced the incumbent prime minister, Binyamin Netanyahu. "I was elected by the people, not by the Knesset [parliament]," Mr Barak observed bitterly this week. That, however, is a moot point under Israel's hybrid system of government. The prime minister is directly elected, and cannot be deposed by the Knesset, except in extreme circumstances. But there are

two ballots, one for the prime minister and one for the parliament, and many people split their vote. Though Mr Barak did well, his party did not, winning only 26 seats in the 120-seat Knesset. No wonder that, despite his popular mandate, Mr Barak has found it hard to govern a disparate coalition in a fragmented parliament.

If Mr Barak's inning is indeed coming to an early end, he has largely himself to blame. His priority should have

10 Million Orphans

For the children who have lost their parents to AIDS, grief is only the beginning of their troubles. The disease's lasting victims.

By Tom Masland And Rod Nordland

Even on the mean streets of Homa Bay, a fishing center of 750,000 on Lake Victoria, the children stand out: Kenya has 350,000 AIDS orphans, and 35,000 of them live here. Many of those who have not been forcibly removed to the orphanage are street children—pickpockets and beggars, prostitutes and thieves. To Hamis Otieno, 14, and his brother, Rashid Faraji, 10, the streets of Homa Bay were their last, best hope. Their father had died of AIDS in 1995; their mother turned to prostitution and abandoned them soon after. Relatives, unable to provide for the boys, cast them out. The brothers made their way by bus to Nairobi, 150 miles away, where they stole, begged and worked as drug couriers. But after a year, hungry and alone, the boys went home; hustling promised to be easier on the less competitive streets of Homa Bay. Soon after their arrival, however, they caught what in their world counts as a break: they were picked up and taken by force to an orphanage. There, every one of the children is an AIDS orphan. But then, that is hardly surprising: in Homa Bay, some 50 to 70 percent of the adults are HIV-positive. "So many have died," says Hamis, "so many."

In the nations south of the Sahara, almost two decades of AIDS deaths—2.2 million in 1998 alone, and a still untallied but certainly greater number in 1999—is leaving a sea of orphans in its wake. By the end of this year, 10.4 million of the children under 15 will have lost their mothers or both parents to AIDS. Before the current epidemic, the perennial cataclysms of war and famine orphaned 2 percent of the region's children; AIDS makes that figure look benign (graphic). A generation of orphans threatens to undermine economic development, for children without parents can seldom afford education. And many AIDS orphans end up "roaming the streets, prime targets for gangs [and] militia and creating more child armies like those that participated in massacres in West Africa," says Dr. Peter Piot, executive director of UNAIDS. But worse lies ahead. The number of AIDS orphans in the region is projected to double or triple by 2010.

It is not only the raw numbers that make this orphan crisis unlike any ever seen. The children, who have often watched their parents die alone and in pain, are left in a world where AIDS has unraveled such traditional safety nets as the extended family, and in households where not a single adult is able to earn a living. Josephine Ssenyonga, 69, lives on a small farm in the Rakai district of Uganda, where AIDS has been cutting through the population like a malevolent scythe for 14 years: 32 percent of the under-15 population, a total of 75,000 children, have been orphaned in Rakai. Of the four daughters and nine sons Ssenyonga raised, 11 are dead. Her son Joseph left her with eight children; Francis left four; Peter left three. "At first there were 22, living in that small hut over there," she says. "My children did not leave me any means to look after these young ones. All they had was sold to help treat them." Overwhelmed, she took the children to the hut one day. "I told them to shut the door so we could all starve to death inside and join the others," Ssenyonga says. She changed her mind when a daughter returned home to help, and World Vision provided a three-room house for them all.

Bernadette Nakayima, 70, lives in Uganda's Masaka district, where 110,000 of the 342,000 children are orphans. Nakayima lost every one of her 11 children to AIDS. "All these left me with 35 grandchildren to look after," she says. "I was a woman struck with sorrow beyond tears." But she is not alone: one out of every four families in Uganda is now caring for an AIDS orphan, says Pelucy Ntambirweki of the Ugandan Women's Effort to Save Orphans (UWESO).

When AIDS takes a parent, it usually takes a childhood, too, for if no other relative steps in, the oldest child becomes the head of a household. Yuda Sanyu Kitali was 10 in 1992 when his mother died of AIDS; the disease had killed his father in 1986. Sanyu had to drop out of school, of course, as did his younger brother, Emmanuel Kulabigwo, now 16, and sister, Margaret Nalubega, 15: when their parents died, so did any hope of affording academic fees. "No one came to claim us or to offer help," says Sanyu. A year after the children were orphaned, the grass-thatched house their father had built in the Rakai district collapsed in a heavy rain. "Since I was the oldest, I had to build another house," Sanyu says. He did his best with mud, poles, reeds and banana fiber. The children grew cassavas and greens on the land their parents left them, but they still went to sleep hungry many nights. As Sanyu tells his story Emmanuel nods silently. Margaret sits on a papyrus mat in the corner, staring at a wall and hiding a tear in her dirty brown dress.

Most orphans are taken in by their extended families, if they are taken in by anyone, but the sheer number of these lost children fills orphanages, too. Ethembeni House, run by the Salvation Army in downtown Johannesburg, has 38 children 5 or younger. All of them have tested HIV-positive. All were abandoned: a vagrant found the newborn Moses, now 3, in a dumpster; a woman handed days-old Simon, now 2, to a street vendor and never returned. The rooms in Ethembeni, lined with cribs, are clean and decorated with pictures of clowns and dolls. Other pictures, of children who died here, line the mantel. Moses points to one: "He's gone," he says. When a stranger enters the room, the children turn expectant faces to her: "Mama, mama," they cry.

In times past it was usually war or neglect or famine or poverty that brought abandoned or orphaned children to the Sanyu Babies Home in Kampala. Now the caseload of 26 is almost entirely AIDS orphans, many of whom have lost not only parents but all their other adult relatives, too. Patricia Namutebi, 3, was brought in as a 1-year-old by a thin, sickly man who said he was her neighbor and that her mother had died of AIDS. Patricia has been sick with one opportunistic infection after another; today she restlessly drags a chair to and fro and swings on the curtains, apart from the other children. Workers at the Babies Home suspect that the man was her father, but it hardly mattered. When they trace abandoned children back to their families, says Joyce Lolindya, administrator of the home, the survivors seem to feel that "it is hard to look after an AIDS victim,

"The number of people who have gone into the coffin-making business— that is something you can see without being an epidemiologist."

—G. SIKIPA, *UNAIDS*

and then also the children of that victim, when you know they will all die." Especially when AIDS carries with it such a social stigma. Unless abandoned AIDS orphans reach an institution like hers, they risk getting sucked into what Godfrey Sikipa of UNAIDS calls "a vicious circle." He adds: "In many cases the orphans, unless we prevent them from going into deeper poverty, will become prostitutes." The fortunate ones become child brides, or the plaything of a sugardaddy. They can only hope that the men will not be among the millions who believe that sex with a virgin cures AIDS.

When an extended family cannot afford to educate all the children in its care—virtually everywhere in Africa governments charge school fees—it is the orphan who is the likeliest dropout. In Zambia, a study cited by the UNAIDS report found, one third of urban children with parents enroll in school, but only one quarter of orphans do. "I wish I could go all the time," says Ben Sengazi, 13, one of Ssenyonga's grandsons. But when the family cannot scrape up the fees, the school turns him away.

Compared with children with parents, AIDS orphans are at far greater risk of malnutrition and of not receiving the health care they need. The little girl named Forget was 4 when her mother died of AIDS last November and she went to live with her grandmother in a village southeast of Harare. Her small body has recently developed ugly lesions, which she scratches constantly. Her grandmother says the causes of the plague are a mystery to her. Although

she is doing what she can for Forget, the assumption by many caregivers is that the orphan, too, is infected with HIV, and that her illness is untreatable. Perhaps that explains one of the puzzles of the AIDS orphans. In 1995 Uganda had 1.2 million of them; based on the number of AIDS deaths and other factors, there should be 1.5 million now, but there are "only" 1.1 million. That is, Uganda is missing 400,000 AIDS orphans. "Either the babies were born [HIV-] positive, or they died from a lack of care," says UWESO's Ntambirweki.

Government and private programs do what they can for AIDS orphans. In Botswana, nongovernmental and community-based organizations provide services ranging from day care to food, clothing and bus fare to and from school. Villages in Malawi have organized communal gardens. Charity groups and orphanages teach the older children AIDS prevention, hoping that the cataclysm that befell the parents will not be visited on the children. World Vision built Sanyu's family a four-room house, paid for his sister and brother's schooling and trained Sanyu in bicycle repair. And after Harriett Namayanja, now 17, lost her parents to AIDS, a loan from a private agency saved her and her eight brothers and sisters. Harriett used the money for sisal grass, from which she weaves doormats. She sells them in Kampala, and with the money, she says, "I am able to look after my younger siblings" and even pay school fees for her brothers. But she and Sanyu are exceptions. Funding has not kept up with the needs of so many orphans, and institutions are stretched almost to the breaking point.

Some 6,000 men and women in sub-Saharan Africa will die of AIDS today. Six thousand more will die tomorrow, and the next day. For the children they leave behind, the tragedy is only beginning.

With Simon Kaheru *in Kampala,* Lara Santoro *in Homa Bay,* Vera Haller *in Johannesburg and* Sharon Begley

The American Century

*From movies to microchips to military might,
Uncle Sam has left his mark around the world*

By Michael Barone

On Dec. 8, 1941, the day after the attack on Pearl Harbor, Franklin D. Roosevelt stood before Congress and called for a declaration of war. "The American people in their righteous might," the president proclaimed, "will win through to absolute victory."

Absolute victory: No compromise, no deals with the enemy. *Righteous might:* Not just a strong America—a virtuous one. *The American people:* A people united, not just the military, or a few elected leaders.

With those 13 words, FDR sketched a history of the 20th century that, if exceedingly short, was also disarmingly accurate. In February 1941, Henry Luce, in his famous "American Century" editorial in *Life*, called on Americans to "accept wholeheartedly our duty and our opportunity as the most powerful and vital nation in the world . . . to exert upon the world the full import of our interests."

And so we have. The most riveting story of the 20th century is the rise of totalitarianism and its defeat at the hands of America. But there are other stories, other chapters. Luce could have no way of knowing it when he penned his editorial, but Americans literally took him at his word, thrusting upon the world the full import of their interests and energies over the course of these hundred years. At the dawn of a new millennium now, one may look back at the old and find it impossible not to recognize an indelible American imprint in virtually every area of human endeavor—in science and medicine, business and industry, arts and letters—it has been Uncle Sam's century. Over the years,

America has been criticized by friend and foe for a dominance both real and perceived. But there is no gainsaying the fact that, if nations were people, Uncle Sam would be the man of the century.

The American legacy is impressive—but it is one no one could have predicted at the dawn of the now departing century. A hundred years ago, America was the largest of the great powers. Its economy had surged ahead of those in Europe. For all of America's sweep and swagger, however, Britain was the dominant world power, with the largest empire and Navy, rivaled only by Germany, with its huge Army and strength in science.

America, for many reasons, was unwilling and unready to inherit the mantle of leadership. The United States was united in name only, the wounds of the Civil War still far from healed. Though wages in the North were twice those in the South, few Southerners deigned to cross the Mason-Dixon line. On both sides of the divide, racial segregation was the order of the day. On the borders, meanwhile, immigrants were pouring in—17 million between 1890 and 1914. The new arrivals gave cold comfort to America's elites. The Poles, Jews, Italians, they feared, couldn't possibly become *true* Americans.

Happily, the elites were wrong—dead wrong. Before too long, an America that had been "a nation of loosely connected islands," as historian Robert Wiebe called it, was becoming a more cohesive and unified whole. The building blocks of the civic life we take for granted today soon began falling into place. The medical profession standardized the curricula of the nation's

medical schools. The practice of law, once open to anyone, was limited to those who had passed state bar exams. Teachers worked from a common curriculum that emphasized English and civics. Education became a transforming

---

U.S. POPULATION:
1900: 75,994,575
2000: 273,482,000[*]

MEDIAN AGE:
1900: 22.9
2000: 35.7

URBAN VS RURAL:
1900: 40% urban, 60% rural
2000: 75% urban, 25% rural

BIRTHRATE:
1900: 32.3 births per thousand
2000: 14.2 births per thousand

IMMIGRANT POPULATION:
1900: 14.7 percent
2000: 7.9 percent

BIGGEST SOURCE OF IMMIGRANTS:
1900: Austria-Hungary
2000: Mexico

[*] ESTIMATE FOR 2000 OR MOST RECENT STATISTIC AVAILABLE

---

engine. The number of kids enrolled in high schools quadrupled from 1890 to 1910. At more rarefied levels, dozens of great research universities were formed.

A new order. The way America worked changed, too. Businesses were transformed from buccaneering, seat-of-the-pants outfits run by ragged ec-

NUMBER OF MILLIONAIRES:

1900: 3,000
2000: 3.5 million

AVERAGE INCOME:

1900: $8,620* a year
2000: $23,812 a year

**DEATHS FROM
INDUSTRIAL ACCIDENTS:**

1900: 35,000 a year
2000: 6,100 a year

AVERAGE WORK WEEK

1900: 60 hours
2000: 44 hours

*ALL MONEY COMPARISONS ARE IN 1999
DOLLARS

centrics into professionally managed organizations. Factories were increasingly run according to the precepts of "scientific" management. The concept was pioneered by Frederick W. Taylor. His time-and-motion studies reduced each task to single steps, allowing managers to maximize production, even by unskilled laborers. Suddenly, the chaotic and unstable economy of the 19th century was a thing of the past.

Nowhere was change so pronounced as in the military. "We are a great nation," Theodore Roosevelt said in 1898, "and we are compelled, whether we will or not, to face the responsibilities that must be faced by all great nations." This was not just rhetoric. In February 1898, as Americans protested Spain's suppression of a revolt in Cuba, Assistant Secretary of the Navy Roosevelt ordered the Pacific fleet to stand ready to attack the Philippines if war came. It did, and before American forces could roust the Spaniards from Cuba, Admiral Dewey sailed into Manila Harbor and destroyed the Spanish fleet. To the surprise and delight of TR, the "splendid little war" sparked enthusiasm among Southerners and Northerners alike. Americans were suddenly possessed of a swaggering new confidence: They could project power far beyond their borders to achieve good ends.

That confidence swelled when Roosevelt, as president, won a treaty to let America build the Panama Canal. American engineers succeeded where

the French had failed, bridging jungles and mountains with an elaborate system of interlocking channels; at the same time, Dr. Walter Reed conquered yellow fever. The lesson, taught in textbooks for years after, was simple—and breathtaking: American expertise could make the world a better place.

But the world was an increasingly perilous place, too. No sooner had the Panama Canal opened, in August 1914, than Europe was plunged into war— which leveraged its own kind of change. President Wilson nationalized the railroads and the shipyards. Newspapers were censored. War critics were jailed. In the meantime, Wilson raised a military of nearly 3 million men, and Americans took pride in helping to win "the war to end wars."

After, America boomed economically. But still it declined to take up the mantle of Britain, now exhausted by wartime costs and slaughter. At home Americans disagreed furiously about Prohibition and, in the Scopes trial of 1925, science and religion. Mass immigration was ended in 1924, but the melting pot kept bubbling. Millions of workers bought cars and fled the teeming tenements on new highways. For a brief, shining moment, Americans seemed freed from the workaday worries of the rest of the world.

So they were thoroughly unprepared for the shocks of the second third of the century—worldwide depression and the rise of totalitarianism. Between 1929 and 1933, the nation's economy shrank by nearly half; 1 in 4 workers was unemployed. Abroad, the wounds of World War I festered, the result, Lenin's Soviet Russia in 1918, Mussolini's Fascist Italy in 1922, Hitler's Nazi Germany in 1933.

Instead of dividing the nation, however, these shocks forged new bonds of common purpose. Popular culture helped. Despite the Depression, radio ownership doubled between 1929 and 1932. Americans went mad for movies. In 1930, in a country of 130 million people, movie attendance hit 90 million a week. The big screen created the strongest popular culture since Dickens and defined for the world a characteristic American style— breezy, friendly, open, optimistic.

All the way. But war clouds soon gathered again. The Sudetenland, Austria, Czechoslovakia—Nazi belligerence knew no bounds. Most Americans, however, were unmoved. It would require another president named Roosevelt to change that. In June 1940, as France surrendered to Hitler and Britain prepared for invasion, FDR started selling arms to Britain and boosted defense spending. Facing re-election, he took the politically risky steps of supporting a military draft, then dispatched 50 destroyers to Britain. Americans supported the moves, and Roosevelt was re-elected. Almost immediately, he won more aid for Britain. After Nazi forces attacked the Soviet Union in the summer of 1941, Roosevelt sent arms to Moscow and blocked oil sales to Japan. Again, Americans applauded: If it required war to stop totalitarianism, so be it.

Then came Pearl Harbor. "We are all in it together—all the way," FDR said in his fireside chat, two days later. "Every single man, woman, and child is a partner in the most tremendous undertaking in our American history." Roosevelt built his war effort on cooperation between big government, big business, big labor. America became "the arsenal of democracy," its industrial might churning out the awesome tools of victory: 7,333 ships, 299,000 aircraft, 634,000 jeeps, 88,000 tanks. The top-secret Manhattan Project, which cost $2 billion— the nation's total economic production in 1940 was $99 billion—produced the atomic bomb. The result was victory over Germany and Japan, confirming America's status as the world's dominant military and economic power.

Just as the first World War had, the war against the Axis powers wrought extraordinary change at home. Americans got used to working productively, and even creatively, in large organizations. Big business, big labor, and big government—with occasional friction— produced a bounteous economy, not another depression. Postwar America's "organization men" and "conformists" produced the baby boom, the habits of the burgeoning middle class reflected in the new universal culture of 1950s television. Church membership reached new highs. Crime fell to record lows.

Confidence in major institutions surged. Americans were bound together by common experiences—the comprehensive high school, the military draft, large corporations, suburbia.

This was also Cold War America. In March 1946, Winston Churchill, now out of office, went to Fulton, Mo., with

CITY WITH THE MOST MILLIONAIRES PER CAPITA:

1900: Buffalo
2000: Seattle

POPULATION OF LOS ANGELES:

1900: 102,479
2000: 3.8 million

CIGARETTES PRODUCED:

1900: 4 billion
2000: 720 billion

DAILY NEWSPAPERS:

1900: 2,226
2000: 1,489

FARM POPULATION

1900: 29,875,000
2000: 4,600,000

NUMBER OF FARMS:

1900: 5,740,000
2000: 2,191,510

DOW JONES INDUSTRIAL AVERAGE:

1900: 68.13
2000: 11,000

PATENTS GRANTED:

1900: 24,656
2000: 147,500

PASSENGER AUTOS REGISTERED IN U.S.:

1900: 8,000
2000: 130 million

HIGHWAY FATALITIES:

1900: 36 per 100 million miles
2000: 1.64 per 100 million miles

MILES OF PAVED ROAD:

1900: 10
2000: 4 million

CARS PRODUCED IN U.S.:

1900: 5,000
2000: 5.5 million

Harry Truman and proclaimed that, because of Joe Stalin, "an iron curtain" had fallen across Eastern Europe.

Americans responded boldly. The Truman Doctrine promised to protect all "free peoples of the world." The Marshall Plan provided vast economic aid to Europe. The NATO treaty of April 1949 was America's first peacetime military alliance. In June 1950, Truman sent troops to Korea to stop the Communist invasion. Defense spending increased, and stayed high for years. America was engaged in a "long, twilight struggle," John Kennedy said. And her people paid for it with high taxes for defense and foreign aid, a military draft, air-raid drills, and listening to Soviet threats of nuclear war over Berlin and Cuba. All that is taken for granted today, but in historic perspective it was extraordinary. "Only a society with enormous confidence in its achievements and in its future," as Henry Kissinger wrote later, "could have mustered the dedication and the resources to strive for a world order in which defeated enemies would be conciliated, stricken allies restored, and adversaries converted."

Doubts set in. It didn't last. Halfway around the globe, a commitment that started with just a few hundred Pentagon advisers escalated into a war with more than half a million American troops—a war that could not be won. Aides to Presidents Kennedy and Johnson had devised a military strategy in Vietnam that was incapable of working. Defense Secretary Robert McNamara scornfully dubbed it, "the social scientists' war."

It was a war many affluent Americans did not find important enough to draft their sons for. McNamara's draft system allowed college students to avoid service. Antiwar movements on elite campuses produced a generation of academics and professionals who regarded the United States and the Communists as morally equivalent. By 1968, many of the planners and supporters of the Vietnam War saw it as deeply immoral. They no longer believed, as the Roosevelts did, in American exceptionalism—the belief that this country was uniquely strong and uniquely good.

In other ways, the postwar system was breaking down. Congress had passed civil rights laws in response to

the nonviolent movement led by Martin Luther King Jr. But black protesters called for violence in response to white oppression.

Big government produced not only war and riots, but also stagflation—high inflation and low economic growth. Big businesses grew less supple and creative, turning out gas guzzlers with "planned obsolescence." Big labor unions stagnated, then lost membership. And the cultural unity of postwar America was splintering. Families with two television sets and several radios no longer watched the same shows and listened to the same music. The universal popular culture of midcentury soon gave way to rival countercultures, many hostile to old values. Starting in the late 1960s, birth rates fell and divorce and births to unwed mothers rose: "the great disruption," as Francis Fukuyama calls it. Crime and welfare dependency tripled from 1965 to 1975.

As the elites lost confidence in America, the American people lost confidence in the elites. Richard Nixon's rhetorical appeals to "the silent majority" rallied only some Americans, and his cool pursuit of geopolitical advantage, the opening to China, and withdrawal from Vietnam failed to engage Americans' yearning for moral purpose, even before his own moral authority was destroyed by Watergate.

Foreign policy elites increasingly saw American strength as malevolent, and were pleased to see it reduced. This was symbolized by the 1977 treaty to relinquish the Panama Canal. Elites, guilty about how America obtained the canal, saw this as necessary to prevent violence in Panama. But most voters still felt pride in this great American achievement, and opposition to the treaty energized Ronald Reagan's nearly successful challenge of President Gerald Ford in 1976.

American pride sank even lower when Iran refused to release 52 Americans held hostage in the U.S. Embassy in November 1979. Under international law, this was an act of war. But for months President Jimmy Carter refused to use force and tried to negotiate, and his half-hearted seven-helicopter rescue attempt in April 1980 failed. Each Carter policy was ap-

ADULTS COMPLETING HIGH SCHOOL:

1900: 15 percent
2000: 83 percent

HOMES WITH ELECTRICITY:

1900: 8 percent
2000: 99.9 percent

PRICE OF A STAMP:

1900: 59 cents*
2000: 33 cents

FEDERAL BUDGET OUTLAY:

1900: $10.3 billion*
2000: $1.7 trillion

DEFENSE EXPENDITURES:

1900: $4 billion*
2000: $268 billion

NATIONAL DEBT:

1900: $24.8 billion*
2000: $5 trillion

PER CAPITA NATIONAL DEBT:

1900: $325*
2000: $23,276

VOTER TURNOUT:

1900: 73.7 percent
2000: 48.9 percent

BOOKS PUBLISHED

1900: 6,536
2000: 65,800

AVERAGE SIZE OF HOUSEHOLD:

1900: 4.76 persons
2000: 2.62 persons

BEER CONSUMPTION:

1900: 58.8 gallons per adult
2000: 31.6 gallons per adult

NUMBER OF BISON:

1900: 400
2000: 200,000

* MONEY COMPARISONS ARE IN 1999 DOLLARS

proved in the polls. But in the end, voters wanted results. Carter was beaten soundly by Reagan, whose threats to use force resulted in the hostages' release just as he was sworn into office.

Reagan embodied the characteristic American style of the 1930s and 1940s movies in which he himself had been a star. He shared most Americans' pride in their country and rejected the guilt complex of the elites. His tax cuts led to two decades of solid economic growth and low inflation, interrupted by recession briefly in 1990–91. Complacent corporate executives were ousted by leveraged buyouts and directors seeking more profits. Big corporations were challenged by tiny start-ups: IBM was replaced as the major high-tech firm by Microsoft. American computers and high-tech—the latest manifestation of 20th-century Americans' scientific and technological expertise—led the world. The peacetime expansions of the 1980s and 1990s produced 40 million new jobs, while the sputtering economies of Europe and Asia produced virtually none. Ordinary Americans' incomes surged and widespread stock ownership resulted in a stock market boom and real gains in wealth for the masses.

Unmatched prowess. Abroad Reagan, despite scorn from the elites, pursued an assertive policy like Harry Truman's. He increased defense spending, sent American troops to Grenada, and supported anti-Communist forces in Central America and Afghanistan. The defense buildup and Reagan's Strategic Defense Initiative convinced Soviet leaders that they could never match the economic and technological prowess of the United States.

Like the two Roosevelts, Reagan insisted on proclaiming the superiority of the American system. In London in 1983, he predicted the demise of the Soviet Union. In Berlin in 1987, he demanded, "Mr. Gorbachev, tear down this wall." By October 1989 the wall was history. The Soviet empire soon followed.

Today, at century's end, America is unquestionably the world's dominant military, economic, and cultural superpower. This has been the work of the American people. The 76 million of 1900 are now the 273 million of 2000.

LIFE EXPECTANCY FOR MEN:

1900: 46.3 years
2000: 73.6 years

LIFE EXPECTANCY FOR WOMEN:

1900: 48.3 years
2000: 79.7 years

MOST POPULAR SONG:

1900: "Good-Bye Dolly Gray"
2000: "Believe"

DEATHS IN CHILDBIRTH:

1900: 9 per thousand
2000: 0.1 per thousand

CANCER DEATHS:

1900: 64 per 100,000
2000: 200 per 100,000

DIVORCED MEN:

1900: 0.3 percent
2000: 8.2 percent

DIVORCED WOMEN:

1900: 0.5 percent
2000: 10.3 percent

The descendants of the immigrants who choked the slums in 1900 are now firmly interwoven into the American fabric. The descendants of the blacks who were excluded by segregation in 1900 now have full civil rights and are surging into the middle classes and upper ranks of society. The new immigrants from Latin America and East Asia who have arrived since the 1965 immigration reform are progressing as their counterparts did a century ago.

The American traditions of excellence fostered by the elite of the first third of the century and the characteristic American openness depicted in the popular culture of the second third of the century gave the American people the strength and the confidence to forge ahead in the last third of the century when so many in the elite lost confidence in their country. Sharing with Ronald Reagan the belief that this country is "a city on a hill," they have won through to absolute victory over totalitarianism, as Franklin Roosevelt promised, and have made this the American century that Henry Luce envisioned.

Test Your Knowledge Form

We encourage you to photocopy and use this page as a tool to assess how the articles in **Annual Editions** expand on the information in your textbook. By reflecting on the articles you will gain enhanced text information. You can also access this useful form on a product's book support Web site at ***http://www.dushkin.com/ online/.***

NAME:

DATE:

_____

TITLE AND NUMBER OF ARTICLE:

_____

BRIEFLY STATE THE MAIN IDEA OF THIS ARTICLE:

_____

LIST THREE IMPORTANT FACTS THAT THE AUTHOR USES TO SUPPORT THE MAIN IDEA:

_____

WHAT INFORMATION OR IDEAS DISCUSSED IN THIS ARTICLE ARE ALSO DISCUSSED IN YOUR TEXTBOOK OR OTHER READINGS THAT YOU HAVE DONE? LIST THE TEXTBOOK CHAPTERS AND PAGE NUMBERS:

_____

LIST ANY EXAMPLES OF BIAS OR FAULTY REASONING THAT YOU FOUND IN THE ARTICLE:

_____

LIST ANY NEW TERMS/CONCEPTS THAT WERE DISCUSSED IN THE ARTICLE, AND WRITE A SHORT DEFINITION:

_____

ANNUAL EDITIONS: World History, Volume II, Seventh Edition

ARTICLE RATING FORM

Here is an opportunity for you to have direct input into the next revision of this volume. We would like you to rate each of the 45 articles listed below, using the following scale:

1. **Excellent: should definitely be retained**
2. **Above average: should probably be retained**
3. **Below average: should probably be deleted**
4. **Poor: should definitely be deleted**

Your ratings will play a vital part in the next revision. So please mail this prepaid form to us just as soon as you complete it. Thanks for your help!

We Want Your Advice

RATING

ARTICLE

1. That Fateful Moment When Two Civilizations Came Face to Face
2. The Potato Connection
3. Making Memories
4. The Dutch in Japan
5. 400 Years of the East India Company
6. The Macartney Embassy to China, 1792–94
7. Coffee, Tea, or Opium?
8. After Centuries of Japanese Isolation, a Fateful Meeting of East and West
9. Chinese Burns: Britain in China 1842–1900
10. The Zulus and the Boer War
11. The First Feminist
12. George Mason: Forgotten Founder, He Conceived the Bill of Rights
13. Founding Rivalries
14. From Mercantilism to 'The Wealth of Nations'
15. As Good As Gold?
16. The Strange Case of the Surgeon at Crowthorne
17. Eyes Wide Open
18. In God's Place
19. The Workshop of a New Society
20. The X Factor
21. The Rock Drill and Civilization
22. The Transatlantic Telegraph Cable

RATING

ARTICLE

23. Father of the Computer Age
24. Greetings From Mars
25. On the Turn—Japan, 1900
26. Home at Last
27. The Maginot Line
28. Women in the Third Reich
29. Exposing the Rape of Nanking
30. His Finest Hour
31. Judgment at Nuremberg
32. The Short-Lived Miracle of DDT
33. The Plan and the Man
34. Korea: Echoes of a War
35. Tibet Through Chinese Eyes
36. The Day We Shot Down the U-2
37. Vietnam's Forgotten Lessons
38. Ten Years of the Chornobyl Era
39. The End of the Cold War: A Russian View
40. Like Herrings in a Barrel
41. The Weather Turns Wild
42. Bombs, Gas and Microbes: The Desperate Efforts to Block the Road to Doomsday
43. Congo's Hidden War
44. 10 Million Orphans
45. The American Century

(Continued on next page)

ANNUAL EDITIONS: WORLD HISTORY, VOLUME II, Seventh Edition

||||||

ABOUT YOU

Name   Date

Are you a teacher? ☐ A student? ☐
Your school's name

Department

Address   City   State   Zip

School telephone #

YOUR COMMENTS ARE IMPORTANT TO US !

Please fill in the following information:
For which course did you use this book?

Did you use a text with this ANNUAL EDITION? ☐ yes ☐ no
What was the title of the text?

What are your general reactions to the Annual Editions concept?

Have you read any particular articles recently that you think should be included in the next edition?

Are there any articles you feel should be replaced in the next edition? Why?

Are there any World Wide Web sites you feel should be included in the next edition? Please annotate.

May we contact you for editorial input? ☐ yes ☐ no
May we quote your comments? ☐ yes ☐ no